THE POETICAL WORKS

OF

THOMAS HOOD.

REPRINTED FROM THE CHANDOS POETS.

With Memoir, Explanatory Notes, &c.

PORTRAIT AND ORIGINAL ILLUSTRATIONS.

LONDON:

FREDERICK WARNE AND CO.,

BEDFORD STREET, STRAND.

THE POETICAL WORKS

OF

THOMAS HOOD.

REPRINTED FROM THE LANSDOWNE POETS

PORTRAIT AND ORIGINAL ILLUSTRATIONS

LONDON:

FREDERICK WARNE AND CO.

BEDFORD STREET, STRAND.

PUBLISHERS' PREFACE.

THE present Edition of Hood's Poems is a complete reprint of all his Poems out of Copyright to the present time, and contains considerably more than any other Non-copyright Edition yet published.

BEDFORD STREET,
   STRAND.

CONTENTS.

ODES AND ADDRESSES.

WHIMS AND ODDITIES.

First Series.

MINOR POEMS.

SONNETS.

COMIC POEMS.

CONTENTS.

PREFATORY MEMOIR.

THOMAS HOOD has a strong hold on the sympathies of Englishmen. His memory is cherished with fondness by his countrymen, probably because he possessed in a high degree that peculiar attribute of the national character—humour. A French satirist once said of the English that *Punch* and *Richard the Third* represented their genius. There is a grain of truth in the assertion. The humour which is susceptible of the ludicrous, when possessed by a man of genius, is also extremely sensitive to the pathetic and tragical ; and it is this power of seeing both the laughable and the sorrowful side of human actions that gives humour a superiority over wit, which is of the imagination purely, while humour " involves the heart, sentiment, and character." " Men of humour," says Coleridge, " are in some degree men of genius ; wits are rarely so, although a man of genius may, amongst other gifts, possess wit—as Shakspeare." And we may add Hood—for wit mingled assuredly with his humour.

This great humorist was born in London in 1799, and was the son of a bookseller of the firm of Vernor and Hood. " The best incident of Hood's boyhood," says Lord Houghton, " was his instruction by a schoolmaster who appreciated his talents, and, as he says, ' made him feel it impossible not to take an interest in learning while he seemed so interested in teaching.' Under the care of this ' decayed dominie,' whom he has so affectionately recorded, he earned a few guineas—his first literary fee—by revising for the press a new edition of ' Paul and Virginia.' "

His mother was a Miss Sands, the daughter of Mr. Sands, the engraver. She was much beloved by her gifted son, who grieved sadly for her when death removed her from his love and care.

Hood's father was a man of cultivated literary tastes, and was the author of two novels which attained some popularity. He died suddenly, leaving his family not very well provided for ; and Thomas (the second son), to relieve his mother of his support, accepted an offer of his uncle, Mr. Sands, and was articled to an engraver. Subsequently he was employed by one of the Le Reux. Of the filial piety of Hood, his accomplished daughter speaks most highly in her charming " Memorials." In the occupation to which his family affection guided him, Hood acquired a skill which afterwards largely aided in the expression of his humour : his pencil became as ready as his pen.

In consequence of his delicate health, he was transferred to the care of a relation at Dundee, where he remained for two years, and made his first appearance in print in the Dundee papers. He became, while there, an earnest reader ; and we are told by Lord Houghton—who was numbered among the personal friends of the poet, and followed him to the tomb—that " as a proof of the seriousness with which he regarded the literary vocation, it may be mentioned that he used to write out his poems in printed characters, believing that that process best enabled him to understand his own peculiarities and faults, and probably unconscious that Coleridge had recommended some such method of criticism when he said he thought ' print settles it.' "

He returned to his former occupation in London in 1821. In that year, an opening which turned his thoughts to literature as a profession occurred. The editor of the *London Magazine*, Mr. John Scott, was killed in a duel, and the magazine passing into the hands of the liberal publishers who befriended Keats, Messrs. Taylor and Hessey, Mr. Hood was engaged by them to assist the editor in correcting the press, and reading contributions offered to their excellent magazine. His first original poem appeared in it July, 1821—" To Hope." In the same year appeared also in this periodical, " Ode to Dr. Kitchener," " The Departure of Summer," and a " Sentimental Journey from Islington to Waterloo Bridge." In the next year some of his very best comic poems were published ; they were of the most original cast. In July, 1822, the really fine poem of "Lycus the Centaur" appeared, together with several smaller poems.

This period must have been one of great enjoyment to the young poet, for the position he held, and his own talents, introduced him to most of the literary celebrities of the day. On the staff of the *London*, or at least frequent contributors to it, were Proctor (Barry Cornwall), Lamb, Talfourd, Hartley Coleridge, &c. His connexion with the writers in the *London* still more deeply affected his after-life, for in 1824 he married a relative of one of the contributors, Jane Reynolds, sister of John Hamilton Reynolds; a poet himself of no little power, though, strangely enough, his productions have been allowed to sink into oblivion. He was the friend of Keats, and in the "Life and Letters of Keats," Lord Houghton thus speaks of him :—"It is to be lamented that Mr. Reynolds' own remarkable verse is not better known. Lord Byron speaks with praise of several pieces, and attributes some to Moore. 'The Fancy,' published under the name of Peter Corcóran, and 'The Garden of Florence,' under that of John Hamilton, are full of merit; especially the former, to which is prefixed one of the liveliest specimens of fictitious biography I know." Jane Reynolds was a sharer in her brother's literary tastes and talent, and was in all truth a *helpmeet* to her gifted husband.

About this time, and conjointly with Reynolds, Hood published the "Odes and Addresses to Great People," which was a perfect success, and caused no little wonder and speculation. Coleridge ascribed it to Lamb. In 1826 appeared the first series of "Whims and Oddities," which had a capital sale. A second edition soon followed, and in 1827 a second Series, dedicated to Sir Walter Scott.

In 1827 the "Plea of the Midsummer Fairies" ought to have shown the British Public that a Poet of great originality had risen up amongst them : but they failed to appreciate the delicate beauty of the poem, and it remained partially unsold. Our readers will, we think, marvel at the want of taste fifty years ago, when they have read it. It is possible, however, that its want of human interest was the cause of its not winning the popularity it deserved ; for, in truth, it seems to need the genius of a Shakspeare to make these graceful fancies acceptable to the unimaginative.

In 1829 Hood became for that year the editor of an Annual called the *Gem*, to which he contributed one of his master-pieces, " Eugene Aram." This wonderful poem was afterwards reprinted in a separate form, with beautiful little engravings by Harvey. In it the tragic power of the humorist was as conspicuous as in any of his later works.

While in town, Hood and his family lived in Robert Street, Adelphi ; but in 1829 he left London, and settled in a pretty cottage at Winchmore Hill, to which he became much attached. The poet's health appears to have been often failing. After a rheumatic fever he went to Brighton, and frequently afterwards to Hastings. He has commemorated his boating excursions there in the lines to Tom Woodgate, an old boatman with whom he frequently went out for a sail.

At Winchmore, in 1830, was born his daughter, Frances Freeling Hood (Mrs. Broderip), who was, we suppose, named after her father's friend, Sir Francis Freeling, Secretary to the Postmaster-General.

In the same year the poet commenced his series of Comic Annuals, which for several years delighted the public, and lit up with glee the hearths of Christmas. Soon after, he supplied the Duke of Devonshire (at the request of the latter) with the well-known List of Titles for the Library door at Chatsworth—in themselves a perfect epitome of wit. For example, among them we find " *Lamb* on the Death of *Wolfe;*" " Tadpoles, or Tales out of *my own Head;*" " On cutting off Heirs with a Shilling ;" " Plurality of Livings with regard to the Commissariat ;" " Boyle on Steam," &c. &c.

Hood wrote the libretto for a little English opera, and helped his brother-in-law, Mr. Reynolds, to dramatize " Gil Blas."

In 1832 he moved to Lake House, Wanstead, and here he wrote his novel " Tylney Hall," which, with the exception of his

"National Tales," is, we believe, the only prose fiction from his pen. The "National Tales" are admirable, both in subject and finish. We recollect how fearfully one of them—the "Spanish Tragedy"—used to haunt our childish imagination, and for how very long a time we thought of a journey in Spain with actual horror; nothing so sensational have we seen since.

At Wanstead Hood also wrote the "Epping Hunt," which has lost something of its point since the time of its production, though still redolent of humour which we can appreciate.

The failure of a firm, in 1834, and other pecuniary misfortunes, threw the poet into difficulties. Like Scott, he honourably refused to become a bankrupt, but resolved rather to pay his debts by extra labour and economy. With this object he disposed of his effects, and started for the Continent as soon as his wife had partially recovered from a serious illness which followed the birth of his son Tom—the late Editor of *Fun.*

Hood's voyage was a boisterous one; for when he crossed to Rotterdam the great storm of 1835 occurred, and besides the peril to which it exposed him, caused him much fatigue, anxiety, and exhaustion.

His memories of his subsequent "Voyage up the Rhine" are embodied in his book so called, which was certainly one of his best works; it is to be regretted that it is (Mrs. Broderip informs us) no longer in print.

A severe illness prostrated Hood at Coblentz; nevertheless his letters from that place are admirable, full of wit and good nature.

During this time the "Comic Annual" came out yearly; and here we must observe that both in that and previously in Whims and Oddities, the pencil as well as the pen of the poet lent admirable aid to the expression of his "merry and witty conceits."

From Coblentz the Hoods moved to Ostend, and from thence, in 1840, the poet went to England on a visit to Dr. Elliot, at Stratford. Here he was seized with a severe attack of spitting blood, and Mrs. Hood came over and joined him.

The life of Hood seems from 1835 to have been a period of

suffering and anxiety, which it needed great fortitude to bear. But through all, his joyous spirit and the unfailing play of his earnest kindly humour bore him victoriously.

About this time Mr. Hood had to enter actions against his publishers, which ruined the sale of the second edition of " Up the Rhine" for that season, as it could not be sold till the actions were decided.

By the advice of his kind friend and physician, Dr. Elliot, Hood now decided on living in England ; and finally the family settled at Camberwell. The poet was delicate and ailing, but he was compelled to work unusually hard, having been engaged by Mr. Colburn to write articles for the *New Monthly*, which were finally to be collected in a volume. Mrs. Broderip draws a touching picture of her father's life at this time :—" He had reasonably calculated," she says, " that a work,* on which he had bestowed the labour of so many painful hours, would have relieved his expenses, and enabled him to go on easily enough. Instead of this, his health had been still further reduced by a dangerous illness, aggravated by anxiety and mental toil ; and a tedious lawsuit, for the fruits of his hardly earned labours (as he truly observed, often attested literally with his blood) was commenced, and fated to drag on its attendant care and harass to the end of his short life, and then remained unfinished."

Very terrible is this picture, and very sad it is to think that such cruel wrong should have blighted that gentle life. In the *New Monthly Magazine* Hood wrote the " Rhymes for the Times," and that awful poem, tragic, and yet humorous, " Miss Kilmansegg." On the death of Hook, the editor of the *New Monthly*, Mr. Colburn offered the editorship to Hood. Soon after he removed to the Elm Tree Road, St. John's Wood.

In the Christmas number of *Punch* for 1844 appeared the famous poem, " The Song of the Shirt." Of this celebrated song Mrs. Hood had, her daughter tells us, prophesied the success. It is said to have done more to benefit the distressed needlewomen than

---

* " Up the Rhine."

anything hitherto urged or done in their behalf. Hood had a most kind and tender heart. His purse and pen were at the service of any one who needed help. The case of Gifford White, a labourer, who in the spring of 1844 was sentenced to transportation for life, for writing a threatening letter to the farmers of Blunti-sham, Huntingdonshire, roused all the generous indignation of Hood. He wrote a most eloquent appeal in the culprit's behalf, which unhappily was of no avail. The panic at the time amongst the farmers, and the obduracy of the Home Secretary, proved in-superable obstacles to the effect of his benevolent efforts ; but to this incident we owe the " Lay of the Labourer,* in the November number of *Hood's Magazine*, 1844, which made its first appearance this year. Hood had worked very hard at this periodical, his daughter tells us ; and it proved a well-merited success. It ranked in the list of its contributors Barry Cornwall, Lord Lytton, Lord Houghton, Dickens, Browning, Moir, Mrs. Norton, James, the Howitts, &c. &c. Mrs. S. C. Hall volunteered to write without payment in the Magazine " as a tribute of veneration to the author of the ' Song of the Shirt.' "

The Hoods had now removed to Devonshire Lodge, Finchley Road, where the poet finally died.

At about this period the failing health of the great humorist, who was suffering from organic disease of the heart—increased of course, by toil and anxiety—induced his friends to lay before the Government his claims, as a literary man, to the grant of a pension. Sir Robert Peel, who admired and appreciated his genius, gladly consented to lay his claims before the Queen ; and in consideration of his uncertain hold on life the pension was granted to his beloved wife.

Hood owed this pension only to his great literary merits, for he was, as he says in his delightful letter to Sir Robert Peel,† " Wholly unconnected with party politics" . . . . his " favourite

---

* It is to be regretted that both this Poem and the Song of the Shirt, being copyright, cannot be included in this collection.

† "Memorials of Hood," vol. ii. p. 240.

theory of government was 'an angel from heaven and a despotism.'"

A noble re-assurance was returned by Sir Robert Peel:—" You may," he says, " write on with the consciousness of independence as free and unfettered as if no communication had ever passed between us."

The remainder of this story is almost too sad to repeat; it has been told with exquisite pathos and tenderness by his gifted daughter* and son. The sufferings of the poet daily increased, but from his dying bed he still supplied the chapters of " Our Family" to his Magazine—drawing and writing in the midst of agony with an endurance which was heroic.

The public, hearing of his danger through the Magazine, truly sympathized with the sorrow of his family. The announcement stated that " His sufferings, which have lately undergone a terrible increase, have been throughout sustained with manly fortitude and Christian resignation. He is perfectly aware of his condition ; and we have no longer any reason or any right to speak ambiguously of a now too certain loss—the loss of a Great Writer— great in the splendour of his copious imagery; in his rare faculty of terse incisive language ; in his powerful pregnancy of thought ; and in his almost Shaksperian versatility of genius—great in the few but noble works he leaves behind—greater still, perhaps, in those he will carry unwritten to his early tomb."

We cannot help thinking that this last sentence contained a great truth. The genius of Hood had grown yearly ; it was not of the firework class, which blazes but once brightly ; it rose gradually, as the sun does—alas ! vanishing before it had quite reached the blaze of noonday.

The last words which his wife heard, as she bent over his dying bed, were—" O Lord ! say Arise, take up thy cross and follow me !"—Dying—dying !" He then sank into a deep slumber, in which his gentle spirit passed to its rest. He was buried in Kensal Green Cemetery. Eighteen months afterwards his widow, the

---

* See " Memorials of Thomas Hood."

faithful partner of his life,—his friend, companion, and helpmate,—
followed him to their eternal home. Hood was an excellent and
tender husband and father, enduring all things for the sake of his
family; in this as in his genius, being a typical Englishman.

In 1852 a too tardy recognition of the honour due to Hood
was made, in consequence of the publication of the following
lines by Eliza Cook :—

> What gorgeous cenotaphs arise
>   Of Parian shrine and granite vault,
> With blazoned claims on purer skies,
>   That shut out earthly flaw and fault!
>
> Who lies below yon splendid tomb,
>   That stretches out so broad and tall?
> The worms will surely ne'er exhume
>   A sleeper locked within such wall.
>
> And see that other stately pile
>   Of chiselled glory—staring out.
> Come, sexton, leave your work awhile,
>   And tell us what we ask about.
>
> So! one belongs to him who held
>   A score of trained and tortured steeds;
> Great circus hero—unexcelled.
>   On what strange stuff Ambition feeds!
>
> The other guards the last repose
>   Of one who shone by juggling craft.
> Methinks when such a temple rose
>   How Esculapius must have laughed.
>
> And see that tomb beneath yon tree!
>   But sexton, tell us where to find
> The grave of him we came to see—
>   Is it not here, or are we blind?

We mean poor Hood's—the man who made
  That song about the "Bridge of Sighs,"
You know the song; well, leave your spade,
  And please to show us where he lies.

What!—there! without a single mark—
  Without a stone—without a line!
Does watchfire Genius leave no spark
  To note its ashes as divine?

Must strangers come to woo his shade,
  Scanning rare beauties as they pass;
And when they pause where he is laid,
  Stop at a trodden mound of grass?

And is it thus?—Well, we suppose
  England is far too poor to spare
A slab of white, where Truth might write
  The title of her Poet Heir.

Let us adorn our city walls
  With senate form and soldier chief
Carve toga folds and laurel stalks,—
  Let marble shine in robe and leaf.

But Hood; "poor Hood!"—the Poet fool
  Who sung of Women's woes and wrongs,
Who taught his Master's Golden Rule—
  Give *him* no statue for his *songs!*

Give him the dust beneath his head,
  Give him a grave—a grave alone—
In Life he dearly won his bread:—
  In Death he was not worth a stone.

Perhaps we rightly think that he
  Who flung God's light round lowly things,
Can soar above in Memory's love,
  Supported by his own strong wings.

Our Shakspeare can be only met
    Within a narrow Playhouse Porch ;
So, Hood, thy spirit need not fret ;
    But hold its own immortal torch.

" Poor Hood !" for whom a people wreathes
    The heart-born flowers that never die.
" Poor Hood !" for whom a requiem breathes
    In every human Toil-wrung sigh.

Let the Horse-tamer's bed be known
    By the rich mausoleum-shrine ;
Give the bold Quack his charnel throne—
    Their works were worthier far than thine.

And let thy Soul serenely sleep
    While pilgrims stand as I have stood ;
To worship at a nameless heap,
    And fondly, sadly say, " Poor Hood !"

The public at once subscribed for a monument befitting the genius of the man thus tenderly mourned ; and the present exquisite one was erected, designed, and executed by Mr. Noble.

On the 18th of July, 1852, it was unveiled, and Lord Houghton (then Mr. Monckton Milnes) made an eloquent oration in praise of the poet. We advise all our readers to go and see the tomb— to make a pilgrimage to the spot hallowed as the resting-place of genius, and there to think tenderly of the gentle, true, and tender Thomas Hood.

Hood's son and daughter survive him ; and it is from the " Memorial" which their filial love has given to the public, that the incidents of this life of the poet are in part taken. They have both inherited a portion of the paternal genius, and are well known in the literary world, on whose sympathies they have also a claim for their father's sake.

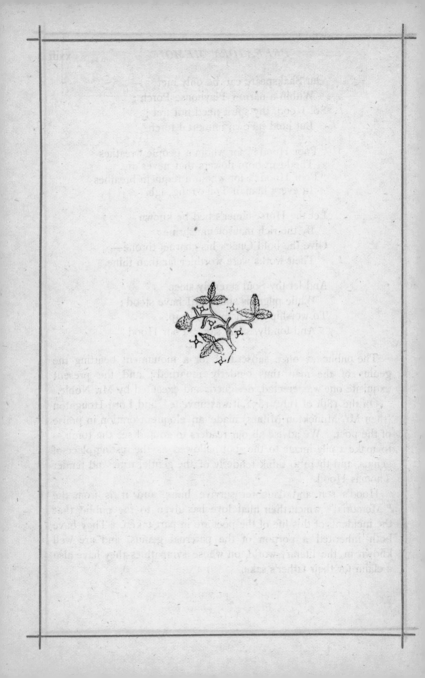

THE POETICAL WORKS

OF

THOMAS HOOD.

ODES AND ADDRESSES.

ODE TO MR. GRAHAM.

THE AERONAUT.

"Up with me!—up with me into the sky!"

WORDSWORTH—*on a Lark!*

DEAR Graham, whilst the busy crowd,
The vain, the wealthy, and the proud,
  Their meaner flights pursue,
Let us cast off the foolish ties
That bind us to the earth, and rise
  And take a bird's-eye view!—

A few more whiffs of my cigar
And then, in Fancy's airy car,
  Have with thee for the skies :—
How oft this fragrant smoke upcurled
Hath borne me from this little world,
  And all that in it lies !—

Away !—away !—the bubble fills—
Farewell to earth and all its hills !—
  We seem to cut the wind !—
So high we mount, so swift we go,
The chimney tops are far below,
  The Eagle's left behind !—

1

Ah me ! my brain begins to swim !—
The world is growing rather dim ;
    The steeples and the trees—
My wife is getting very small !
I cannot see my babe at all !—
    The Dollond, if you please !

Do, Graham, let me have a quiz,
Lord ! what a Lilliput it is,
    That little world of Mogg's !—
Are those the London Docks ?—that channel,
The mighty Thames ?—a proper kennel
    For that small Isle of Dogs !—

What is that seeming tea-urn there ?
That fairy dome, St. Paul's !—I swear
    Wren must have been a Wren !—
And that small stripe ?—it cannot be
The City Road !—Good lack ! to see
    The little ways of men !

Little, indeed !—my eyeballs ache
To find a turnpike.—I must take
    Their tolls upon my trust !—
And where is mortal labour gone ?
Look, Graham, for a little stone
    Mac Adamized to dust !

Look at the horses !—less than flies !—
Oh, what a waste it was of sighs
    To wish to be a Mayor !
What is the honour ?—none at all,
One's honour must be very small
    For such a civic chair !—

And there's Guildhall !—'tis far aloof—
Methinks, I fancy through the roof
    Its little guardian Gogs,
Like penny dolls—a tiny show !—
Well—I must say they're ruled below
    By very little Logs !—

Oh, Graham ! how the upper air
Alters the standards of compare ;
   One of our silken flags
Would cover London all about—
Nay, then—let's even empty out
   Another brace of bags !

Now for a glass of bright Champagne
Above the clouds !—Come, let us drain
   A bumper as we go !—
But hold !—for God's sake do not cant
The cork away—unless you want
   To brain your friends below.

Think ! what a mob of little men
Are crawling just within our ken,
   Like mites upon a cheese !—
Pshaw !—how the foolish sight rebukes
Ambitious thoughts !—can there be *Dukes*
   Of *Gloster* such as these !—

Oh ! what is glory ?—what is fame ?
Hark to the little mob's acclaim,
   'Tis nothing but a hum !—
A few near gnats would trump as loud
As all the shouting of a crowd
   That has so far to come !—

Well—they are wise that choose the near,
A few small buzzards in the ear,
   To organs ages hence !—
Ah me ! how distance touches all ;
It makes the true look rather small,
   But murders poor pretence.

"The world recedes—it disappears !
Heaven opens on my eyes—my ears
   With buzzing noises ring !"—
A fig for Southey's Laureate lore !—
What's Rogers here ?—Who cares for Moore
   That hears the Angels sing !—

A fig for earth, and all its minions !—
We are above the world's opinions,
      Graham ! we'll have our own !—
Look what a vantage height we've got—
Now——*do* you think Sir Walter Scott
      Is such a Great Unknown ?

Speak up !—or hath he hid his name
To crawl thro' " subways" unto fame,
      Like Williams of Cornhill ?—
Speak up, my lad !—when men run small
We'll show what's little in them all,
      Receive it how they will !—

Think now of Irving !—shall he preach
The princes down—shall he impeach
      The potent and the rich,
Merely on ethic stilts—and I
Not moralize at two miles high—
      The true didactic pitch !

Come :—what d'ye think of Jeffrey, sir ?
Is Gifford such a Gulliver
      In Lilliput's Review,
That like Colossus he should stride
Certain small brazen inches wide
      For poets to pass through ?

Look down ! the world is but a spot.
Now say—Is Blackwood's *low* or not,
      For all the Scottish tone ?
It shall not weigh us here—not where
The sandy burden's lost in air—
      Our lading—where is't flown ?

Now—like you Croly's verse indeed—
In heaven—where one cannot read
      The " Warren" on a wall ?
What think you here of that man's fame ?
Tho' Jerdan magnified his name,
      To me 'tis very small !

And, truly, is there such a spell
In those three letters, L. E. L.,
    To witch a world with song?
On clouds the Byron did not sit,
Yet dared on Shakspeare's head to spit,
    And say the world was wrong!

And shall not we? Let's think aloud!
Thus being couched upon a cloud,
    Graham, we'll have our eyes!
We felt the great when we were less,
But we'll retort on littleness
    Now we are in the skies.

O Graham, Graham! how I blame
The bastard blush—the petty shame
    That used to fret me quite—
The little sores I covered then,
No sores on earth, nor sorrows when
    The world is out of sight!

My name is Tims.—I am the man
That North's unseen, diminished clan
    So scurvily abused!
I am the very P. A. Z.
The London Lion's small pin's head
    So often hath refused!

Campbell—(you cannot see him here)—
Hath scorned my *lays:*—do his appear
    Such great eggs from the sky?—
And Longman, and his lengthy Co.
Long, only, in a little Row,
    Have thrust my poems by!

What else?—I'm poor, and much beset
With damned small duns—that is—in debt
    Some grains of golden dust!
But only worth, above, is worth.—
What's all the credit of the earth?
    An inch of cloth on trust!

What's Rothschild here, that wealthy man!
Nay, worlds of wealth?—Oh, if you can
    Spy out—the *Golden Ball!*
Sure as we rose, all money sank:
What's gold or silver now?—the Bank
    Is gone—the 'Change and all!

What's all the ground-rent of the globe?—
Oh, Graham, it would worry Job
    To hear its landlords prate!
But after this survey, I think
I'll ne'er be bullied more, nor shrink
    From men of large estate!

And less, still less, will I submit
To poor mean acres' worth of wit—
    I that have heaven's span—
I that like Shakspeare's self may dream
Beyond the very clouds, and seem
    An Universal Man!

Mark, Graham, mark those gorgeous crowds!
Like Birds of Paradise the clouds
    Are winging on the wind!
But what is grander than their range?
More lovely than their sun-set change?—
    The free creative mind!

Well! the Adults' School's in the air!
The greatest men are lessoned there
    As well as the Lessee!
Oh could Earth's Ellistons thus small
Behold the greatest stage of all,
    How humbled they would be!

"Oh would some Power the giftie gie 'em,
To see themselves as others see 'em,"
    'T would much abate their fuss!
If they could think that from the skies
They are as little in our eyes
    As they can think of us!

Of us? are we gone out of sight?
Lessened! diminished! vanished quite!
   Lost to the tiny town!
Beyond the Eagle's ken—the grope
Of Dollond's longest telescope!
   Graham! we're going down!

Ah me! I've touched a string that opes
The airy valve!—the gas elopes—
   Down goes our bright balloon!—
Farewell the skies! the clouds! I smell
The lower world! Graham, farewell,
   Man of the silken moon!

The earth is close! the City nears—
Like a burnt paper it appears,
   Studded with tiny sparks!
Methinks I hear the distant rout
Of coaches rumbling all about—
   We're close above the Parks!

I hear the watchmen on their beats,
Hawking the hour about the streets.
   Lord! what a cruel jar
It is upon the earth to light!
Well—there's the finish of our flight!
   I've smoked my last cigar!

ODE TO MR. M'ADAM.

"*Let us take to the road.*"—*Beggar's Opera.*

M'ADAM, hail!
Hail, Roadian! hail, Colossus! who dost stand
Striding ten thousand turnpikes on the land!
   Oh universal Leveller! all hail!
To thee, a good, yet stony-hearted man,
   The kindest one, and yet the flintiest going—
To thee—how much for thy commodious plan,
   Lanark Reformer of the Ruts, is Owing!
      The Bristol mail,

Gliding o'er ways hitherto deemed invincible.
  When carrying Patriots now shall never fail
Those of the most "*unshaken* public principle."
    Hail to thee, Scot of Scots !
  Thou northern light, amid those heavy men !
Foe to Stonehenge, yet friend to all beside,
Thou scatterest flints and favours far and wide,
      From palaces to cots ;—
    Dispenser of coagulated good !
    Distributor of granite and of food !
Long may thy fame its even path march on
    E'en when thy sons are dead !
Best benefactor ! though thou giv'st a stone
    To those who ask for bread !

Thy first great trial in this mighty town
Was, if I rightly recollect, upon
    That gentle hill which goeth
Down from "the County" to the Palace gate,
    And, like a river, thanks to thee, now floweth
Past the Old Horticultural Society—
The chemist Cobb's, the house of Howell and James,
Where ladies play high shawl and satin games—
      A little *Hell* of lace !
And past the Athenæum, made of late,
      Severs a sweet variety
Of milliners and booksellers who grace
      Waterloo Place,
Making division, the Muse fears and guesses,
'Twixt Mr. Rivington's and Mr. Hessey's.
Thou stood'st thy trial, Mac ! and shaved the road
From Barber Beaumont's to the King's abode
So well, that paviours threw their rammers by,
Let down their tucked shirt-sleeves, and with a sigh
Prepared themselves, poor souls, to chip or die !

Next, from the palace to the prison, thou
    Didst go, the highway's watchman, to thy beat—
    Preventing though the *rattling* in the street,
      Yet kicking up a row
Upon the stones—ah ! truly watchman-like,
Encouraging thy victims all to strike,

To further thy own purpose, Adam, daily ;—
Thou hast smoothed, alas, the path to the Old Bailey !
    And to the stony bowers
Of Newgate, to encourage the approach,
    By caravan or coach—
Hast strewed the way with flints as soft as flowers.

    Who shall dispute thy name !
Insculpt in stone in every street,
    We soon shall greet
Thy trodden down, yet all unconquered fame !
Where'er we take, even at this time, our way,
Nought see we, but mankind in open air,
Hammering thy fame, as Chantrey would not dare :—
    And with a patient care
Chipping thy immortality all day !
Demosthenes of old—that rare old man—
Prophetically *followed*, Mac ! thy plan :—
    For he, we know,
    (History says so,)
Put *pebbles* in his mouth when he would speak
    The *smoothest* Greek !

  It is " impossible, and cannot be,"
    But that thy genius hath,
    Besides the turnpike, many another path
  Trod, to arrive at popularity,
O'er Pegasus, perchance, thou hast thrown a thigh,
Nor ridden a roadster only ; mighty Mac !
And 'faith I'd swear, when on that wingèd hack,
Thou hast observed the highways in the sky !
Is the path up Parnassus rough and steep,
    And " hard to climb," as Dr. B. would say ?
Dost think it best for Sons of Song to keep
    The noiseless *tenor* of their way ? (see Gray.)
What line of road *should* poets take to bring
    Themselves unto those waters, loved the first !—
Those waters which can wet a man to sing !
    Which, like thy fame, " from *granite* basins burst,
    Leap into life, and, sparkling, woo the thirst ?"

  That thou'rt a proser, even thy birthplace might
Vouchsafe ;—and Mr. Cadell *may*, God wot,

Have paid thee many a pound for many a blot—
        Cadell's a wayward wight !
Although no Walter, still thou art a Scot,
And I can throw, I think, a little light
Upon some works thou hast written for the town—
And published, like a Lilliput Unknown !
    "Highways and Byeways," is thy book, no doubt,
        (One whole edition's out,)
                And next, for it is fair
                        That Fame,
    Seeing her children, should confess she had 'em :—
"Some *Passages* from the life of Adam Blair"—
        (Blair is a Scottish name,)
What are they, but thy own good roads, M'Adam ?

            O ! indefatigable labourer
In the paths of men ! when thou shalt die, 'twill be
A mark of thy surpassing industry,
    That of the monument, which men shall rear
Over thy most inestimable bone,
Thou didst thy very self lay the first stone !—
Of a right ancient line thou comest—through
Each crook and turn we trace the unbroken clue,
Until we see thy sire before our eyes—
Rolling his gravel walks in Paradise !
But he, our great Mac Parent, erred, and ne'er
        Have our walks since been fair !
Yet Time, who, like the merchant, lives on 'Change,
For ever varying, through his varying range,
        Time maketh all things even !
In this strange world, turning beneath high heaven !
    He hath redeemed the Adams, and contrived—
        (How are Time's wonders hived !)
    In pity to mankind and to befriend 'em—
        (Time is above all praise)
That he, who first did make our evil ways,
Re-born in Scotland, should be first to mend 'em !

A FRIENDLY ADDRESS

TO MRS. FRY, IN NEWGATE.

"Sermons in stones."—*As You Like It*.
"Out! out! damned spot."—*Macbeth*.

I LIKE you, Mrs. Fry! I like your name!
  It speaks the very warmth you feel in pressing
In daily act round Charity's great flame—
  I like the crisp Browne way you have of dressing,
Good Mrs. Fry! I like the placid claim
  You make to Christianity—professing
Love, and good *works*—of course you buy of Barton,
Beside the young *fry's* booksellers, Friend Darton!

I like, good Mrs. Fry, your brethren mute—
  Those serious, solemn gentlemen that sport—
I should have said, that *wear*, the sober suit
  Shaped like a court dress—but for heaven's court.
I like your sisters too—sweet Rachel's fruit—
  Protestant nuns! I like their stiff support
Of virtue—and I like to see them clad
With such a difference—just like good from bad!

I like the sober colours—not the wet;
  Those gaudy manufactures of the rainbow—
Green, orange, crimson, purple, violet—
  In which the fair, the flirting, and the vain, go—
The others are a chaste, severer set,
  In which the good, the pious, and the plain, go—
They're moral *standards*, to know Christians by—
In short, they are your *colours*, Mrs. Fry!

As for the naughty tinges of the prism—
  Crimson's the cruel uniform of war—
Blue—hue of brimstone! minds no catechism;
  And green is young and gay—not noted for
Goodness, or gravity, or quietism,
  Till it is saddened down to tea-green, or
Olive—and purple's given to wine, I guess;
And yellow is a convict by its dress!

They're all the devil's liveries, that men
    And women wear in servitude to sin—
But how will they come off, poor motleys, when
    Sin's wages are paid down, and they stand in
The Evil Presence?   You and I know, then
    How all the party colours will begin,
To part—the *Pitt*ite hues will sadden there,
Whereas the *Fox*ite shades will all show fair!

Witness their goodly labours one by one!
    Russet makes garments for the needy poor—
Dove-colour preaches love to all—and *dun*
    Calls every day at Charity's street-door—
Brown studies Scriptures, and bids women shun
    All gaudy furnishing—*olive* doth pour
Oil into wounds: and *drab* and *slate* supply
Scholar and book in Newgate, Mrs. Fry!

Well! Heaven forbid that I should discommend
    The gratis, charitable, jail-endeavour!
When all persuasions in your praises blend—
    The Methodist's creed and cry are, *Fry* for ever!
No—I will be your friend—and, like a friend,
    Point out your very worst defect—Nay, never
Start at that word!   But I *must* ask you why
You keep your school *in* Newgate, Mrs. Fry?

Too well I know the price our mother Eve
    Paid for *her* schooling: but must all her daughters
Commit a petty larceny, and thieve—
    Pay down a crime for "*entrance*" to your "*quarters?*"
Your classes may increase, but I must grieve
    Over your pupils at their bread and waters!
Oh, though it cost you rent—(and rooms run high)—
Keep your school *out* of Newgate, Mrs. Fry!

O save the vulgar soul before it's spoiled!
    Set up your mounted sign *without* the gate—
And there inform the mind before 'tis soiled!
    'Tis sorry writing on a greasy slate!
Nay, if you would not have your labours foiled,
    Take it *inclining* towards a virtuous state,
Not prostrate and laid flat—else, woman meek
The *upright* pencil will but hop and shriek!

Ah, who can tell how hard it is to drain
    The evil spirit from the heart it preys in—
To bring sobriety to life again,
    Choked with the vile Anacreontic raisin—
To wash Black Betty when her black's ingrain—
    To stick a moral lacquer on Moll Brazen,
Of Suky Tawdry's habits to deprive her;
To tame the wild-fowl ways of Jenny Diver!

Ah, who can tell how hard it is to teach
    Miss Nancy Dawson on her bed of straw—
To make long Sal sew up the endless breach
    She made in manners—to write heaven's own law
On hearts of granite.—Nay, how hard to preach,
    In cells, that are not memory's—to draw
The moral thread, through the immoral eye
Of blunt Whitechapel natures, Mrs. Fry!

In vain you teach them baby-work within:
    'Tis but a clumsy botchery of crime;
'Tis but a tedious darning of old sin—
    Come out yourself, and stitch up souls in time—
It is too late for scouring to begin
    When virtue's ravelled out, when all the prime
Is worn away, and nothing sound remains;
You'll fret the fabric out before the stains!

I like your chocolate, good Mrs. Fry!
    I like your cookery in every way;
I like your shrove-tide service and supply;
    I like to hear your sweet *Pandeans* play;
I like the pity in your full-brimmed eye;
    I like your carriage and your silken gray,
Your dove-like habits, and your silent preaching;
But I don't like your Newgatory teaching.

Come out of Newgate, Mrs. Fry! Repair
    Abroad, and find your pupils in the streets.
O, come abroad into the wholesome air,
    And take your moral place, before Sin seats
Her wicked self in the Professor's chair.
    Suppose some morals raw! the true receipt's
To dress them in the pan, but do not try
To cook them in the fire, good Mrs. Fry!

Put on your decent bonnet, and come out!
  Good lack! the ancients did not set up schools
In jail—but at the *Porch!* hinting, no doubt,
  That Vice should have a lesson in the rules
Before 'twas whipt by law.—O come about,
  Good Mrs. Fry! and set up forms and stools
All down the Old Bailey, and thro' Newgate-street,
But not in Mr. Wontner's proper seat!

Teach Lady Barrymore, if, teaching, you
  That peerless Peeress can absolve from dolour;
Teach her it is not virtue to pursue
  Ruin of blue, or any other colour;
Teach her it is not Virtue's crown to rue,
  Month after month, the unpaid drunken dollar;
Teach her that "flooring Charleys" is a game
Unworthy one that bears a Christian name.

O come and teach our children—that arn't *ours*—
  That heaven's straight pathway is a narrow way,
Not Broad St. Giles's, where fierce Sin devours
  Children, like Time—or rather they both prey
On youth together—meanwhile Newgate low'rs
  Even like a black cloud at the close of day,
To shut them out from any more blue sky:
Think of these helpless wretches, Mrs. Fry!

You are not nice—go into their retreats,
  And make them Quakers, if you will.—'Twere best
They wore straight collars, and their shirts sans *pleats;*
  That they had hats *with* brims—that they were drest
In garbs without *lappels*—than shame the streets
  With so much raggedness.—You may invest
Much cash this way—but it will cost its price,
To give a good, round, real *cheque* to Vice!

In brief—Oh teach the child its moral rote,
  Not *in* the way from which 'twill not depart—
But *out*—out—out! Oh, bid it walk remote!
  And if the skies are closed against the smart,
Even let him wear the singled-breasted coat,
  For that ensureth singleness of heart,—
Do what you will, his every want supply,
Keep him—but *out* of Newgate, Mrs. Fry!

ODE TO RICHARD MARTIN, ESQUIRE,

M.P. FOR GALWAY.*

"*Martin*, in this, has proved himself a very good Man!"—*Boxiana*.

How many sing of wars,
Of Greek and Trojan jars—
The butcheries of men!
The Muse hath a "Perpetual Ruby Pen!"
Dabbling with heroes and the blood they spill;
But no one sings the man
That, like a pelican,
Nourishes Pity with his tender *Bill!*

Thou Wilberforce of hacks!
Of whites as well as blacks,
Piebald and dapple gray,
Chestnut and bay—
No poet's eulogy thy name adorns!
But oxen, from the fens
Sheep—in their pens,
Praise thee, and red cows with their winding horns!
Thou art sung on brutal pipes!
Drovers may curse thee,
Knackers asperse thee,
And sly M.P.'s bestow their cruel wipes;
But the old horse neighs thee,
And zebras praise thee,
Asses, I mean—that have as many stripes!

Hast thou not taught the Drover to forbear,
In Smithfield's muddy, murderous, vile environ—
Staying his lifted bludgeon in the air!
Bullocks don't wear
Oxide of iron!
The cruel Jarvy thou hast summoned oft,
Enforcing mercy on the coarse Yahoo,
That thought his horse the *courser* of the two—
Whilst Swift smiled down aloft!—

---

* The author of the Act of Parliament for the Prevention of Cruelty to
Animals. He was member for Galway in the first Parliament after the union
of Great Britain and Ireland. Died, 1834.

O worthy pair ! for this, when ye inhabit
Bodies of birds—(if so the spirit shifts
From flesh to feather)—when the clown uplifts
His hands against the sparrow's nest, to *grab* it—
He shall not harm the MARTINS and the *Swifts !*

Ah ! when Dean Swift was *quick*, how he enhanced
The horse !—and humbled biped man like Plato !
But now he's dead, the charger is mischanced—
Gone backward in the world—and not advanced—
            Remember Cato !
Swift was the horse's champion—not the King's
            Whom Southey sings,
Mounted on Pegasus—would he were thrown !
He'll wear that ancient hackney to the bone,
Like a mere clothes-horse airing royal things !
Ah well-a-day ! the ancients did not use
Their steeds so cruelly !—let it debar men
From wonted rowelling and whip's abuse—
            Look at the ancients' *Muse !*
            Look at their *Carmen !*

O, Martin ! how thine eye—
That one would think had put aside its lashes—
            That can't bear gashes
Thro' any horse's side, must ache to spy
That horrid window fronting Fetter-lane—
For there's a nag the crows have picked for victual,
            Or some man painted in a bloody vein—
            Gods ! is there no *Horse-spital !*
That such raw shows must sicken the humane !
            Sure Mr. Whittle
            Loves thee but little,
To let that poor horse linger in his *pane !*

O build a Brookes's Theatre for horses !
O wipe away the national reproach—
            And find a decent Vulture for their corses !
            And in thy funeral track
Four sorry steeds shall follow in each coach !
            Steeds that confess " the luxury of *woe !*"
True mourning steeds, in no extempore black,
            And many a wretched hack

Shall sorrow for thee—sore with kick and blow
And bloody gash—it is the Indian knack—
(Save that the savage is his own tormentor)—
Banting shall weep too in his sable scarf—
The biped woe the quadruped shall enter,
    And Man and Horse go half and half,
As if their griefs met in a common *Centaur !*

ODE TO THE GREAT UNKNOWN.

"O breathe not his name !"—MOORE.

THOU Great Unknown !
I do not mean Eternity, nor Death,
    That vast incog !
For I suppose thou hast a living breath,
Howbeit we know not from whose lungs 'tis blown,
    Thou man of fog !
Parent of many children—child of none !
    Nobody's son !
Nobody's daughter—but a parent still !
Still but an ostrich parent of a batch
Of orphan eggs—left to the world to hatch.
    Superlative Nil !
A vox and nothing more—yet not Vauxhall ;
A head in papers, yet without a curl !
    Not the Invisible Girl !
No hand—but a handwriting on a wall—
    A popular nonentity,
Still called the same—without identity !
    A lark, heard out of sight—
A nothing shined upon—invisibly bright,
    "Dark with excess of light !"
Constable's literary John-a-nokes—
The real Scottish wizard—and not witch.
    Nobody—in a niche ;
    Every one's hoax !
    Maybe Sir Walter Scott—
    Perhaps not !
Why dost thou so conceal and puzzle curious folks?

Thou—whom the second-sighted never saw,
The Master Fiction of fictitious history !
            Chief Nong tong paw !
No mister in the world—and yet all mystery !
The "tricksy spirit" of a Scotch Cock Lane—
A *novel* Junius puzzling the world's brain—
A man of magic—yet no talisman !
A man of clair obscure—not he o' the moon !
            A star—at noon.
A non-descriptus in a caravan,
A private—of no corps—a northern light
    In a dark lantern—Bogie in a crape—
            A figure—but no shape ;
            A vizor—and no knight ;
    The real abstract hero of the age ;
    The staple Stranger of the stage ;
A Some One made in every man's presumption,
Frankenstein's monster—but instinct with gumption ;
Another strange state captive in the north,
    Constable-guarded in an iron mask—
            Still let me ask,
            Hast thou no silver-platter,
No door-plate, or no card—or some such matter,
To scrawl a name upon, and then cast forth ?

Thou Scottish Barmecide, feeding the hunger
Of Curiosity with airy gammon !
            Thou mystery-monger,
Dealing it out like middle cut of salmon,
That people buy and can't make head or tail of it ;
(Howbeit that puzzle never hurts the sale of it ;)
Thou chief of authors mystic and abstractical,
That lay their proper bodies on the shelf—
Keeping thyself so truly to thyself,
            Thou Zimmerman made practical !
Thou secret fountain of a Scottish style,
            That, like the Nile,
Hideth its source wherever it is bred,
            But still keeps disemboguing
            (Not disembroguing)
Thro' such broad sandy mouths without a head !
Thou disembodied author—not yet dead—

The whole world's literary Absentee !
    Ah ! wherefore hast thou fled,
Thou learned Nemo—wise to a degree,
    Anonymous LL.D. !

Thou nameless captain of the nameless gang
That do—and inquests cannot say who did it !
    Wert thou at Mrs. Donatty's death-pang ?
Hast thou made gravy of Weare's watch—or hid it ?
Hast thou a Blue-Beard chamber ? Heaven forbid it !
    I should be very loth to see thee hang !
I hope thou hast an alibi well planned,
An innocent, altho' an ink-black hand.
    Tho' thou hast newly turned thy private bolt on
      The curiosity of all invaders—
    I hope thou art merely closeted with Colton,
Who knows a little of the *Holy Land*,
    Writing thy next new novel—The Crusaders !

      Perhaps thou wert even born
To be Unknown.—Perhaps hung, some foggy morn,
At Captain Coram's charitable wicket,
      Pinned to a ticket
That Fate had made illegible, foreseeing
The future great unmentionable being.—
      Perhaps thou hast ridden
A scholar poor on St. Augustine's Back,
Like Chatterton, and found a dusty pack
    Of Rowley novels in an old chest hidden ;
A little hoard of clever simulation,
    That took the town—and Constable has bidden
Some hundred pounds for a continuation—
To keep and clothe thee in genteel starvation.

I liked thy Waverley—first of thy breeding ;
    I liked its modest " sixty years ago,"
As if it was not meant for ages' reading.
    I don't like Ivanhoe,
Tho' Dymoke does—it makes him think of clattering
      In iron overalls before the king,
Secure from battering, to ladies flattering,
    Tuning his challenge to the gauntlet's ring —

Oh better far than all that anvil clang
   It was to hear thee touch the famous string
Of Robin Hood's tough bow and make it twang,
   Rousing him up, all verdant, with his clan,
         Like Sagittarian Pan !

I like Guy Mannering—but not that sham son
Of Brown.—I like that literary Sampson,
Nine-tenths a Dyer, with a smack of Porson.
I like Dirk Hatteraick, that rough sea Orson
        That slew the Gauger ;
And Dandie Dinmont, like old Ursa Major
And Merrilies, young Bertram's old defender,
        That Scottish Witch of Endor,
That doomed thy fame.   She was the Witch, I take it,
To tell a great man's fortune—or to make it !

I like thy Antiquary.   With his fit on,
   He makes me think of Mr. Britton,
Who has—or had—within his garden wall,
A *miniature Stone Henge,* so very small
        The sparrows find it difficult to sit on ;
And Dousterswivel, like Poyais' M'Gregor ;
And Edie Ochiltree, that old *Blue Beggar,*
        Painted so cleverly,
I think thou surely knowest Mrs. Beverly !
I like thy Barber—him that fired the *Beacon*—
But that's a tender subject now to speak on !

   I like long-armed Rob Roy.—His very charms
Fashioned him for renown !—In sad sincerity,
   The man that robs or writes must have long arms,
If he's to hand his deeds down to posterity !
Witness Miss Biffin's posthumous prosperity,
Her poor brown crumpled mummy (nothing more)
        Bearing the name she bore,
A thing Time's tooth is tempted to destroy !
But Roys can never die—why else, in verity,
Is Paris echoing with " Vive le *Roy !*"
   Aye, Rob shall live again, and deathless Di
Vernon, of course, shall often live again—
Whilst there's a stone in Newgate, or a chain,
        Who can pass by

Nor feel the Thief's in prison and at hand?
There be Old Bailey Jarvys on the stand!

I like thy Landlord's Tales!—I like that Idol
Of love and Lammermoor—the blue-eyed maid
That led to church the mounted cavalcade,
   And then pulled up with such a bloody bridal!
Throwing equestrian Hymen on his haunches—
I like the family (not silver) branches
       That hold the tapers
   To light the serious legend of Montrose.—
I like M'Aulay's second-sighted vapours,
As if he could not walk or talk alone,
Without the Devil—or the Great Unknown—
   Dalgetty is the dearest of Ducrows!
I like St. Leonard's Lily—drenched with dew!
I like thy Vision of the Covenanters,
That bloody-minded Graham shot and slew.
     I like the battle lost and won;
      The hurly burly's bravely done,
The warlike gallops and the warlike canters!
I like that girded chieftain of the ranters,
Ready to preach down heathens, or to grapple,
      With one eye on his sword
      And one upon the Word—
How *he* would cram the Caledonian Chapel!
I like stern Claverhouse, though he doth dapple
   His raven steed with blood of many a corse—
I like dear Mrs. Headrigg, that unravels
   Her texts of Scripture on a trotting horse—
She is so like Rae Wilson when he travels!

I like thy Kenilworth—but I'm not going
   To take a Retrospective Re-Review
Of all thy dainty novels—merely showing
   The old familiar faces of a few,
     The question to renew,
How thou canst leave such deeds without a name,
Forego the unclaimed dividends of fame,
Forego the smiles of literary houris—
Mid Lothian's trump, and Fife's shrill note of praise,
   And all the Carse of Gowrie's,

When thou might'st have thy statue in Cromarty—
    Or see thy image on Italian trays,
Betwixt Queen Caroline and Buonaparté,
    Be painted by the Titian of R. A.'s,
Or vie in sign-boards with the Royal Guelph!
    P'rhaps have thy bust set cheek by jowl with Homer's,
P'rhaps send our plaster proxies of thyself
    To other Englands with Australian roamers—
        Mayhap, in Literary Owhyhee
        Displace the native wooden gods, or be
The China-Lar of a Canadian shelf!

It is not modesty that bids thee hide—
She never wastes her blushes out of sight:
        It is not to invite
    The world's decision, for thy fame is tried—
    And thy fair deeds are scattered far and wide,
Even royal heads are with thy readers reckoned—
    From men in trencher caps to trencher scholars
        In crimson collars,
And learned sergeants in the Forty-Second!
Whither by land or sea art thou not beckoned?
Mayhap exported from the Frith of Forth,
Defying distance and its dim control;
    Perhaps read about Stromness, and reckoned worth
A brace of Miltons for capacious soul—
    Perhaps studied in the whalers, further north,
And set above ten Shakspeares near the pole!

Oh, when thou writest by Aladdin's lamp,
With such a giant genius at command,
        For ever at thy stamp,
To fill thy treasury from Fairy Land,
When haply thou might'st ask the pearly hand
Of some great British Vizier's eldest daughter,
        Tho' princes sought her,
And lead her in procession hymeneal,
Oh, why dost thou remain a Beau Ideal!
Why stay, a ghost, on the Lethean Wharf,
Enveloped in Scotch mist and gloomy fogs?
Why, but because thou art some puny Dwarf,
Some hopeless Imp, like Riquet with the Tuft,

Fearing, for all thy wit, to be rebuffed,
Or bullied by our great reviewing Gogs?

What in this masquing age
Maketh Unknowns so many and so shy?
What but the critic's page?
One hath a cast, he hides from the world's eye;
Another hath a wen—he wont show where;
A third has sandy hair,
A hunch upon his back, or legs awry,
Things for a vile reviewer to espy!
Another has a mangel-wurzel nose—
Finally, this is dimpled,
Like a pale crumpet face, or that is pimpled,
Things for a monthly critic to expose—
Nay, what is thy own case—that being small,
Thou chooses to be nobody at all!

Well, thou art prudent, with such puny bones—
E'en like Elshender, the mysterious elf,
That shadowy revelation of thyself—
To build thee a small hut of haunted stones—
For certainly the first pernicious man
That ever saw thee, would quickly draw thee
In some vile literary caravan—
Shown for a shilling
Would be thy killing,
Think of Crachami's miserable span .
No tinier frame the tiny spark could dwell in
Than there it fell in—
But when she felt herself a show, she tried
To shrink from the world's eye, poor dwarf! and died!

O since it was thy fortune to be born
A dwarf on some Scotch *Inch*, and then to flinch
From all the Gog-like jostle of great men,
Still with thy small crow pen
Amuse and charm thy lonely hours forlorn—
Still Scottish story daintily adorn,
Be still a shade—and when this age has fled,
When we poor sons and daughters of reality
Are in our graves forgotten and quite dead,

And Time destroys our mottoes of morality—
The lithographic hand of Old Mortality
Shall still restore thy emblem on the stone,
    A featureless death's head,
And rob Oblivion ev'n of the Unknown!

ADDRESS TO MR. DYMOKE,

THE CHAMPION OF ENGLAND.*

"Arma Virumque cano !"—VIRGIL.

MR. DYMOKE ! Sir Knight ! if I may be so bold—
    (I'm a poor simple gentleman just come to town,)
Is your armour put by, like the sheep in a fold ?—
    Is your gauntlet ta'en up, which you lately flung down ?

Are you—who *that* day rode so mailed and admired,
    Now sitting at ease in a library chair ?
Have you sent back to Astley the war-horse you hired,
    With a cheque upon Chambers to settle the fare ?

---

* The office of Champion of England ceased in the person of this gentleman, who defied all gainsayers of the Sovereign's right to the throne for
the last time at the coronation of George IV., 1821. At the coronation of
William IV. and Victoria the Great Banquet and the Champion were
omitted. Mr. Dymoke was created a Baronet, 1841, by Lord Melbourne,
in recompense (says the editor of "Men of the Times") for the loss of the
Championship. Sir Henry Dymoke was the son of the Rev. John Dymoke,
of Scrivelsby, Lincolnshire.

The following verses appeared in the *London Magazine* of September, 1812,
p. 236. The "Duke and Marquis" were Wellington and Anglesey.

THE CHAMPION'S FAREWELL.

OTIUM CUM DIGNITATE.

Here ! bring me my breeches, my armour is over ;
    Farewell for some time to my tin pantaloons ;
Double-milled kerseymere is a kind of leg clover,
    Good luck to broad cloth for a score or two moons !

Here ! hang up my helmet, and reach me my beaver,
    This avoirdupois weight of glory must fall ;
I think on my life that again I shall never
    Take my head in a sauce-pan to Westminster Hall.

Oh, why was my family born to be martial ?
    'Tis a mercy this grand show-off-fight-day is up !

What's become of the cup?   Great tin-plate worker? say?
    Cup and ball is a game which some people deem fun!
Oh! *three golden balls* haven't lured you to play
    Rather false, Mr. D., to all pledges but one?

How defunct is the show that was chivalry's mimic!
    The breastplate—the feathers—the gallant array!
So fades, so grows dim, and so dies, Mr. Dymoke!
    The day of brass breeches! as Wordsworth would say!

Perchance in some village remote, with a cot,
    And a cow, and a pig, and a barn-door, and all;—
You show to the parish that peace is your lot,
    And plenty—tho' absent from Westminster Hall!

And of course you turn every accoutrement now
    To its separate use, that your wants may be well met;—
You toss in your breastplate your pancakes, and grow
    A salad of mustard and cress in your helmet.

And you delve the fresh earth with your falchion, less bright
    Since hung up in sloth from its Westminster task;—
And you bake your own bread in your tin; and, Sir Knight,
    Instead of your brow, put your beer in the casque!

I do not think Cato was much over-partial
    To back through the dishes, with me and my cup.

By the blood of the Dymokes, I'll sit in my lodgings,
    And the gauntlet resign for "neat gentleman's doe;"
If I ride I *will* ride, and no longer be dodging
    My horse's own tail 'twixt Duke, Marquis & Co.

No more at my horsemanship folks shall make merry,
    For I'll ship man and horse, and "show off" not on shore;
No funnies for me! I will ride in a wherry;
    They feathered my skull, but I'll feather my oar.

So, Thomas, take Cato and put on his halter,
    And give him some beans, since I now am at peace;
If a Champion is wanted, pray go to Sir Walter,
    And he'll let you out Marmions at sovereigns apiece.

The ladies admired the piebald nag vastly,
    And clapped his old sober-sides into the street;
Here's a cheque upon Child, so, my man, go to Astley,
    Pay the charge of a charger, and take a receipt.

How delightful to sit by your beans and your peas,
    With a goblet of gooseberry gallantly clutched,
And chat of the blood that had deluged the Pleas,
    And drenched the King's Bench—if the glove had been touched!

If Sir Columbine Daniel, with knightly pretensions,
    Had snatched your " best doe,"—he'd have flooded the floor;—
Nor would even the best of his earthly inventions,
    " Life Preservers," have floated him out of his gore !

Oh, you and your horse ! what a couple was there !
    The man and his *backer*—to win a great fight !
Though the trumpet was loud—you'd an undisturbed air !
    And the nag snuffed the feast and the fray *sans* affright !

Yet strange was the course which the good Cato bore
    When he waddled tail-wise with the cup to his stall ;
For though his departure was at the front door,
    Still he went the back way out of Westminster Hall.

He went—and 'twould puzzle historians to say,
    When they trust Time's conveyance to carry your *mail*—
Whether caution or courage inspired him that day,
    For, though he retreated, he never turned tail.

By my life, he's a wonderful charger !—the best !
    Though not for a Parthian corps !—yet for you !—
Distinguished alike at a fray and a feast,
    What a Horse for a grand Retrospective Review !

What a creature to keep a hot warrior cool
    When the sun's in the face, and the shade's far aloof !—
What a *tail-piece* for Bewick !—or piebald for Poole
    To bear him in safety from Elliston's hoof !

Well ; hail to Old Cato ! the hero of scenes !
    May Astley or age ne'er his comforts abridge ;—
Oh, long may he munch Amphitheatre beans,
    Well " pent up in Utica" over the Bridge !

And to you, Mr. Dymoke, Cribb's rival, I keep
    Wishing all country pleasures, the bravest and best !
And oh ! when you come to the Hummums to sleep,
    May you lie " like a warrior taking his rest !"

ODE TO JOSEPH GRIMALDI, SENIOR.*

" This fellow's wise enough to play the fool,
  And to do that well craves a kind of wit."—*Twelfth Night.*

JOSEPH ! they say thou'st left the stage,
    To toddle down the hill of life,
And taste the flannelled ease of age,
    Apart from pantomimic strife—
" Retired—(for Young would call it so)—
The world shut out"—in Pleasant Row !

And hast thou really washed at last
    From each white cheek the red half moon?
And all thy public Clownship cast,
    To play the Private Pantaloon?
All youth—all ages—yet to be,
Shall have a heavy miss of thee !

Thou didst not preach to make us wise—
    Thou hadst no finger in our schooling—
Thou didst not "lure us to the skies"—
    Thy simple, simple trade was—Fooling !
And yet, Heaven knows ! we could—we can
Much " better spare a better man !"

Oh, had it pleased the gout to take
    The reverend Croly from the stage,
Or Southey, for our quiet's sake,
    Or Mr. Fletcher, Cupid's sage,
Or, d——e ! namby pamby Poole—
Or any other clown or fool !

Go, Dibdin—all that bear the name,
    Go, Byway Highway man ! go ! go !
Go, Skeffy—man of painted fame,
    But leave thy partner, painted Joe !
I could bear Kirby on the wane,
Or Signor Paulo with a sprain !

---

* The celebrated clown, who took leave of the Stage in 1828, at Drury
Lane Theatre.   He was born in 1779 and died 1837.

Had Joseph Wilfred Parkins made
　　His gray hair scarce in private peace—
Had Waithman sought a rural shade—
　　Or Cobbett ta'en a turnpike lease
Or Lisle Bowles gone to *Balaam* Hill—
I think I could be cheerful still !

Had Medwin left off, to his praise,
　　Dead lion kicking, like—a friend !—
Had long, long Irving gone his ways,
　　To muse on death at *Ponder's End*—
Or Lady Morgan taken leave
Of Letters—still I might not grieve !

But, Joseph—everybody's Jo !
　　Is gone—and grieve I will and must !
As Hamlet did for Yorick, so
　　Will I for thee, (tho' not yet dust,)
And talk as he did when he missed
The kissing-crust that he had kissed !

Ah, where is now thy rolling head !
　　Thy winking, reeling, *drunken* eyes,
(As old Catullus would have said,)
　　Thy oven-mouth, that swallowed pies—
Enormous hunger—monstrous drouth !
Thy pockets greedy as thy mouth !

Ah, where thy ears, so often cuffed !—
　　Thy funny, flapping, filching hands !—
Thy partridge body, always stuffed
　　With waifs and strays, and contrabands !—
Thy foot—like Berkeley's *Foote*—for why ?
'Twas often made to wipe an eye !

Ah, where thy legs—that witty pair—
　　For " great wits jump"—and so did they !
Lord ! how they leaped in lamp-light air !
　　Capered—and bounced—and strode away !—
That years should tame the legs—alack !
I've seen spring thro' an Almanack !

But bounds will have their bound—the shocks
   Of Time will cramp the nimblest toes;
And those that frisked in silken clocks
   May look to limp in fleecy hose—
One only (Champion of the ring)
Could ever make his Winter—Spring!

And gout, that owns no odds between
   The toe of Czar and toe of Clown,
Will visit—but I did not mean
   To moralize, though I am grown
Thus sad—Thy going seemed to beat
A muffled drum for Fun's retreat!

And, may be—'tis no time to smother
   A sigh, when two prime wags of London,
Are gone—thou, Joseph, one—the other
   A Joe!—"sic transit gloria *Munden!*"
A third departure some insist on—
Stage-apoplexy threatens Liston!—

Nay, then, let Sleeping Beauty sleep
   With ancient "*Dozey*" to the dregs—
Let Mother Goose wear mourning deep,
   And put a hatchment o'er her eggs!
Let Farly weep—for Magic's man
Is gone—his Christmas Caliban!

Let Kemble, Forbes, and Willet rain,
   As tho' they walked behind thy bier—
For since thou wilt not play again,
   What matters—if in heaven or here!
Or in thy grave, or in thy bed!—
There's *Quick,** might just as well be dead!

Oh, how will thy departure cloud
   The lamp-light of the little breast!
The Christmas child will grieve aloud
   To miss his broadest friend and best—
Poor urchin! what avails to him
The cold New Monthly's *Ghost of Grimm?*

---

* One of the old actors of "Rapid."

For who like thee could ever stride
   Some dozen paces to the mile !—
The motley, medley coach provide—
   Or like Joe Frankenstein compile
The *vegetable man* complete !—
A proper *Covent Garden* feat !

Oh, who like thee could ever drink,
   Or eat—swill—swallow—bolt—and choke !
Nod, weep, and hiccup—sneeze and wink ?—
   Thy very yawn was quite a joke !
Tho' Joseph Junior acts no ill,
"There's no Fool like the old Fool" still !

Joseph, farewell ! dear funny Joe !
   We met with mirth—we part in pain !
For many a long, long year must go,
   Ere Fun can see thy like again—
For Nature does not keep great stores
Of perfect Clowns—that are not *Boors !*

ADDRESS TO SYLVANUS URBAN,* ESQ.,

EDITOR OF THE GENTLEMAN'S MAGAZINE.

"Dost thou not suspect my years ?"—*Much Ado about Nothing*.

OH ! Mr. Urban ! never must *thou* lurch
   A sober age made serious drunk by thee ;
Hop in thy pleasant way from church to church,
   And nurse thy little bald Biography.

Oh, my Sylvanus ! what a heart is thine !
   And what a page attends thee ! Long may I
Hang in demure confusion o'er each line
   That asks thy little questions with a sigh !

---

* The *nom de plume*, used by all editors of this magazine, which was first
published by Edward Cave in 1731.

Old tottering years have nodded to their falls,
  Like pensioners that creep about and die ;—
But thou, Old Parr of periodicals,
  Livest in monthly immortality !

How sweet !—as Byron of his infant said—
  "Knowledge of objects" in thine eye to trace ;
To see the mild no-meanings of thy head,
  Taking a quiet nap upon thy face !

How dear through thy Obituary to roam,
  And not a name of any name to catch !
To meet thy Criticism walking home,
  Averse from rows, and never calling "Watch !"

Rich is thy page in soporific things—
  Composing compositions—lulling men—
Faded old posies of unburied rings—
  Confessions dozing from an opiate pen :—

Lives of Right Reverends that have never lived—
  Deaths of good people that have really died—
Parishioners—hatched—husbanded—and wived,
  Bankrupts and Abbots breaking side by side !

The sacred query—the remote response—
  The march of serious minds, extremely slow—
The graver's cut at some right aged sconce,
  Famous for nothing many years ago !

B. asks of C. if Milton e'er did write
  "Comus," obscured beneath some Ludlow lid ;—
And C., next month, an answer doth indite,
  Informing B. that Mr. Milton did !

X. sends the portrait of a genuine flea,
  Caught upon Martin Luther years agone ;
And Mr. Parkes of Shrewsbury, draws a bee,
  Long dead, that gathered honey for King John.

There is no end of thee—there is no end,
  Sylvanus, of thy A, B, C, D-merits !
Thou dost, with alphabets, old walls attend,
  And poke the letters into holes, like ferrets !

Go on, Sylvanus !—Bear a wary eye,
    The churches cannot yet be quite run out !
Some parishes yet must have been passed by—
    There's Bullock-Smithy has a church no doubt !

Go on—and close the eyes of distant ages !
    Nourish the names of the undoubted dead !
So Epicures shall pick thy lobster-pages,
    Heavy and lively, though but seldom *red.*

Go on ! and thrive ! Demurest of odd fellows !
    Bottling up dulness in an ancient bin !
Still live ! still prose ! continue still to tell us
    Old truths ! no strangers, though we take them in !

AN ADDRESS TO THE STEAM WASHING COMPANY.

> "*Archer.* How many are there, *Scrub ?*
> *Scrub.* Five and forty, sir."—*Beaux Stratagem.*

> "For shame—let the linen alone."—
> *Merry Wives of Windsor.*

MR. SCRUB—Mr. Slop—or whoever you be !
The Cock of Steam Laundries—the head Patentee
Of Associate Cleansers—Chief founder and prime
Of the firm for the wholesale distilling of grime—
Copartners and dealers in linen's propriety—
That make washing public—and wash in society—
O lend me your ear ! if that ear can forego,
For a moment, the music that bubbles below—
From your new Surrey Geysers all foaming and hot—
That soft "*simmer's* sang" so endeared to the Scot—
If your hands may stand still, or your steam, without danger—
If your suds will not cool, and a mere simple stranger,
Both to you and to washing, may put in a rub—
O wipe out your Amazon arms from the tub—
And lend me your ear—let me modestly plead
For a race that your labours may soon supersede—
For a race that, now washing no living affords—
Like Grimaldi, must leave their aquatic old boards,
Not with pence in their pockets to keep them at ease,
Not with bread in the funds—or investments of cheese—

But to droop like sad willows that lived by a stream,
Which the sun has sucked up into vapour and steam.
Ah, look at the Laundress, before you begrudge
Her hard daily bread to that laudable drudge—
When chanticleer singeth his earliest matins,
She slips her amphibious feet in her pattens,
And beginneth her toil while the morn is still gray,
As if she was washing the night into day—
Not with sleeker or rosier fingers Aurora
Beginneth to scatter the dewdrops before her;
Not Venus that rose from the billows so early,
Looked down on the foam with a forehead more *pearly*—
Her head is involved in an aërial mist,
And a bright-beaded bracelet encircles her wrist;
Her visage glows warm with the ardour of duty;
She's Industry's moral—she's all moral beauty!
Growing brighter and brighter at every rub—
Would any man ruin her?—No, Mr. Scrub!
No man that is manly would work her mishap—
No man that is manly would covet her cap—
Nor her apron—her hose—nor her gown made of stuff—
Nor her gin—nor her tea—nor her wet pinch of snuff!
Alas! so *she* thought—but that slippery hope
Has betrayed her, as tho' she had trod on her soap!
And she—whose support—like the fishes that fly,
Was to have her fins wet, must now drop from her sky—
She whose living it was, and a part of her fare,
To be damped once a day, like the great white sea bear,
With her hands like a sponge, and her head like a mop—
Quite a living absorbent that revelled in slop—
She that paddled in water, must walk upon sand,
And sigh for her deeps like a turtle on land!
   Lo, then, the poor Laundress, all wretched she stands,
Instead of a counterpane, wringing her hands!
All haggard and pinched, going down in life's vale,
With no faggot for burning, like Allan-a-dale!
No smoke from her flue, and no steam from her pane,
There once she watched heaven, fearing God and the rain—
Or gazed o'er her bleach-field so fairly engrossed,
Till the lines wandered idle from pillar to post!
Ah, where are the playful young pinners—ah, where
The harlequin quilts that cut capers in air—

The brisk waltzing stockings—the white and the black,
That danced on the tight-rope, or swung on the slack—
The light sylph-like garments so tenderly pinned,
That blew into shape, and embodied the wind!
There was white on the grass—there was white on the spray—
Her garden—it looked like a garden of May!
But now all is dark—not a shirt's on a shrub—
You've ruined her prospects in life, Mr. Scrub!
You've ruined her custom—now families drop her—
From her silver reduced—nay, reduced from her *copper!*
The last of her washing is done at her eye,
One poor little kerchief that never gets dry!
From mere lack of linen she can't lay a cloth,
And boils neither barley nor alkaline broth—
But her children come round her as victuals grow scant,
And recall, with foul faces, the source of their want—
When she thinks of their poor little mouths to be fed,
And then thinks of her trade that is utterly dead,
And even its pearlashes laid in the grave—
Whilst her tub is a dry rotting, stave after stave,
And the greatest of Coopers, ev'n he that they dub
Sir Astley, can't bind up her heart or her tub—
Need you wonder she curses your bones, Mr. Scrub?
Need you wonder, when steam has deprived her of bread,
If she prays that the evil may visit *your* head—
Nay, scald all the heads of your Washing Committee—
If she wishes you all the soot blacks of the city—
In short, not to mention all plagues without number,
If she wishes you all in the *Wash* at the Humber!
    Ah, perhaps, in some moment of drouth and despair,
When her linen got scarce, and her washing grew rare—
When the sum of her suds might be summed in a bowl,
And the rusty cold iron quite entered her soul—
When, perhaps, the last glance of her wandering eye
Had caught "the Cock Laundresses' Coach" going by,
Or her lines that hung idle, to waste the fine weather,
And she thought of her wrongs and her rights both together,
In a lather of passion that frothed as it rose,
Too angry for grammar, too lofty for prose,
On her sheet—if a sheet were still left her—to write,
Some remonstrance like this then, perchance, saw the light—

LETTER OF REMONSTRANCE FROM BRIDGET JONES

TO THE NOBLEMEN AND GENTLEMEN FORMING THE WASHING COMMITTEE.

IT'S a shame, so it is—men can't Let alone
Jobs as is Woman's right to do—and go about there Own—
Theirs Reforms enuff Alreddy without your new schools
For washing to sit Up—and push the Old Tubs from their stools !
But your just like the Raddicals—for upsetting of the Sudds
When the world wagged well enuff—and Women washed your old
    dirty duds,
I'm Certain sure Enuff your Ann Sisters had no steem Indians,
    that's Flat—
But I warrant your Four Fathers went as Tidy and gentlemanny
    for all that—
I suppose your the Family as lived in the Great Kittle
I see on Clapham Commun, some times a very considerable
    period back when I were little,
And they Said it went with Steem—But that was a joke !
For I never see none come of it—that's out of it—but only sun
    Smoak—
And for All your Power of Horses about your Indians you never
    had but Two
In my time to draw you About to Fairs—and hang you, you know
    that's true !
And for All your fine Perspectuses—howsomever you bewhich
    'em,
Theirs as Pretty ones off Primerows Hill, as ever a one at
    Mitchum,
Thof I cant sea What Prospectives and washing has with one an-
    other to Do—
It ant as if a Bird'seye Hankicher could take a Birdsigh view !
But Thats your look out—I've not much to do with that—But
    pleas God to hold up fine,
Id show you caps and pinners and small things as lilliwhit as Ever
    crosst the Line,
Without going any Father off then Little Parodies Place,
And Thats more than you Can—and Ill say it behind your face—

But when Folks talks of washing, it ant for you to Speak—
As kept Dockter Pattyson out of his Shirt for a Weak!
Thinks I, when I heard it—Well, there's a pretty go!
That comes o' not marking of things or washing out the marks,
  and Huddling 'em up so!
Till Their friends comes and owns them, like drownded corpeses
  in a Vault,
But may Hap you havint Larned to spel—and That ant your
  Fault,
Only you ought to leafe the Linnins to them as has Larned—
For if it warnt for Washing—and whare Bills is concarned
What's the Yuse, of all the world, for a Wommans Headication,
And Their Being maid Schollards of Sundays—fit for any Citya-
  tion.

Well, what I says is This—when every Kittle has its spout,
Theirs no nead for Companys to puff steem about!
To be sure its very Well, when Their ant enuff Wind
For blowing up Boats with—but not to hurt human kind
Like that Pearkins with his Blunderbush, that's loaded with hot
  water,
Thof a X Sherrif might' know Better, than make things for
  slaughtter,
As if War warnt Cruel enuff—wherever it befalls,
Without shooting poor sogers, with sich scalding hot balls—
But thats not so Bad as a Sett of Bear Faced Scrubbs
As joins their Sopes together, and sits up Steem rubbing Clubs,
For washing Dirt Cheap—and eating other Peple's grubs!
Which is all verry Fine for you and your Patent Tea,
But I wonders How Poor Wommen is to get Their Beau-He!
They must drink Hunt wash (the only wash God nose there will
  be!)
And their Little drop of Somethings as they takes for their Goods,
When you and your Steem has ruined (G—d forgive mee) their
  lively Hoods,
Poor Wommen as was born to Washing in their youth!
And now must go and Larn other Buisnesses Four Sooth!
But if so be They leave their Lines what are they to go at—
They won't do for Angell's—nor any Trade like That,
Nor we cant Sow Babby Work—for that's all Bespoke—
For the Queakers in Bridle! and a vast of the confined folk

Do their own of Themselves—even the bettermost of em—aye,
    and evn them of middling degrees—
Why Lauk help you Babby Linen ant Bread and Cheese !
Nor we can't go a hammering the roads into Dust,
But we must all go and be Bankers—like Mr. Marshes and Mr.
    Chamberses—and that's what we must !
God nose you oght to have more Concern for our Sects,
When you nose you have sucked us and hanged round our
    Mutherly necks,
And remembers what you Owes to Wommen Besides washing—
You ant, blame you ! like Men to go a slushing and sloshing
In mop caps, and pattins, adoing of Females Labers
And prettily jeared At you great Horse God Meril things, ant you
    now by your next door naybors—
Lawk I thinks I see you with your Sleaves tuckt up
No more like Washing than is drownding of a Pupp,
And for all Your Fine Water Works going round and round,
They'll scrunch your Bones some day—I'll be bound,
And no more nor be a gudgement—for it cant come to good
To sit up agin Providince, which your a doing—nor not fit It
    should,
For man warnt maid for Wommens starvation,
Nor to do away Laundrisses as is Links of the Creation—
And cant be dun without in any Country But a naked Hottinpot
    Nation.
Ah, I wish our Minister would take one of your Tubbs
And preach a Sermon in it, and give you some good rubs—
But I warrants you reads (for you cant spel we nose) nyther
    Bybills or good Tracks,
Or youd no better than Taking the close off one's Backs—
And let your neighbors oxin and Asses alone—
And every Thing thats hern—and give every one their Hone !

    Well, its God for us Al, and every Washer Wommen for herself,
And so you might, without shoving any of us off the shelf,
But if you warnt Noddis you Let wommen abe
And pull of Your Pattins—and leave the washing to we
That nose what's what—Or mark what I say,
Youl make a fine Kittle of fish of Your Close some Day—
When the Aulder men wants Their Bibs, and their ant nun at all,
And Cris mass cum—and never a Cloth to lay in Gild Hall,

Or send a damp shirt to his Woship the Mare
Till hes rumatiz Poor Man, and cant set uprite to do good in his Harm-Chare—
Besides Miss-Matching Larned Ladys Hose, as is sent for you not to wash (for you dont wash) but to stew
And make Peples Stockins yeller as oght to be Blew,
With a vast more like That—and all along ot Steem,
Which warnt meand by Nater for any sich skeam—
But thats your Losses, and youl have to make It Good,
And I cant say I'm Sorry afore God if you shoud,
For men mought Get their Bread a great many ways
Without taking ourn—aye, and Moor to your Prays
You might go and skim the creme off Mr. Muck-Adams milky ways—that's what you might,
Or bete Carpets—or get into Parleamint—or drive Crabrolays from morning to night,
Or, if you must be of our sects, be Watchmen, and slepe upon a poste !
(Which is an od way of sleping, I must say—and a very hard pillow at most,)
Or you might be any trade, as we are not on that I'm awares,
Or be Watermen now, (not Water-wommen,) and roe peple up and down Hungerford stares,
Or if You Was even to Turn Dust Men a *dry sifting* Dirt !
But you oughtint to Hurt Them as never Did You no Hurt !

Yourn with Anymocity,
BRIDGET JONES.

ODE TO CAPTAIN PARRY.*

" By the North Pole, I do challenge thee !"—*Love's Labour's Lost.*

PARRY, my man ! has thy brave leg
　　Yet struck its foot against the peg
　　　　On which the world is spun ?

---

* The Arctic Navigator, Sir William Parry, was born 1790, died 1855. He made four voyages to the North Pole. This ode was written on his third voyage.

Or hast thou found No Thoroughfare
Writ by the hand of Nature there
　　Where man has never run!

Hast thou yet traced the Great Unknown
Of channels in the Frozen Zone,
　　Or held at Icy Bay,
Hast thou still missed the proper track
For homeward Indiamen that lack
　　A bracing by the way?

Still hast thou wasted toil and trouble
On nothing but the North-Sea Bubble
　　Of geographic scholar?
Or found new ways for ships to shape,
Instead of winding round the Cape,
　A short cut thro' the collar!

Hast found the way that sighs were sent to*
The Pole—tho' God knows whom they went to!
　　That track revealed to Pope—
Or if the Arctic waters sally,
Or terminate in some blind alley,
　　A chilly path to grope?

Alas! tho' Ross, in love with snows,
Has painted them *couleur de rose*,
　　It is a dismal doom,
As Claudio saith, to winter thrice,
" In regions of thick-ribbèd ice"—
　　All bright—and yet all gloom!

'Tis well for Gheber souls that sit
Before the fire and worship it
　　With pecks of Wallsend coals,
With feet upon the fender's front,
Roasting their corns—like Mr. Hunt—
　　To speculate on poles.

---

* " And waft a sigh from Indus to the Pole."—*Eloisa to Abelard*.

'Tis easy for our Naval Board—
'Tis easy for our Civic Lord
   Of London and of ease,
That lies in ninety feet of down,
With fur on his nocturnal gown,
    To talk of Frozen Seas !

'Tis fine for Monsieur Ude to sit,
And prate about the mundane spit,
   And babble of *Cook's* track—
He'd roast the leather off his toes,
Ere he would trudge thro' polar snows,
    To plant a British *Jack !*

Oh, not the proud licentious great,
That travel on a carpet skate,
   Can value toils like thine !
What 'tis to take a Hecla range,
Through ice unknown to Mrs. Grange,
    And alpine lumps of brine !

But we, that mount the Hill o' Rhyme,
Can tell how hard it is to climb
   The lofty slippery steep.
Ah ! there are more Snow Hills than that
Which doth black Newgate, like a hat,
    Upon its forehead keep.

Perchance thou'rt now—while I am writing—
Feeling a bear's wet grinder biting
   About thy frozen spine !
Or thou thyself art eating whale,
Oily, and underdone, and stale,
    That, haply, crossed thy line !

But I'll not dream such dreams of ill—
Rather will I believe thee still
   Safe cellared in the snow—
Reciting many a gallant story,
Of British kings and British glory,
    To crony Esquimaux—

Cheering that dismal game where Night
Makes one slow move from black to white
   Thro' all the tedious year—
Or smitten by some fond frost fair,
That combed out crystals from her hair,
   Wooing a seal-skin Dear !

So much a long communion tends,
As Byron says, to make us friends
   With what we daily view—
God knows the daintiest taste may come
To love a nose that's like a plum,
   In marble, cold and blue !

To dote on air, an oily fleece !
As tho' it hung from Helen o' Greece—
   They say that love prevails
Ev'n in the veriest polar land—
And surely she may steal thy hand
   That used to steal thy nails !

But ah, ere thou art fixt to marry,
And take a polar Mrs. Parry,
   Think of a six months' gloom—
Think of the wintry waste, and hers,
Each furnished with a dozen *furs*,
   Think of thine icy *dome !*

Think of the children born to *blubber !*
Ah me ! hast thou an Indian rubber
   Inside !—to hold a meal
For months—about a stone and half
Of whale, and part of a sea calf—
   A fillet of salt veal !—

Some walrus ham—no trifle but
A decent steak—a solid cut
   Of seal—no wafer slice !
A reindeer's tongue and drink beside !
Gallons of Sperm—not rectified !
   And pails of water-ice !

Oh, canst thou fast and then feast thus?
Still come away, and teach to us
   Those blessèd alternations—
To-day to run our dinners fine,
To feed on air and then to dine
   With Civic Corporations—

To save th' Old Bailey's daily shilling,
And then to take a half-year's filling
   In P. N.'s pious Row—
When asked to Hock and haunch o' ven'son,
Thro' something we have worn our pens on
   For Longman and his Co.

O come and tell us what the Pole is—
Whether it singular and sole is—
   Or straight, or crooked bent—
If very thick or very thin—
Made of what wood—and if akin
   To those there be in Kent.

There's Combe, there's Spurzheim, and there's Gall,
Have talked of polls—yet, after all,
   What has the public learned?
And Hunt's account must still defer—
He sought the *poll* at Westminster—
   And is not yet *returned!*

Alvanly asks if whist, dear soul,
Is played in snow-storms near the Pole,
   And how the fur-man deals?
And Eldon doubts if it be true,
That icy Chancellors really do
   Exist upon the *seals!*

Barrow, by well-fed office grates,
Talks of his own bechristened Straits;
   And longs that he were there;
And Croker, in his cabriolet,
Sighs o'er his brown horse, at his Bay,
   And pants to cross the *mer!*

O come away, and set us right,
And, haply, throw a northern light
   On questions such as these :—
Whether, when this drowned world was lost,
The surflux waves were locked in frost,
   And turned to Icy Seas!

Is Ursa Major white or black?
Or do the Polar tribes attack
   Their neighbours—and what for?
Whether they ever play at cuffs,
And then, if they take off their muffs
   In pugilistic war?

Tell us, is *Winter* champion there,
As in our milder fighting air?
   Say, what are *Chilly* loans?
What cures they have for rheums beside,
And if their hearts get ossified
   From eating bread of bones?

Whether they are such dwarfs—the quicker
To circulate the vital liquor*—
   And then, from head to heel—
How short the Methodist must choose
Their dumpy envoys not to lose
   Their toes in spite of zeal?

Whether 'twill soften or sublime it
To preach of Hell in such a climate—
   Whether may Wesley hope
To win their souls—or that old function
Of seals—with the extreme of unction—
   Bespeaks them for the Pope?

Whether the lamps will e'er be " learnèd"
Where six months' " midnight oil" is burnèd,
   Or letters must defer
With people that have never conned
An A, B, C, but live beyond
   The *Sound of Lancaster !*

---

* Buffon.

O come away at any rate—
Well hast thou earned a downier state—
　　With all thy hardy peers—
Good lack, thou must be glad to smell dock,
And rub thy feet with opodeldock,
　　After such frosty years.

Mayhap, some gentle dame at last,
Smit by the perils thou hast passed,
　　However coy before,
Shall bid thee now set up thy rest
In that *Brest Harbour*, Woman's breast,
　　And tempt the Fates no more.

———◆———

ADDRESS TO R. W. ELLISTON, ESQUIRE,

THE GREAT LESSEE !*

" Do you know, you villain, that I am at this moment the greatest man living ?"—*Wild Oats.*

Oh! Great Lessee! Great Manager! Great Man!
Oh, Lord High Elliston! Immortal Pan
Of all the pipes that play in Drury Lane!
Macready's master! Westminster's high *Dane!*
(As Galway Martin, in the House's walls,
Hamlet and Doctor Ireland justly calls!)
Friend to the sweet and ever-smiling Spring!
Magician of the lamp and prompter's ring!
Drury's Aladdin!　Whipper-in of Actors!
Kicker of rebel-preface-malefactors!
Glass-blowers' corrector!　King of the cheque-taker!
At once Great Leamington and Winston-Maker!
Dramatic Bolter of plain *Bunns* and Cakes!
In silken *hose* the most reformed of *Rakes!*
Oh, Lord High Elliston! lend me an ear!
(Poole is away, and Williams shall keep clear)

---

* Of Drury Lane Theatre.　He was born 1774; died 1831.

While I, in little slips of prose, not verse,
Thy splendid course, as pattern-work, rehearse !

Bright was thy youth—thy manhood brighter still—
The greatest Romeo upon Holborn Hill—
Lightest comedian of the pleasant day,
When Jordan threw her sunshine o'er a play !
When fair Thalia held a merry reign,
And Wit was at her Court in Drury Lane !
Before the day when Authors wrote, of course,
The " Entertainment *not* for Man but Horse."
Yet these, though happy, were but subject times,
And no man cares for bottom-steps that climbs—
Far from my wish it is to stifle down
The hours that saw thee snatch the Surrey crown :
Tho' now thy hand a mightier sceptre wields,
Fair was thy reign in sweet St. George's Fields.
Dibdin was *Premier*—and a golden *age*
For a short time enriched the subject stage.
Thou hadst, than other Kings, more peace-and-plenty ;
Ours but one Bench could boast, whilst thou hadst twenty ;
But the times changed—and Booth-acting no more
Drew Rulers' shillings to the gallery door.
Thou didst, with bag and baggage, wander thence,
Repentant, like thy neighbour Magdalens !

Next, the Olympic Games were tried, each feat
Practised, the most bewitching in Wych Street.

*　　*　　*　　*　　*　　*　　*

Rochester there in dirty ways again
Revelled—and lived once more in Drury Lane :
But thou, R. W. ! kept'st thy moral ways,
Pit-lecturing 'twixt the farces and the plays,
A lamplight Irving to the butcher boys
That soiled the benches and that made a noise :—
Rebuking—Half a Robert, Half a Charles—
The well-billed Man that called for promised Carles ;
" Sir !—Have you yet to know !   Hush—hear me out !
A man—pray silence !—may be down with gout,
Or want—or, Sir—aw !—listen !—may be fated,
Being in debt, to be incarcerated !

You—in the back !—can scarcely hear a line !
Down from those benches—butchers—they are *mine !*"

Lastly—and thou wert built for it by nature !—
Crowned was thy head in Drury Lane The*a*tre !
Gentle George Robins saw that it was good,
And Renters clucked around thee in a brood.
King thou wert made of Drury and of Kean !
Of many a lady and of many a Quean !
With Poole and Larpent was thy reign begun—
But now thou turnest from the Dead and Dun,
Hook's in thine eye, to write thy plays, no doubt,
And Colman lives to cut the damnlets out !
Oh, worthy of the house ! the King's commission !
Isn't thy condition " a most blessed condition ?"
Thou reignest over Winston, Kean, and all,
The very lofty and the very small—
Showest the plumbless Bunn the way to kick—
Keepest a Williams for thy veriest stick—
Seest a Vestris in her sweetest moments,
Without the danger of newspaper comments—
Tellest Macready, as none dared before,
Thine open mind from the half-open door !—
(Alas ! I fear he has left Melpomene's crown,
To be a Boniface in Buxton town !)—
Thou holdst the watch, as half-price people know,
And callest to them, to a moment—" Go !"
Teachest the sapient Sapio how to sing—
Hangest a cat most oddly by the wing—
(To prove, no doubt, the endless free list ended,
And all, except the public press, suspended,)
Hast known the length of a Cubitt-foot—and kissed
The pearly whiteness of a Stephens' wrist—
Kissing and pitying—tender and humane !
" By Heaven she loves me ! Oh, it is too plain !"
A sigh like this thy trembling passion slips,
Dimpling the warm Madeira at thy lips !

Go on, Lessee ! Go on, and prosper well !
Fear not, though forty Glass-blowers should rebel—
Show them how thou hast long befriended them,
And teach Dubois their treason to condemn !

Go on ! addressing pits in prose and worse !
Be long, be slow, be anything but terse—
Kiss to the gallery the hand that's gloved—
Make Bunn the Great, and Winston the Beloved,
Ask the two shilling Gods for leave to dun
With words the cheaper Deities in the *One !*
Kick Mr. Poole unseen from scene to scene,
Cane Williams still, and stick to Mr. Kean,
Warn from the benches all the rabble rout ;
Say, those are *mine*—" In parliament, or out !"
Swing cats—for in thy house there's surely space—
O Beasley, for such pastime, planned the place !
Do anything !—Thy fame, thy fortune, nourish !
Laugh and grow fat ! be eloquent, and flourish !
Go on—and but in this reverse the thing,
Walk backward with wax lights before the King—
Go on ! Spring ever in thine eye ! Go on !
Hope's favourite child ! ethereal Elliston !

ODE TO W. KITCHENER, M.D.*

AUTHOR OF THE COOK'S ORACLE—OBSERVATIONS ON VOCAL MUSIC—THE
ART OF INVIGORATING AND PROLONGING LIFE—PRACTICAL OBSERVA-
TIONS ON TELESCOPES, OPERA GLASSES, AND SPECTACLES—THE HOUSE-
KEEPER'S LEDGER—AND THE PLEASURE OF MAKING A WILL.

"I rule the roast, as Milton says !"—*Caleb Quotem.*

OH ! multifarious man !
Thou Wondrous, Admirable Kitchen Crichton :
Born to enlighten
The laws of Optics, Peptics, Music, Cooking—
Master of the Piano—and the Pan—
As busy with the kitchen as the skies !
Now looking
At some rich stew thro' Galileo's eyes—
Or boiling eggs—timed to a metronome—

---

* Born 1775, died 1827.

As much at home
In spectacles as in mere isinglass—
In the art of frying brown—as a digression
On music and poetical expression—
Whereas, how few of all our cooks, alas !
Could tell Calliope from " Callipee !"
          How few there be
Could leave the lowest for the highest stories,
          (Observatories,)
And turn, like thee, Diana's calculator,
However *cook's* synonymous with *Kater!**
          Alas ! still let me say,
          How few could lay
The carving-knife beside the tuning-fork,
Like the proverbial *Jack* ready for any work !

Oh, to behold thy features in thy book !
Thy proper head and shoulders in a plate,
          How it would look !
With one raised eye watching the dial's date,
And one upon the roast, gently cast down—
          Thy chops—done nicely brown—
The garnished brow—with " a few leaves of bay"—
          The hair—" done Wiggy's way !"
And still one studious finger near thy brains,
          As if thou wert just come
          From editing some
New soup—or hashing Dibdin's cold remains !
Or, Orpheus-like—fresh from thy dying strains
Of music—Epping luxuries of sound,
          As Milton says, " in many a bout
          Of linkèd sweetness long drawn out,"
Whilst all thy tame stuffed leopards listened round !

Oh, rather thy whole length reveal,
Standing like Fortune—on the jack—thy wheel.
(Thou art, like Fortune, full of chops and changes,
Thou hast a fillet too before thine eye !)

---

* Captain Kater, the Moon's Surveyor.

Scanning our kitchen and our vocal ranges,
As tho' it were the same to sing or fry—
Nay, so it is—hear how Miss Paton's throat
    Makes "fritters" of a note !
And how Tom Cook (Fryer and Singer born
  By name and nature) oh ! how night and morn
     He for the nicest public taste doth dish up
The good things from that *Pan* of music, Bishop !
And is not reading near akin to feeding,
  Or why should *Oxford Sausages* be fit
    Receptacles for wit ?
Or why should Cambridge put its little, smart,
    Minced brains into a *Tart ?*
Nay, then, thou wert but wise to frame receipts,
    Book-treats,
Equally to instruct the Cook and cram her—
  Receipts to be devoured, as well as read,
    The Culinary Art in gingerbread—
    The Kitchen's *Eaten* Grammar !

Oh, very pleasant is thy motley page—
  Ay, very pleasant in its chatty vein—
    So—in a kitchen—would have talked Montaigne,
That merry Gascon—humourist, and sage !
Let slender minds with single themes engage,
  Like Mr. Bowles with his eternal Pope—
Or Haydon on perpetual Haydon—or
  Hume on " Twice three make four,"
Or Lovelass upon wills—Thou goest on
Plaiting ten topics, like Tate Wilkinson !
  Thy brain is like a rich Kaleidoscope,
Stuffed with a brilliant medley of odd bits,
  And ever shifting on from change to change,
Saucepans—old Songs—Pills—Spectacles—and Spits !
  Thy range is wider than a Rumford Range !
Thy grasp a miracle !—till I recall
Th' indubitable cause of thy variety—
Thou art, of course, th' Epitome of all!
That spying—frying—singing—mixed Society
Of Scientific Friends, who used to meet
Welsh Rabbits—and thyself—in Warren Street !

Oh, hast thou still those Conversazioni,*
Where learned visitors discoursed—and fed?
       There came Belzoni,
Fresh from the ashes of Egyptian dead—
     And gentle Poki—and that Royal Pair,
     Of whom thou didst declare—
" Thanks to the greatest *Cooke* we ever read—
They were—what *Sandwiches* should be—half *bred!*"
There famed M'Adam from his manual toil
Relaxed—and freely owned he took thy hints
     On " making *Broth* with *Flints*"—
There Parry came and showed thee polar oil
For melted butter—Combe with his medullary
      Notions about the *Skullery*,
And Mr. Poole, too partial to a broil—
There witty Rogers came, that punning elf!
      Who used to swear thy book
       Would really look
A *Delphic* " Oracle," if laid on *Delf*—
There, once a month, came Campbell and discussed
His own—and thy own—"*Magazine of Taste*"—
     There Wilberforce the Just
Came in his old black suit, till once he traced
   Thy sly advice to *Poachers* of Black Folks,
     That " do not break their *yolks*,"—
Which huffed him home, in grave disgust and haste!

    There came John Clare, the poet, nor forbore
Thy *Patties*—thou wert hand-and-glove with Moore,
Who called thee "*Kitchen Addison*"—for why?
Thou givest rules for Health and Peptic Pills,
Forms for made dishes, and receipts for Wills,
" *Teaching us how to live and how to die!*"
There came thy Cousin-Cook, good Mrs. Fry—
There Trench, the Thames Projector, first brought on
      His sine *Quay* non—
There Martin would drop in on Monday eves,
Or Fridays, from the pens, and raise his breath
     'Gainst cattle days and death—

---

* Dr. Kitchener's conversazioni were the resort of all the wits and celebrities of the day.

Answered by Mellish, feeder of fat beeves,
  Who swore that Frenchmen never could be eager
  For fighting on soup meagre—
"And yet (as thou wouldst add) the French have seen
      A Marshall *Tureen!*"

Great was thy Evening Cluster!—often graced
With Dollond—Burgess—and Sir Humphry Davy!
'Twas there M'Dermot first inclined to Taste—
There Colburn learned the art of making paste
For puffs—and Accum analysed a gravy,
Colman—the Cutter of Coleman Street, 'tis said
Came there—and Parkins with his Ex-wise-head,
(His claim to letters)—Kater, too, the Moon's
Crony—and Graham, lofty on balloons—
There Croly stalked with holy humour heated,
Who wrote a light horse play, which Yates completed—
      And Lady Morgan, that grinding organ,
And Brasbridge telling anecdotes of spoons—
Madame Valbrèque thrice honoured thee, and came
With great Rossini, his own bow and fiddle—
The Dibdins—Tom, Charles, Frognall—came with tuns
Of poor old books, old puns!
And even Irving spared a night from fame—
And talked—till thou didst stop him in the middle,
      To serve round *Tewah-diddle.**

Then all the guests rose up, and sighed good-bye!
So let them :—thou thyself art still a *Host!*
  Dibdin—Cornaro—Newton—Mrs. Fry!
  Mrs. Glasse, Mr. Spec!—Lovelass—and Weber,
  Mathews in Quot'em—Moore's fire-worshipping Gheber—
Thrice-worthy Worthy, seem by thee engrossed!
Howbeit the Peptic Cook still rules the roast,
Potent to hush all ventriloquial snarling—
And ease the bosom pangs of indigestion!
      Thou art, sans question,
The Corporation's love—its Doctor *Darling!*
Look at the Civic Palate—nay, the bed

---

* The Doctor's composition for a *night-cap.*

Which set dear Mrs. Opie on supplying
    " Illustrations of *Lying !*"
Ninety square feet of down from heel to head
    It measured, and I dread
Was haunted by that terrible night *Mare*,
A monstrous burthen on the corporation !
Look at the Bill of Fare, for one day's share,
Sea-turtles by the score—Oxen by droves,
Geese, turkeys, by the flock—fishes and loaves
    Countless, as when the Lilliputian nation
Was making up the huge man-mountain's ration !

Oh ! worthy Doctor ! surely thou hast driven
The squatting Demon from great Garratt's breast—
    (His honour seemed to rest !—)
And what is thy reward ?—Hath London given
Thee public thanks for thy important service?
    Alas ! not even
The tokens it bestowed on Howe and Jervis !—
Yet could I speak as Orators should speak
Before the worshipful the Common Council,
(Utter my bold bad grammar and pronounce ill,)
Thou shouldst not miss thy Freedom, for a week,
Richly engrossed on vellum :—Reason urges
That he who rules our cookery—that he ·
Who edits soups and gravies, ought to be
A *Citizen*, where sauce can make a *Burgess !**

---

* The *London Magazine* for October, 1821, contains a review of Dr. Kitchener's *Cook's Oracle*, supposed to be written by Hood ; and in the November number of the same journal is the following ode :—

ODE TO DR. KITCHENER.

Ye Muses nine inspire,
And stir up my poetic fire ;
Teach my burning soul to speak
    With a bubble and a squeak !
Of Dr. Kitchener I fain would sing,
Till pots, and pans, and mighty kettles ring.

O culinary Sage !
(I do not mean the herb in use,
That always goes along with goose),
    How have I feasted on thy page !

AN ADDRESS TO THE VERY REVEREND JOHN IRELAND, D.D.

THE DEAN AND CHAPTER OF WESTMINSTER.

CHARLES FYNES CLINTON, LL.D.
THOMAS CAUSTON, D.D.
HOWEL HOLLAND EDWARDS, M.A.
JOSEPH ALLEN, M.A.
LORD HENRY FITZROY, M.A.
THE BISHOP OF EXETER.

W. M. H. EDWARD BENTINCK.
JAMES WEBBER, B.D.
WILLIAM SHORT, D.D.
JAMES TOURNAY, D.D.
ANDREW BELL, D.D.
GEORGE HOLCOMBE, D.D.

"Sure the Guardians of the Temple can never think they get enough."
Citizen of the World.

OH, very reverend Dean and Chapter,
    Exhibitors of giant men,
Hail to each surplice-backed Adapter
    Of England's dead, in her Stone den !
Ye teach us properly to prize
    Two-shilling Grays, and Gays, and Handels,
And, to throw light upon our eyes
    Deal in Wax Queens like old wax candles.

"When like a lobster boiled, the morn
From black to red began to turn,"
Till midnight, when I went to bed,
And clapped my *tewah-diddle* on my head.

Who is there cannot tell
    Thou lead'st a life of living well?
"What baron, or squire, or knight of the shire,
Lives half so well as a holy Fry-er?"
    In doing well thou must be reckon'd
    The first, and Mrs. Fry the second ;
And twice a Job—for in thy feverish toils
Thou wast all over roasts, as well as boils.

Thou wast indeed no dunce,
To treat thy subjects and thyself at once.
    Many a hungry poet eats
        His brains like thee,
        But few there be
Could live so long on their receipts.
What living soul or sinner
Would slight thy invitation to a dinner,

Oh, reverend showmen, rank and file,
    Call in your shillings, two and two;
March with them up the middle aisle,
    And cloister them from public view.
Yours surely are the dusty dead,
    Gladly ye look from bust to bust,
Setting a price on each great head,
    To make it come down with the dust.

Oh, as I see you walk along
    In ample sleeves and ample back
A pursy and well-ordered throng,
    Thoroughly fed, thoroughly black!
In vain I strive me to be dumb—
    You keep each bard like fatted kid,
Grind bones for bread like Fee faw fum!
    And drink from skulls as Byron did!

Ought with the Danaïdes to dwell,
    Draw gravy in a cullender, and hear
    Forever in his ear
The pleasant tinkling of thy dinner bell.

    Immortal Kitchener! thy fame
    Shall keep itself when Time makes game
Of other men's. Yea, it shall keep all weathers,
And thou shalt be upheld by the pen-feathers.
Yea, by the sauce of Michael Kelly,
    Thy name shall perish never,
    But be magnified forever,
By all whose eyes are bigger than their belly

    Yea, till the world is done
    To a turn, and Time puts out the Sun,
Shall live the endless echo of thy name,
But as for thy more fleshy frame,
Oh, Death's carnivorous teeth will tittle
Thee out of breath, and eat it for cold victual.
But still thy fame shall be among the nations
Preserved to the last course of generations.

    Ah, me! my soul is touched with sorrow
    To think how flesh must pass away;
    So mutton that is warm to-day
    Is cold and turned to hashes on the morrow!
        Farewell; I would say more, but I
        Have other fish to fry.

The profitable Abbey is
    A sacred 'Change for stony stock,
Not that a speculation 'tis—
    The profit's founded on a rock.
Death, Dean, and Doctors, in each nave
    Bony investments have inurned !
And hard 'twould be to find a grave
    From which "no money is returned !"

Here many a pensive pilgrim, brought
    By reverence for those learned bones,
Shall often come and walk your short
    Two-shilling* fare upon the stones.—
Ye have that talisman of Wealth,
    Which puddling chemists sought of old,
Till ruined out of hope and health ;—
    The Tomb's the stone that turns to gold !

Oh, licensed cannibals, ye eat
    Your dinners from your own dead race,
Think Gray, preserved, a "funeral meat,"
    And Dryden, deviled, after grace,
A relish ;—and you take your meal
    From Rare Ben Jonson underdone,
Or, whet your holy knives on Steele,
    To cut away at Addison !

O say, of all this famous age,
    Whose learned bones your hopes expect,
Oh have ye numbered Rydal's sage,
    Or Moore among your Ghosts elect ?
Lord Byron was not doomed to make
    You richer by his final sleep—
Why don't ye warn the Great to take
    Their ashes to no other heap ?

---

* Since this poem was written, Dr. Ireland and those in authority under him have reduced the fares. It is gratifying to the English People to know, that while butchers' meat is rising, tombs are falling. (Note by the author.)

Southey's reversion have ye got?
With Coleridge, for his body, made
A bargain?—has Sir Walter Scott,
Like Peter Schlemihl, sold his shade?
Has Rogers haggled hard, or sold
His features for your marble shows,
Or Campbell bartered, ere he's cold,
All interest in his " *bone* repose?"

Rare is your show, ye righteous men!
Priestly Politos—rare, I ween;
But should ye not *outside* the Den
Paint up what *in* it may be seen?
A long green Shakspeare, with a deer
Grasped in the many folds it died in—
A Butler stuffed from ear to ear,
Wet White Bears weeping o'er a Dry-den!

Paint Garrick up like Mr. Papp,
A Giant of some inches high;
Paint Handel up, that organ chap,
With you, as grinders, in his eye;
Depict some plaintive antique thing,
And say th' original may be seen;—
Blind Milton with a dog and string
May be the Beggar o' Bethnal Green!

Put up in Poet's Corner, near
The little door, a platform small;
Get there a monkey—never fear,
You'll catch the gapers one and all!
Stand each of ye a Body Guard,
A Trumpet under either fin,
And yell away in Palace Yard
" All dead! All dead! Walk in! Walk in!"

(But when the people are inside,
Their money paid—I pray you, bid
The keepers not to mount and ride
A race around each coffin lid.—
Poor Mrs. Bodkin thought last year,
That it was hard—the woman clacks—

To have so little in her ear—
    And be so hurried through the Wax !—)

" Walk in ! two shillings only ! come !
    Be not by country grumblers funked !—
Walk in, and see th' illustrious dumb !
    The Cheapest House for the defunct !"
Write up, 'twill breed some just reflection,
    And every rude surmise 'twill stop—
Write up, that you have no connection
    (In large)—with any other shop !

And still, to catch the Clowns the more,
    With samples of your shows in Wax,
Set some old Harry near the door
    To answer queries with his *axe.*—
Put up some general begging-trunk—
    Since the last broke by some mishap,
You've all a bit of General Monk,
    From the respect you bore his Cap !

ODE TO H. BODKIN, ESQUIRE,

SECRETARY TO THE SOCIETY FOR THE SUPPRESSION OF
MENDICITY.*

" This is your charge—you shall comprehend all vagrom men."
                           Much Ado About Nothing.

HAIL, King of Shreds and Patches, hail,
    Disperser of the Poor !
Thou Dog in office, set to bark
    All beggars from the door !

---

* The Society for the Suppression of Mendicity was instituted in 1813. Mr.
Bodkin made himself notorious by his active prosecution of beggars and vaga-
bonds.

Great overseer of overseers,
    And Dealer in old rags !
Thy public duty never fails,
    Thy ardour never flags !

Oh, when I take my walks abroad,
    How many Poor I *miss !*
Had Doctor Watts walked now-a-days
    He would have written this !

So well thy Vagrant catchers prowl,
    So clear thy caution keeps
The path—O, Bodkin, sure thou hast
    The eye that never sleeps !

No Belisarius pleads for alms,
    No Benbow lacketh legs ;
The pious man in black is now
    The only man that begs !

Street-Handels are disorganized,
    Disbanded every band !—
The silent *scraper* at the door
    Is scarce allowed to stand !

The Sweeper brushes with his broom,
    The Carstairs with his chalk
Retires—the Cripple leaves his stand,
    But cannot sell his walk.

The old Wall-blind resigns the wall,
    The Camels hide their humps,
The Witherington without a leg
    Mayn't beg upon his stumps !

Poor Jack is gone, that used to doff
    His battered tattered hat,
And show his dangling sleeve, alas !
    There seemed no arm in that !

Oh ! it was such a sin to air
   His true blue naval rags,
Glory's own trophy, like St. Paul,
   Hung round with holy flags !

Thou knowest best.   I meditate,
   My Bodkin, no offence !
Let us, henceforth, but guard our pounds,
   Thou dost protect our pence !

Well art thou pointed 'gainst the Poor,
   For, when the Beggar Crew
Bring their petitions, thou art paid,
   Of course, to " run them through."

Doubtless thou art what Hamlet meant
   To wretches the last friend :
What ills can mortals have, they can't
   " With a bare *Bodkin*" end ?

WHIMS AND ODDITIES.

𝔉𝔦𝔯𝔰𝔱 𝔖𝔢𝔯𝔦𝔢𝔰.

"O Cicero! Cicero! if to pun be a crime, 'tis a crime I have learned of thee.
O Bias! Bias! if to pun be a crime, by thy example I was biassed."

SCRIBLERUS.

𝔇𝔢𝔡𝔦𝔠𝔞𝔱𝔦𝔬𝔫.

TO THE REVIEWERS.

What is a modern Poet's fate?
To write his thoughts upon a slate;—
The Critic spits on what is done,—
Gives it a wipe,—and all is gone.

MORAL REFLECTIONS ON THE CROSS OF ST. PAUL'S.

I.

THE man that pays his pence, and goes
 Up to thy lofty cross, St. Paul,
Looks over London's naked nose,
  Women and men:
  The world is all beneath his ken,
 He sits above the *Ball.*
He seems on Mount Olympus' top,
Among the Gods, by Jupiter! and lets drop
  His eyes from the empyreal clouds
  On mortal crowds.

II.

Seen from these skies,
How small those emmets in our eyes!
Some carry little sticks—and one
His eggs—to warm them in the sun:

   Dear ! what a hustle,
   And bustle !
And there's my aunt. I know her by her waist,
   So long and thin,
   And so pinched in,
Just in the pismire taste.

III.

Oh ! what are men ?—Beings so small,
   That, should I fall
   Upon their little heads, I must
Crush them by hundreds into dust !

IV.

And what is life ? and all its ages—
   There's seven stages !
Turnham Green ! Chelsea ! Putney ! Fulham !
   Brentford ! and Kew !
   And Tooting, too !
And oh ! what very little nags to pull 'em.
Yet each would seem a horse indeed,
  If here at Paul's tip-top we'd got 'em ;
Although, like Cinderella's breed,
  They're mice at bottom.
Then let me not despise a horse,
Though he looks small from Paul's high cross !
Since he would be,—as near the sky,
   —Fourteen hands high.

V.

What is this world with London in its lap ?
   Mogg's Map.
The Thames that ebbs and flows in its broad channel ?
   A *tidy* kennel.
The bridges stretching from its banks ?
   Stone planks.
Oh me ! hence could I read an admonition
   To mad Ambition !
But that he would not listen to my call,
Though I should stand upon the cross, and *ball !*

A VALENTINE.

I.

OH ! cruel heart ! ere these posthumous papers
    Have met thine eyes, I shall be out of breath ;
Those cruel eyes, like two funereal tapers,
    Have only lighted me the way to death.
Perchance, thou wilt extinguish them in vapours,
    When I am gone, and green grass covereth
Thy lover, lost ; but it will be in vain—
It will not bring the vital spark again.

II.

Ah ! when those eyes, like tapers, burned so blue,
    It seemed an omen that we must expect
The sprites of lovers : and it boded true,
    For I am half a sprite—a ghost elect ;
Wherefore I write to thee this last adieu,
    With my last pen—before that I effect
My exit from the stage ; just stopped before
The tombstone steps that lead us to death's door.

III.

Full soon these living eyes, now liquid bright,
    Will turn dead dull, and wear no radiance, save
They shed a dreary and inhuman light,
    Illumed within by glow-worms of the grave ;
These ruddy cheeks, so pleasant to the sight,
    These lusty legs, and all the limbs I have,
Will keep Death's carnival, and, foul or fresh,
Must bid farewell, a long farewell, to flesh !

IV.

Yea, and this very heart, that dies for thee,
    As broken victuals to the worms will go ;
And all the world will dine again but me—
    For I shall have no stomach ;—and I know,

When I am ghostly, thou wilt sprightly be
    As now thou art; but will not tears of woe
Water thy spirits, with remorse adjunct,
When thou dost pause, and think of the defunct?

V.

And when thy soul is buried in a sleep,
    In midnight solitude, and little dreaming
Of such a spectre—what, if I should creep
    Within thy presence in such dismal seeming?
Thine eyes will stare themselves awake, and weep,
    And thou wilt cross thyself with treble screaming,
And pray, with mingled penitence and dread
That I were less alive—or not so dead.

VI.

Then will thy heart confess thee, and reprove
    This wilful homicide which thou hast done:
And the sad epitaph of so much love
    Will eat into thy heart, as if in stone:
And all the lovers that around thee move,
    Will read my fate, and tremble for their own;
And strike upon their heartless breasts, and sigh,
" Man, born of woman, must of woman die!"

VII.

Mine eyes grow dropsical—I can no more—
    And what is written thou may'st scorn to read,
Shutting thy tearless eyes.—'Tis done—'tis o'er—
    My hand is destined for another deed.
But one last word wrung from its aching core,
    And my lone heart in silentness will bleed;
Alas! it ought to take a life to tell
That one last word—that fare—fare—fare thee well!

LOVE.

O LOVE ! what art thou, Love ? the ace of hearts,
 Trumping earth's kings and queens, and all its suits ;
A player, masquerading many parts
 In life's odd carnival ;—A boy that shoots,
From ladies' eyes, such mortal woundy darts ;
 A gardener, pulling heart's-ease up by the roots ;
The Puck of Passion—partly false—part real—
A marriageable maiden's "beau-ideal."

O Love, what art thou, Love ? a wicked thing,
 Making green misses spoil their work at school ;
A melancholy man, cross-gartering ?
 Grave ripe-faced wisdom made an April fool ?
A youngster tilting at a wedding-ring ?
 A sinner, sitting on a cuttie stool ?
A Ferdinand de Something in a hovel,
Helping Matilda Rose to make a novel ?

O Love ! what art thou, Love ? one that is bad
 With palpitations of the heart—like mine—
A poor bewildered maid, making so sad
 A necklace of her garters—fell design !
A poet, gone unreasonably mad,
 Ending his sonnets with a hempen line ?
O Love !—but whither now ? forgive me, pray ;
I'm not the first that Love hath led astray.

"PLEASE TO RING THE BELLE."

I.

I'LL tell you a story that's not in Tom Moore :—
Young Love likes to knock at a pretty girl's door :
So he call'd upon Lucy—'twas just ten o'clock—
Like a spruce single man, with a smart double knock.

II.

Now, a handmaid, whatever her fingers be at,
Will run like a puss when she hears a *rat*-tat:
So Lucy ran up—and in two seconds more
Had questioned the stranger and answered the door.

III.

The meeting was bliss; but the parting was woe;
For the moment will come when such comers must go:
So she kissed him, and whispered—poor innocent thing—
" The next time you come, love, pray come with a ring."

———

A RECIPE—FOR CIVILIZATION.

The following Poem—is from the Pen of DOCTOR KITCHENER !—the most heterogeneous of Authors, but at the same time—in the Sporting Latin of Mr. Egan,—a real Homo-*genius*, or a Genius of a Man ! in the Poem, his CULINARY ENTHUSIASM, as usual, *boils over!* and makes it seem written, as he describes himself (see The Cook's Oracle)—with the Spit in one hand !—and the Frying-Pan in the other,—While in the style of the rhymes it is Hudibrastic,——as if in the ingredients of Versification, he had been assisted by his BUTLER !

As a Head Cook, Optician—Physician, Music Master—Domestic Economist and Death-bed Attorney !—I have celebrated The Author elsewhere with approbation :—And cannot now place him upon the Table *as a Poet*,—— without still being his LAUDER, a phrase which those persons whose course of classical reading recalls the INFAMOUS FORGERY on *The Immortal Bard of Avon !*——will find easy to understand.

SURELY, those sages err who teach
That man is known from brutes by speech,
Which hardly severs man from woman,
But not th' inhuman from the human,—
Or else might parrots claim affinity,
And dogs be doctors by latinity,—
Not t' insist, (as might be shown,)
That beasts have gibberish of their own,
Which once was no dead tongue, though we
Since Æsop's days have lost the key ;
Nor yet to hint dumb men,—and, still, not
Beasts that could gossip though they will not,

But play at dummy like the monkeys,
For fear mankind should make them flunkies.
Neither can man be known by feature
Or form, because so like a creature,
That some grave men could never shape
Which is the aped and which the ape,
Nor by his gait, nor by his height,
Nor yet because he's black or white,
But *rational*,—for so we call
The only Cooking Animal!
The only one who brings his bit
Of dinner to the pot or spit,
For where's the lion e'er was hasty,
To put his ven'son in a pasty?
Ergo, by logic, we repute,
That he that cooks is not a brute,—
But Equus brutum est, which means,
If a horse had sense he'd boil his beans,
Nay, no one but a horse would forage
On naked oats instead of porridge,
Which proves if brutes and Scotchmen vary,
The difference is culinary.
Further, as man is known by feeding
From brutes,—so men from men, in breeding,
Are still distinguished as they eat,
And raw in manners raw in meat,—
Look at the polished nations hight
The civilized—the most polite
Is that which bears the praise of nations
For dressing eggs two hundred fashions,
Whereas, at savage feeders look,—
The less refined the less they cook ;
From Tartar grooms that merely straddle
Across a steak and warm their saddle,
Down to the Abyssinian squaw,
That bolts her chops and collops raw,
And, like a wild beast, cares as little
To dress her person as her victual,—
For gowns, and gloves, and caps, and tippets,
Are beauty's sauces, spice, and sippets,
And not by shamble bodies put on,
But those who roast and boil their mutton ;

So Eve and Adam wore no dresses
Because they lived on watercresses,
And till they learned to cook their crudities,
Went blind as beetles to their nudities.
For niceness comes from th' inner side,
(As an ox is drest before his hide,)
And when the entrail loathes vulgarity
The outward man will soon cull rarity,
For 'tis th' effect of what we eat
To make a man look like his meat,
As insects show their food's complexions ;
Thus fopling's clothes are like confections :
But who, to feed a jaunty coxcomb,
Would have an Abyssinian ox come ?—
Or serve a dish oi fricassees,
To clodpoles in a coat of frieze ?
Whereas a black would call for buffalo
Alive—and, no doubt, eat the offal too.
Now (this premised) it follows then
That certain culinary men
Should first go forth with pans and spits
To bring the heathens to their wits,
(For all wise Scotchmen of our century
Know that first steps are alimentary ;
And, as we have proved, flesh pots and saucepans
Must pave the way for Wilberforce plans ;)
But Bunyan erred to think the near gate
To take man's soul, was battering Ear gate,
When reason should have worked her course
As men of war do—when their force
Can't take a town by open courage,
They steal an entry with its forage.
What reverend bishop, for example,
Could preach horned Apis from his temple ?
Whereas a cook would soon unseat him,
And make his own churchwardens eat him.
Not Irving could convert those vermin,
Th' Anthropophages, by a sermon ;
Whereas your Osborne,* in a trice,
Would "take a shin of beef and spice,"—

---

* Cook to the late Sir Joseph Banks.

And raise them such a savoury smother,
No Negro would devour his brother,
But turn his stomach round as loth
As Persians, to the old black broth,—
For knowledge oftenest makes an entry,
As well as true love, through the pantry,
Where beaux that came at first for feeding
Grow gallant men and get good breeding ;—
Exempli gratia—in the West,
Ship-traders say there swims a nest
Lined with black natives, like a rookery,
But coarse as carrion crows at cookery.—
This race, though now call'd O. Y. E. men,
(To show they are more than A. B. C. men,)
Was once so ignorant of our knacks
They laid their mats upon their backs,
And grew their quartern loaves for luncheon
On trees that baked them in the sunshine.
As for their bodies, they were coated,
(For painted things are so denoted ;)
But, the naked truth is stark primevals,
That said their prayers to timber devils,
Allowed polygamy—dwelt in wigwams,—
And, when they meant a feast, ate big yams,—
And why?—because their savage nook
Had ne'er been visited by Cook,—
And so they fared till our great chief,
Brought them, not Methodists, but beef
In tubs,—and taught them how to live,
Knowing it was too soon to give,
Just then, a homily on their sins,
(For cooking ends ere grace begins,)
Or hand his tracts to the untractable
Till they could keep a more exact table—
For nature has her proper courses,
And wild men must be backed like horses,
Which, jockeys know, are never fit
For riding till they've had a bit
I' the mouth ; but then, with proper tackle,
You may trot them to a tabernacle.
Ergo (I say) he first made changes
In the heathen modes, by kitchen ranges,

And taught the king's cook, by convincing
Process, that chewing was not mincing,
And in her black fist thrust a bundle
Of tracts abridged from Glasse and Rundell,
Where, ere she had read beyond Welsh rabbits,
She saw the spareness of her habits,
And round her loins put on a striped
Towel, where fingers might be wiped,
And then her breast clothed like her ribs,
(For aprons lead of course to bibs,)
And, by the time she had got a meat-
Screen, veiled her back, too, from the heat—
As for her gravies and her sauces,
(Though they reformed the royal fauces,)
Her forcemeats and ragouts,—I praise not,
Because the legend further says not,
Except, she kept each Christian high-day,
And once upon a fat good Fry-day
Ran short of logs, and told the Pagan
That turn'd the spit, to chop up Dagon!

THE LAST MAN.

'Twas in the year two thousand and one,
A pleasant morning of May,
I sat on the gallows-tree all alone,
A chaunting a merry lay,—
To think how the pest had spared my life,
To sing with the larks that day!

When up the heath came a jolly knave,
Like a scarecrow, all in rags:
It made me crow to see his old duds
All abroad in the wind, like flags :—
So up he came to the timber's foot
And pitched down his greasy bags.

Good Lord! how blithe the old beggar was!
At pulling out his scraps,—
The very sight of his broken orts
Made a work in his wrinkled chaps :

"Come down," says he, " you Newgate bird,
And have a taste of my snaps!"——

Then down the rope, like a tar from the mast,
I slided, and by him stood ;
But I wished myself on the gallows again
When I smelt that beggar's food,
A foul beef-bone and a mouldy crust ;
" Oh !" quoth he, " the heavens are good !"

Then after this grace he cast him down :
Says I, " You'll get sweeter air
A pace or two off, on the windward side,"
For the felons' bones lay there.
But he only laugh'd at the empty skulls,
And offer'd them part of his fare.

" I never harm'd *them*, and they wont harm me :
Let the proud and the rich be cravens !"
I did not like that strange beggar man,
He looked so up at the heavens.
Anon he shook out his empty old poke ;
" There's the crumbs," saith he, " for the ravens !"

It made me angry to see his face,
It had such a jesting look ;
But while I made up my mind to speak,
A small case-bottle he took :
Quoth he, " Though I gather the green watercress,
My drink is not of the brook !"

Full manners-like he tendered the dram ;
Oh, it came of a dainty cask !
But whenever it came to his turn to pull,
" Your leave, good sir, I must ask ;
But I always wipe the brim with my sleeve,
When a hangman sups at my flask !"

And then he laughed so loudly and long,
The churl was quite out of breath ;
I thought the very Old One was come
To mock me before my death,
And wished I had buried the dead men's bones
That were lying about the heath !

But the beggar gave me a jolly clap—
" Come, let us pledge each other,
For all the wide world is dead beside,
And we are brother and brother—
I've a yearning for thee in my heart,
As if we had come of one mother.

" I've a yearning for thee in my heart
That almost makes me weep,
For as I passed from town to town
The folks were all stone-asleep,—
But when I saw thee sitting aloft,
It made me both laugh and leap !"

Now a curse (I thought) be on his love,
And a curse upon his mirth,—
An' if it were not for that beggar man
I'd be the King of the earth,—
But I promised myself an hour should come
To make him rue his birth—

So down we sat and boused again
Till the sun was in mid-sky,
When, just when the gentle west-wind came,
We hearkened a dismal cry ;
" Up, up, on the tree," quoth the beggar man,
" Till these horrible dogs go by !"

And lo ! from the forest's far-off skirts,
They came all yelling for gore,
A hundred hounds pursuing at once,
And a panting hart before,
Till he sunk down at the gallows' foot,
And there his haunches they tore !

His haunches they tore, without a horn
To tell when the chase was done ;
And there was not a single scarlet coat
To flaunt it in the sun !—
I turned, and looked at the beggar man,
And his tears dropt one by one !

And with curses sore he chid at the hounds,
Till the last dropt out of sight;
Anon, saith he, " Let's down again,
And ramble for our delight,
For the world's all free, and we may choose
A right cozy barn for to-night!"

With that, he set up his staff on end,
And it fell with the point due West;
So we fared that way to a city great,
Where the folks had died of the pest—
It was fine to enter in house and hall,
Wherever it liked me best;—

For the porters all were stiff and cold,
And could not lift their heads;
And when we came where their masters lay,
The rats leapt out of the beds:
The grandest palaces in the land
Were as free as workhouse sheds.

But the beggar man made a mumping face,
And knocked at every gate:
It made me curse to hear how he whined,
So our fellowship turned to hate,
And I bade him walk the world by himself,
For I scorned so humble a mate!

So *he* turned right, and *I* turned left,
As if we had never met;
And I chose a fair stone house for myself,
For the city was all to let;
And for three brave holidays drank my fill
Of the choicest that I could get.

And because my jerkin was coarse and worn,
I got me a proper vest;
It was purple velvet, stitched o'er with gold,
And a shining star at the breast!—
'Twas enough to fetch old Joan from her grave
To see me so purely drest!

But Joan was dead and under the mould,
And every buxom lass ;
In vain I watched, at the window pane,
For a Christian soul to pass !
But sheep and kine wandered up the street,
And browsed on the new-come grass.

When lo ! I spied the old beggar man,
And lustily he did sing !—
His rags were lapped in a scarlet cloak,
And a crown he had like a King ;
So he stepped right up before my gate
And danced me a saucy fling !

Heaven mend us all !—but, within my mind,
I had killed him then and there ;
To see him lording so braggart-like
That was born to his beggar's fare,
And how he had stolen the royal crown
His betters were meant to wear.

But God forbid that a thief should die
Without his share of the laws !
So I nimbly whipt my tackle out,
And soon tied up his claws,—
I was judge, myself, and jury, and all,
And solemnly tried the cause.

But the beggar man would not plead, but cried
Like a babe without its corals,
For he knew how hard it is apt to go
When the law and a thief have quarrels,—
There was not a Christian soul alive
To speak a word for his morals.

Oh, how gaily I doffed my costly gear,
And put on my work-day clothes ;
I was tired of such a long Sunday life,—
And never was one of the sloths ;
But the beggar man grumbled a weary deal,
And made many crooked mouths.

So I hauled him off to the gallows' foot,
And blinded him in his bags;
'Twas a weary job to heave him up,
For a doomed man always lags;
But by ten of the clock he was off his legs
In the wind, and airing his rags!

So there he hung, and there I stood,
The LAST MAN left alive,
To have my own will of all the earth:
Quoth I, now I shall thrive!
But when was ever honey made
With one bee in a hive?

My conscience began to gnaw my heart,
Before the day was done,
For other men's lives had all gone out,
Like candles in the sun!—
But it seemed as if I had broke, at last,
A thousand necks in one!

So I went and cut his body down
To bury it decentlie;—
God send there were any good soul alive
To do the like by me!
But the wild dogs came with terrible speed,
And bade me up the tree!

My sight was like a drunkard's sight,
And my head began to swim,
To see their jaws all white with foam,
Like the ravenous ocean brim:—
But when the wild dogs trotted away
Their jaws were bloody and grim!

Their jaws were bloody and grim, good Lord!
But the beggar man, where was he?—
There was naught of him but some ribbons of rags
Below the gallows' tree.
I know the Devil, when I am dead,
Will send his hounds for me!—

I've buried my babies one by one,
And dug the deep hole for Joan,
And covered the faces of kith and kin,
And felt the old churchyard stone
Go cold to my heart, full many a time,
But I never felt so lone !

For the lion and Adam were company,
And the tiger him beguiled :
But the simple kine are foes to my life,
And the household brutes are wild.
If the veriest cur would lick my hand,
I could love it like a child !

And the beggar man's ghost besets my dream
At night, to make me madder,—
And my wretched conscience within my breast
Is like a stinging adder ;
I sigh when I pass the gallows' foot,
And look at the rope and ladder !—

For hanging looks sweet,—but, alas ! in vain
My desperate fancy begs,—
I must turn my cup of sorrows quite up,
And drink it to the dregs,—
For there is not another man alive,
In the world, to pull my legs !

FAITHLESS SALLY BROWN.

AN OLD BALLAD.

Young Ben he was a nice young man,
    A carpenter by trade ;
And he fell in love with Sally Brown,
    That was a lady's maid.

But as they fetched a walk one day,
    They met a press-gang crew ;
And Sally she did faint away,
    Whilst Ben he was brought to.

The Boatswain swore with wicked words,
    Enough to shock a saint,
That though she did seem in a fit,
    'Twas nothing but a feint.

" Come, girl," said he, " hold up your head,
    He'll be as good as me ;
For when your swain is in our boat,
    A boatswain he will be."

So when they'd made their game of her,
    And taken off her elf,
She roused, and found she only was
    A coming to herself.

" And is he gone, and is he gone ?"
    She cried, and wept outright :
" Then I will to the water side,
    And see him out of sight."

A waterman came up to her,
    " Now, young woman," said he,
" If you weep on so, you will make
    Eye-water in the sea."

" Alas ! they've taken my beau Ben
    To sail with old Benbow ;"
And her woe began to run afresh,
    As if she'd said Gee woe !

Says he, " They've only taken him
    To the Tender ship, you see ;"
" The Tender ship," cried Sally Brown,
    " What a hard-ship that must be !

" Oh ! would I were a mermaid now,
    For then I'd follow him ;
But oh !—I'm not a fish-woman,
    And so I cannot swim.

" Alas ! I was not born beneath
    The Virgin and the Scales,
So I must curse my cruel stars,
    And walk about in Wales."

Now Ben had sailed to many a place
    That's underneath the world ;
But in two years the ship came home,
    And all her sails were furled.

But when he called on Sally Brown,
    To see how she went on,
He found she'd got another Ben,
    Whose Christian name was John.

" O Sally Brown, O Sally Brown,
    How could you serve me so ?
I've met with many a breeze before,
    But never such a blow."

Then reading on his 'bacco box,
    He heaved a bitter sigh,
And then began to eye his pipe,
    And then to pipe his eye.

And then he tried to sing " All's Well,"
    But could not though he tried ;
His head was turned, and so he chewed
    His pigtail till he died.

His death, which happened in his berth,
    At forty-odd befell :
They went and told the sexton, and
    The sexton toll'd the bell.

———◆———

BACKING THE FAVOURITE.

On a pistol, or a knife !
For I'm weary of my life,—
    My cup has nothing sweet left to flavour it ;
My estate is out at nurse,
And my heart is like my purse,—
    And all through backing of the Favourite !

At dear O'Neil's first start,
I sported all my heart,—
   Oh, Becher, he never marred a braver hit!
For he crossed her in her race,
And made her lose her place,
   And there was an end of that Favourite!

Anon, to mend my chance,
For the Goddess of the Dance*
   I pined, and told my enslaver it!—
But she wedded in a canter,
And made me a Levanter,
   In foreign lands to sigh for the Favourite!

Then next Miss M. A. Tree
I adored, so sweetly she
   Could warble like a nightingale and quaver it,—
But she left that course of life
To be Mr. Bradshaw's wife,
   And all the world lost on the Favourite!

But out of sorrow's surf
Soon I leaped upon the turf,
   Where fortune loves to wanton it and waver it;—
But standing on the pet,
"O my bonny, bonny Bet!"
   Black and yellow pulled short up with the Favourite!

Thus flung by all the crack,
I resolved to cut the pack,—
   The second-raters seemed then a safer hit!
So I laid my little odds
Against Memnon!   O ye Gods!
   Am I always to be floored by the Favourite!

---

* The late favourite of the King's Theatre who left the pas seul of life for a perpetual *Ball.* Is not that her effigy now commonly borne about by the Italian image vendors—an ethereal form holding a wreath with both hands above her head—and her husband, in emblem, beneath her foot?

THE MERMAID OF MARGATE.

"Alas! what perils do environ
That man who meddles with a siren!"—*Hubibras.*

On Margate beach, where the sick one roams,
    And the sentimental reads;
Where the maiden flirts, and the widow comes
    Like the ocean—to cast her weeds;—

Where urchins wander to pick up shells,
    And the Cit to spy at the ships,—
Like the water gala at Sadler's Wells,
    And the Chandler for watery dips;—

There's a maiden sits by the ocean brim,
    As lovely and fair as sin!
But woe, deep water and woe to him,
    That she snareth like Peter Fin!

Her head is crowned with pretty sea-wares,
    And her locks are golden and loose,
And seek to her feet, like other folks' heirs,
    To stand, of course, in her shoes!

And all day long she combeth them well,
    With a sea-shark's prickly jaw;
And her mouth is just like a rose-lipped shell,
    The fairest that man e'er saw!

And the Fishmonger, humble as love may be,
    Hath planted his seat by her side;
"Good even, fair maid! Is thy lover at sea,
    To make thee so watch the tide?"

She turned about with her pearly brows,
    And clasped him by the hand;
"Come, love, with me; I've a bonny house
    On the golden Goodwin Sand."

And then she gave him a siren kiss,
    No honeycomb e'er was sweeter;
Poor wretch! how little he dreamt for this
    That Peter should be salt-Peter:

And away with her prize to the wave she leapt,
 Not walking, as damsels do,
With toe and heel, as she ought to have stept,
 But she hopt like a Kangaroo ;

One plunge, and then the victim was blind,
 Whilst they gallopped across the tide ;
At last, on the bank he waked in his mind,
 And the Beauty was by his side.

One half on the sand, and half in the sea,
 But his hair began to stiffen ;
For when he looked where her feet should be,
 She had no more feet than Miss Biffen !

But a scaly tail, of a dolphin's growth,
 In the dabbling brine did soak :
At last she opened her pearly mouth,
 Like an oyster, and thus she spoke :

"You crimpt my father, who was a skate,—
 And my sister you sold—a maid ;
So here remain for a fish'ry fate,
 For lost you are, and betrayed !"

And away she went, with a seagull's scream,
 And a splash of her saucy tail ;
In a moment he lost the silvery gleam
 That shone on her splendid mail !

The sun went down with a blood-red flame,
 And the sky grew cloudy and black,
And the tumbling billows like leap-frog came,
 Each over the other's back !

Ah me ! it had been a beautiful scene,
 With the safe terra-firma round ;
But the green water-hillocks all seem'd to him
 Like those in a churchyard ground ;

And Christians love in the turf to lie,
 Not in watery graves to be ;
Nay, the very fishes will sooner die
 On the land than in the sea.

And whilst he stood, the watery strife
  Encroached on every hand,
And the ground decreased,—his moments of life
  Seemed measured, like Time's, by sand ;

And still the waters foamed in, like ale,
  In front, and on either flank,
He knew that Goodwin and Co. must fail,
  There was such a run on the bank.

A little more, and a little more,
  The surges came tumbling in,
He sang the evening hymn twice o'er,
  And thought of every sin !

Each flounder and plaice lay cold at his heart,
  As cold as his marble slab ;
And he thought he felt, in every part,
  The pincers of scalded crab.

The squealing lobsters that he had boiled,
  And the little potted shrimps,
All the horny prawns he had ever spoiled,
  Gnawed into his soul, like imps !

And the billows were wandering to and fro,
  And the glorious sun was sunk,
And Day, getting black in the face, as though
  Of the night-shade she had drunk !

Had there been but a smuggler's cargo adrift,
  One tub, or keg, to be seen,
It might have given his spirits a lift
  Or an *anker* where *Hope* might lean !

But there was not a box or a beam afloat,
  To raft him from that sad place ;
Not a skiff, not a yawl, or a mackerel boat,
  Nor a smack upon Neptune's face.

At last, his lingering hopes to buoy,
  He saw a sail and a mast,
And called " Ahoy !"—but it was not a boy,
  And so the vessel went past.

6

And with saucy wing that flapped in his face,
   The wild bird about him flew,
With a shrilly scream, that twitted his case,
   " Why, thou art a sea-gull too !"

And lo ! the tide was over his feet ;
   Oh ! his heart began to freeze,
And slowly to pulse :—in another beat
   The wave was up to his knees !

He was deafened amidst the mountain tops,
   And the salt spray blinded his eyes,
And washed away the other salt drops
   That grief had caused to arise :—

But just as his body was all afloat,
   And the surges above him broke,
He was saved from the hungry deep by a boat
   Of Deal—(but builded of oak.)

The skipper gave him a dram, as he lay,
   And chafed his shivering skin ;
And the Angel returned that was flying away
   With the spirit of Peter Fin !

AS IT FELL UPON A DAY.

OH ! what's befallen Bessy Brown,
   She stands so squalling in the street ;
She's let her pitcher tumble down,
   And all the water's at her feet !

The little schoolboys stood about,
   And laughed to see her pumping, pumping ;
Now with a curtsey to the spout,
   And then upon her tiptoes jumping.

Long time she waited for her neighbours
   To have their turns :—but she must lose
The watery wages of her labours,—
   Except a little in her shoes !

Without a voice to tell her tale,
   And ugly transport in her face;
All like a jugless nightingale,
   She thinks of her bereavèd case.

At last she sobs—she cries—she screams !—
   And pours her flood of sorrows out,
From eyes and mouth, in mingled streams,
   Just like the lion on the spout.

For well poor Bessy knows her mother
   Must lose her tea, for water's lack,
That Sukey burns—and baby-brother
   Must be dry-rubbed with huck-a-back !

A FAIRY TALE.

On Hounslow Heath—and close beside the road,
As western travellers may oft have seen,—
A little house some years ago there stood,
    A miniken abode ;
And built like Mr. Birkbeck's all of wood :
The walls of white, the window-shutters green,—
Four wheels it hath at North, South, East, and West,
    (Though now at rest)
On which it used to wander to and fro,
Because its master ne'er maintain'd a rider,
    Like those who trade in Paternoster Row ;
But made his business travel for itself,
    Till he had made his pelf,
And then retired—if one may call it so,
    Of a roadsider.

Perchance, the very race and constant riot
Of stages, long and short, which thereby ran,
Made him more relish the repose and quiet
    Of his now sedentary caravan ;
Perchance, he loved the ground because 'twas common,
    And so he might impale a strip of soil
    That furnished, by his toil,
Some dusty greens, for him and his old woman ;—

And five tall hollyhocks, in dingy flower,
Howbeit, the thoroughfare did no ways spoil
His peace, unless, in some unlucky hour,
A stray horse came, and gobbled up his bow'r.

But tired of always looking at the coaches,
The same to come,—when they had seen them one day!
    And, used to brisker life, both man and wife
Began to suffer N U E's approaches,
And feel retirement like a long wet Sunday,—
So, having had some quarters of school breeding,
They turned themselves, like other folks, to reading ;
But setting out where others nigh have done,
    And being ripened in the seventh stage,
        The childhood of old age,
Began, as other children have begun,—
Not with the pastorals of Mr. Pope,
        Or Bard of Hope,
Or Paley ethical, or learned Porson,—
But spelt, on Sabbaths, in St. Mark, or John,
And then relax'd themselves with Whittington,
        Or Valentine and Orson—
But chiefly fairy tales they loved to con,
And being easily melted in their dotage,
        Slobber'd,—and kept
        Reading,—and wept
Over the white Cat, in their wooden cottage.

      Thus reading on—the longer
They read, of course, their childish faith grew stronger
In Gnomes, and Hags, and Elves, and Giants grim,—
If talking Trees and Birds revealed to him,
She saw the flight of Fairyland's fly-waggons,
    And magic fishes swim
In puddle ponds, and took old crows for dragons,—
Both were quite drunk from the enchanted flagons ;
When as it fell upon a summer's day,
    As the old man sat a feeding
      On the old babe-reading,
Beside his open street-and-parlour door,
      A hideous roar
Proclaimed a drove of beasts was coming by the way.

Long-horned, and short, of many a different breed,
Tall, tawny brutes, from famous Lincoln-levels
   Or Durham feed;
With some of those unquiet black dwarf devils
   From nether side of Tweed,
   Or Firth of Forth;
Looking half wild with joy to leave the North,—
With dusty hides, all mobbing on together,—
When,—whether from a fly's malicious comment
Upon his tender flank, from which he shrank;
   Or whether
Only in some enthusiastic moment,—
However, one brown monster, in a frisk,
Giving his tail a perpendicular whisk,
Kicked out a passage through the beastly rabble;
And after a pas seul,—or, if you will, a
Horn-pipe before the Basket-maker's villa,
   Leapt o'er the tiny pale,—
Backed his beefsteaks against the wooden gable,
And thrust his brawny bell-rope of a tail
   Right o'er the page,
   Wherein the sage
Just then was spelling some romantic fable.

The old man, half a scholar, half a dunce,
Could not peruse,—who could?—two tales at once;
   And being huffed
At what he knew was none of Riquet's Tuft;
   Banged-to the door,
But most unluckily enclosed a morsel
Of the intruding tail, and all the tassel :—
   The monster gave a roar,
And bolting off with speed increased by pain,
The little house became a coach once more,
And, like Macheath, " took to the road" again!

Just then, by fortune's whimsical decree,
The ancient woman stooping with her crupper
Towards sweet home, or where sweet home should be,
Was getting up some household herbs for supper;
Thoughtful of Cinderella, in the tale,
And quaintly wondering if magic shifts

Could o'er a common pumpkin so prevail,
To turn it to a coach ;—what pretty gifts
Might come of cabbages, and curly kale ;
Meanwhile she never heard her old man's wail,
Nor turned, till home had turned a corner, quite
　　　　　Gone out of sight !

At last, conceive her, rising from the ground,
Weary of sitting on her russet clothing
　　　　　And looking round
　　　　　Where rest was to be found,
There was no house—no villa there—no nothing !
　　　　　No house !
　　　　　The change was quite amazing ;
It made her senses stagger for a minute,
The riddle's explication seemed to harden ;
But soon her superannuated *nous*
Explain'd the horrid mystery ;—and raising
Her hand to heaven, with the cabbage in it,
　　　　　On which she meant to sup,—
"Well ! this *is* Fairy Work ! I'll bet a farden,
Little Prince Silverwings has ketch'd me up,
And set me down in some one else's garden !"

THE FALL OF THE DEER.

[From an old MS.]

Now the loud Crye is up, and harke !
The barkye Trees give back the Bark ;
The House Wife heares the merrie rout,
And runnes,—and lets the beere run out,
Leaving her Babes to weepe,—for why ?
She likes to heare the Deer Dogges crye,
And see the wild Stag how he stretches
The naturall Buck-skin of his Breeches,
Running like one of Human kind
Dogged by fleet Bailiffes close behind—
As if he had not payde his Bill
For Ven'son, or was owing still

For his two Hornes, and soe did get
Over his Head and Ears in Debt ;—
Wherefore he strives to paye his Waye
With his long Legges the while he maye :—
But he is chased, like Silver Dish,
As well as anye Hart may wish
Except that one whose Heart doth beat
So faste it hasteneth his Feet ;—
And runninge soe he holdeth Death
Four Feet from him,—till his Breath
Faileth, and slacking Pace at last,
From runninge slow he standeth faste,
With hornie Bayonettes at baye
To baying Dogges around, and they
Pushing him sore, he pusheth sore,
And goreth them that seek his Gore,—
Whatever Dogge his Horne doth rive
Is dead—as sure as he's alive !
Soe that courageous Hart doth fight
With Fate, and calleth up his might,
And standeth stout that he may fall
Bravelye, and be avenged of all,
Nor like a Craven yeeld his Breath
Under the Jawes of Dogges and Death !

DECEMBER AND MAY.

" Crabbed Age and Youth cannot live together."
SHAKSPEARE.

SAID Nestor, to his pretty wife, quite sorrowful one day,
" Why, dearest, will you shed in pearls those lovely eyes away,
You ought to be more fortified." " Ah, brute, be quiet, do,
I know I'm not so fortyfied, nor fiftyfied, as you !

" Oh, men are vile deceivers all, as I have ever heard,
You'd die for me you swore, and I—I took you at your word.
I was a tradesman's widow then—a pretty change I've made ;
To live and die the wife of one, a widower by trade !"

" Come, come, my dear, these flighty airs declare, in sober truth,
You want as much in age, indeed, as I can want in youth;
Besides, you said you liked old men, though now at me you huff."
" Why, yes," she said, " and so I do—but you're not old enough!"

" Come, come, my dear, let's make it up, and have a quiet hive;
I'll be the best of men—I mean, I'll be the best *alive!*
Your grieving so will kill me, for it cuts me to the core."
" I thank ye, sir, for telling me—for now I'll grieve the more!"

A WINTER NOSEGAY.

OH, withered winter blossoms,
Dowager-flowers,—the December vanity,
In antiquated visages and bosoms.
What are ye planned for,
Unless to stand for
Emblems, and peevish morals of humanity?
There is my Quaker Aunt,
A Paper-Flower,—with a formal border
No breeze could e'er disorder,
Pouting at that old beau—the Winter Cherry,
A puckered berry;
And Box, like a tough-lived annuitant,—
Verdant alway—
From quarter-day even to quarter-day;
And poor old Honesty, as thin as want,
Well named—God-wot;
Under the baptism of the water-pot,
The very apparition of a plant;
And why,
Dost hold thy head so high,
Old Winter-Daisy;
Because thy virtue never was infirm,
Howe'er thy stalk be crazy?
That never wanton fly, or blighting worm,
Made holes in thy most perfect indentation?
'Tis likely that sour leaf,
To garden thief,

Forcepped or winged, was never a temptation ;—
Well,—still uphold thy wintry-reputation ;
Still shalt thou frown upon all lovers' trial :
And when, like Grecian maids, young maids of ours
　　　　Converse with flow'rs,
Then thou shalt be the token of denial.
　　　Away ! dull weeds,
Born without beneficial use or needs !
Fit only to deck out cold winding sheets ;
And then not for the milkmaid's funeral-bloom,
　　　　Or fair Fidele's tomb——
　　　　　To tantalize,—vile cheats !
Some prodigal bee, with hope of after-sweets,
　　　　Frigid and rigid,
　　　　As if ye never knew
　　　　One drop of dew,
Or the warm sun resplendent ;
Indifferent of culture and of care,
Giving no sweets back to the fostering air,
　　　Churlishly independent—
　　　　I hate ye, of all breeds ;
Yea, all that live so selfishly—to self,
And not by interchange of kindly deeds—
　　　　Hence !—from my shelf !

EQUESTRIAN COURTSHIP.

It was a young maiden went forth to ride,
And there was a wooer to pace by her side ;
His horse was so little, and hers so high,
He thought his Angel was up in the sky.

His love was great, though his wit was small ;
He bade her ride easy—and that was all.
The very horses began to neigh,—
Because their betters had nought to say.

They rode by elm, and they rode by oak,
They rode by a churchyard, and then he spoke :
" My pretty maiden, if you'll agree,
You shall always amble through life with me."

The damsel answered him never a word,
But kicked the grey mare, and away she spurred.
The wooer still followed behind the jade,
And enjoyed—like a wooer—the dust she made.

They rode thro' moss, and they rode thro' more,—
The gallant behind and the lass before :—
At last they came to a miry place,
And there the sad wooer gave up the chase.

Quoth he, " If my nag was better to ride,
I'd follow her over the world so wide.
Oh, it is not my love that begins to fail,
But I've lost the last glimpse of the grey mare's tail !"

SHE IS FAR FROM THE LAND.

Cables entangling her,
Shipspars for mangling her,
Ropes, sure of strangling her ;
Blocks over-dangling her ;
Tiller to batter her,
Topmast to shatter her,
Tobacco to spatter her ;
Boreas blustering,
Boatswain quite flustering,
Thunder-clouds mustering
To blast her with sulphur—
If the deep don't engulf her ;
Sometimes fear's scrutiny
Pries out a mutiny,
Sniffs conflagration,
Or hints at starvation :—
All the sea-dangers,
Buccaneers, rangers,
Pirates and Salle-men,
Algerine galleymen,
Tornadoes and typhons,
And horrible syphons,
And submarine travels
Thro' roaring sea-navels,

Everything wrong enough,
Long-boat not long enough,
Vessel not strong enough;
Pitch marring frippery,
The deck very slippery,
And the cabin—built sloping,
The Captain a-toping,
And the mate a blasphemer,
That names his Redeemer,
With inward uneasiness;
The cook known, by greasiness,
The victuals beslubber'd,
Her bed—in a cupboard;
Things of strange christening,
Snatched in her listening,
Blue lights and red lights
And mention of dead-lights,
And shrouds made a theme of,
Things horrid to dream of,—
And *buoys* in the water
To fear all exhort her;
Her friend no Leander,
Herself no sea-gander,
And ne'er a cork jacket
On board of the packet;
The breeze still a-stiffening,
The trumpet quite deafening;
Thoughts of repentance,
And doomsday and sentence;
Everything sinister,
Not a church minister,—
Pilot a blunderer,
Coral reefs under her,
Ready to sunder her;
Trunks tipsy-topsy,
The ship in a dropsy;
Waves oversurging her,
Sirens a-dirgeing her;
Sharks all expecting her,
Swordfish dissecting her,
Crabs with their hand-vices
Punishing land vices;

Sea-dogs and unicorns,
Things with no puny horns,
Mermen carnivorous—
" Good Lord deliver us !"

THE STAG-EYED LADY.

A MOORISH TALE.

Scheherazade immediately began the following story.

ALI BEN ALI (did you never read
   His wondrous acts that chronicles relate,—
How there was one in pity might exceed
   The sack of Troy ?) magnificent he sate
Upon the throne of greatness—great indeed,
   For those that he had under him were great—
The horse he rode on, shod with silver nails,
Was a Bashaw—Bashaws have horses' tails.

Ali was cruel—a most cruel one !
   'Tis rumoured he had strangled his own mother—
Howbeit such deeds of darkness he had done,
   'Tis thought he would have slain his elder brother
And sister too—but happily that none
   Did live within *harm's* length of one another,
Else he had sent the Sun in all its blaze
To endless night, and shorten'd the Moon's days.

Despotic power, that mars a weak man's wit,
   And makes a bad man—absolutely bad,
Made Ali wicked—to a fault :—'tis fit
   Monarchs should have some check-strings ; but he had
No curb upon his will—no, not a *bit*—
   Wherefore he did not reign well—and full glad
His slaves had been to hang him—but they faltered,
And let him live unhanged—and still unaltered,

Until he got a sage bush of a beard,
   Wherein an Attic owl might roost—a trail

Of bristly hair—that, honoured and unsheared,
   Grew downward like old women and cow's tail,
Being a sign of age—some grey appeared,
   Mingling with duskier brown its warnings pale ;
But yet not so poetic as when Time
Comes like Jack Frost, and whitens it in rime.

Ben Ali took the hint, and much did vex
   His royal bosom that he had no son,
No living child of the more noble sex,
   To stand in his Morocco shoes—not one
To make a negro-pollard—or tread necks
   When he was gone—doomed, when his days were done,
To leave the very city of his fame
Without an Ali to keep up his name.

Therefore he chose a lady for his love,
   Singling from out the herd one stag-eyed dear ;
So called, because her lustrous eyes, above
   All eyes, were dark, and timorous, and clear ;
Then, through his Muftis piously he strove,
   And drummèd with proxy-prayers Mohammed's ear,
Knowing a boy for certain must come of it,
Or else he was not praying to his *Profit*.

Beer will grow *mothery*, and ladies fair
   Will grow like beer : so did that stag-eyed dame :
Ben Ali hoping for a son and heir,
   Boyed up his hopes, and even chose a name
Of mighty hero that his child should bear ;
   He made so certain ere his chicken came :
But oh ! all worldly wit is little worth,
Nor knoweth what to-morrow will bring forth.

To-morrow came, and with to-morrow's sun
   A little daughter to this world of sins,—
Miss-fortunes never come alone—so one
   Brought on another, like a pair of twins !
Twins ! female twins !—it was enough to stun
   Their little wits and scare them from their skins
To hear their father stamp, and curse and swear,
Pulling his beard because he had no heir,

Then strove their stag-eyed mother to calm down
   This his paternal rage, and thus addrest :
" O ! most Serene ! why dost thou stamp and frown,
   And box the compass of the royal chest ?
Ah ! thou wilt mar that portly trunk, I own
   I love to gaze on !—Pr'ythee, thou hadst best
Pocket thy fists.   Nay, love, if you so thin
Your beard, you'll want a wig upon your chin !"

But not her words, nor e'en her tears, could slack
   The quicklime of his rage, that hotter grew ;
He called his slaves to bring an ample sack
   Wherein a woman might be *poked*—a few
Dark grimly men felt pity and looked black
   . At this sad order ; but their slaveships knew
When any dared demur, his sword so bending
Cut off the " head and front of their offending."

For Ali had a sword, much like himself,
   A crooked blade, guilty of human gore—
The trophies it had lopped from many an elf
   Were stuck at his *head*-quarters by the score—
Nor yet in peace he laid it on the shelf,
   But jested with it, and his wit cut sore ;
So that (as they of Public Houses speak)
He often did his dozen *butts* a week.

Therefore his slaves, with most obedient fear,
   Came with the sack the lady to enclose ;
In vain from her stag-eyes " the big round tears
   Coursed one another down her innocent nose ;"
In vain her tongue wept sorrow in their ears ;
   Though there were some felt willing to oppose,
Yet when their heads came in their heads, that minute,
Though 'twas a piteous *case*, they put her in it.

And when the sack was tied, some two or three
   Of these black undertakers slowly brought her
To a kind of Moorish Serpentine ; for she
   Was doom'd to have *a winding sheet of water*.
Then farewell, earth—farewell to the green tree—
   Farewell, the sun—the moon—each little daughter !

She's shot from off the shoulders of a black,
Like a bag of Wall's End from a coalman's back.

The waters oped, and the wide sack full-filled
   All that the waters oped, as down it fell ;
Then closed the wave, and then the surface rilled
   A ring above her, like a water-knell ;
A moment more, and all its face was stilled,
   And not a guilty heave was left to tell
That underneath its calm and blue transparence
A dame lay drownèd in her sack, like Clarence.

But Heaven beheld, and awful witness bore,
   The moon in black eclipse deceased that night,
Like Desdemona smothered by the Moor,
   The lady's natal star with pale affright
Fainted and fell—and what were stars before,
   Turned comets as the tale was brought to light :
And all looked downward on the fatal wave,
And made their own reflections on her grave.

Next night a head—a little lady head,
   Pushed through the waters a most glassy face,
With weedy tresses, thrown apart and spread,
   Combed by live ivory, to show the space
Of a pale forehead, and two eyes that shed
   A soft blue mist, breathing a bloomy grace
Over their sleepy lids—and so she raised
Her *aqua*line nose above the stream, and gazed.

She oped her lips—lips of a gentle blush,
   So pale it seemed near drowned to a white,—
She oped her lips, and forth there sprang a gush
   Of music bubbling through the surface light ;
The leaves are motionless, the breezes hush
   To listen to the air—and through the night
There come these words of a most plaintive ditty,
Sobbing as it would break all hearts with pity :

THE WATER PERI'S SONG.

Farewell, farewell, to my mother's own daughter,
   The child that she wet-nursed is lapped in the wave ;
The *Mussul*man coming to fish in this water,
   Adds a tear to the flood that weeps over her grave.

This sack is her coffin, this water's her bier,
　This greyish *bath* cloak is her funeral pall;
And, stranger, O stranger! this song that you hear
　Is her epitaph, elegy, dirges, and all!

Farewell, farewell, to the child of Al Hassan,
　My mother's own daughter—the last of her race—
She's a corpse, the poor body! and lies in this basin,
　And sleeps in the water that washes her face.

REMONSTRATORY ODE,

FROM THE ELEPHANT AT EXETER 'CHANGE, TO MR. MATHEWS,
AT THE ENGLISH OPERA-HOUSE.

" See with what courteous action
He beckons you to a more removed ground."—*Hamlet.*

[WRITTEN BY A FRIEND.]

I.

Oh, Mr. Mathews! Sir!
(If a plain elephant may speak his mind,
And that I have a mind to speak I find
　　By my inward stir)
I long have thought, and wished to say, that we
Mar our well-merited prosperity
　　By being such near neighbours;
My keeper now hath lent me pen and ink,
Shoved in my truss of lunch, and tub of drink,
　　And left me to my labours.
The whole menagerie is in repose,
The Coatamundi is in his Sunday clothes,
Watching the Lynx's most unnatural doze;
The Panther is asleep and the Macaw;
The Lion is engaged on something raw;
　　The white bear cools his chin
　　'Gainst the wet tin;
And the confined old Monkey's in the straw.

All the nine little Lionets are lying
Slumbering in milk, and sighing ;
   Miss Cross is sipping ox-tail soup,
    In her front coop,
So here's the happy mid-day moment ;—yes,
I seize it, Mr. Mathews, to address
   A word or two
    To you
On the subject of the ruin which must come
By both being in the Strand, and both at home
On the same nights ; two treats
   So very near each other,
   As, oh my brother !
To play old gooseberry with both receipts.

II.

  When you begin
Your summer fun, three times a week, at eight,
   And carriages roll up, and cits roll in,
I feel a change in Exeter 'Change's change.
And, dash my trunk, I hate
To ring my bell, when you ring yours, and go
With a diminished glory through *my* show !
  It is most strange ;
But crowds that meant to see me eat a stack,
And sip a water-butt or so, and crack
  A root of mangel-wurzel with my foot,
  Eat little children's fruit,
   Pick from the floor small coins,
And then turn slowly round and show my India-rubber loins:
   'Tis strange—most strange, but true,
That these same crowds seek *you !*
Pass *my* abode, and pay at *your* next door !
It makes me roar
With anguish when I think of this ; I go
With sad severity my nightly rounds
   Before one poor front row,
   My fatal funny foe !
And when I stoop, as duty bids, I sigh
And feel that, while poor elephantine I
  Pick up a sixpence, you pick up the pounds !

III.

Could you not go?
Could you not take the Coburg or the Surrey?
Or Sadler's Wells,—(I am not in a hurry,
I never am!) for the next season?—oh!
          Woe! woe! woe!
To both of us, if we remain; for not
In silence will I bear my altered lot,
To have you merry, sir, at my expense;
          No man of any sense,
No true great person (and we both are great
In our own ways) would tempt another's fate.
I would myself depart
In Mr. Cross's cart;
But, like Othello, "am not easily moved."
There's a nice house in Tottenham Court, they say,
Fit for a single gentleman's small play;
          And more conveniently near your home:
          You'll easily go and come.
Or get a room in the City—in some street—
Coachmaker's Hall, or the Paul's Head,
          Cateaton Street;
Any large place, in short, in which to get your bread;
          But do not stay, and get
          Me into the Gazette!

IV.

          Ah! The Gazette;
I press my forehead with my trunk, and wet
My tender cheek with elephantine tears,
          Shed of a walnut size
          From my wise eyes,
To think of ruin after prosperous years.
          What a dread case would be
          For me—large me!
To meet at Basinghall Street, the first and seventh
          And the eleventh!
To undergo (D———n!)
          My last examination!
To cringe, and to surrender,
Like a criminal offender,

All my effects—my bell-pull, and my bell,
My bolt, my stock of hay, my new deal cell.
  To *post* my ivory, sir !
And have some curious commissioner
Very irreverently search my trunk ;
  'Sdeath ! I should die
With rage, to find a tiger in possession
 Of my abode ; up to his yellow knees
In my old straw ; and my profound profession
Entrusted to two beasts of assignees !

v.

The truth is simply this,—if you *will* stay
  Under my very nose,
  Filling your rows
Just at my feeding time, to see *your* play,
  My mind's made up,
  No more at nine I sup,
Except on Tuesdays, Wednesdays, Fridays, Sundays,
  From eight to eleven,
  As I hope for heaven,
On Thursdays, and on Saturdays, and Mondays,
 I'll squeak and roar, and grunt without cessation,
 And utterly confound your recitation.
And, mark me ! all my friends of the furry snout
  Shall join a chorus shout,
We will be heard—we'll spoil
Your wicked ruination toil.
  Insolvency must ensue
  To you, sir, you ;
Unless you move your opposition shop,
  And let me stop.

vi.

I have no more to say :—I do not write
 In anger, but in sorrow ; I must look
However to my interests every night,
 And they detest your " Memorandum-book."
If we could join our forces—I should like it ;
  You do the dialogue, and I the songs.
  A voice to me belongs ;

(The Editors of the *Globe* and *Traveller* ring
With praises of it, when I hourly sing
    God save the King.)
If such a bargain could be schemed I'd strike it!
  I think, too, I could do the Welsh old man
  In the Youthful Days, if dressed upon your plan;
And the attorney in your Paris trip,—
    I'm large about the hip!
Now think of this!—for we cannot go on
  As next door rivals, that my mind declares.
I must be penniless, or you be gone!
We must live separate, or else have shares.
    I am a friend or foe
    As you take this;
  Let me your profitable hubbub miss,
Or be it " Mathews, Elephant, and Co. !"

THE IRISH SCHOOLMASTER.

I.

ALACK ! 'tis melancholy theme to think
How Learning doth in rugged states abide,
And, like her bashful owl, obscurely blink,
In pensive glooms and corners, scarcely spied;
Not, as in Founders' Halls and domes of pride,
Served with grave homage, like a tragic queen,
But with one lonely priest compelled to hide,
In midst of foggy moors and mosses green,
In that clay cabin hight the College of Kilreen !

II.

This College looketh South and West alsoe,
Because it hath a cast in windows twain;
Crazy and cracked they be, and wind doth blow
Thorough transparent holes in every pane,
Which Dan, with many paines, makes whole again
With nether garments, which his thrift doth teach,
To stand for glass, like pronouns, and when rain
Stormeth, he puts, " once more unto the breach,"
Outside and in, tho' broke, yet so he mendeth each.

III.

And in the midst a little door there is,
Whereon a board that doth congratulate
With painted letters, red as blood I wis,
Thus written,

　　"CHILDREN TAKEN IN TO BATE:"
And oft, indeed, the inward of that gate,
Most ventriloque, doth utter tender squeak,
And moans of infants that bemoan their fate,
In midst of sounds of Latin, French, and Greek,
Which, all i' the Irish tongue, he teacheth them to speak.

IV.

For some are meant to right illegal wrongs,
And some for Doctors of Divinitie,
Whom he doth teach to murder the dead tongues,
And so win academical degree ;
But some are bred for service of the sea,
Howbeit, their store of learning is but small.
For mickle waste he counteth it would be
To stock a head with bookish wares at all,
Only to be knocked off by ruthless cannon ball.

V.

Six babes he sways,—some little and some big,
Divided into classes six ;—alsoe,
He keeps a parlour boarder of a pig,
That in the College fareth to and fro,
And picketh up the urchins' crumbs below,—
And eke the learned rudiments they scan,
And thus his A, B, C, doth wisely know,—
Hereafter to be shown in caravan,
And raise the wonderment of many a learned man.

VI.

Alsoe, he schools some tame familiar fowls,
Whereof, above his head, some two or three
Sit darkly squatting, like Minerva's owls,
But on the branches of no living tree,
And overlook the learned family ;

While, sometimes, Partlet, from her gloomy perch,
Drops feather on the nose of Dominie,
Meanwhile, with serious eye, he makes research
In leaves of that sour tree of knowledge—now a birch.

VII.

No chair he hath, the awful Pedagogue,
Such as would magisterial hams imbed,
But sitteth lowly on a beechen log,
Secure in high authority and dread :
Large, as a dome for learning, seemed his head,
And like Apollo's, all beset with rays,
Because his locks are so unkempt and red,
And stand abroad in many several ways :—
No laurel crown he wears, howbeit his cap is baize,

VIII.

And, underneath, a pair of shaggy brows
O'erhang as many eyes of gizzard hue,
That inward giblet of a fowl, which shows
A mongrel tint, that is ne brown ne blue ;
His nose,—it is a coral to the view ;
Well nourished with Pierian Potheen,—
For much he loves his native mountain dew ;—
But to depict the dye would lack, I ween,
A bottle-red, in terms, as well as bottle-green.

IX.

As for his coat, 'tis such a jerkin short
As Spenser had, ere he composed his Tales ;
But underneath he hath no vest, nor aught,
So that the wind his airy breast assails ;
Below, he wears the nether garb of males,
Of crimson plush, but non-plushed at the knee ;—
Thence further down the native red prevails,
Of his own naked fleecy hosiery :—
Two sandals, without soles, complete his cap-a-pee.

X.

Nathless, for dignity, he now doth lap
His function in a magisterial gown,

That shows more countries in it than a map,—
Blue tint, and red, and green, and russet brown,
Besides some blots, standing for country town ;
And eke some rents, for streams and rivers wide ;
But, sometimes, bashful when he looks adown,
He turns the garment of the other side,
Hopeful that so the holes may never be espied !

XI.

And soe he sits, amidst the little pack,
That look for shady or for sunny noon,
Within his visage, like an almanack,—
His quiet smile foretelling gracious boon :
But when his mouth droops down, like rainy moon,
With horrid chill each little heart unwarms,
Knowing that infant show'rs will follow soon,
And with forebodings of near wrath and storms
They sit, like timid hares, all trembling on their forms.

XII.

Ah ! luckless wight, who cannot then repeat
" Corduroy Colloquy,"—or " Ki, Kæ, Kod,"—
Full soon his tears shall make his turfy seat
More sodden, though already made of sod,
For Dan shall whip him with the word of God,—
Severe by rule, and not by nature mild,
He never spoils the child and spares the rod,
But spoils the rod and never spares the child,
And soe with holy rule deems he is reconciled.

XIII.

But, surely, the just sky will never wink
At men who take delight in childish throe,
And stripe the nether-urchin like a pink
Or tender hyacinth, inscribed with woe ;
Such bloody Pedagogues, when they shall know,
By useless birches, that forlorn recess,
Which is no holiday, in Pit below,
Will hell not seem designed for their distress,—
A melancholy place, that is all bottomlesse ?

XIV.

Yet would the Muse not chide the wholesome use
Of needful discipline, in due degree.
Devoid of sway, what wrongs will time produce,
Whene'er the twig untrained grows up a tree.
This shall a Carder, that a Whiteboy be,
Ferocious leaders of atrocious bands,
And Learning's help be used for infamie,
By lawless clerks, that, with their bloody hands,
In murdered English write Rock's murderous commands.

XV.

But ah ! what shrilly cry doth now alarm
The sooty fowls that dozed upon the beam,
All sudden fluttering from the brandished arm,
And cackling chorus with the human scream ;
Meanwhile, the scourge plies that unkindly seam,
In Phelim's brogues, which bares his naked skin,
Like traitor cap in warlike fort, I deem,
That falsely lets the fierce besieger in,
Nor seeks the Pedagogue by other course to win.

XVI.

No parent dear he hath to heed his cries ;—
Alas ! his parent dear is far aloof,
And deep his Seven-Dial cellar lies,
Killed by kind cudgel-play, or gin of proof ;
Or climbeth, catwise, on some London roof,
Singing, perchance, a lay of Erin's Isle,
Or, whilst he labours, weaves a fancy-woof,
Dreaming he sees his home,—his Phelim smile ;
Ah me ! that luckless imp, who weepeth all the while !

XVII.

Ah ! who can paint that hard and heavy time,
When first the scholar lists in learning's train,
And mounts her rugged steep, enforced to climb,
Like sooty imp, by sharp posterior pain,
From bloody twig, and eke that Indian cane,

Wherein, alas ! no sugared juices dwell,
For this, the while one stripling's sluices drain
Another weepeth over chilblains fell,
Always upon the heel, yet never to be well !

XVIII.

Anon a third, for his delicious root,
Late ravished from his tooth by elder chit,
So soon is human violence afoot,
So hardly is the harmless biter bit !
Meanwhile, the tyrant, with untimely wit
And mouthing face, derides the small one's moan,
Who, all lamenting for his loss, doth sit,
Alack,—mischance comes seldomtimes alone,
But aye the worried dog must rue more curs than one.

XIX.

For lo ! the Pedagogue, with sudden drub,
Smites his scald head, that is already sore,—
Superfluous wound,—such is misfortune's rub !
Who straight makes answer with redoubled roar,
And sheds salt tears twice faster than before,
That still with backward fist he strives to dry ;
Washing, with brackish moisture, o'er and o'er,
His muddy cheek, that grows more foul thereby,
Till all his rainy face looks grim as rainy sky.

XX.

So Dan, by dint of noise, obtains a peace,
And with his natural untender knack,
By new distress, bids former grievance cease,
Like tears dried up with rugged huckaback,
That sets the mournful visage all awrack ;
Yet soon the childish countenance will shine
Even as thorough storms the soonest slack,
For grief and beef in adverse ways incline,
This keeps, and that decays, when duly soaked in brine.

XXI.

Now all is hushed, and with a look profound,
The Dominie lays ope the learned page ;

(So be it called) although he doth expound
Without a book both Greek and Latin sage ;
Now telleth he of Rome's rude infant age,
How Romulus was bred in savage wood
By wet-nurse wolf, devoid of wolfish rage ;
And laid foundation-stone of walls of mud,
But watered it, alas ! with warm fraternal blood.

XXII.

Anon, he turns to that Homeric war,
How Troy was sieged like Londonderry town ;
And stout Achilles at his jaunting-car
Dragged mighty Hector with a bloody crown :
And eke the bard, that sung of their renown,
In garb of Greece most beggar-like and torn,
He paints, with colly, wand'ring up and down,
Because, at once, in seven cities born ;
And so, of parish rights, was all his days forlorn.

XXIII.

Anon, through old Mythology he goes,
Of gods defunct, and all their pedigrees,
But shuns their scandalous amours, and shows
How Plato wise, and clear-eyed Socrates,
Confessed not to those heathen hes and shes ;
But through the clouds of the Olympic cope
Beheld St. Peter, with his holy keys,
And owned their love was naught, and bowed to Pope,
Whilst all their purblind race in Pagan mist did grope.

XXIV.

From such quaint themes he turns, at last, aside,
To new philosophies, that still are green,
And shows what railroads have been track'd to guide
The wheels of great political machine ;
If English corn should go abroad, I ween,
And gold be made of gold, or paper sheet ;
How many pigs be born to each spalpeen ;
And, ah ! how man shall thrive beyond his meat,—
With twenty souls alive, to one square sod of peat !

XXV.

Here, he makes end; and all the fry of youth,
   That stood around with serious look intense,
Close up again their gaping eyes and mouth,
   Which they had opened to his eloquence,
   As if their hearing were a threefold sense;
But now the current of his words is done,
   And whether any fruits shall spring from thence,
   In future time, with any mother's son,
It is a thing, God wot! that can be told by none.

XXVI.

Now by the creeping shadows of the noon,
   The hour is come to lay aside their lore;
The cheerful Pedagogue perceives it soon,
   And cries, "Begone!" unto the imps,—and four
Snatch their two hats, and struggle for the door,
   Like ardent spirits vented from a cask,
   All blithe and boisterous,—but leave two more,
With Reading made Uneasy for a task,
To weep, whilst all their mates in merry sunshine bask,

XXVII.

Like sportive Elfins, on the verdant sod,
   With tender moss so sleekly overgrown,
That doth not hurt, but kiss, the sole unshod,
   So soothly kind is Erin to her own!
And one, at Hare and Hound, plays all alone,—
   For Phelim's gone to tend his step-dame's cow;
   Ah! Phelim's step-dame is a cankered crone!
Whilst other twain play at an Irish row,
And, with shillelah small, break one another's brow!

XXVIII.

But careful Dominie, with ceaseless thrift,
   Now changeth ferula for rural hoe;
But, first of all, with tender hand doth shift
   His college gown, because of solar glow,

And hangs it on a bush, to scare the crow:
Meanwhile he plants in earth the dappled bean,
Or trains the young potatoes all a-row,
Or plucks the fragrant leek for pottage green,
With that crisp curly herb called Kale in Aberdeen.

XXIX.

And so he wisely spends the fruitful hours,
Linked each to each by labour, like a bee;
Or rules in Learning's hall, or trims her bow'rs;
Would there were many more such wights as he,
To sway each capital academie
Of Cam and Isis, for, alack! at each
There dwells, I wot, some dronish Dominie;
That does no garden work, nor yet doth teach,
But wears a floury head, and talks in flow'ry speech!

THE SEA-SPELL.

"Cauld, cauld, he lies beneath the deep."
Old Scotch Ballad.

I.

It was a jolly mariner!
The tallest man of three,—
He loosed his sail against the wind,
And turned his boat to sea:
The ink-black sky told every eye
A storm was soon to be!

II.

But still that jolly mariner
Took in no reef at all,
For, in his pouch, confidingly
He wore a baby's caul;
A thing, as gossip-nurses know,
That always brings a squall!

III.

His hat was new, or newly glazed,
Shone brightly in the sun ;
His jacket, like a mariner's,
True blue, as e'er was spun ;
His ample trousers, like St. Paul,
Bore forty stripes save one.

IV.

And now the fretting foaming tide
He steered away to cross ;
The bounding pinnace played a game
Of dreary pitch and toss ;
A game that, on the good dry land,
Is apt to bring a loss !

V.

Good Heaven befriend that little boat,
And guide her on her way !
A boat, they say, has canvas wings,
But cannot fly away !
Though like a merry singing bird,
She sits upon the spray !

VI.

Still east by south the little boat,
With tawny sail kept beating :
Now out of sight, between two waves,
Now o'er th' horizon fleeting :
Like greedy swine that feed on mast,—
The waves her mast seemed eating !

VII.

The sullen sky grew black above,
The wave as black beneath ;
Each roaring billow showed full soon
A white and foamy wreath ;
Like angry dogs that snarl at first,
And then display their teeth.

VIII.

The boatman looked against the wind,
The mast began to creak,
The wave, per saltum, came and dried,
In salt upon his cheek !
The pointed wave against him reared,
As if it owned a pique !

IX.

Nor rushing wind, nor gushing wave,
That boatman could alarm,
But still he stood away to sea,
And trusted in his charm ;
He thought by purchase he was safe,
And armed against all harm !

X.

Now thick and fast and far aslant,
The stormy rain came pouring,
He heard upon the sandy bank
The distant breakers roaring,—
A groaning intermitting sound,
Like Gog and Magog snoring !

XI.

The seafowl shrieked around the mast,
Ahead the grampus tumbled,
And far off, from a copper cloud,
The hollow thunder rumbled ;
It would have quailed another heart,
But his was never humbled.

XII.

For why ? he had that infant's caul ;
And wherefore should he dread ?
Alas ! alas ! he little thought,
Before the ebb-tide sped,
That like that infant he should die,
And with a watery head !

XIII.

The rushing brine flowed in apace ;
His boat had ne'er a deck ;
Fate seemed to call him on, and he
Attended to her beck ;
And so he went, still trusting on,
Though reckless—to his wreck !

XIV.

For as he left his helm, to heave
The ballast bags a-weather,
Three monstrous seas came roaring on,
Like lions leagued together.
The two first waves the little boat
Swam over like a feather.

XV.

The two first waves were past and gone,
And sinking in her wake ;
The hugest still came leaping on,
And hissing like a snake,
Now helm a-lee ! for through the midst
The monster he must take !

XVI.

Ah me ! it was a dreary mount !
Its base as black as night,
Its top of pale and livid green,
Its crest of awful white,
Like Neptune with a leprosy,—
And so it reared upright !

XVII.

With quaking sails the little boat
Climbed up the foaming heap ;
With quaking sails it paused awhile,
At balance on the steep :
Then rushing down the nether slope,
Plunged with a dizzy sweep !

XVIII.

Look, how a horse, made mad with fear,
  Disdains his careful guide ;
So now the headlong headstrong boat,
  Unmanaged, turns aside,
And straight presents her reeling flank
  Against the swelling tide !

XIX.

The gusty wind assaults the sail ;
  Her ballast lies a-lee !
The sheets to windward, taunt and stiff !
  Oh ! the Lively—where is she ?
Her capsized keel is in the foam,
  Her pennon's in the sea !

XX.

The wild gull, sailing overhead,
  Three times beheld emerge
The head of that bold mariner,
  And then she screamed his dirge !
For he had sunk within his grave,
  Lapped in a shroud of surge !

XXI.

The ensuing wave, with horrid foam,
  Rushed o'er and covered all,—
The jolly boatman's drowning scream
  Was smothered by the squall ;
Heaven never heard his cry, nor did
  The ocean heed his *caul*.

FAITHLESS NELLY GRAY.

A PATHETIC BALLAD.

BEN BATTLE was a soldier bold,
  And used to war's alarms :
But a cannon-ball took off his legs,
  So he laid down his arms !

Now as they bore him off the field,
  Said he, " Let others shoot,
For here I leave my second leg,
  And the Forty-second Foot !"

The army-surgeons made him limbs :
  Said he,—" They're only pegs :
But there's as wooden members quite
  As represent my legs !"

Now Ben he loved a pretty maid,
  Her name was Nelly Gray ;
So he went to pay her his devours
  When he'd devoured his pay !

But when he called on Nelly Gray,
  She made him quite a scoff ;
And when she saw his wooden legs,
  Began to take them off !

" O Nelly Gray ! O Nelly Gray !
  Is this your love so warm ?
The love that loves a scarlet coat,
  Should be more uniform !"

Said she, " I loved a soldier once,
  For he was blithe and brave ;
But I will never have a man
  With both legs in the grave !

" Before you had those timber toes,
  Your love I did allow,
But then, you know, you stand upon
  Another footing now !"

"O Nelly Gray ! O Nelly Gray !
  For all your jeering speeches,
At duty's call I left my legs
  In Badajos's *breaches !*"

" Why, then," said she, "you've lost the feet
  Of legs in war's alarms,
And now you cannot wear your shoes
  Upon your feats of arms !"

" O, false and fickle Nelly Gray ;
　　I know why you refuse :—
Though I've no feet—some other man
　　Is standing in my shoes !

" I wish I ne'er had seen your face ;
　　But, now, a long farewell !
For you will be my death ;—alas !
　　You will not be my *Nell !*"

Now when he went from Nelly Gray,
　　His heart so heavy got—
And life was such a burthen grown,
　　It made him take a knot !

So round his melancholy neck
　　A rope he did entwine,
And, for his second time in life,
　　Enlisted in the Line !

One end he tied around a beam,
　　And then removed his pegs,
And, as his legs were off,—of course,
　　He soon was off his legs !

And there he hung till he was dead
　　As any nail in town,—
For though distress had cut him up,
　　It could not cut him down !

A dozen men sat on his corpse,
　　To find out why he died—
And they buried Ben in four cross-roads,
　　With a *stake* in his inside !

Second Series.

BIANCA'S DREAM.

A VENETIAN STORY.

I.

Bianca!—fair Bianca!—who could dwell
  With safety on her dark and hazel gaze,
Nor find there lurked in it a witching spell,
  Fatal to balmy nights and blessèd days?
The peaceful breath that made the bosom swell,
  She turned to gas, and set it in a blaze;
Each eye of hers had Love's Eupyrion in it,
That he could light his link at in a minute.

II.

So that, wherever in her charms she shone,
  A thousand breasts were kindled into flame;
Maidens who cursed her looks forgot their own,
  And beaux were turned to flambeaux where she came;
All hearts indeed were conquered but her own,
  Which none could ever temper down or tame:
In short, to take our haberdasher's hints,
She might have written over it—"from Flints."

III.

She was, in truth, the wonder of her sex,
  At least in Venice—where with eyes of brown,
Tenderly languid, ladies seldom vex
  An amorous gentle with a needless frown;
Where gondolas convey guitars by pecks,
  And Love at casements climbeth up and down,
Whom for his tricks and custom in that kind,
Some have considered a Venetian blind.

IV.

Howbeit, this difference was quickly taught,
　　Amongst more youths who had this cruel jailor,
To hapless Julio—all in vain he sought
　　With each new moon his hatter and his tailor;
In vain the richest padusoy he bought,
　　And went in bran new beaver to assail her—
As if to show that Love had made him *smart*
All over—and not merely round his heart.

V.

In vain he laboured thro' the sylvan park
　　Bianca haunted in—that where she came,
Her learnèd eyes in wandering might mark
　　The twisted cipher of her maiden name,
Wholesomely going thro' a course of bark;
　　No one was touched or troubled by his flame,
Except the Dryads, those old maids that grow
In trees—like wooden dolls in embryo.

VI.

In vain complaining elegies he writ,
　　And taught his tuneful instrument to grieve,
And sang in quavers how his heart was split,
　　Constant beneath her lattice with each eve;
She mocked his wooing with her wicked wit,
　　And slashed his suit so that it matched his sleeve,
Till he grew silent at the vesper star,
And quite despairing, hamstringed his guitar.

VII.

Bianca's heart was coldly frosted o'er
　　With snows unmelting—an eternal sheet;
But his was red within him, like the core
　　Of old Vesuvius, with perpetual heat;
And oft he longed internally to pour
　　His flames and glowing lava at her feet;
But when his burnings he began to spout,
She stopped his mouth, and put the *crater* out.

VIII.

Meanwhile he wasted in the eyes of men,
　So thin, he seemed a sort of skeleton-key
Suspended at Death's door—so pale—and then
　He turned as nervous as an aspen tree;
The life of man is threescore years and ten,
　But he was perishing at twenty-three,
For people truly said, as grief grew stronger,
"It could not shorten his poor life—much longer."

IX.

For why, he neither slept, nor drank, nor fed,
　Nor relished any kind of mirth below;
Fire in his heart, and frenzy in his head,
　Love had become his universal foe,
Salt in his sugar—nightmare in his bed;
　At last, no wonder wretched Julio,
A sorrow-ridden thing, in utter dearth
Of hope—made up his mind to cut her girth!

X.

For hapless lovers always died of old,
　Sooner than chew reflection's bitter cud;
So Thisbe stuck herself, what time 'tis told
　The tender-hearted mulberries wept blood;
And so poor Sappho, when her boy was cold,
　Drowned her salt tear-drops in a salter flood,
Their fame still breathing, tho' their breath be past,
For those old *suitors* lived beyond their last.

XI.

So Julio went to drown—when life was dull,
　But took his corks, and merely had a bath;
And once, he pulled a trigger at his skull,
　But merely broke a window in his wrath;
And once, his hopeless being to annul,
　He tied a packthread to a beam of lath,
A line so ample, 'twas a query whether
'Twas meant to be a halter or a tether.

XII.

Smile not in scorn, that Julio did not thrust
　　His sorrows thro'—'tis horrible to die !
And come down with our little all of dust,
　　That dun of all the duns to satisfy :
To leave life's pleasant city as we must,
　　In Death's most dreary spunging-house to lie,
Where even all our personals must go
To pay the debt of Nature that we owe !

XIII.

So Julio lived :—'twas nothing but a pet
　　He took at life—a momentary spite ;
Besides, he hoped that time would some day get
　　The better of love's flame, however bright ;
A thing that time has never compassed yet,
　　For love, we know, is an immortal light ;
Like that old fire, that, quite beyond a doubt,
Was always in—for none have found it out.

XIV.

Meanwhile, Bianca dreamed—'twas once when Night
　　Along the darkened plain began to creep,
Like a young Hottentot, whose eyes are bright,
　　Altho' in skin as sooty as a sweep :
The flowers had shut their eyes—the zephyr light
　　Was gone, for it had rocked the leaves to sleep ;
And all the little birds had laid their heads
Under their wings—sleeping in feather beds.

XV.

Lone in her chamber sat the dark-eyed maid,
　　By easy stages jaunting thro' her prayers,
But list'ning sidelong to a serenade,
　　That robbed the saints a little of their shares :
For Julio underneath the lattice played
　　His Deh Vieni, and such amorous airs,
Born only underneath Italian skies,
Where every fiddle has a Bridge of Sighs.

XVI.

Sweet was the tune—the words were even sweeter—
    Praising her eyes, her lips, her nose, her hair,
With all the common tropes wherewith in metre
    The hackney poets overcharge their fair.
Her shape was like Diana's, but completer ;
    Her brow with Grecian Helen's might compare :
Cupid, alas ! was cruel Sagittarius,
Julio—the weeping water-man Aquarius.

XVII.

Now, after listing to such laudings rare,
    'Twas very natural indeed to go—
What if she did postpone one little prayer—
    To ask her mirror, " if it was not so ?"
'Twas a large mirror, none the worse for wear,
    Reflecting her at once from top to toe :
And there she gazed upon that glossy track,
That showed her front face tho' it " gave her back."

XVIII.

And long her lovely eyes were held in thrall,
    By that dear page where first the woman reads :
That Julio was no flatterer, none at all,
    She told herself—and then she told her beads ;
Meanwhile, the nerves insensibly let fall
    Two curtains fairer than the lily breeds ;
For Sleep had crept and kissed her unawares,
Just at the half-way milestone of her prayers.

XIX.

Then like a drooping rose so bended she,
    Till her bowed head upon her hand reposed ;
But still she plainly saw, or seemed to see,
    That fair reflection, tho' her eyes were closed,
A beauty-bright as it was wont to be,
    A portrait Fancy painted while she dozed :
'Tis very natural, some people say,
To dream of what we dwell on in the day.

XX.

Still shone her face—yet not, alas! the same,
　　But 'gan some dreary touches to assume,
And sadder thoughts, with sadder changes came—
　　Her eyes resigned their light, her lips their bloom,
Her teeth fell out, her tresses did the same,
　　Her cheeks were tinged with bile, her eyes with rheum:
There was a throbbing at her heart within,
For oh! there was a shooting in her chin.

XXI.

And lo! upon her sad desponding brow,
　　The cruel trenches of besieging age,
With seams, but most unseemly, 'gan to show
　　Her place was booking for the seventh stage;
And where her raven traces used to flow,
　　Some locks that Time had left her in his rage,
And some mock ringlets, made her forehead shady,
A compound (like our Psalms) of tête and braidy.

XXII.

Then for her shape—alas! how Saturn wrecks,
　　And bends, and corkscrews all the frame about,
Doubles the hams, and crooks the straightest necks,
　　Draws in the nape, and pushes forth the snout,
Makes backs and stomachs concave or convex;
　　Witness those pensioners called In and Out,
Who all day watching first and second rater,
Quaintly unbend themselves—but grow no straighter.

XXIII.

So Time with fair Bianca dealt, and made
　　Her shape a bow, that once was like an arrow;
His iron hand upon her spine he laid,
　　And twisted all awry her " winsome marrow,"
In truth it was a change!—she had obeyed
　　The holy Pope before her chest grew narrow,
But spectacles and palsy seemed to make her
Something between a Glassite and a Quaker.

XXIV.

Her grief and gall meanwhile were quite extreme,
   And she had ample reason for her trouble ;
For what sad maiden can endure to seem
   Set in for singleness, tho' growing double.
The fancy maddened her ; but now the dream,
   Grown thin by getting bigger, like a bubble,
Burst,—but still left some fragments of its size,
That, like the soapsuds, smarted in her eyes.

XXV.

And here—just here—as she began to heed
   The real world, her clock chimed out its score ;
A clock it was of the Venetian breed,
   That cried the hour from one to twenty-four ;
The works moreover standing in some need
   Of workmanship, it struck some dozens more ;
A warning voice that clenched Bianca's fears,
Such strokes referring doubtless to her years.

XXVI.

At fifteen chimes she was but half a nun,
   By twenty she had quite renounced the veil ;
She thought of Julio just at twenty-one,
   And thirty made her very sad and pale,
To paint that ruin where her charms would run ;
   At forty all the maid began to fail,
And thought no higher, as the late dream crossed her,
Of single blessedness, than single Gloster.

XXVII.

And so Bianca changed ;—the next sweet even,
   With Julio in a black Venetian bark,
Rowed slow and stealthily—the hour, eleven,
   Just sounding from the tower of old St. Mark.
She sat with eyes turned quietly to heav'n,
   Perchance rejoicing in the grateful dark
That veiled her blushing cheek—for Julio brought her,
Of course—to break the ice upon the water.

XXVIII.

But what a puzzle is one's serious mind
    To open ;—oysters, when the ice is thick,
Are not so difficult and disinclined ;
    And Julio felt the declaration stick
About his throat in a most awful kind ;
    However, he contrived by bits to pick
His trouble forth—much like a rotten cork
Groped from a long-neck'd bottle with a fork.

XXIX.

But love is still the quickest of all readers ;
    And Julio spent besides those signs profuse
That English telegraphs and foreign pleaders,
    In help of language, are so apt to use ;
Arms, shoulders, fingers, all were interceders,
    Nods, shrugs, and bends—Bianca could not choose
But soften to his suit with more facility,
He told his story with so much agility.

XXX.

" Be thou my park, and I will be thy dear,
    (So he began at last to speak or quote ;)
Be thou my bark, and I thy gondolier,
    (For passion takes this figurative note ;)
Be thou my light, and I thy chandelier ;
    Be thou my dove, and I will be thy cote :
My lily be, and I will be thy river ;
Be thou my life—and I will be thy liver."

XXXI.

This, with more tender logic of the kind,
    He poured into her small and shell-like ear,
That timidly against his lids inclined ;
    Meanwhile her eyes glanced on the silver sphere
That even now began to steal behind
    A dewy vapour, which was lingering near,
Wherein the dull moon crept all dim and pale,
Just like a virgin putting on the veil :

XXXII.

Bidding adieu to all her sparks—the stars,
    That erst had wooed and worshipped in her train,
Saturn and Hesperus, and gallant Mars—
    Never to flirt with heavenly eyes again.
Meanwhile, remindful of the convent bars,
    Bianca did not watch these signs in vain,
But turned to Julio at the dark eclipse,
With words, like verbal kisses, on her lips.

XXXIII.

He took the hint full speedily, and, backed
    By love, and night, and the occasion's meetness,
Bestowed a something on her cheek that smacked
    (Tho' quite in silence) of ambrosial sweetness,
That made her think all other kisses lacked
    Till then, but what she knew not, of completeness :
Being used but sisterly salutes to feel,
Insipid things—like sandwiches of veal.

XXXIV.

He took her hand, and soon she felt him wring
    The pretty fingers all instead of one ;
Anon his stealthy arm began to cling
    About her waist that had been clasped by none ;
Their dear confessions I forbear to sing,
    Since cold description would but be outrun :
For bliss and Irish watches have the pow'r,
In twenty minutes, to lose half an hour !

MARY'S GHOST.

A PATHETIC BALLAD.

I.

'Twas in the middle of the night,
    To sleep young William tried ;
When Mary's ghost came stealing in,
    And stood at his bed-side.

II.

O William dear ! O William dear !
　My rest eternal ceases ;
Alas ! my everlasting peace
　Is broken into pieces.

III.

I thought the last of all my cares
　Would end with my last minute ;
But tho' I went to my long home,
　I didn't stay long in it.

IV.

The body-snatchers they have come,
　And made a snatch at me ;
It's very hard them kind of men
　Wont let a body be !

V.

You thought that I was buried deep,
　Quite decent like and chary,
But from her grave in Mary-bone,
　They've come and boned your Mary

VI.

The arm that used to take your arm
　Is took to Dr. Vyse ;
And both my legs are gone to walk
　The hospital at Guy's.

VII.

I vowed that you should have my hand,
　But fate gives us denial ;
You'll find it there, at Dr. Bell's,
　In spirits and a phial.

VIII.

As for my feet, the little feet
　You used to call so pretty,
There's one, I know, in Bedford Row,
　The t'other's in the City.

IX.

I can't tell where my head is gone,
    But Doctor Carpue can ;
As for my trunk, it's all packed up
    To go by Pickford's van.

X.

I wish you'd go to Mr. P.
    And save me such a ride ;
I don't half like the outside place,
    They've took for my inside.

XI.

The cock it crows—I must be gone !
    My William, we must part !
But I'll be yours in death, altho'
    Sir Astley has my heart.

XII.

Don't go to weep upon my grave,
    And think that there I be ;
They haven't left an atom there
    Of my anatomie.

THE PROGRESS OF ART.

I.

O HAPPY time !—Art's early days !
When o'er each deed, with sweet self-praise,
    Narcissus-like I hung !
When great Rembrandt but little seemed,
And such Old Masters all were deemed
    As nothing to the young !

II.

Some scratchy strokes—abrupt and few,
So easily and swift I drew,
    Sufficed for my design ;
My sketchy, superficial hand
Drew solids at a dash—and spanned
    A surface with a line.

III.

Not long my eye was thus content,
But grew more critical—my bent
   Essayed a higher walk;
I copied leaden eyes in lead—
Rheumatic hands in white and red,
   And gouty feet—in chalk.

IV.

Anon my studious art for days
Kept making faces—happy phrase,
   For faces such as mine!
Accomplished in the details then,
I left the minor parts of men,
   And drew the form divine.

V.

Old Gods and Heroes—Trojan—Greek,
Figures—long after the antique,
   Great Ajax justly feared;
Hectors, of whom at night I dreamt,
And Nestor, fringed enough to tempt
   Bird-nesters to his beard.

VI.

A Bacchus, leering on a bowl,
A Pallas that out-stared her owl,
   A Vulcan—very lame;
A Dian stuck about with stars,
With my right hand I murdered Mars—
   (One Williams did the same.)

VII.

But tired of this dry work at last,
Crayon and chalk aside I cast,
   And gave my brush a drink!
Dipping—" as when a painter dips
In gloom of earthquake and eclipse,"—
   That is—in Indian ink.

VIII.

Oh then, what black Mont Blancs arose,
Crested with soot, and not with snows:
  What clouds of dingy hue!
In spite of what the bard has penned,
I fear the distance did not "lend
  Enchantment to the view."

IX.

Not Radcliffe's brush did e'er design
Black Forests half so black as mine,
  Or lakes so like a pall;
The Chinese cake dispersed a ray
Of darkness, like the light of Day
  And Martin over all.

X.

Yet urchin pride sustained me still,
I gazed on all with right good will,
  And spread the dingy tint;
" No holy Luke helped me to paint,
The devil surely, not a Saint,
  Had any finger in't!"

XI.

But colours came!—like morning light,
With gorgeous hues, displacing night,
  Or Spring's enlivened scene:
At once the sable shades withdrew;
My skies got very, very blue;
  My trees extremely green.

XII.

And washed by my cosmetic brush,
How Beauty's cheek began to blush;
  With lock of auburn stain—
(Not Goldsmith's Auburn)—nut-brown hair,
That made her loveliest of the fair;
  Not "loveliest of the plain!"

XIII.

Her lips were of vermilion hue ;
Love in her eyes, and Prussian blue,
    Set all my heart in flame !
A young Pygmalion, I adored
The maids I made—but time was stored
    With evil—and it came !

XIV.

Perspective dawned—and soon I saw
My houses stand against its law ;
    And " keeping" all unkept !
My beauties were no longer things
For love and fond imaginings ;
    But horrors to be wept !

XV.

Ah ! why did knowledge ope my eyes ?
Why did I get more artist wise ?
    It only serves to hint,
What grave defects and wants are mine ;
That I'm no Hilton in design—
    In nature no De Wint !

XVI.

Thrice happy time !—Art's early days !
When o'er each deed, with sweet self-praise,
    Narcissus-like I hung !
When great Rembrandt but little seemed,
And such Old Masters all were deemed
    As nothing to the young !

A LEGEND OF NAVARRE.

I.

'Twas in the reign of Lewis, called the Great,
    As one may read on his triumphal arches,
The thing befell I'm going to relate,
    In course of one of those " pomposo" marches
He loved to make, like any gorgeous Persian,
Partly for war, and partly for diversion.

II.

Some wag had put it in the royal brain
    To drop a visit at an old chateau,
Quite unexpected, with his courtly train;
    The monarch liked it—but it happened so,
That Death had got before them by a post,
And they were " reckoning without their *host*,"

III.

Who died exactly as a child should die,
    Without one groan or a convulsive breath,
Closing without one pang his quiet eye,
    Sliding composedly from sleep—to death;
A corpse so placid ne'er adorned a bed,
He seemed not quite—but only rather dead.

IV.

All night the widowed Baroness contrived
    To shed a widow's tears; but on the morrow
Some news of such unusual sort arrived,
    There came strange alteration in her sorrow;
From mouth to mouth it passed, one common humming
Throughout the house—the King! the King is coming!

V.

The Baroness, with all her soul and heart,
    A loyal woman, (now called ultra-loyal,)
Soon thrust all funeral concerns apart,
    And only thought about a banquet-royal;
In short, by aid of earnest preparation;
The visit quite dismissed the visitation.

VI.

And, spite of all her grief for the ex-mate,
    There was a secret hope she could not smother,
That some one, early, might replace " the late,"
    It was too soon to think about another ;
Yet let her minutes of despair be reckoned
Against her hope, which was but for *a second.*

VII.

She almost thought that being thus bereft
    Just then, was one of Time's propitious touches ;
A thread in such a nick so nicked, it left
    Free opportunity to be a duchess ;
Thus all her care was only to look pleasant,
But as for tears—she dropped them—for the present.

VIII.

Her household, as good servants ought to try,
    Looked like their lady—anything but sad,
And giggled even that they might not cry,
    To damp fine company ; in truth they had
No time to mourn, thro' choking turkeys' throttles,
Scouring old laces, and reviewing bottles.

IX.

Oh what a hubbub for the house of woe !
    All, resolute to one irresolution,
Kept tearing, swearing, plunging to and fro,
    Just like another French mob-revolution.
There lay the corpse that could not stir a muscle,
But all the rest seemed Chaos in a bustle.

X.

The Monarch came : oh ! who could ever guess
    The Baroness had been so late a weeper !
The kingly grace and more than graciousness,
    Buried the poor defunct some fathoms deeper,—
Could he have had a glance—alas, poor being !
Seeing would certainly have led to *D*—ing.

XI.

For casting round about her eyes to find
    Some one to whom her chattels to endorse,
The comfortable dame at last inclined
    To choose the cheerful Master of the Horse ;
He was so gay—so tender—the complete
Nice man—the sweetest of the monarch's suite.

XII.

He saw at once and entered in the lists—
    Glance unto glance made amorous replies ;
They talked together like two egotists,
    In conversation all made up of *eyes :*
No couple ever got so right consort-ish
Within two hours—a courtship rather shortish.

XIII.

At last, some sleepy, some by wine opprest,
    The courtly company began " nid noddin ;"
The King first sought his chamber, and the rest
    Instanter followed by the course he trod in.
I shall not please the scandalous by showing
The order, or disorder of their going.

XIV.

The old chateau, before that night, had never
    Held half so many underneath its roof ;
It tasked the Baroness's best endeavour,
    And put her best contrivance to the proof,
To give them chambers up and down the stairs,
In twos and threes, by singles, and by pairs.

XV.

She had just lodging for the whole—yet barely ;
    And some, that were both broad of back and tall,
Lay on spare beds that served them very sparely ;
    However, there were beds enough for all ;
But living bodies occupied so many,
She could not let the dead one take up any !

XVI.

The act was certainly not over decent :
    Some small respect, e'en after death she owed him,
Considering his death had been so recent ;
    However, by command, her servants stowed him,
(I am ashamed to think how he was slubbered,)
Stuck bolt upright within a corner cupboard !

XVII.

And there he slept as soundly as a post,
    With no more pillow than an oaken shelf :
Just like a kind accommodating host,
    Taking all inconvenience on himself ;
None else slept in that room, except a stranger,
A decent man, a sort of Forest Ranger :

XVIII.

Who, whether he had gone too soon to bed,
    Or dreamt himself into an appetite,
Howbeit, he took a longing to be fed,
    About the hungry middle of the night ;
So getting forth, he sought some scrap to eat,
Hopeful of some stray pasty or cold meat.

XIX.

The casual glances of the midnight moon,
    Bright'ning some antique ornaments of brass,
Guided his gropings to that corner soon,
    Just where it stood, the coffin-safe, alas !
He tried the door—then shook it—and in course
Of time it opened to a little force.

XX.

He put one hand in, and began to grope ;
    The place was very deep and quite as dark as
The middle night ;—when lo ! beyond his hope,
    He felt a something cold, in fact, the carcase ;
Right overjoyed, he laughed, and blest his luck
At finding, as he thought, this haunch of buck !

XXI.

Then striding back for his *couteau-de-chasse*,
   Determined on a little midnight lunching,
He came again and probed about the mass,
   As if to find the fattest bit for munching ;
Not meaning wastefully to cut it all up,
But only to abstract a little collop.

XXII.

But just as he had struck one greedy stroke,
   His hand fell down quite powerless and weak ;
For when he cut the haunch it plainly spoke
   As haunch of ven'son never ought to speak ;
No wonder that his hand could go no further—
Whose could ?—to carve cold meat that bellowed, "Murther!"

XXIII.

Down came the Body with a bounce, and down
   The Ranger sprang, a staircase at a spring,
And bawled enough to waken up a town ;
   Some thought that *they* were murdered, some, the King,
And, like Macduff, did nothing for a season,
But stand upon the spot and bellow, "Treason !"

XXIV.

A hundred nightcaps gathered in a mob,
   Torches drew torches, swords brought swords together,
It seemed so dark and perilous a job ;
   The Baroness came trembling like a feather
Just in the rear, as pallid as a corse,
Leaning against the Master of the Horse.

XXV.

A dozen of the bravest up the stair,
   Well lighted and well watched, began to clamber ;
They sought the door—they found it—they were there—
   A dozen heads went poking in the chamber ;
And lo ! with one hand planted on his hurt,
There stood the Body bleeding thro' his shirt,—

XXVI.

No passive corse—but like a duellist
  Just smarting from a scratch—in fierce position,
One hand advanced, and ready to resist;
  In fact, the Baron doffed the apparition,
Swearing those oaths the French delight in most,
And for the second time "gave up the ghost !"

XXVII.

A living miracle !—for why ?—the knife
  That cuts so many off from grave gray hairs,
Had only carved him kindly into life :
  How soon it changed the posture of affairs !
The difference one person more or less
Will make in families, is past all guess.

XXVIII.

There stood the Baroness—no widow yet :
  Here stood the Baron—" in the body" still :
There stood the Horses' Master in a pet,
  Choking with disappointment's bitter pill,
To see the hope of his reversion fail,
Like that of riding on a donkey's tail.

XXIX.

The Baron lived—'twas nothing but a trance :
  The lady died—'twas nothing but a death :
The cupboard-cut served only to enhance
  This postscript to the old Baronial breath :
He soon forgave, for the revival's sake,
A little *chop* intended for a *steak !*

THE DEMON SHIP.

'TWAS off the Wash—the sun went down—the sea looked black and grim,
For stormy clouds, with murky fleece, were mustering at the brim ;
Titanic shades ! enormous gloom !—as if the solid night
Of Erebus rose suddenly to seize upon the light !

It was a time for mariners to bear a wary eye,
With such a dark conspiracy between the sea and sky!

Down went my helm—close reefed—the tack held freely in my
    hand—
With ballast snug—I put about, and scudded for the land.
Loud hissed the sea beneath her lea—my little boat flew fast,
But faster still the rushing storm came borne upon the blast.
Lord! what a roaring hurricane beset the straining sail!
What furious sleet, with level drift, and fierce assaults of hail!
What darksome caverns yawned before! what jagged steeps behind!
Like battle-steeds, with foamy manes, wild tossing in the wind.
Each after each sank down astern, exhausted in the chase,
But where it sank another rose and galloped in its place;
As black as night—they turned to white, and cast against the cloud
A snowy sheet, as if each surge upturned a sailor's shroud:
Still flew my boat; alas! alas! her course was nearly run!
Behold yon fatal billow rise—ten billows heaped in one!
With fearful speed the dreary mass came rolling, rolling, fast,
As if the scooping sea contained one only wave at last!
Still on it came, with horrid roar, a swift pursuing grave;
It seemed as though some cloud had turned its hugeness to a wave!
Its briny sleet began to beat beforehand in my face—
I felt the rearward keel begin to climb its swelling base!
I saw its alpine hoary head impending over mine!
Another pulse—and down it rushed—an avalanche of brine!
Brief pause had I, on God to cry, or think of wife and home;
The waters closed—and when I shrieked, I shrieked below the
    foam!
Beyond that rush I have no hint of any after deed—
For I was tossing on the waste, as senseless as a weed.

*   *   *   *   *

"Where am I?—in the breathing world, or in the world of death?"
With sharp and sudden pang I drew another birth of breath;
My eyes drank in a doubtful light, my ears a doubtful sound—
And was that ship a *real* ship whose tackle seemed around?
A moon, as if the earthly moon, was shining up aloft;
But were those beams the very beams that I had seen so oft?
A face, that mocked the human face, before me watched alone;
But were those eyes the eyes of man that looked against my own?

Oh, never may the moon again disclose me such a sight
As met my gaze, when first I looked, on that accursèd night!
I've seen a thousand horrid shapes begot of fierce extremes
Of fever; and most frightful things have haunted in my dreams—
Hyenas—cats—blood-loving bats—and apes with hateful stare—
Pernicious snakes, and shaggy bulls—the lion, and she-bear—
Strong enemies, with Judas looks, of treachery and spite—
Detested features, hardly dimmed and banished by the light!
Pale-sheeted ghosts, with gory locks, upstarting from their tombs—
All phantasies and images that flit in midnight glooms—
Hags, goblins, demons, lemures, have made me all aghast,—
But nothing like that GRIMLY ONE who stood beside the mast!

His cheek was black—his brow was black—his eyes and hair as
  dark:
His hand was black, and where it touched, it left a sable mark;
His throat was black, his vest the same, and when I looked
  beneath,
His breast was black—all, all was black, except his grinning teeth.
His sooty crew were like in hue, as black as Afric slaves!
Oh, horror! e'en the ship was black that ploughed the inky waves!

"Alas!" I cried, "for love of truth and blessed mercy's sake!
Where am I? in what dreadful ship? upon what dreadful lake?
What shape is that, so very grim, and black as any coal?
It is Mahound, the Evil One, and he has gained my soul!
Oh, mother dear! my tender nurse! dear meadows that beguiled
My happy days, when I was yet a little sinless child,—
My mother dear—my native fields, I never more shall see:
I'm sailing in the Devil's Ship, upon the Devil's Sea!"

Loud laughed that SABLE MARINER, and loudly in return
His sooty crew sent forth a laugh that rang from stem to stern—
A dozen pair of grimly cheeks were crumpled on the nonce—
As many sets of grinning teeth came shining out at once:
A dozen gloomy shapes at once enjoyed the merry fit,
With shriek and yell, and oaths as well, like Demons of the Pit.
They crowed their fill, and then the Chief made answer for the
  whole;—
"Our skins," said he, "are black ye see, because we carry coal;
You'll find your mother sure enough, and see your native fields—
For this here ship has picked you up—the Mary Ann of Shields!"

A TRUE STORY.

Of all our pains, since man was curst,
I mean of body, not the mental,
To name the worst, among the worst,
The dental sure is transcendental;
Some bit of masticating bone,
That ought to help to clear a shelf,
But let its proper work alone,
And only seems to gnaw itself;
In fact, of any grave attack
On victual there is little danger,
'Tis so like coming to the *rack*,
As well as going to the manger.

Old Hunks—it seemed a fit retort
Of justice on his grinding ways—
Possessed a grinder of the sort,
That troubled all his latter days.
The best of friends fall out, and so
His teeth had done some years ago,
Save some old stumps with ragged root,
And they took turn about to shoot;
If he drank any chilly liquor,
They made it quite a point to throb;
But if he warmed it on the hob,
Why then they only twitched the quicker.

One tooth—I wonder such a tooth
Had never killed him in his youth—
One tooth he had with many fangs,
That shot at once as many pangs,
It had a universal sting;
One touch of that ecstatic stump
Could jerk his limbs and make him jump,
Just like a puppet on a string;
And what was worse than all, it had
A way of making others bad.
There is, as many know, a knack,
With certain farming undertakers,
And this same tooth pursued their track,
By adding *achers* still to *achers*!

One way there is, that has been judged
A certain cure, but Hunks was loth
To pay the fee, and quite begrudged
To lose his tooth and money both;
In fact, a dentist and the wheel
Of Fortune are a kindred cast,
For after all is drawn, you feel
It's paying for a blank at last;
So Hunks went on from week to week,
And kept his torment in his cheek;
Oh! how it sometimes set him rocking,
With that perpetual gnaw—gnaw—gnaw,
His moans and groans were truly shocking,
And loud,—altho' he held his jaw.
Many a tug he gave his gum
And tooth, but still it would not come,
Tho' tied by string to some firm thing,
He could not draw it, do his best,
By draw'rs, altho' he tried a chest.

At last, but after much debating,
He joined a score of mouths in waiting,
Like his, to have their troubles out.
Sad sight it was to look about
At twenty faces making faces,
With many a rampant trick and antic,
For all were very horrid cases,
And made their owners nearly frantic.
A little wicket now and then
Took one of these unhappy men,
And out again the victim rushed,
While eyes and mouth together gushed;
At last arrived our hero's turn,
Who plunged his hands in both his pockets,
And down he sat, prepared to learn
How teeth are charmed to quit their sockets.

Those who have felt such operations,
Alone can guess the sort of ache,
When his old tooth began to break
The thread of old associations;
It touched a string in every part,
It had so many tender ties;

One chord seemed wrenching at his heart,
And two were tugging at his eyes ;
" Bone of his bone," he felt of course,
As husbands do in such divorce ;
At last the fangs gave way a little,
Hunks gave his head a backward jerk,
And lo ! the cause of all this work,
Went—where it used to send his victual !

The monstrous pain of this proceeding
Had not so numbed his miser wit,
But in this slip he saw a hit
To save, at least, his purse from bleeding ;
So when the dentist sought his fees,
Quoth Hunks, " Let's finish, if you please."
" How, finish ! why, it's out !"—" Oh ! no—
'Tis you are out, to argue so ;
I'm none of your before-hand tippers.
My tooth is in my head no doubt,
But, as you say you pulled it out,
Of course it's there—between your nippers."
" Zounds, sir ! d'ye think I'd sell the truth
To get a fee ? no, wretch, I scorn it !"
But Hunks still asked to see the tooth,
And swore by gum ! he had not drawn it.

His end obtained, he took his leave,
A secret chuckle in his sleeve ;
The joke was worthy to produce one,
To think, by favour of his wit,
How well a dentist had been bit
By one old stump, and that a loose one !
The thing was worth a laugh, but mirth
Is still the frailest thing on earth :
Alas ! how often when a joke
Seems in our sleeve, and safe enough,
There comes some unexpected stroke,
And hangs a weeper on the cuff !

Hunks had not whistled half a mile,
When, planted right against a stile,
There stood his foeman, Mike Mahoney,

A vagrant reaper, Irish born,
That helped to reap our miser's corn,
But had not helped to reap his money,
A fact that Hunks remembered quickly;
His whistle all at once was quelled,
And when he saw how Michael held
His sickle, he felt rather sickly.

Nine souls in ten, with half his fright,
Would soon have paid the bill at sight,
But misers (let observers watch it)
Will never part with their delight
Till well demanded by a hatchet—
They live hard—and they die to match it.
Thus Hunks prepared for Mike's attacking,
Resolved not yet to pay the debt,
But let him take it out in hacking;
However, Mike began to stickle
In words before he used the sickle;
But mercy was not long attendant:
From words at last he took to blows,
And aimed a cut at Hunks's nose,
That made it what some folks are not—
A member very independent.

Heaven knows how far this cruel trick
Might still have led, but for a tramper
That came in danger's very nick,
To put Mahoney to the scamper.
But still compassion met a damper;
There lay the severed nose, alas!
Beside the daisies on the grass,
"Wee, crimson-tipt" as well as they,
According to the poet's lay:
And there stood Hunks, no sight for laughter.
Away went Hodge to get assistance,
With nose in hand, which Hunks ran after,
But somewhat at unusual distance.
In many a little country place
It is a very common case
To have but one residing doctor,
Whose practice rather seems to be
No practice, but a rule of three,

Physician—surgeon—drug-decoctor ;
Thus Hunks was forced to go once more
Where he had ta'en his tooth before.
His mere name made the learned man hot,—
" What ! Hunks again within my door !
I'll pull his nose ;" quoth Hunks, " You cannot."

The doctor looked and saw the case
Plain as the nose *not* on his face.
" Oh ! hum—ha—yes—I understand."
But then arose a long demur,
For not a finger would he stir
Till he was paid his fee in hand ;
That matter settled, there they were,
With Hunks well strapped upon his chair.

The opening of a surgeon's job—
His tools, a chestful or a drawerful—
Are always something very awful,
And give the heart the strangest throb ;
But never patient in his funks
Looked half so like a ghost as Hunks,
Or surgeon half so like a devil
Prepared for some infernal revel :
His huge black eye kept rolling, rolling,
Just like a bolus in a box :
His fury seemed above controlling,
He bellowed like a hunted ox :
" Now, swindling wretch, I'll show thee how
We treat such cheating knaves as thou ;
Oh ! sweet is this revenge to sup ;
I have thee by the nose—it's now
My turn—and I will turn it up."

Guess how the miser liked the scurvy
And cruel way of venting passion ;
The snubbing folks in this new fashion
Seemed quite to turn him topsy-turvy ;
He uttered prayers, and groans, and curses,
For things had often gone amiss
And wrong with him before, but this
Would be the worst of all *reverses !*

In fancy he beheld his snout
Turned upward like a pitcher's spout;
There was another grievance yet,
And fancy did not fail to show it,
That he must throw a summerset,
Or stand upon his head to blow it.

And was there then no argument
To change the doctor's vile intent,
And move his pity?—yes, in truth,
And that was—paying for the tooth.
"Zounds! pay for such a stump! I'd rather——"
But here the menace went no farther,
For with his other ways of pinching,
Hunks had a miser's love of snuff,
A recollection strong enough
To cause a very serious flinching;
In short, he paid and had the feature
Replaced as it was meant by nature;
For tho' by this 'twas cold to handle,
(No corpse's could have felt more horrid,)
And white just like an end of candle,
The doctor deemed and proved it too,
That noses from the nose will do
As well as noses from the forehead;
So, fixed by dint of rag and lint,
The part was bandaged up and muffled.
The chair unfastened, Hunks arose,
And shuffled out, for once unshuffled;
And as he went, these words he snuffled—
" Well, this *is* ' paying thro' the nose.' "

TIM TURPIN.

A PATHETIC BALLAD.

I.

TIM TURPIN he was gravel-blind,
    And ne'er had seen the skies:
For Nature, when his head was made,
    Forgot to dot his eyes.

II.

So, like a Christmas pedagogue,
  Poor Tim was forced to do—
Look out for pupils ; for he had
  A vacancy for two.

III.

There's some have specs to help their sight
  Of objects dim and small :
But Tim had *specks* within his eyes,
  And could not see at all.

IV.

Now Tim he wooed a servant maid,
  And took her to his arms ;
For he, like Pyramus, had cast
  A wall-eye on her charms.

V.

By day she led him up and down,
  Where'er he wished to jog,
A happy wife, altho' she led
  The life of any dog.

VI.

But just when Tim had lived a month
  In honey with his wife,
A surgeon ope'd his Milton eyes,
  Like oysters, with a knife.

VII.

But when his eyes were opened thus,
  He wished them dark again :
For when he looked upon his wife,
  He saw her very plain.

VIII.

Her face was bad, her figure worse,
  He couldn't bear to eat :
For she was anything but like
  A grace before his meat.

IX.

Now Tim he was a feeling man:
　For when his sight was thick
It made him feel for everything—
　But that was with a stick.

X.

So, with a cudgel in his hand
　It was not light or slim—
He knocked at his wife's head until
　It opened unto him.

XI.

And when the corpse was stiff and cold,
　He took his slaughtered spouse,
And laid her in a heap with all
　The ashes of her house.

XII.

But like a wicked murderer,
　He lived in constant fear
From day to day, and so he cut
　His throat from ear to ear.

XIII.

The neighbours fetched a doctor in:
　Said he, "This wound I dread
Can hardly be sewed up—his life
　Is hanging on a thread."

XIV.

But when another week was gone,
　He gave him stronger hope—
Instead of hanging on a thread,
　Of hanging on a rope.

XV.

Ah! when he hid his bloody work
　In ashes round about,
How little he supposed the truth
　Would soon be sifted out.

XVI.

But when the parish dustman came,
  His rubbish to withdraw,
He found more dust within the heap
  Than he contracted for !

XVII.

A dozen men to try the fact
  Were sworn that very day ;
But though they all were jurors, yet
  No conjurors were they.

XVIII.

Said Tim unto those jurymen,
  You need not waste your breath,
For I confess myself at once
  The author of her death.

XIX.

And, oh ! when I reflect upon
  The blood that I have spilt,
Just like a button is my soul,
  Inscribed with double *guilt !*

XX.

Then turning round his head again,
  He saw before his eyes,
A great judge, and a little judge,
  The judges of a-size !

XXI.

The great judge took his judgment cap,
  And put it on his head,
And sentenced Tim by law to hang
  Till he was three times dead.

XXII.

So he was tried, and he was hung
  (Fit punishment for such)
On Horsham-drop, and none can say
  It was a drop too much.

THE MONKEY-MARTYR.

A FABLE.

"God help thee, said I. but I'll let thee out, cost what it will: so I turned about the cage to get to the door."—STERNE.

'TIS strange, what awkward figures and odd capers
Folks cut, who seek their doctrine from the papers;
But there are many shallow politicians,
Who take their bias from bewildered journals—
  Turn State physicians,
And make themselves fools'-caps of the diurnals.

One of this kind, not human, but a monkey,
Had read himself at last to this sour creed—
That he was nothing but Oppression's flunkey,
And man a tyrant over all his breed.
  He could not read
Of niggers whipt, or over-trampled weavers,
But he applied their wrongs to his own seed,
And nourished thoughts that threw him into fevers.
His very dreams were full of martial beavers,
And drilling Pugs, for liberty pugnacious,
  To sever chains vexatious.
In fact, he thought that all his injured line
Should take up pikes in hand, and never drop 'em
Till they had cleared a road to Freedom's shrine,
Unless perchance the turnpike men should stop 'em.

  Full of this rancour,
Pacing one day beside St. Clement Danes,
  It came into his brains
To give a look in at the Crown and Anchor;
Where certain solemn sages of the nation
Were at that moment in deliberation
How to relieve the wide world of its chains,
  Pluck despots down,
  And thereby crown
Whitee- as well as blackee-man-cipation.
Pug heard the speeches with great approbation,
And gazed with pride upon the Liberators;

            To see mere coalheavers
            Such perfect Bolivars—
Waiters of inns sublimed to innovators—
And slaters dignified as legislators—
Small publicans demanding (such their high sense
Of liberty) an universal licence—
And patten-makers easing Freedom's clogs—
            The whole thing seemed
            So fine, he deemed
The smallest demagogues as great as Gogs!

Pug, with some curious notions in his noddle,
Walked out at last, and turned into the Strand,
            To the left hand,
Conning some portions of the previous twaddle,
And striding with a step that seemed designed
To represent the mighty March of Mind,
            Instead of that slow waddle
Of thought, to which our ancestors inclined.
No wonder, then, that he should quickly find
He stood in front of that intrusive pile,
            Where Cross keeps many a kind
            Of bird confined,
And free-born animal, in durance vile—
A thought that stirred up all the monkey-bile.

            The window stood ajar—
            It was not far,
Nor, like Parnassus, very hard to climb—
The hour was verging on the supper-time,
And many a growl was sent through many a bar.
Meanwhile Pug scrambled upward like a tar,
            And soon crept in,
            Unnoticed in the din
Of tuneless throats, that made the attics ring
With all the harshest notes that they could bring;
            For, like the Jews,
            Wild beasts refuse
In midst of their captivity—to sing.

        Lord! how it made him chafe,
Full of his new emancipating zeal,

To look around upon this brute-bastile,
And see the king of creatures in—a safe !
The desert's denizen in one small den,
Swallowing slavery's most bitter pills—
A bear in bars unbearable.   And then
The fretful porcupine, with all its quills
        Imprisoned in a pen !

    A tiger limited to four feet ten,
        And, still worse lot,
        A leopard to one spot !
        An elephant enlarged,
        But not discharged,
    (It was before the elephant was shot ;)
A doleful wanderoo, that wandered not ;
An ounce much disproportioned to his pound.
        Pug's wrath waxed hot
To gaze upon these captive creatures round ;
Whose claws—all scratching—gave him full assurance
They found their durance vile of vile endurance.

He went above—a solitary mounter
Up gloomy stairs—and saw a pensive group
        Of hapless fowls—
        Cranes, vultures, owls ;
In fact, it was a sort of Poultry Compter,
Where feathered prisoners were doomed to droop :
Here sat an eagle, forced to make a stoop,
Not from the skies, but his impending roof ;
        And there aloof,
A pining ostrich, moping in a coop ;
With other samples of the bird creation,
All caged against their powers and their wills ;
And cramped in such a space, the longest bills
Were plainly bills of least accommodation.
In truth, it was a very ugly scene
To fall to any liberator's share,
To see those wingèd fowls, that once had been
Free as the wind, no freer than fixed air.

      His temper little mended,
Pug from this Bird-cage Walk at last descended

Unto the lion and the elephant,
His bosom in a pant
To see all nature's Free List thus suspended,
And beasts deprived of what she had intended.
They could not even prey
In their own way—
A hardship always reckoned quite prodigious.
Thus he revolved,
And soon resolved
To give them freedom, civil and religious.

That night there were no country cousins, raw
From Wales, to view the lion and his kin:
The keeper's eyes were fixed upon a saw;
The saw was fixed upon a bullock's shin:
Meanwhile with stealthy paw,
Pug hastened to withdraw
The bolt that kept the king of brutes within.
Now, monarch of the forest ! thou shalt win
Precious enfranchisement—thy bolts are undone;
Thou art no longer a degraded creature,
But loose to roam with liberty and nature,
And free of all the jungles about London—
All Hampstead's heathy desert lies before thee !
Methinks I see thee bound from Cross's ark,
Full of the native instinct that comes o'er thee,
And turn a ranger
Of Hounslow Forest and the Regent's Park—
Thin Rhodes's cows—the mail-coach steeds endanger,
And gobble parish watchmen after dark.
Methinks I see thee, with the early lark,
Stealing to Merlin's cave (*thy* cave). Alas,
That such bright visions should not come to pass !
Alas, for freedom, and for freedom's hero !
Alas, for liberty of life and limb !
For Pug had only half unbolted Nero,
When Nero *bolted him !*

DEATH'S RAMBLE.

One day the dreary old King of Death
    Inclined for some sport with the carnal,
So he tied a pack of darts on his back,
    And quietly stole from his charnel.

His head was bald of flesh and of hair,
    His body was lean and lank,
His joints at each stir made a crack, and the cur
    Took a gnaw, by the way, at his shank.

And what did he do with his deadly darts,
    This goblin of grisly bone?
He dabbled and spilled man's blood, and he killed
    Like a butcher that kills his own.

The first he slaughtered it made him laugh,
    (For the man was a coffin-maker),
To think how the mutes, and men in black suits,
    Would mourn for an undertaker.

Death saw two Quakers sitting at church,
    Quoth he, "We shall not differ."
And he let them alone, like figures of stone,
    For he could not maker them stiffer.

He saw two duellists going to fight,
    In fear they could not smother;
And he shot one through at once—for he knew
    They never would shoot each other.

He saw a watchman fast in his box,
    And he gave a snore infernal;
Said Death, "He may keep his breath, for his sleep
    Can never be more eternal."

He met a coachman driving his coach,
    So slow, that his fare grew sick;
But he let him stray on his tedious way,
    For Death only wars on the *quick*.

Death saw a toll-man taking a toll,
 In the spirit of his fraternity ;
But he knew that sort of man would extort
 Though summoned to all eternity.

He found an author writing his life,
 But he let him write no further ;
For Death, who strikes whenever he likes,
 Is jealous of all self-murther !

Death saw a patient that pulled out his purse,
 And a doctor that took the sum ;
But he let them be—for he knew that the " fee"
 Was a prelude to " faw" and " fum."

He met a dustman ringing a bell,
 And he gave him a mortal thrust ;
For himself, by law, since Adam's flaw,
 Is contractor for all our dust.

He saw a sailor mixing his grog,
 And he marked him out for slaughter ;
For on water he scarcely had cared for Death,
 And never on rum-and-water.

Death saw two players playing at cards,
 But the game wasn't worth a dump,
For he quickly laid them flat with a spade,
 To wait for the final trump !

CRANIOLOGY.

'TIS strange how like a very dunce,
Man—with his bumps upon his sconce,
Has lived so long, and yet no knowledge he
Has had, till lately, of Phrenology—
A science that by simple dint of
Head-combing he should find a hint of,
When scratching o'er those little poll-hills,
The faculties throw up like mole-hills ;

A science that, in very spite
Of all his teeth, ne'er came to light,
For though he knew his skull had *grinders,*
Still there turned up no *organ* finders,
Still sages wrote, and ages fled,
And no man's head came in his head—
Not even the pate of Erra Pater,
Knew aught about its pia mater.
At last great Dr. Gall bestirs him—
I don't know but it might be Spurzheim—
Tho' native of a dull and slow land,
And makes partition of our Poll-land ;
At our Acquisitiveness guesses,
And all those necessary *nesses*
Indicative of human habits,
All burrowing in the head like rabbits.
Thus Veneration, he made known,
Had got a lodging at the Crown :
And Music (see Deville's example)
A set of chambers in the Temple ;
That Language taught the tongues close by,
And took in pupils thro' the eye,
Close by his neighbour Computation,
Who taught the eyebrows numeration.

The science thus—to speak in fit
Terms—having struggled from its nit,
Was seized on by a swarm of Scotchmen,
Those scientifical hotch-potch men,
Who have at least a penny dip,
And wallop in all doctorship,
Just as in making broth they smatter
By bobbing twenty things in water :
These men, I say, made quick appliance
And close, to phrenologic science ;
For of all learnèd themes whatever,
That schools and colleges deliver,
There's none they love so near the bodles,
As analysing their own noddles ;
Thus in a trice each northern blockhead
Had got his fingers in his shock head,

And of his bumps was babbling yet worse
Than poor Miss Capulet's dry wet-nurse ;
Till having been sufficient rangers
Of their own heads, they took to strangers',
And found in Presbyterians' polls
The things they hated in their souls ;
For Presbyterians hear with passion
Of organs joined with veneration.
No kind there was of human pumpkin
But at its bumps it had a bumpkin ;
Down to the very lowest gullion,
And oiliest skull of oily scullion.
No great man died but this they *did* do,
They begged his cranium of his widow :
No murderer died by law disaster,
But they took off his sconce in plaster ;
For thereon they could show depending,
" The head and front of his offending :"
How that his philanthropic bump
Was mastered by a baser lump ;
For every bump (these wags insist)
Has its direct antagonist,
Each striving stoutly to prevail,
Like horses knotted tail to tail !
And many a stiff and sturdy battle
Occurs between these adverse cattle,
The secret cause, beyond all question,
Of aches ascribed to indigestion,—
Whereas 'tis but two knobby rivals
Tugging together like sheer devils,
Till one gets mastery, good or sinister,
And comes in like a new prime-minister.

Each bias in some master node is :—
What takes M'Adam where a road is,
To hammer little pebbles less ?
His organ of Destructiveness.
What makes great Joseph so encumber
Debate ? a lumping lump of Number :
Or Malthus rail at babies so ?
The smallness of his Philopro—

What severs man and wife? a simple
Defect of the Adhesive pimple:
Or makes weak women go astray?
Their bumps are more in fault than they.

These facts being found and set in order
By grave M.D.s beyond the Border,
To make them for some months eternal,
Were entered monthly in a journal,
That many a northern sage still writes in,
And throws his little Northern Lights in,
And proves and proves about the phrenos,
A great deal more than I or he knows:
How Music suffers, *par exemple*,
By wearing tight hats round the temple;
What ills great boxers have to fear
From blisters put behind the ear;
And how a porter's Veneration
Is hurt by porters' occupation;
Whether shillelaghs in reality
May deaden Individuality;
Or tongs and poker be creative
Of alterations in th' Amative;
If falls from scaffolds make us less
Inclined to all Constructiveness:
With more such matters, all applying
To heads—and therefore *head*ifying.

———————

A PARTHIAN GLANCE.

" Sweet Memory, wafted by thy gentle gale,
Oft up the stream of time I turn my sail."—ROGERS.

I.

COME, my Crony, let's think upon far-away days,
    And lift up a little Oblivion's veil;
Let's consider the past with a lingering gaze,
    Like a peacock whose eyes are inclined to his tail.

II.

Ay, come, let us turn our attention behind,
　Like those critics whose heads are so heavy, I fear,
That they cannot keep up with the march of the mind,
　And so turn face about for reviewing the rear.

III.

Looking over Time's crupper and over his tail,
　Oh! what ages and pages there are to revise!
And as farther our back-searching glances prevail,
　Like the emmets, "how little we are in our eyes!"

IV.

What a sweet pretty innocent, half a yard long,
　On a dimity lap of true nursery make!
I can fancy I hear the old lullaby song
　That was meant to compose me, but kept me awake.

V.

Methinks I still suffer the infantine throes,
　When my flesh was a cushion for any long pin—
Whilst they patted my body to comfort my woes,
　Oh! how little they dreamt they were driving them in!

VI.

Infant sorrows are strong—infant pleasures as weak—
　But no grief was allowed to indulge in its note;
Did you ever attempt a small "bubble and squeak,"
　Thro' the Dalby's Carminative down in your throat?

VII.

Did you ever go up to the roof with a bounce?
　Did you ever come down to the floor with the same?
Oh! I can't but agree with both ends, and pronounce
　"Head or tails" with a child, an unpleasantish game!

VIII.

Then an urchin—I see myself urchin, indeed,
　With a smooth Sunday face for a mother's delight;

Why should weeks have an end?—I am sure there was need
    Of a Sabbath to follow each Saturday-night.

IX.

Was your face ever sent to the housemaid to scrub?
    Have you ever felt huckaback softened with sand?
Had you ever your nose towelled up to a snub,
    And your eyes knuckled out with the back of the hand?

X.

Then a schoolboy—my tailor was nothing in fault,
    For an urchin will grow to a lad by degrees,—
But how well I remember that "pepper and salt,"
    That was down to the elbows, and up to the knees!

XI.

What a figure it cut when as Norval I spoke!
    With a lanky right leg duly planted before;
Whilst I told of the chief that was killed by my stroke,
    And extended *my* arms as "the arms that he wore!"

XII.

Next a Lover—Oh! say, were you ever in love?
    With a lady too cold—and your bosom too hot!
Have you bowed to a shoe-tie, and knelt to a glove?
    Like a *beau* that desired to be tied in a knot?

XIII.

With the Bride all in white, and your body in blue,
    Did you walk up the aisle—the genteelest of men?
When I think of that beautiful vision anew,
    Oh! I seem but the *biffin* of what I was then!

XIV.

I am withered and worn by a premature care,
    And my wrinkles confess the decline of my days;
Old Time's busy hand has made free with my hair,
    And I'm seeking to hide it—by writing for bays.

A SAILOR'S APOLOGY FOR BOW-LEGS.

THERE'S some is born with their legs straight by natur—
And some is born with bow-legs from the first—
And some that should have growed a good deal straighter,
  But they were badly nursed,
And set, you see, like Bacchus, with their pegs
  Astride of casks and kegs.
I've got myself a sort of bow to larboard
  And starboard,
And this is what it was that warped my legs:

'Twas all along of Poll, as I may say,
That fouled my cable when I ought to slip;
  But on the tenth of May,
  When I gets under weigh,
Down there in Hartfordshire, to join my ship,
  I sees the mail
  Get under sail,
The only one there was to make the trip.
  Well, I gives chase,
  But as she run
  Two knots to one,
There warn't no use in keeping on the race!

Well, casting round about, what next to try on,
  And how to spin,
I spies an ensign with a Bloody Lion,
And bears away to leeward for the inn,
  Beats round the gable,
And fetches up before the coach-horse stable.
Well, there they stand, four kickers in a row,
  And so
I just makes free to cut a brown 'un's cable.
But riding isn't in a seaman's natur;
So I whips out a toughish end of yarn,
And gets a kind of sort of a land-waiter
  To splice me, heel to heel,
  Under the she-mare's keel,
And off I goes, and leaves the inn a-starn!

My eyes! how she did pitch!
And wouldn't keep her own to go in no line,
Tho' I kept bowsing, bowsing at her bow-line,
But always making lee-way to the ditch,
And yawed her head about all sorts of ways.
    The devil sink the craft!
And wasn't she tremendous slack in stays!
We couldn't, no how, keep the inn abaft!
    Well, I suppose
We hadn't run a knot—or much beyond—
(What will you have on it?)—but off she goes,
Up to her bends in a fresh-water pond!
    There I am! all a-back!
So I looks forward for her bridle-gears,
To heave her head round on the t'other tack;
    But when I starts,
    The leather parts,
And goes away right over by the ears!

    What could a fellow do,
Whose legs, like mine, you know, were in the bilboes,
But trim myself upright for bringing-to,
And square his yard-arms and brace up his elbows,
    In rig all snug and clever,
Just while his craft was taking in her water?
I didn't like my berth though, howsomdever,
Because the yarn, you see, kept getting tauter.
Says I—I wish this job was rayther shorter!

    The chase had gained a mile
A-head, and still the she-mare stood a-drinking:
    Now, all the while
Her body didn't take, of course, to shrinking.
Says I, she's letting out her reefs, I'm thinking;
    And so she swelled and swelled,
    And yet the tackle held,
Till both my legs began to bend like winkin.
My eyes! but she took in enough to founder!
And there's my timbers straining every bit,
    Ready to split,
And her tarnation hull a-growing rounder!

Well, there—off Hartford Ness,
We lay both lashed and water-logged together,
            And can't contrive a signal of distress.
Thinks I, we must ride out this here foul weather,
Tho' sick of riding out, and nothing less;
When, looking round, I sees a man a-starn:
" Hollo!" says I, " come underneath her quarter!"
And hands him out my knife to cut the yarn.
So I gets off, and lands upon the road,
And leaves the she-mare to her own consarn,
            A-standing by the water.
If I get on another, I'll be blowed!
And that's the way, you see, my legs got bowed!

JACK HALL.

I.

'TIS very hard when men forsake
This melancholy world, and make
A bed of turf, they cannot take
            A quiet doze,
But certain rogues will come and break
            Their " bone repose."

II.

'Tis hard we can't give up our breath,
And to the earth our earth bequeath,
Without Death Fetches after death,
            Who thus exhume us!
And snatch us from our homes beneath,
            And hearths posthumous.

III.

The tender lover comes to rear
The mournful urn, and shed his tear—
" Her glorious dust," he cries, " is here!"
            Alack! alack!
The while his Sacharissa dear
            Is in a sack!

IV.

'Tis hard one cannot lie amid
The mould beneath a coffin-lid,
But thus the Faculty will bid
    Their rogues break thro' it!
If they don't want us there, why did
    They send us to it?

V.

One of these sacrilegious knaves,
Who crave as hungry vulture craves,
Behaving as the ghoul behaves,
    'Neath churchyard wall—
Mayhap because he fed on graves,
    Was named Jack Hall.

VI.

By day it was his trade to go
Tending the black coach to and fro;
And sometimes at the door of woe,
    With emblems suitable,
He stood with brother Mute, to show
    That life is mutable

VII.

But long before they passed the ferry,
The dead that he had helped to bury
He sacked—(he had a sack to carry
    The bodies off in;)
In fact, he let them have a very
    Short fit of coffin.

VIII.

Night after night, with crow and spade,
He drove this dead but thriving trade,
Meanwhile his conscience never weighed
    A single horsehair;
On corses of all kinds he preyed,
    A perfect corsair!

IX.

At last—it may be, Death took spite,
Or jesting, only meant to fright—
He sought for Jack night after night
                    The churchyards round ;
And soon they met, the man and sprite,
                    In Pancras' ground.

X.

Jack, by the glimpses of the moon,
Perceived the bony knacker soon,
An awful shape to meet at noon
                    Of night and lonely ;
But Jack's tough courage did but swoon
                    A minute only.

XI.

Anon he gave his spade a swing
Aloft, and kept it brandishing,
Ready for what mishaps might spring
                    From this conjunction ;
Funking indeed was quite a thing
                    Beside his function.

XII.

" Hollo !" cried Death, " d'ye wish your sands
Run out ? the stoutest never stands
A chance with me,—to my commands
                    The strongest truckles ;
But I'm your friend—so let's shake hands,
                    I should say—knuckles."

XIII.

Jack, glad to see th' old sprite so sprightly,
And meaning nothing but uprightly,
Shook hands at once, and bowing slightly,
                    His mull did proffer :
But Death, who had no nose, politely
                    Declined the offer.

11

XIV.

Then sitting down upon a bank,
Leg over leg, shank over shank,
Like friends for conversation frank,
                    That had no check on :
Quoth Jack unto the Lean and Lank,
                    "You're Death, I reckon."

XV.

The Jaw-bone grinned :—" I am that same,
You've hit exactly on my name ;
In truth it has some little fame
                    Where burial sod is."
Quoth Jack (and winked), " Of course ye came
                    Here after bodies."

XVI.

Death grinned again and shook his head :—
" I've little business with the dead ;
When they are fairly sent to bed
                    I've done my turn :
Whether or not the worms are fed
                    Is your concern.

XVII.

" My errand here, in meeting you,
Is nothing but a how-d'ye-do ;
I've done what jobs I had—a few,
                    Along this way ;
If I can serve a crony too,
                    I beg you'll say."

XVIII.

Quoth Jack, " Your Honour's very kind :
And now I call the thing to mind,
This parish very strict I find ;
                    But in the next 'un
There lives a very well-inclined
                    Old sort of sexton."

XIX.

Death took the hint, and gave a wink
As well as eyelet-holes can blink;
Then stretching out his arm to link
  The other's arm,—
"Suppose," says he, "we have a drink
  Of something warm."

XX.

Jack nothing loth, with friendly ease
Spoke up at once :—"Why, what ye please;
Hard by there is the Cheshire Cheese,
  A famous tap."
But this suggestion seemed to tease
  The bony chap.

XXI.

"No, no !—your mortal drinks are heady,
And only make my hand unsteady;
I do not even care for Deady,
  And loathe your rum;
But I've some glorious brewage ready,
  My drink is—mum !"

XXII.

And off they set, each right content—
Who knows the dreary way they went?
But Jack felt rather faint and spent,
  And out of breath;
At last he saw, quite evident,
  The Door of Death.

XXIII.

All other men had been unmanned
To see a coffin on each hand,
That served a skeleton to stand
  By way of sentry;
In fact, Death has a very grand
  And awful entry.

XXIV.

Throughout his dismal sign prevails,
His name is writ in coffin nails ;
The mortal darts make area rails ;
   A skull that mocketh
Grins on the gloomy gate, and quails
   Whoever knocketh.

XXV.

And lo ! on either side, arise
Two monstrous pillars—bones of thighs ;
A monumental slab supplies
   The step of stone,
Where waiting for his master lies,
   A dog of bone.

XXVI.

The dog leapt up, but gave no yell,
The wire was pulled, but woke no bell,
The ghastly knocker rose and fell,
   But caused no riot ;
The ways of Death, we all know well,
   Are very quiet.

XXVII.

Old Bones stepped in ; Jack stepped behind :
Quoth Death, " I really hope you'll find
The entertainment to your mind,
   As I shall treat ye —
A friend or two of goblin kind
   I've asked to meet ye."

XXVIII.

And lo ! a crowd of spectres tall,
Like jack-a-lanterns on a wall,
Were standing—every ghastly ball
   An eager watcher.
" My friends," says Death—"friends, Mr. Hall,
   The body-snatcher."

XXIX.

Lord ! what a tumult it produced,
When Mr. Hall was introduced !
Jack even, who had long been used
　　　　To frightful things,
Felt just as if his back was sluiced
　　　　With freezing springs !

XXX.

Each goblin face began to make
Some horrid mouth—ape—gorgon—snake ;
And then a spectre hag would shake
　　　　An airy thighbone ;
And cried (or seemed to cry) I'll break
　　　　Your bone, with *my* bone !

XXXI.

Some ground their teeth—some seemed to spit—
(Nothing, but nothing came of it ;)
A hundred awful brows were knit
　　　　In dreadful spite.
Thought Jack—I'm sure I'd better quit,
　　　　Without good-night.

XXXII.

One skip and hop and he was clear,
And running like a hunted deer,
As fleet as people run by fear
　　　　Well spurred and whipped,
Death, ghosts, and all in that career
　　　　Were quite outstripped.

XXXIII.

But those who live by death must die ;
Jack's soul at last prepared to fly ;
And when his latter end drew nigh,
　　　　Oh ! what a swarm
Of doctors came,—but not to try
　　　　To keep him warm.

XXXIV.

No ravens ever scented prey
So early where a dead horse lay,
Nor vultures sniffed so far away
　　　　　A last convulse:
A dozen "guests" day after day
　　　　　Were "at his pulse."

XXXV.

'Twas strange, altho' they got no fees,
How still they watched by twos and threes:
But Jack a very little ease
　　　　　Obtained from them;
In fact, he did not find M.D.s
　　　　　Worth one D—M.

XXXVI.

The passing bell with hollow toll
Was in his thought—the dreary hole!
Jack gave his eyes a horrid roll,
　　　　　And then a cough.
" There's something weighing on my soul
　　　　　I wish was off:

XXXVII.

" All night it roves about my brains,
All day it adds to all my pains;
It is concerning my remains
　　　　　When I am dead."
Twelve wigs and twelve gold-headed canes
　　　　　Drew near his bed.

XXXVIII.

" Alas !" he sighed, " I'm sore afraid,
A dozen pangs my heart invade;
But when I drove a certain trade
　　　　　In flesh and bone,
There was a little bargain made
　　　　　About my own."

XXXIX.

Twelve suits of black began to close,
Twelve pairs of sleek and sable hose,
Twelve flowing cambric frills in rows,
   At once drew round;
Twelve noses turned against his nose,
    Twelve snubs profound.

XL.

" Ten guineas did not quite suffice,
And so I sold my body twice;
Twice did not do—I sold it thrice:
   Forgive my crimes!
In short, I have received its price
    A dozen times!"

XLI.

Twelve brows got very grim and black,
Twelve wishes stretched him on the rack,
Twelve pairs of hands for fierce attack
   Took up position,
Ready to share the dying Jack
    By long division.

XLII.

Twelve angry doctors wrangled so,
That twelve had struck an hour ago,
Before they had an eye to throw
   On the departed;
Twelve heads turned round at once, and lo!
    Twelve doctors started.

XLIII.

Whether some comrade of the dead,
Or Satan took it in his head,
To steal the corpse—the corpse had fled!
   'Tis only written,
That *" there was nothing in the bed,*
    But twelve were bitten!"

THE WEE MAN.

A ROMANCE.

It was a merry company,
　　And they were just afloat,
When lo! a man, of dwarfish span,
　　Came up and hailed the boat.

"Good morrow to ye, gentle folks,
　　And will you let me in?
A slender space will serve my case,
　　For I am small and thin."

They saw he was a dwarfish man,
　　And very small and thin;
Not seven such would matter much,
　　And so they took him in.

They laughed to see his little hat,
　　With such a narrow brim;
They laughed to note his dapper coat,
　　With skirts so scant and trim.

But barely had they gone a mile,
　　When, gravely, one and all,
At once began to think the man
　　Was not so very small:

His coat had got a broader skirt,
　　His hat a broader brim.
His leg grew stout, and soon plumped out
　　A very proper limb.

Still on they went, and as they went,
　　More rough the billows grew,—
And rose and fell, a greater swell,
　　And he was swelling too!

And lo ! where room had been for seven,
    For six there scarce was space !
For five !—for four !—for three !—not more
    Than two could find a place !

There was not even room for one !
    They crowded by degrees—
Ay—closer yet, till elbows met,
    And knees were jogging knees.

" Good sir, you must not sit a-stern,
    The wave will else come in !"
Without a word he gravely stirred,
    Another seat to win.

" Good sir, the boat has lost her trim,
    You must not sit a-lee !"
With smiling face, and courteous grace,
    The middle seat took he.

But still, by constant quiet growth,
    His back became so wide,
Each neighbour wight, to left and right,
    Was thrust against the side.

Lord ! how they chided with themselves,
    That they had let him in ;
To see him grow so monstrous now,
    That came so small and thin.

On every brow a dewdrop stood,
    They grew so scared and hot,—
" I' the name of all that's great and tall,
    Who are ye, sir, and what ?"

Loud laughed the Gogmagog, a laugh
    As loud as giant's roar—
" When first I came, my proper name
    Was Little—now I'm *Moore !*"

A BUTCHER.

WHOE'ER has gone thro' London Street,
Has seen a Butcher gazing at his meat,
    And how he keeps
      Gloating upon a sheep's
Or bullock's personals, as if his own;
    How he admires his halves
    And quarters—and his calves,
As if in truth upon his own legs grown;
    His fat! *his* suet!
His kidneys peeping elegantly thro' it!
    His thick flank!
    And *his* thin!
      His shank!
      His shin!
Skin of his skin, and bone too of his bone!

With what an air
He stands aloof, across the thoroughfare
Gazing—and will not let a body by,
Tho' buy! buy! buy! be constantly his cry.
Meanwhile with arms akimbo, and a pair
Of Rhodian legs, he revels in a stare
At his Joint Stock—for one may call it so,
    Howbeit without a *Co.*
The dotage of self-love was never fonder
Than he of his brute bodies all a-row;
Narcissus in the wave did never ponder
    With love so strong,
    On his "portrait charmant,"
As our vain Butcher on his carcass yonder.

Look at his sleek round skull!
How bright his cheek, how rubicund his nose is!
    His visage seems to be
    Ripe for beef-tea;
Of brutal juices the whole man is full.
In fact, fulfilling the metempsychosis,
The Butcher is already half a Bull.

"DON'T YOU SMELL FIRE?"

I.

Run !—run for St. Clement's engine !
  For the Pawnbroker's all in a blaze,
And the pledges are frying and singeing—
  Oh ! how the poor pawners will craze !
Now where can the turncock be drinking ?
  Was there ever so thirsty an elf ?
But he still may tope on, for I'm thinking
  That the plugs are as dry as himself.

II.

The engines ! I hear them come rumbling ;
  There's the Phœnix ! the Globe ! and the Sun !
What a row there will be, and a grumbling,
  When the water don't start for a run !
See ! there they come racing and tearing,
  All the street with loud voices is filled ;
Oh ! it's only the firemen a-swearing
  At a man they've run over and killed !

III.

How sweetly the sparks fly away now,
  And twinkle like stars in the sky.
It's a wonder the engines don't play now ;
  But I never saw water so shy !
Why, there isn't enough for a snipe,
  And the fire it is fiercer, alas !
Oh ! instead of the New River pipe,
  They have gone—that they have—to the gas !

IV.

Only look at the poor little P——'s
  On the roof.   Is there anything sadder ?
My dears, keep fast hold, if you please,
  And they wont be an hour with the ladder !

But if anyone's hot in their feet,
    And in very great haste to be saved,
Here's a nice easy bit in the street,
    That M'Adam has lately unpaved!

v.

There is some one—I see a dark shape
    At that window, the hottest of all,—
My good woman, why don't you escape?
    Never think of your bonnet and shawl:
If your dress isn't perfect, what is it
    For once in a way to your hurt?
When your husband is paying a visit
    There, at Number Fourteen, in his shirt!

vi.

Only see how she throws out her *chaney!*
    Her basins, and teapots, and all
The most brittle of *her* goods—or any,
    But they all break in breaking their fall:
Such things are not surely the best
    From a two-storey window to throw—
She might save a good iron-bound chest,
    For there's plenty of people below!

vii.

O dear! what a beautiful flash!
    How it shone through the window and door!
We shall soon hear a scream and a crash,
    When the woman falls thro' with the floor!
There! there! what a volley of flame,
    And then suddenly all is obscured!—
Well—I'm glad in my heart that I came;
    But I hope the poor man is insured!

THE VOLUNTEER.

"The clashing of my armour in my ears
Sounds like a passing bell ; my buckler puts me
In mind of a bier ; this, my broadsword, a pickaxe
To dig my grave."—*The Lover's Progress.*

I.

'Twas in that memorable year
France threatened to put off in
Flat-bottomed boats, intending each
To be a British coffin,
To make sad widows of our wives,
And every babe an orphan :—

II.

When coats were made of scarlet cloaks,
And heads were dredged with flour,
I 'listed in the Lawyers' Corps,
Against the battle hour ;
A perfect Volunteer—for why?
I brought my "will and pow'r."

III.

One dreary day—a day of dread,
Like Cato's, over-cast—
About the hour of six, (the morn
And I were breaking fast,)
There came a loud and sudden sound,
That struck me all aghast !

IV.

A dismal sort of morning roll,
That was not to be eaten :
Although it was no skin of mine,
But parchment that was beaten,
I felt tattooed through all my flesh,
Like any Otaheitan.

V.

My jaws with utter dread enclosed
The morsel I was munching,
And terror locked them up so tight,
My very teeth went crunching
All through my bread and tongue at once,
Like sandwich made at lunching.

VI.

My hand that held the teapot fast,
Stiffened, but yet unsteady,
Kept pouring, pouring, pouring o'er
The cup in one long eddy,
Till both my hose were marked with *tea,*
As they were marked already.

VII.

I felt my visage turn from red
To white—from cold to hot;
But it was nothing wonderful
My colour changed, I wot,
For, like some variable silks,
I felt that I was shot.

VIII.

And looking forth with anxious eye,
From my snug upper storey,
I saw our melancholy corps
Going to beds all gory;
The pioneers seemed very loth
To axe their way to glory.

IX.

The captain marched as mourners march,
The ensign too seemed lagging,
And many more, although they were
No ensigns, took to flagging—
Like corpses in the Serpentine,
Methought they wanted dragging.

X.

But while I watched, the thought of death
Came like a chilly gust,
And lo ! I shut the window down,
With very little lust
To join so many marching men,
That soon might be March dust.

XI.

Quoth I, "Since Fate ordains it so,
Our foe the coast must land on ;"
I felt so warm beside the fire
I cared not to abandon ;
Our hearths and homes are always things
That patriots make a stand on.

XII.

" The fools that fight abroad for home,"
Thought I, "may get a wrong one ;
Let those that have no home, at all
Go battle for a long one."
The mirror here confirmed me this
Reflection, by a strong one :

XIII.

For there, where I was wont to shave,
And deck me like Adonis,
There stood the leader of our foes,
With vultures for his cronies—
No Corsican, but Death himself,
The Bony of all Bonies.

XIV.

A horrid sight it was, and sad,
To see the grisly chap
Put on my crimson livery,
And then begin to clap
My helmet on—ah me ! it felt
Like any felon's cap.

XV.

My plume seemed borrowed from a hearse,
An undertaker's crest;
My epaulettes like coffin-plates;
My belt so heavy pressed,
Four pipeclay cross-roads seemed to lie
At once upon my breast.

XVI.

My brazen breastplate only lacked
A little heap of salt,
To make me like a corpse full dressed,
Preparing for the vault—
To set up what the Poet calls
My everlasting halt.

XVII.

This funeral show inclined me quite
To peace :—and here I am !
Whilst better lions go to war,
Enjoying with the lamb
A lengthened life, that might have been
A martial epigram.

THE WIDOW.

ONE widow at a grave will sob
A little while, and weep, and sigh !
If two should meet on such a job,
They'll have a gossip by-and-by.
If three should come together—why,
Three widows are good company !
If four should meet by any chance,
Four is a number very nice,
To have a rubber in a trice—
But five will up and have a dance !

Poor Mrs. C—— (why should I not
Declare her name?—her name was Cross)
Was one of those the " common lot"
Had left to weep " no common loss ;"
For she had lately buried then
A man, the " very best of men,"
A lingering truth, discovered first
Whenever men " are at the worst."
To take the measure of her woe,
It was some dozen inches deep—
I mean in crape, and hung so low,
It hid the drops she did *not* weep :
In fact, what human life appears,
It was a perfect " veil of tears."
Though ever since she lost " her prop
And stay"—alas ! he wouldn't stay—
She never had a tear to mop,
Except one little angry drop
From Passion's eye, as Moore would say
Because, when Mister Cross took flight,
It looked so very like a spite—
He died upon a washing-day !

Still Widow Cross went twice a week,
As if " to wet a widow's cheek,"
And soothe his grave with sorrow's gravy—
'Twas nothing but a make-believe,
She might as well have hoped to grieve
Enough of brine to float a navy ;
And yet she often seemed to raise
A cambric kerchief to her eye—
A *duster* ought to be the phrase,
Its work was all so very dry.
The springs were locked that ought to flow—
In England or in widow-woman—
As those that watch the weather know,
Such " backward Springs" are not uncommon.

But why did Widow Cross take pains
To call upon the " dear remains"—
Remains that could not tell a jot
Whether she ever wept or not,

Or how his relict took her losses?
Oh! my black ink turns red for shame—
But still the naughty world must learn,
There was a little German came
To shed a tear in "Anna's Urn,"
At the next grave to Mr. Cross's!
For there an angel's virtues slept,
"Too soon did Heaven assert its claim!"
But still her painted face he kept,
"Encompassed in an angel's frame."

He looked quite sad and quite deprived,
His head was nothing but a hat-band;
He looked so lone, and so *un*wived,
That soon the Widow Cross contrived
To fall in love with even *that* band;
And all at once the brackish juices
Came gushing out thro' sorrow's sluices—
Tear after tear too fast to wipe,
Tho' sopped, and sopped, and sopped again—
No leak in sorrow's private pipe,
But like a bursting on the main!
Whoe'er has watched the window-pane—
I mean to say in showery weather—
Has seen two little drops of rain,
Like lovers very fond and fain,
At one another creeping, creeping,
Till both, at last, embrace together:
So fared it with that couple's weeping!
The principle was quite as active—
      Tear unto tear
      Kept drawing near,
Their very blacks became attractive.
To cut a shortish story shorter,
Conceive them sitting *tête-à-tête*—
Two cups—hot muffins on a plate—
With "Anna's Urn" to hold hot water!
The brazen vessel for awhile
Had lectured in an easy song,
Like Abernethy—on the bile—
The scalded herb was getting strong;

All seemed as smooth as smooth could be,
To have a cozy cup of tea.
Alas! how often human sippers
With unexpected bitters meet,
And buds, the sweetest of the sweet,
Like sugar, only meet the nippers!

The Widow Cross, I should have told,
Had seen three husbands to the mould:
She never sought an Indian pyre,
Like Hindoo wives that lose their loves;
But, with a proper sense of fire,
Put up, instead, with "three removes."
Thus, when with any tender words
Or tears she spoke about her loss,
The dear departed Mr. Cross
Came in for nothing but his thirds;
For, as all widows love too well,
She liked upon the list to dwell,
And oft ripped up the old disasters.
She might, indeed, have been supposed
A great *ship* owner; for she prosed
Eternally of her Three Masters!

Thus, foolish woman! while she nursed
Her mild souchong, she talked and reckoned
What had been left her by her first,
And by her last, and by her second.
Alas! not all her annual rents
Could then entice the little German—
Not Mr. Cross's Three per Cents,
Or Consols, ever make him *her* man.
He liked her cash, he liked her houses,
But not that dismal bit of land
She always settled on her spouses.
So taking up his hat and band,
Said he, "You'll think my conduct odd—
But here my hopes no more may linger;
I thought you had a wedding-finger,
But oh!—it is a curtain-rod!"

JOHN TROT.

A BALLAD.

I.

JOHN TROT he was as tall a lad
    As York did ever rear—
As his dear Granny used to say,
    He'd make a grenadier.

II.

A sergeant soon came down to York,
    With ribbons and a frill;
My lads, said he, let broadcast be,
    And come away to drill.

III.

But when he wanted John to 'list,
    In war he saw no fun,
Where what is called a raw recruit
    Gets often over-done.

IV.

Let others carry guns, said he,
    And go to war's alarms,
But I have got a shoulder-knot
    Imposed upon my arms.

V.

For John he had a footman's place
    To wait on Lady Wye—
She was a dumpy woman, tho'
    Her family was high.

VI.

Now when two years had passed away,
    Her lord took very ill,
And left her to her widowhood,
    Of course more dumpy still.

VII.

Said John, I am a proper man,
   And very tall to see;
Who knows, but now her lord is low,
   She may look up to me?

VIII.

A cunning woman told me once,
   Such fortune would turn up;
She was a kind of sorceress,
   But studied in a cup!

IX.

So he walked up to Lady Wye,
   And took her quite amazed,—
She thought, tho' John was tall enough,
   He wanted to be raised.

X.

But John—for why? she was a dame
   Of such a dwarfish sort—
Had only come to bid her make
   Her mourning very short.

XI.

Said he, your lord is dead and cold,
   You only cry in vain;
Not all the cries of London now
   Could call him back again!

XII.

You'll soon have many a noble beau,
   To dry your noble tears—
But just consider this, that I
   Have followed you for years.

XIII.

And tho' you are above me far,
   What matters high degree,
When you are only four foot nine,
   And I am six foot three!

XIV.

For tho' you are of lofty race,
    And I'm a low-born elf;
Yet none among your friends could say,
    You matched beneath yourself.

XV.

Said she, such insolence as this
    Can be no common case;
Tho' you are in my service, sir,
    Your love is out of place.

XVI.

O Lady Wye! O Lady Wye!
    Consider what you do;
How can you be so short with me,
    I am not so with you!

XVII.

Then ringing for her serving men,
    They showed him to the door:
Said they, you turn out better now,
    Why didn't you before?

XVIII.

They stripped his coat, and gave him kicks
    For all his wages due;
And off, instead of green and gold,
    He went in black and blue.

XIX.

No family would take him in,
    Because of his discharge;
So he made up his mind to serve
    The country all at large.

XX.

Huzza! the sergeant cried, and put
    The money in his hand,
And with a shilling cut him off
    From his paternal land.

XXI.

For when his regiment went to fight
    At Saragossa town,
A Frenchman thought he looked too tall
    And so he cut him down !

ODE TO THE CAMELEOPARD.

WELCOME to Freedom's birthplace—and a den !
        Great Anti-climax, hail !
So very lofty in thy front—but then,
        So dwindling at the tail !
In truth, thou hast the most unequal legs !
Has one pair galloped, whilst the other trotted,
Along with other brethren, leopard-spotted,
O'er Afric sand, where ostriches lay eggs ?
Sure thou wert caught in some hard uphill chase,
Those hinder heels still keeping thee in check !
        And yet thou seem'st prepared in any case,
        Tho' they had lost the race,
            To win it—by a neck !

That lengthy neck—how like a crane's it looks !
Art thou the overseer of all the brutes ?
Or dost thou browze on tip-top leaves or fruits—
Or go a bird-nesting amongst the rooks ?
How kindly nature caters for all wants ;
Thus giving unto thee a neck that stretches,
        And high food fetches—
To some a long nose, like the elephant's !

Oh ! had'st thou any organ to thy bellows,
To turn thy breath to speech in human style,
        What secrets thou might'st tell us,
Where now our scientific guesses fail ;
        For instance of the Nile,
Whether those Seven Mouths have any tail.
        Mayhap thy luck too,
From that high head, as from a lofty hill,
Has let thee see the marvellous Timbuctoo—
Or drink of Niger at its infant rill ;

What were the travels of our Major Denham,
  Or Clapperton, to thine
   In that same line,
If thou could'st only squat thee down and pen 'em !

Strange sights, indeed, thou must have overlooked,
With eyes held ever in such vantage-stations !
Hast seen, perchance, unhappy white folks cooked,
And then made free of negro corporations ?
Poor wretches saved from castaway three-deckers—
   By sooty wreckers—
From hungry waves to have a loss still drearier,
To far exceed the utmost aim of Park—
And find themselves, alas ! beyond the mark,
In the *insides* of Africa's interior !
Live on, Giraffe ! genteelest of raff kind !—
Admired by noble and by royal tongues !
   May no pernicious wind,
Or English fog, blight thy exotic lungs !

Live on in happy peace, altho' a rarity,
Nor envy thy poor cousin's more outrageous
   Parisian popularity—
Whose very leopard-rash is grown contagious,
And worn on gloves and ribbons all about,
   Alas ! they'll wear him out !—
So thou shalt take thy sweet diurnal feeds—
When he is stuffed with undigested straw,
Sad food that never visited his jaw !
And staring round him with a brace of beads !

POEMS.

THE PLEA OF THE MIDSUMMER FAIRIES.

To Charles Lamb, Esq.

My dear Friend,—I thank my literary fortune that I am not
reduced, like many better wits, to barter dedications, for the hope
or promise of patronage, with some nominally great man; but
that where true affection points, and honest respect, I am free to
gratify my head and heart by a sincere inscription. An intimacy
and dearness, worthy of a much earlier date than our acquaintance
can refer to, direct me at once to your name: and with this
acknowledgment of your ever kind feeling towards me, I desire to
record a respect and admiration for you as a writer, which no one
acquainted with our literature, save Elia himself, will think dispro-
portionate or misplaced. If I had not these better reasons to
govern me, I should be guided to the same selection by your
intense yet critical relish for the works of our great Dramatist, and
for that favourite play in particular which has furnished the subject
of my verses.

It is my design, in the following poem, to celebrate, by an
allegory, that immortality which Shakspeare has conferred on the
fairy mythology by his " Midsummer Night's Dream." But for him,
those pretty children of our childhood would leave barely their
names to our maturer years; they belong, as the mites upon the
plum, to the bloom of fancy, a thing generally too frail and
beautiful to withstand the rude handling of time: but the Poet
has made this most perishable part of the mind's creation equal
to the most enduring; he has so intertwined the elfins with
human sympathies, and linked them by so many delightful associations with the productions of nature, that they are as real to the
mind's eye as their green magical circles to the outer sense.

It would have been a pity for such a race to go extinct, even
though they were but as the butterflies that hover about the leaves
and blossoms of the visible world.

I am, my dear Friend, yours most truly,

T. Hood.

I.

'Twas in that mellow season of the year,
When the hot sun singes the yellow leaves
Till they be gold,—and with a broader sphere
The Moon looks down on Ceres and her sheaves ;
When more abundantly the spider weaves,
And the cold wind breathes from a chillier clime ;
That forth I fared, on one of those still eves,
Touched with the dewy sadness of the time,
To think how the bright months had spent their prime.

II.

So that, wherever I addressed my way,
I seemed to track the melancholy feet
Of him that is the Father of Decay,
And spoils at once the sour weed and the sweet ;
Wherefore regretfully I made retreat
To some unwasted regions of my brain,
Charmed with the light of summer and the heat,
And bade that bounteous season bloom again,
And sprout fresh flowers in my own domain.

III.

It was a shady and sequestered scene,
Like those famed gardens of Boccaccio,
Planted with his own laurels evergreen,
And roses that for endless summer blow ;
And there were fountain springs to overflow
Their marble basins,—and cool green arcades
Of tall o'erarching sycamores, to throw
Athwart the dappled path their dancing shades,—
With timid conies cropping the green blades.

IV.

And there were crystal pools, peopled with fish,
Argent and gold ; and some of Tyrian skin,
Some crimson-barred ;—and ever at a wish
They rose obsequious till the wave grew thin

As glass upon their backs, and then dived in,
Quenching their ardent scales in watery gloom;
Whilst others with fresh hues rowed forth to win
My changeable regard, for so we doom
Things born of thought to vanish or to bloom.

V.

And there were many birds of many dyes,
From tree to tree still faring to and fro,
And stately peacocks with their splendid eyes,
And gorgeous pheasants with their golden glow,
Like Iris just bedabbled in her bow,
Besides some vocalists, without a name,
That oft on fairy errands come and go,
With accents magical;—and all were tame,
And peckled at my hand where'er I came.

VI.

And for my sylvan company, in lieu
Of Pampinea with her lively peers,
Sat Queen Titania with her pretty crew,
All in their liveries quaint, with elfin gears,
For she was gracious to my childish years,
And made me free of her enchanted round;
Wherefore this dreamy scene she still endears,
And plants her court upon a verdant mound,
Fenced with umbrageous woods and groves profound.

VII.

" Ah me," she cries, " was ever moonlight seen
So clear and tender for our midnight trips?
Go some one forth, and with a trump convene
My lieges all !"—Away the goblin skips
A pace or two apart, and deftly strips
The ruddy skin from a sweet rose's cheek,
Then blows the shuddering leaf between his lips,
Making it utter forth a shrill small shriek,
Like a frayed bird in the grey owlet's beak.

VIII.

And lo! upon my fixed delighted ken
Appeared the loyal Fays.—Some by degrees
Crept from the primrose buds that opened then,
And some from bell-shaped blossoms like the bees,
Some from the dewy meads, and rushy leas,
Flew up like chafers when the rustics pass;
Some from the rivers, others from tall trees
Dropped, like shed blossoms, silent to the grass,
Spirits and elfins small, of every class.

IX.

Peri and Pixy, and quaint Puck the Antic,
Brought Robin Goodfellow, that merry swain;
And stealthy Mab, queen of old realms romantic,
Came too, from distance, in her tiny wain,
Fresh dripping from a cloud—some bloomy rain,
Then circling the bright Moon, had washed her car,
And still bedewed it with a various stain:
Lastly came Ariel, shooting from a star,
Who bears all fairy embassies afar.

X.

But Oberon, that night elsewhere exiled,
Was absent, whether some distempered spleen
Kept him and his fair mate unreconciled,
Or warfare with the Gnome (whose race had been
Sometime obnoxious) kept him from his queen,
And made her now peruse the starry skies
Prophetical with such an absent mien;
Howbeit, the tears stole often to her eyes,
And oft the Moon was incensed with her sighs—

XI.

Which made the elves sport drearily, and soon
Their hushing dances languished to a stand,
Like midnight leaves when, as the Zephyrs swoon,
All on their drooping stems they sink unfanned,—

So into silence drooped the fairy band,
To see their empress dear so pale and still,
Crowding her softly round on either hand,
As pale as frosty snowdrops, and as chill,
To whom the sceptred dame reveals her ill.

XII.

"Alas," quoth she, "ye know our fairy lives
Are leased upon the fickle faith of men ;
Not measured out against fate's mortal knives,
Like human gossamers, we perish when
We fade, and are forgot in worldly ken,—
Though poesy has thus prolonged our date,
Thanks be to the sweet Bard's auspicious pen
That rescued us so long !—howbeit of late
I feel some dark misgivings of our fate.

XIII.

"And this dull day my melancholy sleep
Hath been so thronged with images of woe,
That even now I cannot choose but weep
To think this was some sad prophetic show
Of future horror to befall us so,—
Of mortal wreck and uttermost distress,—
Yea, our poor empire's fall and overthrow,—
For this was my long vision's dreadful stress,
And when I waked my trouble was not less.

XIV.

"Whenever to the clouds I tried to seek,
Such leaden weight dragged these Icarian wings,
My faithless wand was wavering and weak,
And slimy toads had trespassed in our rings—
The birds refused to sing for me—all things
Disowned their old allegiance to our spells ;
The rude bees pricked me with their rebel stings ;
And, when I passed, the valley-lily's bells
Rang out, methought, most melancholy knells.

XV.

"And ever on the faint and flagging air
A doleful spirit with a dreary note
Cried in my fearful ear, ' Prepare ! prepare !'
Which soon I knew came from a raven's throat,
Perched on a cypress bough not far remote,—
A cursed bird, too crafty to be shot,
That alway cometh with his soot-black coat
To make hearts dreary :—for he is a blot
Upon the book of life, as well ye wot !

XVI.

" Wherefore some while I bribed him to be mute,
With bitter acorns stuffing his foul maw,
Which barely I appeased, when some fresh bruit
Startled me all aheap !—and soon I saw
The horridest shape that ever raised my awe,—
A monstrous giant, very huge and tall,
Such as in elder times, devoid of law,
With wicked might grieved the primeval ball,
And this was sure the deadliest of them all !

XVII.

" Gaunt was he as a wolf of Languedoc,
With bloody jaws, and frost upon his crown ;
So from his barren poll one hoary lock
Over his wrinkled front fell far adown,
Well nigh to where his frosty brows did frown
Like jagged icicles at cottage eaves ;
And for his coronal he wore some brown
And bristled ears gathered from Ceres' sheaves,
Entwined with certain sere and russet leaves.

XVIII.

" And lo ! upon a mast reared far aloft,
He bore a very bright and crescent blade,
The which he waved so dreadfully, and oft,
In meditative spite, that, sore dismayed,

I crept into an acorn-cup for shade;
Meanwhile the horrid effigy went by:
I trow his look was dreadful, for it made
The trembling birds betake them to the sky,
For every leaf was lifted by his sigh.

XIX.

" And ever as he sighed, his foggy breath
Blurred out the landscape like a flight of smoke:
Thence knew I this was either dreary Death
Or Time, who leads all creatures to his stroke.
Ah wretched me !"—Here, even as she spoke,
The melancholy Shape came gliding in,
And leaned his back against an antique oak,
Folding his wings, that were so fine and thin,
They scarce were seen against the Dryad's skin.

XX.

Then what a fear seized all the little rout !
Look how a flock of panicked sheep will stare—
And huddle close—and start—and wheel about,
Watching the roaming mongrel here and there,—
So did that sudden Apparition scare
All close aheap those small affrighted things;
Nor sought they now the safety of the air,
As if some leaden spell withheld their wings;
But who can fly that ancientest of Kings?

XXI.

Whom now the Queen, with a forestalling tear
And previous sigh, beginneth to entreat,
Bidding him spare, for love, her lieges dear :
" Alas !" quoth she, " is there no nodding wheat
Ripe for thy crooked weapon, and more meet,—
Or withered leaves to ravish from the tree,—
Or crumbling battlements for thy defeat?
Think but what vaunting monuments there be
Builded in spite and mockery of thee.

XXII.

" O fret away the fabric walls of Fame,
And grind down marble Cæsars with the dust :
Make tombs inscriptionless—raze each high name,
And waste old armours of renown with rust :
Do all of this, and thy revenge is just :
Make such decays the trophies of thy prime,
And check Ambition's overweening lust,
That dares exterminating war with Time,—
But we are guiltless of that lofty crime.

XXIII.

" Frail feeble sprites !—the children of a dream !
Leased on the sufferance of fickle men,
Like motes dependent on the sunny beam,
Living but in the sun's indulgent ken,
And when that light withdraws, withdrawing then ;—
So do we flutter in the glance of youth
And fervid fancy,—and so perish when
The eye of faith grows aged ;—in sad truth,
Feeling thy sway, O Time ! though not thy tooth !

XXIV.

" Where be those old divinities forlorn,
That dwelt in trees, or haunted in a stream ?
Alas ! their memories are dimmed and torn,
Like the remaining tatters of a dream :
So will it fare with our poor thrones, I deem ;—
For us the same dark trench Oblivion delves,
That holds the wastes of every human scheme.
O spare us then,—and these our pretty elves,
We soon, alas ! shall perish of ourselves !"

XXV.

Now as she ended, with a sigh, to name
Those old Olympians, scattered by the whirl
Of fortune's giddy wheel and brought to shame,
Methought a scornful and malignant curl

Showed on the lips of that malicious churl,
To think what noble havocs he had made ;
So that I feared he all at once would hurl
The harmless fairies into endless shade,—
Howbeit he stopped awhile to whet his blade.

XXVI.

Pity it was to hear the elfins' wail,
Rise up in concert from their mingled dread ;
Pity it was to see them, all so pale,
Gaze on the grass as for a dying bed ;
But Puck was seated on a spider's thread,
That hung between two branches of a briar,
And 'gan to swing and gambol heels o'er head,
Like any Southwark tumbler on a wire,
For him no present grief could long inspire.

XXVII.

Meanwhile the Queen with many piteous drops,
Falling like tiny sparks full fast and free,
Bedews a pathway from her throne ; and stops
Before the foot of her arch enemy,
And with her little arms enfolds his knee,
That shows more grisly from that fair embrace ;
But she will ne'er depart. " Alas !" quoth she,
" My painful fingers I will here enlace
Till I have gained your pity for our race.

XXVIII.

" What have we ever done to earn this grudge,
And hate—(if not too humble for thy hating ?)—
Look o'er our labours and our lives, and judge
If there be any ills of our creating :
For we are very kindly creatures, dating
With nature's charities still sweet and bland :
O think this murder worthy of debating !"
Herewith she makes a signal with her hand,
To beckon some one from the Fairy band.

XXIX.

Anon I saw one of those elfin things
Clad all in white like any chorister,
Come fluttering forth on his melodious wings,
That made soft music at each little stir,
But something louder than a bee's demur
Before he lights upon a bunch of broom,
And thus 'gan he with Saturn to confer,—
And O his voice was sweet, touched with the gloom
Of that sad theme that argued of his doom !

XXX.

Quoth he, " We make all melodies our care,
That no false discords may offend the Sun,
Music's great master—tuning everywhere
All pastoral sounds and melodies, each one
Duly to place and season, so that none
May harshly interfere.   We rouse at morn
The shrill sweet lark ; and when the day is done,
Hush silent pauses for the bird forlorn,
That singeth with her breast against a thorn.

XXXI.

" We gather in loud choirs the twittering race,
That make a chorus with their single note ;
And tend on new-fledged birds in every place,
That duly they may get their tunes by rote ;
And oft, like echoes, answering remote,
We hide in thickets from the feathered throng,
And strain in rivalship each throbbing throat,
Singing in shrill responses all day long,
Whilst the glad truant listens to our song.

XXXII.

" Wherefore, great King of Years, as thou dost love
The raining music from a morning cloud,
When vanished larks are carolling above,
To wake Apollo with their pipings loud ;

If ever thou hast heard in leafy shroud
The sweet and plaintive Sappho of the dell,
Show thy sweet mercy on this little crowd,
And we will muffle up the sheepfold bell
Whene'er thou listenest to Philomel."

XXXIII.

Then Saturn thus :—" Sweet is the merry lark,
That carols in man's ear so clear and strong ;
And youth must love to listen in the dark
That tuneful elegy of Tereus' wrong ;
But I have heard that ancient strain too long,
For sweet is sweet but when a little strange,
And I grow weary for some newer song ;
For wherefore had I wings, unless to range
Through all things mutable from change to change ?

XXXIV.

" But wouldst thou hear the melodies of Time,
Listen when sleep and drowsy darkness roll
Over hushed cities, and the midnight chime
Sounds from their hundred clocks, and deep bells toll
Like a last knell over the dead world's soul,
Saying, Time shall be final of all things,
Whose late, last voice must elegize the whole,—
O then I clap aloft my brave broad wings,
And make the wide air tremble while it rings !"

XXXV.

Then next a fair Eve-Fay made meek address,
Saying, "We be the handmaids of the Spring,
In sign whereof, May, the quaint broideress,
Hath wrought her samplers on our gauzy wing.
We tend upon buds' birth and blossoming,
And count the leafy tributes that they owe—
As, so much to the earth—so much to fling
In showers to the brook—so much to go
In whirlwinds to the clouds that made them grow

XXXVI.

" The pastoral cowslips are our little pets,
And daisy stars, whose firmament is green ;
Pansies, and those veiled nuns, meek violets,
Sighing to that warm world from which they screen ;
And golden daffodils, plucked for May's Queen ;
And lonely harebells, quaking on the heath ;
And Hyacinth, long since a fair youth seen,
Whose tuneful voice, turned fragrance in his breath,
Kissed by sad Zephyr, guilty of his death.

XXXVII.

" The widowed primrose weeping to the moon,
And saffron crocus in whose chalice bright
A cool libation hoarded for the noon
Is kept—and she that purifies the light,
The virgin lily, faithful to her white,
Whereon Eve wept in Eden for her shame ;
And the most dainty rose, Aurora's spright,
Our very godchild, by whatever name—
Spare us our lives, for we did nurse the same !"

XXXVIII.

Then that old Mower stamped his heel, and struck
His hurtful scythe against the harmless ground,
Saying, " Ye foolish imps, when am I stuck
With gaudy buds, or like a wooer crowned
With flow'ry chaplets, save when they are found
Withered ?—Whenever have I plucked a rose,
Except to scatter its vain leaves around ?
For so all gloss of beauty I oppose,
And bring decay on every flower that blows.

XXXIX.

" Or when am I so wroth as when I view
The wanton pride of Summer ;—how she decks
The birthday world with blossoms ever new,
As if Time had not lived, and heaped great wrecks

Of years on years?—O then I bravely vex
And catch the gay months in their gaudy plight,
And slay them with the wreaths about their necks,
Like foolish heifers in the holy rite,
And raise great trophies to my ancient might."

XL.

Then saith another, " We are kindly things,
And like her offspring nestle with the dove,—
Witness these hearts embroidered on our wings,
To show our constant patronage of love :—
We sit at even, in sweet bowers above
Lovers, and shake rich odours on the air,
To mingle with their sighs ; and still remove
The startling owl, and bid the bat forbear
Their privacy, and haunt some other where.

XLI.

" And we are near the mother when she sits
Beside her infant in its wicker bed ;
And we are in the fairy scene that flits
Across its tender brain : sweet dreams we shed,
And whilst the tender little soul is fled
Away, to sport with our young elves, the while
We touch the dimpled cheek with roses red,
And tickle the soft lips until they smile,
So that their careful parents they beguile.

XLII.

" O then, if ever thou hast breathed a vow
At Love's dear portal, or at pale moon-rise
Crushed the dear curl on a regardful brow
That did not frown thee from thy honey prize—
If ever thy sweet son sat on thy thighs,
And wooed thee from thy careful thoughts within
To watch the harmless beauty of his eyes,
Or glad thy fingers on his smooth soft skin,
For Love's dear sake, let us thy pity win !"

XLIII.

Then Saturn fiercely thus :—" What joy have I
In tender babes, that have devoured mine own,
Whenever to the light I heard them cry,
Till foolish Rhea cheated me with stone ?
Whereon, till now, is my great hunger shown,
In monstrous dints of my enormous tooth ;
And,—but the peopled world is too full grown
For hunger's edge—I would consume all youth
At one great meal, without delay or ruth !

XLIV.

" For I am well nigh crazed and wild to hear
How boastful fathers taunt me with their breed,
Saying, We shall not die nor disappear,
But in these other selves ourselves succeed,
Even as ripe flowers pass into their seed
Only to be renewed from prime to prime,
All of which boastings I am forced to read,
Besides a thousand challenges to Time
Which bragging lovers have compiled in rhyme.

XLV.

" Wherefore, when they are sweetly met o' nights,
There will I steal, and with my hurried hand
Startle them suddenly from their delights
Before the next encounter hath been planned,
Ravishing hours in little minutes spanned ;
But when they say farewell, and grieve apart,
Then like a leaden statue I will stand,
Meanwhile their many tears encrust my dart,
And with a ragged edge cut heart from heart."

XLVI.

Then next a merry Woodsman, clad in green,
Stept vanward from his mates, that idly stood
Each at his proper ease, as they had been
Nursed in the liberty of old Shérwood,

And wore the livery of Robin Hood,
Who wont in forest shades to dine and sup,—
So came this chief right frankly, and made good
His haunch against his axe, and thus spoke up,
Doffing his cap, which was an acorn's cup :—

XLVII.

"We be small foresters and gay, who tend
On trees, and all their furniture of green,
Training the young boughs airily to bend,
And show blue snatches of the sky between ;
Or knit more close intricacies, to screen
Birds' crafty dwellings as may hide them best,
But most the timid blackbird's—she, that seen,
Will bear black poisonous berries to her nest,
Lest man should cage the darlings of her breast.

XLVIII.

"We bend each tree in proper attitude,
And founting willows train in silvery falls ;
We frame all shady roofs and arches rude,
And verdant aisles leading to Dryads' halls,
Or deep recesses where the Echo calls ;—
We shape all plumy trees against the sky,
And carve tall elms' Corinthian capitals,—
When sometimes, as our tiny hatchets ply,
Men say the tapping woodpecker is nigh.

XLIX.

"Sometimes we scoop the squirrel's hollow cell,
And sometimes carve quaint letters on trees' rind,
That haply some lone musing wight may spell
Dainty Aminta,—Gentle Rosalind,—
Or chastest Laura,—sweetly called to mind
In sylvan solitudes, ere he lies down ;
And sometimes we enrich grey stems with twined
And vagrant ivy,—or rich moss, whose brown
Burns into gold as the warm sun goes down.

L.

"And, lastly, for mirth's sake and Christmas cheer,
We bear the seedling berries, for increase,
To graft the Druid oaks, from year to year,
Careful that mistletoe may never cease ;
Wherefore, if thou dost prize the shady peace
Of sombre forests, or to see light break
Through sylvan cloisters, and in spring release
Thy spirit amongst leaves from careful ake,
Spare us our lives for the Green Dryad's sake."

LI.

Then Saturn, with a frown :—"Go forth, and fell
Oak for your coffins, and thenceforth lay by
Your axes for the rust, and bid farewell
To all sweet birds, and the blue peeps of sky
Through tangled branches, for ye shall not spy
The next green generation of the tree ;
But hence with the dead leaves, whene'er they fly,—
Which in the bleak air I would rather see,
Than flights of the most tuneful birds that be.

LII.

"For I dislike all prime and verdant pets,
Ivy except, that on the aged wall
Preys with its worm-like roots, and daily frets
The crumbled tower it seems to league withal,
King-like, worn down by its own coronal :
Neither in forest haunts love I to won,
Before the golden plumage 'gins to fall,
And leaves the brown bleak limbs with few leaves on,
Or bare—like Nature in her skeleton.

LIII.

"For then sit I amongst the crooked boughs,
Wooing dull Memory with kindred sighs ;
And there in rustling nuptials we espouse,
Smit by the sadness in each other's eyes ;

But Hope must have green bowers and blue skies,
And must be courted with the gauds of spring;
Whilst Youth leans god-like on her lap, and cries,
What shall we always do, but love and sing?—
And Time is reckoned a discarded thing."

LIV.

Here in my dream it made me fret to see
How Puck, the antic, all this dreary while
Had blithely jested with calamity,
With mistimed mirth mocking the doleful style
Of his sad comrades, till it raised my bile
To see him so reflect their grief aside,
Turning their solemn looks to half a smile—
Like a straight stick shown crooked in the tide;
But soon a novel advocate I spied.

LV.

Quoth he—" We teach all natures to fulfil
Their fore-appointed crafts, and instincts meet,—
The bee's sweet alchemy,—the spider's skill,—
The pismire's care to garner up his wheat,—
And rustic masonry to swallows fleet,—
The lapwing's cunning to preserve her nest,—
But most, that lesser pelican, the sweet
And shrilly ruddock, with its bleeding breast,
Its tender pity of poor babes distrest.

LVI.

" Sometimes we cast our shapes, and in sleek skins
Delve with the timid mole, that aptly delves
From our example; so the spider spins,
And eke the silkworm, patterned by ourselves:
Sometimes we travail on the summer shelves
Of early bees, and busy toils commence,
Watched of wise men, that know not we are elves,
But gaze and marvel at our stretch of sense,
And praise our human-like intelligence.

LVII.

"Wherefore, by thy delight in that old tale,
And plaintive dirges the late robins sing,
What time the leaves are scattered by the gale,
Mindful of that old forest burying;
As thou dost love to watch each tiny thing,
For whom our craft most curiously contrives,
If thou hast caught a bee upon the wing,
To take his honey-bag,—spare us our lives,
And we will pay the ransom in full hives."

LVIII.

"Now by my glass," quoth Time, "ye do offend
In teaching the brown bees that careful lore,
And frugal ants, whose millions would have end,
But they lay up for need a timely store,
And travail with the seasons evermore;
Whereas Great Mammoth long hath passed away,
And none but I can tell what hide he wore;
Whilst purblind men, the creatures of a day,
In riddling wonder his great bones survey."

LIX.

Then came an elf, right beauteous to behold,
Whose coat was like a brooklet that the sun
Hath all embroidered with its crooked gold,
It was so quaintly wrought, and overrun
With spangled traceries,—most meet for one
That was a warden of the pearly streams;
And as he stept out of the shadows dun,
His jewels sparkled in the pale moon's gleams,
And shot into the air their pointed beams.

LX.

Quoth he,—"We bear the cold and silver keys
Of bubbling springs and fountains, that below
Course thro' the veiny earth,—which when they freeze
Into hard chrysolites, we bid to flow,

Creeping like subtle snakes, when as they go,
We guide their windings to melodious falls,
At whose soft murmurings, so sweet and low,
Poets have turned their smoothest madrigals,
To sing to ladies in their banquet halls.

LXI.

" And when the hot sun with his steadfast heat
Parches the river god,—whose dusty urn
Drips miserly, till soon his crystal feet
Against his pebbly floor wax faint and burn,
And languid fish, unpoised, grow sick and yearn,—
Then scoop we hollows in some sandy nook,
And little channels dig, wherein we turn
The thread-worn rivulet, that all forsook
The Naiad-lily, pining for her brook.

LXII.

"Wherefore, by thy delight in cool green meads,
With living sapphires daintily inlaid,—
In all soft songs of waters and their reeds,—
And all reflections in a streamlet made,
Haply of thy own love, that, disarrayed,
Kills the fair lily with a livelier white,—
By silver trouts upspringing from green shade,
And winking stars reduplicate at night,
Spare us, poor ministers to such delight."

LXIII.

Howbeit his pleading and his gentle looks
Moved not the spiteful Shade :—Quoth he, "Your taste
Shoots wide of mine, for I despise the brooks
And slavish rivulets that run to waste
In noontide sweats, or, like poor vassals, haste
To swell the vast dominion of the sea,
In whose great presence I am held disgraced,
And neighboured with a king that rivals me
In ancient might and hoary majesty.

LXIV.

" Whereas I ruled in Chaos, and still keep
The awful secrets of that ancient dearth,
Before the briny fountains of the deep
Brimmed up the hollow cavities of earth ;
I saw each trickling Sea-God at his birth,
Each pearly Naiad with her oozy locks,
And infant Titans of enormous girth,
Whose huge young feet yet stumbled on the rocks,
Stunning the early world with frequent shocks.

LXV.

" Where now is Titan, with his cumbrous brood,
That scared the world ?—By this sharp scythe they fell,
And half the sky was curdled with their blood :
So have all primal giants sighed farewell.
No Wardens now by sedgy fountains dwell,
No pearly Naiads.   All their days are done
That strove with Time, untimely, to excel ;
Wherefore I razed their progenies, and none
But my great shadow intercepts the sun !"

LXVI.

Then saith the timid Fay—" O mighty Time !
Well hast thou wrought the cruel Titans' fall,
For they were stained with many a bloody crime :
Great giants work great wrongs—but we are small,
For love goes lowly ;—but Oppression's tall,
And with surpassing strides goes foremost still
Where love indeed can hardly reach at all ;
Like a poor dwarf o'erburdened with goodwill,
That labours to efface the tracks of ill.

LXVII.

" Man even strives with Man, but we eschew
The guilty feud, and all fierce strifes abhor ;
Nay, we are gentle as sweet heaven's dew,
Beside the red and horrid drops of war,

Weeping the cruel hates men battle for,
Which worldly bosoms nourish in our spite;
For in the gentle breast we ne'er withdraw,
But only when all love hath taken flight,
And youth's warm gracious heart is hardened quite.

LXVIII.

" So are our gentle natures intertwined
With sweet humanities, and closely knit
In kindly sympathy with human kind.
Witness how we befriend, with elfin wit,
All hopeless maids and lovers—nor omit
Magical succours unto hearts forlorn:
We charm man's life, and do not perish it;
So judge us by the helps we showed this morn,
To one who held his wretched days in scorn.

LXIX.

" 'Twas nigh sweet Amwell;—for the Queen had tasked
Our skill to-day amidst the silver Lea,
Whereon the noontide sun had not yet basked;
Wherefore some patient man we thought to see,
Planted in mossgrown rushes to the knee,
Beside the cloudy margin cold and dim;
Howbeit no patient fisherman was he
That cast his sudden shadow from the brim,
Making us leave our toils to gaze on him.

LXX.

" His face was ashy pale, and leaden care
Had sunk the levelled arches of his brow,
Once bridges for his joyous thoughts to fare
Over those melancholy springs and slow,
That from his piteous eyes began to flow,
And fell anon into the chilly stream;
Which, as his mimicked image showed below,
Wrinkled his face with many a needless seam,
Making grief sadder in its own esteem.

LXXI.

" And lo ! upon the air we saw him stretch
His passionate arms ; and, in a wayward strain,
He 'gan to elegize that fellow wretch
That with mute gestures answered him again,
Saying, ' Poor slave, how long wilt thou remain
Life's sad weak captive in a prison strong,
Hoping with tears to rust away thy chain,
In bitter servitude to worldly wrong ?
Thou wear'st that mortal livery too long !'

LXXII.

" This, with more spleenful speeches and some tears,
When he had spent upon the imaged wave,
Speedily I convened my elfin peers
Under the lily-cups, that we might save
This woeful mortal from a wilful grave
By shrewd diversions of his mind's regret,
Seeing he was mere melancholy's slave,
That sank wherever a dark cloud he met,
And straight was tangled in her secret net.

LXXIII.

" Therefore, as still he watched the water's flow,
Daintily we transformed, and with bright fins
Came glancing through the gloom ; some from below
Rose like dim fancies when a dream begins,
Snatching the light upon their purple skins ;
Then under the broad leaves made slow retire :
One like a golden galley bravely wins
Its radiant course—another glows like fire—
Making that wayward man our pranks admire.

LXXIV.

" And so he banished thought, and quite forgot
All contemplation of that wretched face ;
And so we wiled him from that lonely spot
Along the river's brink ; till by heaven's grace,

He met a gentle haunter of the place,
Full of sweet wisdom gathered from the brooks,
Who there discussed his melancholy case
With wholesome texts learned from kind nature's books,
Meanwhile he newly trimmed his lines and hooks."

LXXV.

Herewith the Fairy ceased.   Quoth Ariel now—
" Let me remember how I saved a man,
Whose fatal noose was fastened on a bough,
Intended to abridge his sad life's span ;
For haply I was by when he began
His stern soliloquy in life's dispraise,
And overheard his melancholy plan,
How he had made a vow to end his days,
And therefore followed him in all his ways.

LXXVI.

" Through brake and tangled copse, for much he loathed
All populous haunts, and roamed in forests rude,
To hide himself from man.   But I had clothed
My delicate limbs with plumes, and still pursued,
Where only foxes and wild cats intrude,
Till we were come beside an ancient tree
Late blasted by a storm.   Here he renewed
His loud complaints—choosing that spot to be
The scene of his last horrid tragedy.

LXXVII.

" It was a wild and melancholy glen,
Made gloomy by tall firs and cypress dark,
Whose roots, like any bones of buried men,
Pushed through the rotten sod for fear's remark ;
A hundred horrid stems, jagged and stark,
Wrestled with crooked arms in hideous fray,
Besides sleek ashes with their dappled bark,
Like crafty serpents climbing for a prey,
With many blasted oaks mossgrown and grey.

LXXVIII.

"But here upon his final desperate clause
Suddenly I pronounced so sweet a strain,
Like a panged nightingale, it made him pause,
Till half the frenzy of his grief was slain,
The sad remainder oozing from his brain
In timely ecstasies of healing tears,
Which through his ardent eyes began to drain—
Meanwhile the deadly Fates unclosed their shears :
So pity me and all my fated peers !"

LXXIX.

Thus Ariel ended, and was some time hushed :
When with the hoary Shape a fresh tongue pleads,
And red as rose the gentle Fairy blushed
To read the record of her own good deeds :—
"It chanced," quoth she, "in seeking through the meads
For honeyed cowslips, sweetest in the morn,
Whilst yet the buds were hung with dewy beads,
And Echo answered to the huntsman's horn,
We found a babe left in the swarths forlorn.

LXXX.

"A little, sorrowful, deserted thing,
Begot of love, and yet no love begetting ;
Guiltless of shame, and yet for shame to wring ;
And too soon banished from a mother's petting,
To churlish nurture and the wide world's fretting,
For alien pity and unnatural care ;
Alas ! to see how the cold dew kept wetting
His childish coats, and dabbled all his hair,
Like gossamers across his forehead fair.

LXXXI.

"His pretty pouting mouth, witless of speech,
Lay half-way open like a rose-lipped shell ;
And his young cheek was softer than a peach,
Whereon his tears, for roundness, could not dwell,

But quickly rolled themselves to pearls, and fell,
Some on the grass, and some against his hand,
Or haply wandered to the dimpled well,
Which love beside his mouth had sweetly planned,
Yet not for tears, but mirth and smilings bland.

LXXXII.

" Pity it was to see those frequent tears
Falling regardless from his friendless eyes ;
There was such beauty in those twin blue spheres,
As any mother's heart might leap to prize ;
Blue were they, like the zenith of the skies
Softened betwixt two clouds, both clear and mild ;
Just touched with thought, and yet not over wise,
They showed the gentle spirit of a child,
Not yet by care or any craft defiled.

LXXXIII.

" Pity it was to see the ardent sun
 Scorching his helpless limbs—it shone so warm ;
For kindly shade or shelter he had none,
Nor mother's gentle breast, come fair or storm.
Meanwhile I bade my pitying mates transform
Like grasshoppers, and then, with shrilly cries,
All round the infant noisily we swarm,
Haply some passing rustic to advise—
Whilst providential Heaven our care espies,

LXXXIV.

" And sends full soon a tender-hearted hind,
Who, wondering at our loud unusual note,
Strays curiously aside, and so doth find
The orphan child laid in the grass remote,
And laps the foundling in his russet coat,
Who thence was nurtured in his kindly cot :
But how he prospered let proud London quote,
How wise, how rich, and how renowned he got,
And chief of all her citizens, I wot.

14

LXXXV.

"Witness his goodly vessels on the Thames,
Whose holds were fraught with costly merchandize—
Jewels from Ind, and pearls for courtly dames,
And gorgeous silks that Samarcand supplies :
Witness that Royal Bourse he bade arise,
The mart of merchants from the East and West ;
Whose slender summit, pointing to the skies,
Still bears, in token of his grateful breast,
The tender grasshopper, his chosen crest—

LXXXVI.

"The tender grasshopper, his chosen crest,
That all the summer, with a tuneful wing,
Makes merry chirpings in its grassy nest,
Inspirited with dew to leap and sing :
So let us also live, eternal King !
Partakers of the green and pleasant earth :
Pity it is to slay the meanest thing,
That, like a mote, shines in the smile of mirth :
Enough there is of joy's decrease and dearth !

LXXXVII.

"Enough of pleasure, and delight, and beauty,
Perished and gone, and hasting to decay ;
Enough to sadden even thee, whose duty
Or spite it is to havoc and to slay :
Too many a lovely race razed quite away,
Hath left large gaps in life and human loving :
Here then begin thy cruel war to stay,
And spare fresh sighs, and tears, and groans, reproving
Thy desolating hand for our removing."

LXXXVIII.

Now here I heard a shrill and sudden cry,
And, looking up, I saw the antic Puck
Grappling with Time, who clutched him like a fly
Victim of his own sport,—the jester's luck !

He, whilst his fellows grieved, poor wight, had stuck
His freakish gauds upon the Ancient's brow,
And now his ear, and now his beard, would pluck ;
Whereas the angry churl had snatched him now,
Crying, "Thou impish mischief, who art thou ?"

LXXXIX.

"Alas !" quoth Puck, "a little random elf,
Born in the sport of nature, like a weed,
For simple sweet enjoyment of myself,
But for no other purpose, worth, or need ;
And yet withal of a most happy breed ;
And there is Robin Goodfellow besides,
My partner dear in many a prankish deed
To make Dame Laughter hold her jolly sides,
Like merry mummers twain on holy tides.

XC.

"'Tis we that bob the angler's idle cork,
Till e'en the patient man breathes half a curse ;
We steal the morsel from the gossip's fork,
And curdling looks with secret straws disperse,
Or stop the sneezing chanter at mid verse :
And when an infant's beauty prospers ill,
We change, some mothers say, the child at nurse ;
But any graver purpose to fulfil,
We have not wit enough, and scarce the will.

XCI.

"We never let the canker melancholy
To gather on our faces like a rust,
But gloss our features with some change of folly,
Taking life's fabled miseries on trust,
But only sorrowing when sorrow must :
We ruminate no sage's solemn cud,
But own ourselves a pinch of lively dust
To frisk upon a wind,—whereas the flood
Of tears would turn us into heavy mud.

XCII.

Beshrew those sad interpreters of nature,
Who gloze her lively universal law,
As if she had not formed our cheerful feature
To be so tickled with the slightest straw !
So let them vex their mumping mouths, and draw
The corners downward, like a wat'ry moon,
And deal in gusty sighs and rainy flaw—
We will not woo foul weather all too soon,
Or nurse November on the lap of June.

XCIII.

" For ours are winging sprites, like any bird,
That shun all stagnant settlements of grief ;
And even in our rest our hearts are stirred,
Like insects settled on a dancing leaf :
This is our small philosophy in brief,
Which thus to teach hath set me all agape :
But dost thou relish it ? O hoary chief !
Unclasp thy crooked fingers from my nape,
And I will show thee many a pleasant scrape."

XCIV.

Then Saturn thus :—shaking his crooked blade
O'erhead, which made aloft a lightning flash
In all the fairies' eyes, dismally frayed !
His ensuing voice came like the thunder crash—
Meanwhile the bolt shatters some pine or ash—
" Thou feeble, wanton, foolish, fickle thing !
Whom nought can frighten, sadden, or abash,—
To hope my solemn countenance to wring
To idiot smiles !—but I will prune thy wing !

XCV.

" Lo ! this most awful handle of my scythe
Stood once a Maypole, with a flowery crown,
Which rustics danced around, and maidens blithe,
To wanton pipings ;—but I plucked it down,

And robed the May Queen in a churchyard gown,
Turning her buds to rosemary and rue ;
And all their merry minstrelsy did drown,
And laid each lusty leaper in the dew ;
So thou shalt fare—and every jovial crew !"

XCVI.

Here he lets go the struggling imp, to clutch
His mortal engine with each grisly hand,
Which frights the elfin progeny so much,
They huddle in a heap, and trembling stand
All round Titania, like the queen bee's band,
With signs and tears and very shrieks of woe !
Meanwhile, some moving argument I planned,
To make the stern Shade merciful,—when lo !
He drops his fatal scythe without a blow !

XCVII.

For, just at need, a timely Apparition*
Steps in between, to bear the awful brunt ;
Making him change his horrible position,
To marvel at this comer, brave and blunt,
That dares Time's irresistible affront,
Whose strokes have scarred even the gods of old ;
Whereas this seemed a mortal, at mere hunt
For coneys, lighted by the moonshine cold,
Or stalker of stray deer, stealthy and bold.

XCVIII.

Who, turning to the small assembled fays,
Doffs to the lily queen his courteous cap,
And holds her beauty for awhile in gaze,
With bright eyes kindling at this pleasant hap ;
And thence upon the fair moon's silver map,
As if in question of this magic chance,
Laid like a dream upon the green earth's lap ;
And then upon old Saturn turns askance,
Exclaiming, with a glad and kindly glance :—

---

* Shakspeare.

XCIX.

" Oh, these be Fancy's revellers by night !
Stealthy companions of the downy moth—
Diana's motes, that flit in her pale light,
Shunners of sunbeams in diurnal sloth ;
These be the feasters on night's silver cloth,—
The gnat with shrilly trump is their covener,
Forth from their flowery chambers, nothing loth,
With lulling tunes to charm the air serener,
Or dance upon the grass to make it greener.

C.

" These be the pretty genii of the flow'rs,
Daintily fed with honey and pure dew—
Midsummer's phantoms in her dreaming hours,
King Oberon, and all his merry crew,
The darling puppets of romance's view ;
Fairies, and sprites, and goblin elves we call them,
Famous for patronage of lovers true ;
No harm they act, neither shall harm befall them,
So do not thus with crabbed frowns appal them."

CI.

O what a cry was Saturn's then !—it made
The fairies quake.   " What care I for their pranks,
However they may lovers choose to aid,
Or dance their roundelays on flow'ry banks ?
Long must they dance before they earn my thanks,—
So step aside, to some far safer spot,
Whilst with my hungry scythe I mow their ranks,
And leave them in the sun, like weeds to rot,
And with the next day's sun to be forgot."

CII.

Anon, he raised afresh his weapon keen ;
But still the gracious Shade disarmed his aim,
Stepping with brave alacrity between,
And made his sere arm powerless and tame.

His be perpetual glory, for the shame
Of hoary Saturn in that grand defeat!
But I must tell, how here Titania came
With all her kneeling lieges, to entreat
His kindly succour, in sad tones, but sweet.

CIII.

Saying, "Thou seest a wretched queen before thee,
The fading power of a failing land,
Who for her kingdom kneeleth to implore thee,
Now menaced by this tyrant's spoiling hand;
No one but thee can hopefully withstand
That crooked blade he longeth so to lift.
I pray thee blind him with his own vile sand,
Which only times all ruins by its drift,
Or prune his eagle wings that are so swift.

CIV.

"Or take him by that sole and grizzled tuft,
That hangs upon his bald and barren crown;
And we will sing to see him so rebuffed,
And lend our little mights to pull him down,
And make brave sport of his malicious frown,
For all his boastful mockery o'er men;
For thou wast born I know for this renown,
By my most magical and inward ken,
That readeth ev'n at Fate's forestalling pen.

CV.

"Nay, by the golden lustre of thine eye,
And by thy brow's most fair and ample span,
Thought's glorious palace, framed for fancies high,
And by thy cheek thus passionately wan,
I know the signs of an immortal man,—
Nature's chief darling, and illustrious mate,
Destined to foil old Death's oblivious plan,
And shine untarnished by the fogs of Fate,
Time's famous rival till the final date!

CVI.

" O shield us then from this usurping Time,
And we will visit thee in moonlight dreams ;
And teach thee tunes to wed unto thy rhyme,
And dance about thee in all midnight gleams,
Giving thee glimpses of our magic schemes,
Such as no mortal's eye hath even seen :
And, for thy love to us in our extremes,
Will ever keep thy chaplet fresh and green,
Such as no poet's wreath hath ever been !

CVII.

" And we'll distil thee aromatic dews,
To charm thy sense, when there shall be no flow'rs ;
And flavoured syrups in thy drinks infuse,
And teach the nightingale to haunt thy bow'rs.
And with our games divert thy weariest hours,
With all that elfin wits can e'er devise.
And, this churl dead, there'll be no hasting hours
To rob thee of thy joys, as now joy flies :"—
Here she was stopped by Saturn's furious cries.

CVIII.

Whom, therefore, the kind Shade rebukes anew,
Saying, " Thou haggard Sin, go forth, and scoop
Thy hollow coffin in some churchyard yew,
Or make th' autumnal flowers turn pale, and droop ;
Or fell the bearded corn, till gleaners stoop
Under fat sheaves—or blast the piny grove ;
But here thou shalt not harm this pretty group,
Whose lives are not so frail and feebly wove,
But leased on Nature's loveliness and love.

CIX.

" 'Tis these that free the small entangled fly,
Caught in the venomed spider's crafty snare ;
These be the petty surgeons that apply
The healing balsams to the wounded hare,

Bedded in bloody fern, no creature's care !
These be providers for the orphan brood,
Whose tender mother hath been slain in air,
Quitting with gaping bill her darling's food,
Hard by the verge of her domestic wood.

CX.

" 'Tis these befriend the timid trembling stag,
When, with a bursting heart beset with fears,
He feels his saving speed begin to flag ;
For then they quench the fatal taint with tears,
And prompt fresh shifts in his alarumed ears,
So piteously they view all bloody morts ;
Or if the gunner, with his arm, appears,
Like noisy pies and jays, with harsh reports,
They warn the wildfowl of his deadly sports.

CXI.

" For these are kindly ministers of nature,
To soothe all covert hurts and dumb distress ;
Pretty they be, and very small of stature—
For mercy still consorts with littleness ;
Wherefore the sum of good is still the less,
And mischief grossest in this world of wrong ;
So do these charitable dwarfs redress
The tenfold ravages of giants strong,
To whom great malice and great might belong.

CXII.

" Likewise to them are Poets much beholden
For secret favours in the midnight glooms ;
Brave Spenser quaffed out of their goblets golden,
And saw their tables spread of prompt mushrooms
And heard their horns of honeysuckle blooms
Sounding upon the air most soothing soft,
Like humming bees busy about the brooms—
And glanced this fair queen's witchery full oft,
And in her magic wain soared far aloft.

CXIII.

" Nay I myself, though mortal, once was nursed
By fairy gossips, friendly at my birth,
And in my childish ear glib Mab rehearsed
Her breezy travels round our planet's girth,
Telling me wonders of the moon and earth;
My gramarye at her grave lap I conned,
Where Puck hath been convened to make me mirth;
I have had from Queen Titania tokens fond,
And toyed with Oberon's permitted wand.

CXIV.

" With figs and plums and Persian dates they fed me,
And delicate cates after my sunset meal,
And took me by my childish hand, and led me
By craggy rocks crested with keeps of steel,
Whose awful bases deep dark woods conceal,
Staining some dead lake with their verdant dyes:
And when the West sparkled at Phœbus' wheel,
With fairy euphrasy they purged mine eyes,
To let me see their cities in the skies.

CXV.

" 'Twas they first schooled my young imagination
To take its flights like any new-fledged bird,
And showed the span of wingèd meditation
Stretched wider than things grossly seen or heard.
With sweet swift Ariel how I soared and stirred
The fragrant blooms of spiritual bow'rs!
'Twas they endeared what I have still preferred,
Nature's blest attributes and balmy pow'rs,
Her hills and vales and brooks, sweet birds and flow'rs!

CXVI.

"Wherefore with all true loyalty and duty
Will I regard them in my honouring rhyme,
With love for love, and homages to beauty,
And magic thoughts gathered in night's cool clime,

With studious verse trancing the dragon Time,
Strong as old Merlin's necromatic spells,
So these dear monarchs of the summer's prime
Shall live unstartled by his dreadful yells,
Till shrill larks warn them to their flowery cells."

CXVII.

Look how a poisoned man turns livid black,
Drugged with a cup of deadly hellebore,
That sets his horrid features all at rack,—
So seemed these words into the ear to pour
Of ghastly Saturn, answering with a roar
Of mortal pain and spite and utmost rage,
Wherewith his grisly arm he raised once more,
And bade the clustered sinews all engage,
As if at one fell stroke to wreck an age.

CXVIII.

Whereas the blade flashed on the dinted ground,
Down through his steadfast foe, yet made no scar
On that immortal Shade, or death-like wound;
But Time was long benumbed, and stood ajar,
And then with baffled rage took flight afar,
To weep his hurt in some Cimmerian gloom,
Or meaner fames (like mine) to mock and mar,
Or sharp his scythe for royal strokes of doom,
Whetting its edge on some old Cæsar's tomb.

CXIX.

Howbeit he vanished in the forest shade,
Distantly heard as if some grumbling pard,
And, like Narcissus, to a sound decayed;
Meanwhile the fays clustered the gracious Bard,
The darling centre of their dear regard:
Besides of sundry dances on the green,
Never was mortal man so brightly starred,
Or won such pretty homages, I ween.
"Nod to him, Elves!" cries the melodious queen.

CXX.

"Nod to him, Elves, and flutter round about him,
And quite enclose him with your pretty crowd,
And touch him lovingly, for that, without him,
The silkworm now had spun our dreary shroud ;
But he hath all dispersed death's tearful cloud,
And Time's dread effigy scared quite away :
Bow to him then, as though to me ye bowed,
And his dear wishes prosper and obey
Wherever love and wit can find a way !

CXXI.

"'Noint him with fairy dews of magic savours,
Shaken from orient buds still pearly wet,
Roses and spicy pinks,—and, of all favours,
Plant in his walks the purple violet,
And meadow-sweet under the hedges set,
To mingle breaths with dainty eglantine
And honeysuckles sweet,—nor yet forget
Some pastoral flowery chaplets to entwine,
To vie the thoughts about his brow benign !

CXXII.

"Let no wild things astonish him or fear him,
But tell them all how mild he is of heart,
Till e'en the timid hares go frankly near him,
And eke the dappled does, yet never start ;
Nor shall their fawns into the thickets dart,
Nor wrens forsake their nests among the leaves,
Nor speckled thrushes flutter far apart ;
But bid the sacred swallow haunt his eaves,
To guard his roof from lightning and from thieves.

CXXIII.

"Or when he goes the nimble squirrel's visitor,
Let the brown hermit bring his hoarded nuts,
For, tell him, this is Nature's kind Inquisitor,—
Though man keeps cautious doors that conscience shuts,

For conscious wrong all curious quest rebuts ;
Nor yet shall bees uncase their jealous stings,
However he may watch their straw-built huts ;
So let him learn the crafts of all small things,
Which he will hint most aptly when he sings."

CXXIV.

Here she leaves off, and with a graceful hand
Waves thrice three splendid circles round his head ;
Which, though deserted by the radiant wand,
Wears still the glory which her waving shed,
Such as erst crowned the old Apostle's head,
To show the thoughts there harboured were divine,
And on immortal contemplations fed :
Goodly it was to see that glory shine
Around a brow so lofty and benign !

CXXV.

Goodly it was to see the elfin brood
Contend for kisses of his gentle hand,
That had their mortal enemy withstood,
And stayed their lives, fast ebbing with the sand.
Long while this strife engaged the pretty band ;
But now bold Chanticleer, from farm to farm,
Challenged the dawn creeping o'er eastern land,
And well the fairies knew that shrill alarm,
Which sounds the knell of every elfish charm.

CXXVI.

And soon the rolling mist, that 'gan arise
From plashy mead and undiscovered stream,
Earth's morning incense to the early skies,
Crept o'er the failing landscape of my dream.
Soon faded then the Phantom of my theme—
A shapeless Shade, that fancy disavowed,
And shrank· to nothing in the mist extreme.
Then flew Titania,—and her little crowd,
Like flocking linnets, vanished in a cloud.

HERO AND LEANDER.

To S. T. Coleridge, Esq

It is not with a hope my feeble praise
Can add one moment's honour to thine own,
That with thy mighty name I grace these lays;
I seek to glorify myself alone :
For that same precious favour thou hast shown
To my endeavour in a bygone time,
And by this token, I would have it known
Thou art my friend, and friendly to my rhyme !
It is my dear ambition now to climb
Still higher in my thought—if my bold pen
May thrust on contemplations more sublime.
But I am thirsty for thy praise, for when
We gain applauses from the great in name,
We seem to be partakers of *their* fame.

I.

Oh Bards of old ! what sorrows have ye sung,
And tragic stories, chronicled in stone—
Sad Philomel restored her ravished tongue,
And transformed Niobe in dumbness shown ;
Sweet Sappho on her love for ever calls,
And Hero on the drowned Leander falls !

II.

Was it that spectacles of sadder plights,
Should make our blisses relish the more high ?
Then all fair dames, and maidens, and true knights,
Whose flourished fortunes prosper in Love's eye,
Weep here, unto a tale of ancient grief,
Traced from the course of an old bas-relief.

III.

There stands Abydos !—here is Sestos' steep,
Hard by the gusty margin of the sea,
Where sprinkling waves continually do leap ;
And that is where those famous lovers be,
A builded gloom shot up into the grey,
As if the first tall watch-tow'r of the day.

IV.

Lo! how the lark soars upward and is gone;
Turning a spirit as he nears the sky,
His voice is heard, though body there is none,
And rain-like music scatters from on high;
But Love would follow with a falcon spite,
To pluck the minstrel from his dewy height.

V.

For Love hath framed a ditty of regrets,
Tuned to the hollow sobbings on the shore,
A vexing sense, that with like music frets,
And chimes this dismal burthen o'er and o'er,
Saying, Leander's joys are past and spent,
Like stars extinguished in the firmament.

VI.

For ere the golden crevices of morn
Let in those regal luxuries of light,
Which all the variable east adorn,
And hang rich fringes on the skirts of night,
Leander, weaning from sweet Hero's side,
Must leave a widow where he found a bride.

VII.

Hark! how the billows beat upon the sand!
Like pawing steeds impatient of delay;
Meanwhile their rider, ling'ring on the land,
Dallies with love, and holds farewell at bay
A too short span.   How tedious slow is grief!
But parting renders time both sad and brief.

VIII.

" Alas (he sighed), that this first glimpsing light,
Which makes the wide world tenderly appear,
Should be the burning signal for my flight,
From all the world's best image, which is here;
Whose very shadow, in my fond compare,
Shines far more bright than Beauty's self elsewhere."

IX.

Their cheeks are white as blossoms of the dark,
Whose leaves close up and show the outward pale,
And those fair mirrors where their joys did spark,
All dim and tarnished with a dreary veil,
No more to kindle till the night's return,
Like stars replenished at Joy's golden urn.

X.

Ev'n thus they creep into the spectral grey,
That cramps the landscape in its narrow brim,
As when two shadows by old Lethe stray,
He clasping her, and she entwining him;
Like trees wind-parted that embrace anon,
True love so often goes before 'tis gone.

XI.

For what rich merchant but will pause in fear,
To trust his wealth to the unsafe abyss?
So Hero dotes upon her treasure here,
And sums the loss with many an anxious kiss,
Whilst her fond eyes grow dizzy in her head,
Fear aggravating fear with shows of dread.

XII.

She thinks how many have been sunk and drowned,
And spies their snow-white bones below the deep,
Then calls huge congregated monsters round,
And plants a rock wherever he would leap;
Anon she dwells on a fantastic dream,
Which she interprets of that fatal stream.

XIII.

Saying, "That honeyed fly I saw was thee,
Which lighted on a water-lily's cup,
When, lo! the flow'r, enamoured of my bee,
Closed on him suddenly and locked him up,
And he was smothered in her drenching dew;
Therefore this day thy drowning I shall rue."

XIV.

But next, remembering her virgin fame,
She clips him in her arms and bids him go,
But seeing him break loose, repents her shame,
And plucks him back upon her bosom's snow;
And tears unfix her iced resolve again,
As steadfast frosts are thawed by show'rs of rain.

XV.

O for a type of parting ! Love to love
Is like the fond attraction of two spheres,
Which needs a godlike effort to remove,
And then sink down their sunny atmospheres,
In rain and darkness on each ruined heart,
Nor yet their melodies will sound impart.

XVI.

So brave Leander sunders from his bride;
The wrenching pang disparts his soul in twain;
Half stays with her, half goes towards the tide—
And life must ache, until they join again.
Now wouldst thou know the wideness of the wound
Mete every step he takes upon the ground.

XVII.

And for the agony and bosom-throe,
Let it be measured by the wide vast air,
For that is infinite, and so is woe,
Since parted lovers breathe it everywhere.
Look how it heaves Leander's labouring chest,
Panting, at poise, upon a rocky crest !

XVIII.

From which he leaps into the scooping brine,
That shocks his bosom with a double chill;
Because, all hours, till the slow sun's decline,
That cold divorcer will betwixt them still;
Wherefore he likens it to Styx' foul tide,
Where life grows death upon the other side.

XIX.

Then sadly he confronts his twofold toil
Against rude waves and an unwilling mind,
Wishing, alas ! with the stout rower's toil,
That like a rower he might gaze behind,
And watch that lonely statue he hath left
On her bleak summit, weeping and bereft !

XX.

Yet turning oft, he sees her troubled locks
Pursue him still the furthest that they may ;
Her marble arms that overstretch the rocks,
And her pale passioned hands that seem to pray
In dumb petition to the gods above !
Love prays devoutly when it prays for love !

XXI.

Then with deep sighs he blows away the wave,
That hangs superfluous tears upon his cheek,
And bans his labour like a hopeless slave,
That, chained in hostile galley, faint and weak,
Plies on despairing through the restless foam,
Thoughtful of his lost love and far-off home.

XXII.

The drowsy mist before him chill and dank,
Like a dull lethargy o'erleans the sea,
Where he rows on against the utter blank,
Steering as if to dim eternity,—
Like Love's frail ghost departing with the dawn ;
A failing shadow in the twilight drawn.

XXIII.

And soon is gone,—or nothing but a faint
And failing image in the eye of thought,
That mocks his model with an after-paint,
And stains an atom like the shape she sought;
Then with her earnest vows she hopes to fee,
The old and hoary majesty of sea.

XXIV.

"O King of waves, and brother of high Jove,
Preserve my sumless venture there afloat ;
A woman's heart, and its whole wealth of love,
Are all embarked upon that little boat ;
Nay, but two loves, two lives, a double fate,
A perilous voyage for so dear a freight.

XXV.

"If impious mariners be stained with crime,
Shake not in awful rage thy hoary locks ;
Lay by thy storms until another time,
Lest my frail bark be dashed against the rocks :
Or rather smooth thy deeps, that he may fly
Like Love himself, upon a seeming sky !

XXVI.

"Let all thy herded monsters sleep beneath,
Nor gore him with crooked tusks, or wreathèd horns ;
Let no fierce sharks destroy him with their teeth,
Nor spine-fish wound him with their venomed thorns ;
But if he faint, and timely succour lack,
Let ruthful dolphins rest him on their back.

XXVII.

Let no false dimpling whirlpools suck him in,
Nor slimy quicksands smother his sweet breath ;
Let no jagged corals tear his tender skin,
Nor mountain billows bury him in death."
And with that thought forestalling her own fears,
She drowned his painted image in her tears.

XXVIII.

By this, the climbing sun, with rest repaired,
Looked through the gold embrasures of the sky,
And asked the drowsy world how she had fared ;
The drowsy world shone brightened in reply ;
And smiling off her fogs, his slanting beam
Spied young Leander in the middle stream.

XXIX.

His face was pallid, but the hectic morn
Had hung a lying crimson on his cheeks,
And slanderous sparkles in his eyes forlorn;
So death lies ambushed in consumptive streaks;
But inward grief was writhing o'er its task,
As heart-sick jesters weep behind the mask.

XXX.

He thought of Hero and the lost delight,
Her last embracings, and the space between;
He thought of Hero and the future night,
Her speechless rapture and enamoured mien,
When, lo! before him, scarce two galleys' space,
His thought's confronted with another face!

XXXI.

Her aspect's like a moon divinely fair,
But makes the midnight darker that it lies on;
'Tis so beclouded with her coal-black hair
That densely skirts her luminous horizon,
Making her doubly fair, thus darkly set,
As marble lies advantaged upon jet.

XXXII.

She's all too bright, too argent, and too pale,
To be a woman :—but a woman's double,
Reflected on the wave so faint and frail,
She tops the billows like an air-blown bubble;
Or dim creation of a morning dream,
Fair as the wave-bleached lily of the stream.

XXXIII.

The very rumour strikes his seeing dead:
Great beauty like great fear first stuns the sense:
He knows not if her lips be blue or red,
Nor if her eyes can give true evidence:
Like murder's witness swooning in the court,
His sight falls senseless by its own report.

XXXIV.

Anon resuming, it declares her eyes
Are tinct with azure, like two crystal wells,
That drink the blue complexion of the skies,
Or pearls outpeeping from their silvery shells:
Her polished brow, it is an ample plain,
To lodge vast contemplations of the main.

XXXV.

Her lips might corals seem, but corals near,
Stray through her hair like blossoms on a bower;
And o'er the weaker red still domineer,
And make it pale by tribute to more power;
Her rounded cheeks are of still paler hue,
Touched by the bloom of water, tender blue.

XXXVI.

Thus he beholds her rocking on the water,
Under the glossy umbrage of her hair,
Like pearly Amphitrite's fairest daughter
Naiad, or Nereid—or Syren fair,
Mislodging music in her pitiless breast,
A nightingale within a falcon's nest.

XXXVII.

They say there be such maidens in the deep,
Charming poor mariners, that all too near
By mortal lullabies fall dead asleep,
As drowsy men are poisoned through the ear;
Therefore Leander's fears begin to urge,
This snowy swan is come to sing his dirge.

XXXVIII.

At which he falls into a deadly chill,
And strains his eyes upon her lips apart;
Fearing each breath to feel that prelude shrill,
Pierce through his marrow, like a death-blown dart
Shot sudden from an Indian's hollow cane,
With mortal venom fraught, and fiery pain.

XXXIX.

Here then, poor wretch, how he begins to crowd
A thousand thoughts within a pulse's space;
There seemed so brief a pause of life allowed,
His mind stretched universal, to embrace
The whole wide world, in an extreme farewell—
A moment's musing—but an age to tell.

XL.

For there stood Hero, widowed at a glance,
The foreseen sum of many a tedious fact,
Pale cheeks, dim eyes, and withered countenance,
A wasting ruin that no wasting lacked;
Time's tragic consequents ere time began,
A world of sorrow in a tear-drop's span.

XLI.

A moment's thinking is an hour in words—
An hour of words is little for some woes;
Too little breathing a long life affords,
For love to paint itself by perfect shows;
Then let his love and grief unwronged lie dumb,
Whilst Fear, and that it fears, together come.

XLII.

As when the crew, hard by some jutty cape,
Struck pale and panicked by the billows' roar,
Lay by all timely measures of escape,
And let their bark go driving on the shore;
So frayed Leander, drifting to his wreck,
Gazing on Scylla, falls upon her neck.

XLIII.

For he hath all forgot the swimmer's art,
The rower's cunning, and the pilot's skill,
Letting his arms fall down in languid part,
Swayed by the waves, and nothing by his will,
Till soon he jars against that glossy skin,
Solid like glass, though seemingly as thin.

XLIV.

Lo! how she startles at the warning shock,
And straightway girds him to her radiant breast,
More like his safe smooth harbour than his rock;
Poor wretch, he is so faint and toil-opprest,
He cannot loose him from his grappling foe,
Whether for love or hate, she lets not go.

XLV.

His eyes are blinded with the sleety brine,
His ears are deafened with the wildering noise;
He asks the purpose of her fell design,
But foamy waves choke up his struggling voice;
Under the ponderous sea his body dips,
And Hero's name dies bubbling on his lips.

XLVI.

Look how a man is lowered to his grave;
A yearning hollow in the green earth's lap;
So he is sunk into the yawning wave,
The plunging sea fills up the watery gap;
Anon he is all gone, and nothing seen,
But likeness of green turf and hillocks green.

XLVII.

And where he swam, the constant sun lies sleeping,
Over the verdant plain that makes his bed;
And all the noisy waves go freshly leaping,
Like gamesome boys over the churchyard dead;
The light in vain keeps looking for his face,
Now screaming seafowl settle in his place.

XLVIII.

Yet weep and watch for him though all in vain!
Ye moaning billows, seek him as ye wander!
Ye gazing sunbeams, look for him again!
Ye winds, grow hoarse with asking for Leander!
Ye did but spare him for more cruel rape,
Sea-storm and ruin in a female shape!

XLIX.

She says 'tis love hath bribed her to this deed,
The glancing of his eyes did so bewitch her,
O bootless theft ! unprofitable meed !
Love's treasury is sacked, but she no richer ;
The sparkles of his eyes are cold and dead,
And all his golden looks are turned to lead !

L.

She holds the casket, but her simple hand
Hath spilled its dearest jewel by the way ;
She hath life's empty garment at command,
But her own death lies covert in the prey ;
As if a thief should steal a tainted vest,
Some dead man's spoil, and sicken of his pest.

LI.

Now she compels him to her deeps below,
Hiding his face beneath her plenteous hair,
Which jealously she shakes all round her brow,
For dread of envy, though no eyes are there
But seals', and all brute tenants of the deep,
Which heedless through the wave their journeys keep.

LII.

Down and still downwards through the dusky green
She bore him, murmuring with joyous haste
In too rash ignorance, as he had been
Born to the texture of that watery waste ;
That which she breathed and sighed, the emerald wave,
How could her pleasant home become his grave !

LIII.

Down and still downward through the dusky green
She bore her treasure, with a face too nigh
To mark how life was altered in its mien,
Or how the light grew torpid in his eye,
Or how his pearly breath unprisoned there,
Flew up to join the universal air.

LIV.

She could not miss the throbbings of his heart,
Whilst her own pulse so wantoned in its joy;
She could not guess he struggled to depart,
And when he strove no more, the hapless boy!
She read his mortal stillness for content,
Feeling no fear where only love was meant.

LV.

Soon she alights upon her ocean-floor,
And straight unyokes her arms from her fair prize:
Then on his lovely face begins to pore,
As if to glut her soul;—her hungry eyes
Have grown so jealous of her arms' delight;
It seems, she hath no other sense but sight.

LVI.

But O sad marvel! O most bitter strange!
What dismal magic makes his cheek so pale,
Why will he not embrace,—why not exchange
Her kindly kisses;—wherefore not exhale
Some odorous message from life's ruby gates,
Where she his first sweet embassy awaits?

LVII.

Her eyes, poor watchers, fixed upon his looks,
Are grappled with a wonder near to grief,
As one, who pores on undeciphered books,
Strains vain surmise, and dodges with belief;
So she keeps gazing with a mazy thought,
Framing a thousand doubts that end in naught.

LVIII.

Too stern inscription for a page so young,
The dark translation of his look was death!
But death was written in an alien tongue,
And learning was not by to give it breath;
So one deep woe sleeps buried in its seal,
Which Time, untimely, hasteth to reveal.

LIX.

Meanwhile she sits unconscious of her hap,
Nursing Death's marble effigy, which there
With heavy head lies pillowed in her lap,
And elbows all unhinged :—his sleeking hair
Creeps o'er her knees, and settles where his hand
Leans with lax fingers crooked against the sand ;

LX.

And there lies spread in many an oozy trail,
Like glossy weeds hung from a chalky base,
That shows no whiter than his brow is pale ;
So soon the wintry death had bleached his face
Into cold marble,—with blue chilly shades,
Showing wherein the freezy blood pervades.

LXI.

And o'er his steadfast cheek a furrowed pain
Hath set, and stiffened like a storm in ice,
Showing by drooping lines the deadly strain
Of mortal anguish ;—yet you might gaze twice
Ere Death it seemed, and not his cousin, Sleep,
That through those creviced lids did underpeep.

LXII.

But all that tender bloom about his eyes,
Is death's own vi'lets, which his utmost rite
It is to scatter when the red rose dies ;
For blue is chilly, and akin to white :
Also he leaves some tinges on his lips,
Which he hath kissed with such cold frosty nips.

LXIII.

"Surely," quoth she, " he sleeps, the senseless thing,
Oppressed and faint with toiling in the stream !"
Therefore she will not mar his rest, but sing
So low, her tune shall mingle with his dream ;
Meanwhile, her lily fingers tasks to twine
His uncrispt locks uncurling in the brine.

LXIV.

" O lovely boy !"—thus she attuned her voice,—
" Welcome, thrice welcome, to a sea-maid's home,
My love-mate thou shalt be, and true heart's choice ;
How have I longed such a twin-self should come,—
A lonely thing, till this sweet chance befell,
My heart kept sighing like a hollow shell.

LXV.

" Here thou shalt live, beneath this secret dome,
An ocean bower, defended by the shade
Of quiet waters ; a cool emerald gloom
To lap thee all about.   Nay, be not frayed,
Those are but shady fishes that sail by
Like antic clouds across my liquid sky !

LXVI.

" Look how the sunbeam burns upon their scales,
And shows rich glimpses of their Tyrian skins,
They flash small lightnings from their vigorous tails,
And winking stars are kindled at their fins ;
These shall divert thee in thy weariest mood,
And seek thy hand for gamesomeness and food.

LXVII.

" Lo ! those green pretty leaves with tassel bells,
My flowrets those, that never pine for drouth ;
Myself did plant them in the dappled shells,
That drink the wave with such a rosy mouth,—
Pearls wouldst thou have beside ? crystals to shine ?
I had such treasures once,—now they are thine.

LXVIII.

" Now, lay thine ear against this golden sand,
And thou shalt hear the music of the sea,
Those hollow tunes it plays against the land,—
Is't not a rich and wondrous melody ?
I have lain hours, and fancied in its tone
I heard the languages of ages gone !

LXIX.

"I too can sing when it shall please thy choice,
And breathe soft tunes through a melodious shell,
Though heretofore I have but set my voice
To some long sighs, grief harmonized, to tell
How desolate I fared ;—but this sweet change
Will add new notes of gladness to my range !

LXX.

"Or bid me speak and I will tell thee tales,
Which I have framed out of the noise of waves ;
Ere now I have communed with senseless gales,
And held vain colloquies with barren caves ;
But I could talk to thee whole days and days,
Only to word my love a thousand ways.

LXXI.

"But if thy lips will bless me with their speech,
Then ope, sweet oracles ! and I'll be mute ;
I was born ignorant for thee to teach,
Nay all love's lore to thy dear looks impute ;
Then ope thine eyes, fair teachers, by whose light
I saw o give away my heart aright !"

LXXII.

But cold and deaf the sullen creature lies,
Over her knees, and with concealing clay,
Like hoarding Avarice locks up his eyes,
And leaves the world impoverished of day ;
Then at his cruel lips she bends to plead,
But there the door is closed against her need.

LXXIII.

Surely he sleeps—so her false wits infer !
Alas ! poor sluggard, ne'er to wake again !
Surely he sleeps, yet without any stir
That might denote a vision in his brain ;
Or if he does not sleep, he feigns too long,
Twice she hath reached the ending of her song.

LXXIV.

Therefore 'tis time she tells him to uncover
Those radiant jesters, and disperse her fears,
Whereby her April face is shaded over,
Like rainy clouds just ripe for showering tears ;
Nay, if he will not wake, so poor she gets,
Herself must rob those locked up cabinets.

LXXV.

With that she stoops above his brow, and bids
Her busy hands forsake his tangled hair,
And tenderly lift up those coffer-lids,
That she may gaze upon the jewels there,
Like babes that pluck an early bud apart,
To know the dainty colour of its heart.

LXXVI.

Now, picture one, soft creeping to a bed,
Who slowly parts the fringe-hung canopies,
And then starts back to find the sleeper dead ;
So she looks in on his uncovered eyes,
And seeing all within so drear and dark,
Her own bright soul dies in her like a spark.

LXXVII.

Backward she falls, like a pale prophetess,
Under the swoon of holy divination :
And what had all surpassed her simple guess,
She now resolves in this dark revelation ;
Death's very mystery—oblivious death ;
Long sleep—deep night, and an entranced breath.

LXXVIII.

Yet life, though wounded sore, not wholly slain,
Merely obscured, and not extinguished, lies ;
Her breath that stood at ebb, soon flows again,
Heaving her hollow breast with heavy sighs,
And light comes in and kindles up the gloom,
To light her spirit from its transient tomb.

LXXIX.

Then like the sun, awakened at new dawn,
With pale bewildered face she peers about,
And spies blurred images obscurely drawn,
Uncertain shadows in a haze of doubt;
But her true grief grows shapely by degrees,
A perished creature lying on her knees.

LXXX.

And now she knows how that old Murder preys,
Whose quarry on her lap lies newly slain;
How he roams all abroad and grimly slays,
Like a lean tiger in Love's own domain;
Parting from mates,—and oft in flowery lawns
Bereaves mild mothers of their milky fawns

LXXXI.

O too dear knowledge ! O pernicious earning !
Foul curse engraven upon beauty's page !
Ev'n now the sorrow of that deadly learning
Ploughs up her brow, like an untimely age,
And on her cheek stamps verdict of death's truth,
By canker blights upon the bud of youth !

LXXXII.

For as unwholesome winds decay the leaf,
So her cheeks' rose is perished by her sighs,
And withers in the sickly breath of grief;
Whilst unacquainted rheum bedims her eyes,
Tears, virgin tears, the first that ever leapt
From those young lids, now plentifully wept.

LXXXIII.

Whence being shed, the liquid crystalline
Drops straightway down, refusing to partake
In gross admixture with the baser brine,
But shrinks and hardens into pearls opaque,
Hereafter to be worn on arms and ears ;
So one maid's trophy is another's tears !

LXXXIV.

" O foul Arch-Shadow, thou old cloud of Night,
(Thus in her frenzy she began to wail,)
Thou blank oblivion—blotter out of light,
Life's ruthless murderer, and dear love's bale !
Why hast thou left thy havoc incomplete,
Leaving me here, and slaying the more sweet ?

LXXXV.

"Lo ! what a lovely ruin thou hast made,
Alas ! alas ! thou hast no eyes to see,
And blindly slew'st him in misguided shade.
Would I had lent my doting sense to thee !
But now I turn to thee, a willing mark,
Thine arrows miss me in the aimless dark !

LXXXVI.

" O doubly cruel !—twice misdoing spite,
But I will guide thee with my helping eyes,
Or walk the wide world through, devoid of sight,
Yet thou shalt know me by my many sighs.
Nay, then thou shouldst have spared my rose, false Death,
And known Love's flow'r by smelling his sweet breath ;

LXXXVII.

" Or, when thy furious rage was round him dealing,
Love should have grown from touching of his skin,
But like cold marble thou art all unfeeling,
And hast no ruddy springs of warmth within,
And being but a shape of freezing bone,
Thy touching only turned my love to stone !

LXXXVIII.

" And here, alas ! he lies across my knees,
With cheeks still colder than the stilly wave,
The light beneath his eyelids seems to freeze,
Here then, since Love is dead and lacks a grave,
O come and dig it in my sad heart's core—
That wound will bring a balsam for its sore !

LXXXIX.

" For art thou not a sleep where sense of ill
Lies stingless, like a sense benumbed with cold,
Healing all hurts only with sleep's good will,
So shall I slumber, and perchance behold
My living love in dreams—O happy night,
That lets me company his banished spright!

XC.

"O poppy Death!—sweet poisoner of sleep!
Where shall I seek for thee, oblivious drug,
That I may steep thee in my drink, and creep
Out of life's coil.   Look, Idol! how I hug
Thy dainty image in this strict embrace,
And kiss this clay-cold model of thy face!

XCI.

" Put out, put out these sun-consuming lamps,
I do but read my sorrows by their shine,
O come and quench them with thy oozy damps,
And let my darkness intermix with thine ;
Since love is blinded, wherefore should I see?
Now love is death—death will be love to me!

XCII.

" Away, away, this vain complaining breath,
It does but stir the troubles that I weep,
Let it be hushed and quieted, sweet Death,
The wind must settle ere the wave can sleep—
Since love is silent, I would fain be mute,
O Death, be gracious to my dying suit!"

XCIII.

Thus far she pleads, but pleading nought avails her,
For Death, her sullen burden, deigns no heed,
Then with dumb craving arms, since darkness fails her,
She prays to heav'n's fair light, as if her need
Inspired her there were Gods to pity pain,
Or end it—but she lifts her arms in vain!

XCIV.

Poor gilded Grief! the subtle light by this
With mazy gold creeps through her watery mine,
And, diving downward through the green abyss,
Lights up her palace with an amber shine;
There, falling on her arms—the crystal skin
Reveals the ruby tide that fares within.

XCV.

Look how the fulsome beam would hang a glory
On her dark hair, but the dark hairs repel it;
Look how the perjured glow suborns a story
On her pale lips, but lips refuse to tell it;
Grief will not swerve from grief, however told
On coral lips, or charactered in gold;

XCVI.

Or else, thou maid! safe anchored on Love's neck,
Listing the hapless doom of young Leander,
Thou wouldst not shed a tear for that old wreck,
Sitting secure where no wild surges wander;
Whereas the woe moves on with tragic pace,
And shows its sad reflection in thy face.

XCVII.

Thus having travelled on, and tracked the tale,
Like the true course of an old bas-relief,
Where Tragedy pursues her progress pale,
Brood here awhile upon that sea-maid's grief,
And take a deeper imprint from the frieze
Of that young Fate, with Death upon her knees.

XCVIII.

Then whilst the melancholy muse withal
Resumes her music in a sadder tone,
Meanwhile the sunbeam strikes upon the wall,
Conceive that lovely siren to live on,
Ev'n as Hope whispered, the Promethean light
Would kindle up the dead Leander's sprite.

XCIX.

" 'Tis light," she says, " that feeds the glittering stars,
And those were stars set in his heavenly brow,
But this salt cloud, this cold sea-vapour, mars
Their radiant breathing, and obscures them now,
Therefore I'll lay him in the clear blue air,
And see how these dull orbs will kindle there."

C.

Swiftly as dolphins glide, or swifter yet,
With dead Leander in her fond arms' fold,
She cleaves the meshes of that radiant net,
The sun hath twined above of liquid gold,
Nor slacks, till on the margin of the land,
She lays his body on the glowing sand.

CI.

There, like a pearly waif, just past the reach
Of foamy billows he lies cast.   Just then,
Some listless fishers, straying down the beach,
Spy out this wonder.   Thence the curious men,
Low crouching, creep into a thicket brake,
And watch her doings till their rude hearts ache.

CII.

First she begins to chafe him till she faints,
Then falls upon his mouth with kisses many,
And sometimes pauses in her own complaints
To list his breathing, but there is not any,—
Then looks into his eyes where no light dwells,
Light makes no pictures in such muddy wells.

CIII.

The hot sun parches his discovered eyes,
The hot sun beats on his discoloured limbs,
The sand is oozy whereupon he lies,
Soiling his fairness ; then away she swims,
Meaning to gather him a daintier bed,
Plucking the cool fresh weeds, brown, green, and red.

CIV.

But, simple-witted thief, while she dives under,
Another robs her of her amorous theft ;
The ambushed fishermen creep forth to plunder,
And steal the unwatched treasure she has left ;
Only his void impression dints the sands !
Leander is purloined by stealthy hands !

CV.

Lo ! how she shudders off the beaded wave !
Like Grief all over tears, and senseless falls,
His void imprint seems hollowed for her grave,
Then, rising on her knees, looks round and calls
On Hero ! Hero ! having learned this name
Of his last breath, she calls him by the same.

CVI.

Then with her frantic hands she rends her hairs,
And casts them forth, sad keepsakes to the wind,
As if in plucking those she plucked her cares ;
But grief lies deeper, and remains behind
Like a barbed arrow, rankling in her brain,
Turning her very thoughts to throbs of pain.

CVII.

Anon her tangled locks are left alone,
And down upon the sand she meekly sits,
Hard by the foam as humble as a stone,
Like an enchanted maid beside her wits,
That ponders with a look serene and tragic,
Stunned by the mighty mystery of magic.

CVIII.

Or think of Ariadne's utter trance,
Crazed by the flight of that disloyal traitor,
Who left her gazing on the green expanse
That swallowed up his track,—yet this would mate her,
Ev'n in the cloudy summit of her woe,
When o'er the far sea-brim she saw him go.

CIX.

For even so she bows, and bends her gaze
O'er the eternal waste, as if to sum
Its waves by weary thousands all her days,
Dismally doomed! meanwhile the billows come,
And coldly dabble with her quiet feet,
Like any bleaching stones they wont to greet.

CX.

And thence into her lap have boldly sprung,
Washing her weedy tresses to and fro,
That round her crouching knees have darkly hung,
But she sits careless of waves' ebb and flow,
Like a lone beacon on a desert coast,
Showing where all her hope was wrecked and lost.

CXI.

Yet whether in the sea or vaulted sky,
She knoweth not her love's abrupt resort,
So like a shape of dreams he left her eye,
Winking with doubt.   Meanwhile, the churl's report
Has thronged the beach with many a curious face,
That peeps upon her from its hiding place.

CXII.

And here a head, and there a brow half seen,
Dodges behind a rock.   Here on his hands,
A mariner his crumpled cheeks doth lean
Over a rugged crest.   Another stands,
Holding his harmful arrow at the head,
Still checked by human caution and strange dread.

CXIII.

One stops his ears,—another close beholder
Whispers unto the next his grave surmise ;
This crouches down,—and just above his shoulder,
A woman's pity saddens in her eyes,
And prompts her to befriend that lonely grief,
With all sweet helps of sisterly relief,

CXIV.

And down the sunny beach she paces slowly,
With many doubtful pauses by the way;
Grief hath an influence so hushed and holy—
Making her twice attempt, ere she can lay
Her hand upon that sea-maid's shoulder white,
Which makes her startle up in wild affright.

CXV.

And, like a seal, she leaps into the wave
That drowns the shrill remainder of her scream;
Anon the sea fills up the watery cave,
And seals her exit with a foamy seam—
Leaving those baffled gazers on the beach
Turning in uncouth wonder each to each.

CXVI.

Some watch, some call, some see her head emerge,
Wherever a brown weed falls through the foam;
Some point to white eruptions of the surge:
But she is vanished to her shady home,
Under the deep, inscrutable—and there
Weeps in a midnight made of her own hair.

CXVII.

Now here, the sighing winds, before unheard,
Forth from their cloudy caves begin to blow,
Till all the surface of the deep is stirred,
Like to the panting grief it hides below;
And heaven is covered with a stormy rack,
Soiling the waters with its inky black.

CXVIII.

The screaming fowl resigns her finny prey,
And labours shoreward with a bending wing,
Rowing against the wind her toilsome way;
Meanwhile the curling billows chafe, and fling
Their dewy frost still further on the stones,
That answer to the wind with hollow groans.

CXIX.

And here and there a fisher's far-off bark
Flies with the sun's last glimpse upon its sail,
Like a bright flame amid the waters dark,
Watched with the hope and fear of maidens pale;
And anxious mothers that upturn their brows,
Freighting the gusty wind with frequent vows,

CXX.

For that the horrid deep has no sure track
To guide love safe into his homely haven.
And lo! the storm grows blacker in its wrath,
O'er the dark billow brooding like a raven,
That bodes of death and widow's sorrowing,
Under the dusky covering of his wing.

CXXI.

And so day ended.   But no vesper spark
Hung forth its heavenly sign; but sheets of flame
Played round the savage features of the dark,
Making night horrible.   That night there came
A weeping maiden to high Sestos' steep,
And tore her hair and gazed upon the deep.

CXXII.

And waved aloft her bright and ruddy torch,
Whose flame the boastful wind so rudely fanned,
That oft it would recoil, and basely scorch
The tender covert of her sheltering hand;
Which yet, for love's dear sake, disdained retire,
And, like a glorying martyr, braved the fire.

CXXIII.

For that was love's own sign and beacon guide
Across the Hellespont's wide weary space,
Wherein he nightly struggled with the tide;
Look what a red it forges on her face,
As if she blushed at holding such a light,
Even in the unseen presence of the night!

CXXIV.

Whereas her tragic cheek is truly pale,
And colder than the rude and ruffian air
That howls into her ear a horrid tale
Of storm, and wreck, and uttermost despair,
Saying, " Leander floats amid the surge,
And those are dismal waves that sing his dirge."

CXXV.

And hark !—a grieving voice, trembling and faint,
Blends with the hollow sobbings of the sea ;
Like the sad music of a siren's plaint,
But shriller than Leander's voice should be,
Unless the wintry death had changed its tone—
Wherefore she thinks she hears his spirit moan.

CXXVI.

For now, upon each brief and breathless pause,
Made by the raging winds, it plainly calls
On Hero ! Hero !—whereupon she draws
Close to the dizzy brink, that ne'er appals
Her brave and constant spirit to recoil,
However the wild billows toss and toil.

CXXVII.

" Oh ! dost thou live under the deep deep sea ?
I thought such love as thine could never die ;
If thou hast gained an immortality,
From the kind pitying sea-god, so will I ;
And this false cruel tide that used to sever
Our hearts, shall be our common home for ever !

CXXVIII.

" There we will sit and sport upon one billow,
And sing our ocean ditties all the day,
And lie together on the same green pillow,
That curls above us with its dewy spray ;
And ever in one presence live and dwell,
Like two twin pearls within the selfsame shell."

CXXIX.

One moment, then, upon the dizzy verge
She stands, with face upturned against the sky;
A moment more, upon the foamy surge
She gazes, with a calm despairing eye;
Feeling that awful pause of blood and breath
Which life endures when it confronts with death;

CXXX.

Then from the giddy steep she madly springs,
Grasping her maiden robes, that vainly kept
Panting abroad, like unavailing wings,
To save her from her death.—The sea-maid wept,
And in a crystal cave her corse enshrined,
No meaner sepulchre should Hero find!

LYCUS, THE CENTAUR.

FROM AN UNROLLED MANUSCRIPT OF APOLLONIUS CURIUS.

To J. H. Reynolds, Esq.

My dear Reynolds,—You will remember "Lycus."—It was written in the pleasant spring-time of our friendship, and I am glad to maintain that association by connecting your name with the poem. It will gratify me to find that you regard it with the old partiality for the writings of each other which prevailed in those days. For my own sake, I must regret that your pen goes now into far other records than those which used to delight me.

Your true Friend and Brother,
T. Hood.

THE ARGUMENT.

Lycus, detained by Circe in her magical dominion, is beloved by a Water Nymph, who, desiring to render him immortal, has recourse to the Sorceress. Circe gives her an incantation to pronounce, which should turn Lycus into a horse; but the horrible effect of the charm causing her to break off in the midst, he becomes a Centaur.

Who hath ever been lured and bound by a spell
To wander, fore-doomed, in that circle of hell

Where Witchery works with her will like a god,
Works more than the wonders of time at a nod,—
At a word,—at a touch,—at a flash of the eye,
But each form is a cheat, and each sound is a lie,
Things born of a wish—to endure for a thought,
Or last for long ages—to vanish to nought,
Or put on new semblance? O Jove, I had given
The throne of a kingdom to know if that heaven
And the earth and its streams were of Circe, or whether
They kept the world's birthday and brightened together!
For I loved them in terror, and constantly dreaded
That the earth where I trod, and the cave where I bedded,
The face I might dote on, should live out the lease
Of the charm that created, and suddenly cease;
And I gave me to slumber, as if from one dream
To another—each other—and drank of the stream
Like a first taste of blood, lest as water I quaffed
Swift poison, and never should breathe from the draught,—
Such drink as her own monarch husband drained up
When he pledged her, and Fate closed his eyes in the cup.
And I plucked of the fruit with held breath, and a fear
That the branch would start back and scream out in my ear;
For once, at my suppering, I plucked in the dusk
An apple, juice-gushing and fragrant of musk;
But by daylight my fingers were crimsoned with gore,
And the half-eaten fragment was flesh at the core;
And once—only once—for the love of its blush,
I broke a bloom bough, but there came such a gush
On my hand, that it fainted away in weak fright,
While the leaf-hidden woodpecker shrieked at the sight;
And oh! such an agony thrilled in that note,
That my soul, startling up, beat its wings in my throat,
As it longed to be free of a body whose hand
Was doomed to work torments a Fury had planned!

There I stood without stir, yet how willing to flee,
As if rooted and horror-turned into a tree,—
Oh! for innocent death,—and to suddenly win it,
I drank of the stream, but no poison was in it;
I plunged in its waters, but ere I could sink,
Some invisible fate pulled me back to the brink;

I sprang from the rock, from its pinnacle height,
But fell on the grass, with a grasshopper's flight;
I ran at my fears—they were fears and no more,
For the bear would not mangle my limbs, nor the boar,
But moaned,—all their brutalized flesh could not smother,
The horrible truth,—we were kin to each other!

They were mournfully gentle, and grouped for relief,
All foes in their skin, but all friends in their grief:
The leopard was there,—baby-mild in its feature;
And the tiger, black barred, with the gaze of a creature
That knew gentle pity; the bristle-backed boar,
His innocent tusks stained with mulberry gore;
And the laughing hyena—but laughing no more;
And the snake, not with magical orbs to devise
Strange death, but with woman's attraction of eyes;
The tall ugly ape, that still bore a dim shine
Through his hairy eclipse of a manhood divine;
And the elephant stately, with more than its reason,
How thoughtful in sadness! but this is no season
To reckon them up from the lag-bellied toad
To the mammoth, whose sobs shook his ponderous load.
There were woes of all shapes, wretched forms, when I came,
That hung down their heads with a human-like shame;
The elephant hid in the boughs, and the bear
Shed over his eyes the dark veil of his hair;
And the womanly soul turning sick with disgust,
Tried to vomit herself from her serpentine crust;
While all groaned their groans into one at their lot,
As I brought them the image of what they were not.

Then rose a wild sound of the human voice choking
Through vile brutal organs—low tremulous croaking;
Cries swallowed abruptly—deep animal tones
Attuned to strange passion, and full-uttered groans;
All shuddering weaker, till hushed in a pause
Of tongues in mute motion and wide-yearning jaws;
And I guessed that those horrors were meant to tell o'er
The tale of their woes; but the silence told more
That writhed on their tongues: and I knelt on the sod,
And prayed with my voice to the cloud-stirring God,
For the sad congregation of suppliants there,
That upturned to his heaven brute faces of prayer;

And I ceased, and they uttered a moaning so deep,
That I wept for my heart-ease,—but they could not weep,
And gazed with red eyeballs, all wistfully dry,
At the comfort of tears in a stag's human eye.
Then I motioned them round, and, to soothe their distress,
I caressed, and they bent them to meet my caress,
Their necks to my arm, and their heads to my palm,
And with poor grateful eyes suffered meekly and calm
Those tokens of kindness, withheld by hard fate
From returns that might chill the warm pity to hate ;
So they passively bowed—save the serpent, that leapt
To my breast like a sister, and pressingly crept
In embrace of my neck, and with close kisses blistered
My lips in rash love,—then drew backward, and glistered
Her eyes in my face, and loud hissing affright,
Dropt down, and swift started away from my sight !

This sorrow was theirs, but thrice wretched my lot,
Turned brute in my soul, though my body was not
When I fled from the sorrow of womanly faces,
That shrouded their woe in the shade of lone places,
And dashed off bright tears, till their fingers were wet,
And then wiped their lids with long tresses of jet :
But I fled—though they stretched out their hands, all entangled
With hair, and blood-stained of the breasts they had mangled—
Though they called—and perchance but to ask, had I seen
Their loves, or to tell the vile wrongs that had been ·
But I stayed not to hear, lest the story should hold
Some hell-form of words, some enchantment once told,
Might translate me in flesh to a brute ; and I dreaded
To gaze on their charms, lest my faith should be wedded
With some pity,—and love in that pity perchance—
To a thing not all lovely ; for once at a glance
Methought, where one sat, I descried a bright wonder
That flowed like a long silver rivulet under
The long fenny grass, with so lovely a breast,
Could it be a snake-tail made the charm of the rest ?

So I roamed in that circle of horrors, and Fear
Walked with me, by hills, and in valleys, and near
Clustered trees for their gloom—not to shelter from heat
But lest a brute-shadow should grow at my feet ;

And besides that full oft in the sunshiny place,
Dark shadows would gather like clouds on its face,
In the horrible likeness of demons, (that none
Could see, like invisible flames in the sun;)
But grew to one monster that seized on the light,
Like the dragon that strangles the moon in the night;
Fierce sphinxes, long serpents, and asps of the South;
Wild birds of huge beak, and all horrors that drouth
Engenders of slime in the land of the pest,
Vile shapes without shape, and foul bats of the West,
Bringing Night on their wings; and the bodies wherein
Great Brahma imprisons the spirits of sin,
Many-handed, that blent in one phantom fight
Like a Titan, and threatfully warred with the light;
I have heard the wild shriek that gave signal to close,
When they rushed on that shadowy Python of foes;
That met with sharp beaks and wide gaping of jaws,
With flapping of wings, and fierce grasping of claws,
And whirls of long tails :—I have seen the quick flutter
Of fragments dissevered,—and necks stretched to utter
Long screamings of pain,—the swift motion of blows,
And wrestling of arms—to the flight at the close,
When the dust of the earth startled upward in rings,
And flew on the whirlwind that followed their wings.

Thus they fled—not forgotten—but often to grow
Like fears in my eyes, when I walked to and fro
In the shadows, and felt from some beings unseen
The warm touch of kisses, but clean or unclean
I knew not, nor whether the love I had won
Was of heaven or hell—till one day in the sun,
In its very noon-blaze, I could fancy a thing
Of beauty, but faint as the cloud-mirrors fling
On the gaze of the shepherd that watches the sky,
Half-seen and half-dreamed in the soul of his eye.
And when in my musings I gazed on the stream,
In motionless trances of thought, there would seem
A face like that face, looking upward through mine;
With its eyes full of love, and the dim-drowned shine
Of limbs and fair garments, like clouds in that blue
Serene :—there I stood for long hours but to view

Those fond earnest eyes that were ever uplifted
Towards me, and winked as the water-weed drifted
Between ; but the fish knew that presence, and plied
Their long curvy tails, and swift darted aside.

There I gazed for lost time, and forgot all the things
That once had been wonders—the fishes with wings,
And the glimmer of magnified eyes that looked up
From the glooms of the bottom like pearls in a cup,
And the huge endless serpent of silvery gleam,
Slow winding along like a tide in the stream.
Some maid of the waters, some Naiad, methought
Held me dear in the pearl of her eye—and I brought
My wish to that fancy ; and often I dashed
My limbs in the water, and suddenly splashed
The cool drops around me, yet clung to the brink,
Chilled by watery fears, how that Beauty might sink
With my life in her arms to her garden, and bind me
With its long tangled grasses, or cruelly wind me
In some eddy to hum out my life in her ear,
Like a spider-caught bee,—and in aid of that fear
Came the tardy remembrance—Oh falsest of men !
Why was not that beauty remembered till then ?
My love, my safe love, whose glad life would have run
Into mine—like a drop—that our fate might be one,
That now, even now, maybe, clasped in a dream,
That form which I gave to some jilt of the stream,
And gazed with fond eyes that her tears tried to smother
On a mock of those eyes that I gave to another !

Then I rose from the stream, but the eyes of my mind,
Still full of the tempter, kept gazing behind
On her crystalline face, while I painfully leapt
To the bank, and shook off the curst waters, and wept
With my brow in the reeds ; and the reeds to my ear
Bowed, bent by no wind, and in whispers of fear,
Growing small with large secrets, foretold me of one
That loved me,—but oh ! to fly from her, and shun
Her love like a pest—though her love was as true
To mine as her stream to the heavenly blue ;
For why should I love her with love that would bring
All misfortune, like Hate, on so joyous a thing ?

Because of her rival,—even her whose witch-face
I had slighted, and therefore was doomed in that place
To roam, and had roamed, where all horrors grew rank,
Nine days ere I wept with my brow on that bank ;
Her name be not named, but her spite would not fail
To our love like a blight ; and they told me the tale
Of Scylla, and Picus, imprisoned to speak
His shrill-screaming woe through a woodpecker's beak.

Then they ceased—I had heard as the voice of my star
That told me the truth of my fortunes—thus far
I had read of my sorrow ; and lay in the hush
Of deep meditation,—when lo ! a light crush
Of the reeds, and I turned and looked round in the night
Of new sunshine, and saw, as I sipped of the light
Narrow-winking, the realized nymph of the stream,
Rising up from the wave with the bend and the gleam
Of a fountain, and o'er her white arms she kept throwing
Bright torrents of hair, that went flowing and flowing
In falls to her feet, and the blue waters rolled
Down her limbs like a garment, in many a fold,
Sun-spangled, gold-broidered, and fled far behind,
Like an infinite train.   So she came and reclined
In the reeds, and I hungered to see her unseal
The buds of her eyes that would ope and reveal
The blue that was in them ; and they ope'd, and she raised
Two orbs of pure crystal, and timidly gazed
With her eyes on my eyes ; but their colour and shine
Was of that which they looked on, and mostly of mine—
For she loved me,—except when she blushed, and they sank,
Shame-humbled, to number the stones on the bank,
Or her play-idle fingers, while lisping she told me
How she put on her veil, and in love to behold me,
Would wing through the sun till she fainted away
Like a mist, and then flew to her waters and lay
In love-patience long hours, and sore dazzled her eyes
In watching for mine 'gainst the midsummer skies.
But now they were healed,—O my heart, it still dances
When I think of the charm of her changeable glances,
And my image how small when it sank in the deep
Of her eyes where her soul was,—alas ! now they weep,

And none knoweth where. In what stream do her eyes
Shed invisible tears? Who beholds where her sighs
Flow in eddies, or sees the ascent of the leaf
She has plucked with her tresses? Who listens her grief
Like a far fall of waters, or hears where her feet
Grow emphatic among the loose pebbles, and beat
Them together? Ah! surely her flowers float adown
To the sea unaccepted, and little ones drown
For need of her mercy,—even he whose twin-brother
Will miss him for ever; and the sorrowful mother
Imploreth in vain for his body to kiss
And cling to, all dripping and cold as it is,
Because that soft pity is lost in hard pain!
We loved,—how we loved!—for I thought not again
Of the woes that were whispered like fears in that place
If I gave me to beauty. Her face was the face
Far away, and her eyes were the eyes that were drowned
For my absence,—her arms were the arms that sought round,
And clasped me to nought; for I gazed and became
Only true to my falsehood, and had but one name
For two loves, and called ever on Ægle, sweet maid
Of the sky-loving waters,—and was not afraid
Of the sight of her skin;—for it never could be,
Her beauty and love were misfortunes to me!

Thus our bliss had endured for a time-shortened space,
Like a day made of three, and the smile of her face
Had been with me for joy,—when she told me indeed
Her love was self-tasked with a work that would need
Some short hours, for in truth 'twas the veriest pity
Our love should not last, and then sang me a ditty,
Of one with warm lips that should love her, and love her
When suns were burnt dim and long ages past over.
So she fled with her voice, and I patiently nested
My limbs in the reeds, in still quiet, and rested
Till my thoughts grew extinct, and I sank in a sleep
Of dreams,—but their meaning was hidden too deep
To be read what their woe was;—but still it was woe
That was writ on all faces that swam to and fro
In that river of night;—and the gaze of their eyes
Was sad,—and the bend of their brows,—and their cries

Were seen, but I heard not. The warm touch of tears
Travelled down my cold cheeks, and I shook till my fears
Awaked me, and lo ! I was couched in a bower,
The growth of long summers reared up in an hour !
Then I said, in the fear of my dream, I will fly
From this magic, but could not, because that my eye
Grew love-idle among the rich blooms ; and the earth
Held me down with its coolness of touch, and the mirth
Of some bird was above me,—who, even in fear,
Would startle the thrush ? and methought there drew near
A form as of Ægle,—but it was not the face
Hope made, and I knew the witch-queen of that place,
Even Circe the Cruel, that came like a Death
Which I feared, and yet fled not, for want of my breath.
There was thought in her face, and her eyes were not raised
From the grass at her foot, but I saw, as I gazed,
Her spite—and her countenance changed with her mind
As she planned how to thrall me with beauty, and bind
My soul to her charms,—and her long tresses played
From shade into shine and from shine into shade,
Like a day in mid-autumn,—first fair, O how fair !
With long snaky locks of the adderblack hair
That clung round her neck,—those dark locks that I prize,
For the sake of a maid that once loved me with eyes
Of that fathomless hue,—but they changed as they rolled,
And brightened, and suddenly blazed into gold
That she combed into flames, and the locks that fell down
Turned dark as they fell, but I slighted their brown,
Nor loved, till I saw the light ringlets shed wild,
That innocence wears when she is but a child ;
And her eyes,—O I ne'er had been witched with their shine,
Had they been any other, my Ægle, than thine !

　　Then I gave me to magic, and gazed till I maddened
In the full of their light,—but I saddened and saddened
The deeper I looked,—till I sank on the snow
Of her bosom, a thing made of terror and woe,
And answered its throb with the shudder of fears,
And hid my cold eyes from her eyes with my tears,
And strained her white arms with the still languid weight
Of a fainting distress. There she sat like the Fate

That is nurse unto Death, and bent over in shame
To hide me from her—the true Ægle—that came
With the words on her lips the false witch had foregiven
To make me immortal—for now I was even
At the portals of Death, who but waited the hush
Of world-sounds in my ear to cry welcome, and rush
With my soul to the banks of his black-flowing river.
O would it had flown from my body for ever,
Ere I listened those words, when I felt with a start,
The life-blood rush back in one throb to my heart,
And saw the pale lips where the rest of that spell
Had perished in horror—and heard the farewell
Of that voice that was drowned in the dash of the stream !
How fain had I followed, and plunged with that scream
Into death, but my being indignantly lagged
Through the brutalized flesh that I painfully dragged
Behind me :—" O Circe ! O mother of Spite !
Speak the last of that curse ! and imprison me quite
In the husk of a brute,—that no pity may name
The man that I was,—that no kindred may claim
The monster I am !   Let me utterly be
Brute-buried, and Nature's dishonour with me
Uninscribed !"—But she listened my prayer, that was praise
To her malice, with smiles, and advised me to gaze
On the river for love,—and perchance she would make
In pity a maid without eyes for my sake,
And she left me like Scorn.   Then I asked of the wave,
What monster I was, and it trembled and gave
The true shape of my grief, and I turned with my face
From all waters for ever, and fled through that place,
Till with horror more strong than all magic I passed
Its bounds, and the world was before me at last.

There I wandered in sorrow, and shunned the abodes
Of men, that stood up in the likeness of Gods,
But I saw from afar the warm shine of the sun
On their cities, where man was a million, not one ;
And I saw the white smoke of their altars ascending,
That showed where the hearts of the many were blending,
And the wind in my face brought shrill voices that came
From the trumpets that gathered whole bands in one fame

17

As a chorus of man,—and they streamed from the gates
Like a dusky libation poured out to the Fates.
But at times there were gentler processions of peace
That I watched with my soul in my eyes till their cease,
There were women! there men! but to me a third sex
I saw them all dots—yet I loved them as specks:
And oft to assuage a sad yearning of eyes
I stole near the city, but stole covert-wise
Like a wild beast of love, and perchance to be smitten
By some hand that I rather had wept on than bitten!
Oh, I once had a haunt near a cot where a mother
Daily sat in the shade with her child, and would smother
Its eyelids in kisses, and then in its sleep
Sang dreams in its ear of its manhood, while deep
In a thicket of willows I gazed o'er the brooks
That murmured between us and kissed them with looks;
But the willows unbosomed their secret, and never
I returned to the spot I had startled for ever,
Though I oft longed to know, but could ask it of none,
Was the mother still fair, and how big was her son?

For the haunters of fields they all shunned me by flight,
The men in their horror, the women in fright;
None ever remained save a child once that sported
Among the wild bluebells, and playfully courted
The breeze; and beside him a speckled snake lay
Tight strangled, because it had hissed him away
From the flower at his finger; he rose and drew near
Like a Son of Immortals, one born to no fear,
But with strength of black locks and with eyes azure bright
To grow to large manhood of merciful might.
He came, with his face of bold wonder, to feel
The hair of my side, and to lift up my heel,
And questioned my face with wide eyes; but when under
My lids he saw tears,—for I wept at his wonder,
He stroked me, and uttered such kindliness then,
That the once love of women, the friendship of men
In past sorrow, no kindness e'er came like a kiss
On my heart in its desolate day such as this!
And I yearned at his cheeks in my love, and down bent,
And lifted him up in my arms with intent

To kiss him,—but he cruel-kindly, alas!
Held out to my lips a plucked handful of grass!
Then I dropt him in horror, but felt as I fled
The stone he indignantly hurled at my head,
That dissevered my ear,—but I felt not, whose fate
Was to meet more distress in his love than his hate!

Thus I wandered, companioned of grief and forlorn,
Till I wished for that land where my being was born,
But what was that land with its love, where my home
Was self-shut against me; for why should I come
Like an after-distress to my grey-bearded father,
With a blight to the last of his sight?—let him rather
Lament for me dead, and shed tears in the urn
Where I was not, and still in fond memory turn
To his son even such as he left him.   Oh, how
Could I walk with the youth once my fellows, but now
Like Gods to my humbled estate?—or how bear
The steeds once the pride of eyes and the care
Of my hands?   Then I turned me self-banished, and came
Into Thessaly here, where I met with the same
As myself.   I have heard how they met by a stream
In games, and were suddenly changed by a scream
That made wretches of many, as she rolled her wild eyes
Against heaven, and so vanished.—The gentle and wise
Lose their thoughts in deep studies, and others their ill
In the mirth of mankind where they mingle them still.

THE TWO PEACOCKS OF BEDFONT.

I.

ALAS! that breathing Vanity should go
   Where Pride is buried,—like its very ghost,
Uprisen from the naked bones below,
   In novel flesh, clad in the silent boast
Of gaudy silk that flutters to and fro,
   Shedding its chilling superstition most
On young and ignorant natures—as it wont
To haunt the peaceful churchyard of Bedfont!

II.

Each Sabbath morning, at the hour of prayer,
  Behold two maidens, up the quiet green
Shining, far distant, in the summer air
  That flaunts their dewy robes and breathes between
Their downy plumes,—sailing as if they were
  Two far-off ships,—until they brush between
The churchyard's humble walls, and watch and wait
On either side of the wide opened gate.

III.

And there they stand—with haughty necks before
  God's holy house, that points towards the skies—
Frowning reluctant duty from the poor,
  And tempting homage from unthoughtful eyes :
And Youth looks lingering from the temple door,
  Breathing its wishes in unfruitful sighs,
With pouting lips,—forgetful of the grace,
Of health, and smiles, on the heart-conscious face ;

IV.

Because that Wealth, which has no bliss beside,
  May wear the happiness of rich attire ;
And those two sisters, in their silly pride,
  May change the soul's warm glances for the fire
Of lifeless diamonds ;—and for health denied,—
  With art, that blushes at itself, inspire
Their languid cheeks—and flourish in a glory
That has no life in life, nor after-story.

V.

The aged priest goes shaking his grey hair
  In meekest censuring, and turns his eye
Earthward in grief, and heavenward in prayer,
  And sighs, and clasps his hands, and passes by
Good-hearted man ! what sullen soul would wear
  Thy sorrow for a garb, and constantly
Put on thy censure, that might win the praise
Of one so grey in goodness and in days?

VI.

Also the solemn clerk partakes the shame
   Of this ungodly shine of human pride,
And sadly blends his reverence and blame
   In one grave bow, and passes with a stride
Impatient :—many a red-hooded dame
   Turns her pained head, but not her glance, aside
From wanton dress, and marvels o'er again,
That heaven hath no wet judgments for the vain.

VII.

"I have a lily in the bloom at home,"
   Quoth one, "and by the blessed Sabbath day
I'll pluck my lily in its pride, and come
   And read a lesson upon vain array;
And when stiff silks are rustling up, and some
   Give place, I'll shake it in proud eyes and say—
Making my reverence,—'Ladies, an' you please,
King Solomon's not half so fine as these.' "

VIII.

Then her meek partner, who has nearly run
   His earthly course,—"Nay, Goody, let your text
Grow in the garden.   We have only one—
   Who knows that these dim eyes may see the next?
Summer will come again, and summer sun,
   And lilies too,—but I were sorely vext
To mar my garden, and cut short the blow
Of the last lily I may live to grow."

IX.

"The last!" quoth she, "and though the last it were—
   Lo! those two wantons, where they stand so proud
With waving plumes, and jewels in their hair,
   And painted cheeks, like Dagons to be bowed
And curtseyed to!—last Sabbath after prayer,
   I heard the little Tomkins ask aloud
If they were angels—but I made him know
God's bright ones better, with a bitter blow!"

X.

So speaking, they pursue the pebbly walk
    That leads to the white porch the Sunday throng,
Hand-coupled urchins in restrained talk,
    And anxious pedagogue that chastens wrong,
And posied churchwarden with solemn stalk,
    And gold-bedizened beadle flames along,
And gentle peasant clad in buff and green,
Like a meek cowslip in the spring serene;

XI.

And blushing maiden—modestly arrayed
    In spotless white,—still conscious of the glass;
And she, the lonely widow, that hath made
    A sable covenant with grief,—alas!
She veils her tears under the deep, deep shade,
    While the poor kindly-hearted, as they pass,
Bend to unclouded childhood, and caress
Her boy,—so rosy!—and so fatherless!

XII.

Thus, as good Christians ought, they all drew near
    The fair white temple, to the timely call
Of pleasant bells that tremble in the ear.
    Now the last frock, and scarlet hood, and shawl
Fade into dusk, in the dim atmosphere
    Of the low porch, and heaven has won them all,—
Saving those two, that turn aside and pass
In velvet blossom, where all flesh is grass.

XIII.

Ah me! to see their silken manors trailed
    In purple luxuries—with restless gold,—
Flaunting the grass where widowhood has wailed
    In blotted black,—over the heapy mould
Panting wave-wantonly!   They never quailed
    How the warm vanity abused the cold;
Nor saw the solemn faces of the gone
Sadly uplooking through transparent stone:

XIV.

But swept their dwellings with unquiet light,
  Shocking the awful presence of the dead ;
Where gracious natures would their eyes benight,
  Nor wear their being with a lip too red,
Nor move too rudely in the summer bright
  Of sun, but put staid sorrow in their tread,
Meting it into steps, with inward breath,
In very pity to bereaved death.

XV.

Now in the church, time-sobered minds resign
  To solemn prayer, and the loud chaunted hymn,—
With glowing picturings of joys divine
  Painting the mistlight where the roof is dim ;
But youth looks upward to the window shine,
  Warming with rose and purple and the swim
Of gold, as if thought-tinted by the stains
Of gorgeous light through many-coloured panes ;

XVI.

Soiling the virgin snow wherein God hath
  Enrobed his angels,—and with absent eyes
Hearing of Heaven, and its directed path,
  Thoughtful of slippers,—and the glorious skies
Clouding with satin,—till the preacher's wrath
  Consumes his pity, and he glows and cries,
With a deep voice that trembles in its might,
And earnest eyes grown eloquent in light :

XVII.

" O that the vacant eye would learn to look
  On very beauty, and the heart embrace
True loveliness, and from this holy book
  Drink the warm-breathing tenderness and grace
Of love indeed ! O that the young soul took
  Its virgin passion from the glorious face
Of fair religion, and addressed its strife,
To win the riches of eternal life !

XVIII.

" Doth the vain heart love glory that is none,
　　And the poor excellence of vain attire?
O go, and drown your eyes against the sun,
　　The visible ruler of the starry quire,
Till boiling gold in giddy eddies run,
　　Dazzling the brain with orbs of living fire;
And the faint soul down darkens into night,
And dies a burning martyrdom to light.

XIX.

" O go, and gaze—when the low winds of ev'n
　　Breathe hymns, and Nature's many forests nod
Their gold-crowned heads; and the rich blooms of heav'n
　　Sun-ripened give their blushes up to God;
And mountain-rocks and cloudy steeps are riv'n
　　By founts of fire, as smitten by the rod
Of heavenly Moses,—that your thirsty sense
May quench its longings of magnificence!

XX.

" Yet suns shall perish—stars shall fade away—
　　Day into darkness—darkness into death—
Death into silence; the warm light of day,
　　The blooms of summer, the rich glowing breath
Of even—all shall wither and decay,
　　Like the frail furniture of dreams beneath
The touch of morn—or bubbles of rich dyes
That break and vanish in the aching eyes."

XXI.

They hear, soul-blushing, and repentant shed
　　Unwholesome thoughts in wholesome tears, and pour
Their sin to earth,—and with low drooping head
　　Receive the solemn blessing, and implore
Its grace—then soberly with chastened tread,
　　They meekly press towards the gusty door,
With humbled eyes that go to gaze upon
The lowly grass—like him of Babylon.

XXII.

The lowly grass !—O water-constant mind !
   Fast-ebbing holiness !—soon-fading grace
Of serious thought, as if the gushing wind
   Through the low porch had washed it from the face
For ever !   How they lift their eyes to find
   Old vanities.   Pride wins the very place
Of meekness, like a bird, and flutters now
With idle wings on the curl-conscious brow !

XXIII.

And lo ! with eager looks they seek the way
   Of old temptation at the lowly gate ;
To feast on feathers, and on vain array,
   And painted cheeks, and the rich glistering state
Of jewel-sprinkled locks.   But where are they,
   The graceless haughty ones that used to wait
With lofty neck, and nods, and stiffened eye ?
None challenge the old homage bending by.

XXIV.

In vain they look for the ungracious bloom
   Of rich apparel where it glowed before,—
For Vanity has faded all to gloom,
   And lofty Pride has stiffened to the core,
For impious Life to tremble at its doom,—
   Set for a warning token evermore,
Whereon, as now, the giddy and the wise
Shall gaze with lifted hands and wond'ring eyes.

XXV.

The aged priest goes on each Sabbath morn,
   But shakes not sorrow under his grey hair ;
The solemn clerk goes lavendered and shorn,
   Nor stoops his back to the ungodly pair ;
And ancient lips that puckered up in scorn,
   Go smoothly breathing to the house of pray'r ;
And in the garden-plot, from day to day,
The lily blooms its long white life away.

XXVI.

And where two haughty maidens used to be,
    In pride of plume, where plumy Death had trod,
Trailing their gorgeous velvets wantonly,
    Most unmeet pall, over the holy sod;
There, gentle stranger, thou may'st only see
    Two sombre Peacocks.——Age, with sapient nod
Marking the spot, still tarries to declare
How they once lived, and wherefore they are there.

MINOR POEMS.

FAIR INES.

I.

O saw ye not fair Ines?
She's gone into the West,
To dazzle when the sun is down,
And rob the world of rest :
She took our daylight with her,
The smiles that we love best,
With morning blushes on her cheek,
And pearls upon her breast.

II.

O turn again, fair Ines,
Before the fall of night,
For fear the Moon should shine alone,
And stars unrivalled bright ;
And blessed will the lover be
That walks beneath their light,
And breathes the love against thy cheek
I dare not even write !

III.

Would I had been, fair Ines,
That gallant cavalier,
Who rode so gaily by thy side,
And whispered thee so near !
Were there no bonny dames at home,
Or no true lovers here,
That he should cross the seas to win
The dearest of the dear ?

IV.

I saw thee, lovely Ines,
Descend along the shore,
With bands of noble gentlemen,
And banners waved before:
And gentle youth and maidens gay,
And snowy plumes they wore;
It would have been a beauteous dream,—
If it had been no more!

V.

Alas, alas, fair Ines,
She went away with song,
With Music waiting on her steps,
And shoutings of the throng;
But some were sad, and felt no mirth,
But only Music's wrong,
In sounds that sang Farewell, Farewell,
To her you've loved so long.

VI.

Farewell, farewell, fair Ines,
That vessel never bore
So fair a lady on its deck,
Nor danced so light before,—
Alas for pleasure on the sea,
And sorrow on the shore!
The smile that blest one lover's heart
Has broken many more!

THE DEPARTURE OF SUMMER.

SUMMER is gone on swallows' wings,
And Earth has buried all her flowers:
No more the lark, the linnet sings,
But Silence sits in faded bowers.
There is a shadow on the plain
Of Winter ere he comes again,—

There is in woods a solemn sound
Of hollow warnings whispered round,
As Echo in her deep recess
For once had turned a prophetess.
Shuddering Autumn stops to list,
And breathes his fear in sudden sighs,
With clouded face, and hazel eyes
That quench themselves, and hide in mist.

Yes, Summer's gone like pageant bright;
Its glorious days of golden light
Are gone—the mimic suns that quiver,
Then melt in Time's dark-flowing river.
Gone the sweetly-scented breeze
That spoke in music to the trees;
Gone for damp and chilly breath,
As if fresh blown o'er marble seas,
Or newly from the lungs of Death.
Gone its virgin roses' blushes,
Warm as when Aurora rushes
Freshly from the god's embrace,
With all her shame upon her face.
Old Time hath laid them in the mould;
Sure he is blind as well as old,
Whose hand relentless never spares
Young cheeks so beauty-bright as theirs!
Gone are the flame-eyed lovers now
From where so blushing-blest they tarried
Under the hawthorn's blossom-bough,
Gone; for Day and Night are married.
All the light of love is fled:
Alas! that negro breasts should hide
The lips that were so rosy red,
At morning and at even-tide!

Delightful Summer! then adieu
Till thou shalt visit us anew:
But who without regretful sigh
Can say, adieu, and see thee fly?
Not he that e'er hath felt thy power,
His joy expanding like a flower
That cometh after rain and snow,
Looks up at heaven, and learns to glow:

Not he that fled from Babel-strife
To the green Sabbath-land of life,
To dodge dull Care 'mid clustered trees,
And cool his forehead in the breeze,—
Whose spirit, weary-worn perchance,
Shook from its wings a weight of grief,
And perched upon an aspen leaf,
For every breath to make it dance.

Farewell !—on wings of sombre stain,
That blacken in the last blue skies,
Thou fly'st ; but thou wilt come again
On the gay wings of butterflies.
Spring at thy approach will sprout
Her new Corinthian beauties out,
Leaf-woven homes, where twitter-words
Will grow to songs, and eggs to birds ;
Ambitious buds shall swell to flowers,
And April smiles to sunny hours.
Bright days shall be, and gentle nights
Full of soft breath and echo-lights,
As if the god of sun-time kept
His eyes half open while he slept.
Roses shall be where roses were,
Not shadows, but reality ;
As if they never perished there,
But slept in immortality :
Nature shall thrill with new delight,
And Time's relumined river run
Warm as young blood, and dazzling bright,
As if its source were in the sun !

But say, hath Winter then no charms ?
Is there no joy, no gladness warms
His aged heart ? no happy wiles
To cheat the hoary one to smiles ?
Onward he comes—the cruel North
Pours his furious whirlwind forth
Before him—and we breathe the breath
Of famished bears that howl to death.
Onward he comes from rocks that blanch
O'er solid streams that never flow,

His tears all ice, his locks all snow,
Just crept from some huge avalanche—
A thing half-breathing and half-warm,
As if one spark began to glow
Within some statue's marble form,
Or pilgrim stiffened in the storm.
O ! will not Mirth's light arrows fail
To pierce that frozen coat of mail ?
O ! will not Joy but strive in vain
To light up those glazed eyes again ?

No ! take him in, and blaze the oak,
And pour the wine, and warm the ale ;
His sides shall shake to many a joke,
His tongue shall thaw in many a tale,
His eyes grow bright, his heart be gay,
And even his palsy charmed away.
What heeds he then the boisterous shout
Of angry winds that scold without,
Like shrewish wives at tavern door ?
What heeds he then the wild uproar
Of billows bursting on the shore ?
In dashing waves, in howling breeze,
There is a music that can charm him ;
When safe, and sheltered, and at ease,
He hears the storm that cannot harm him.

But hark ! those shouts ! that sudden din
Of little hearts that laugh within.
O ! take him where the youngsters play,
And he will grow as young as they !
They come ! they come ! each blue-eyed Sport,
The Twelfth-Night King and all his court—
'Tis Mirth fresh crowned with mistletoe !
Music with her merry fiddles,
Joy " on light fantastic toe,"
Wit with all his jests and riddles,
Singing and dancing as they go.
And Love, young Love, among the rest,
A welcome—nor unbidden guest.

But still for Summer dost thou grieve ?
Then read our Poets—they shall weave

A garden of green fancies still,
Where thy wish may rove at will.
They have kept for after treats
The essences of summer sweets,
And echoes of its songs that wind
In endless music through the mind:
They have stamped in visible traces
The " thoughts that breathe," in words that shine—
The flights of soul in sunny places—
To greet and company with thine.
These shall wing thee on to flowers—
The past or future, that shall seem
All the brighter in thy dream
For blowing in such desert hours.
The summer never shines so bright
As thought of in a winter's night;
And the sweetest, loveliest rose
Is in the bud before it blows.
The dear one of the lover's heart
Is painted to his longing eyes,
In charms she ne'er can realize—
But when she turns again to part.
Dream thou then, and bind thy brow
With wreath of fancy roses now,
And drink of Summer in the cup
Where the Muse hath mixed it up;
The " dance, and song, and sunburnt mirth,"
With the warm nectar of the earth:
Drink! 'twill glow in every vein,
And thou shalt dream the winter through:
Then waken to the sun again,
And find thy Summer Vision true!

SONG.

FOR MUSIC.

A LAKE and a fairy boat
To sail in the moonlight clear,—
And merrily we would float
From the dragons that watch us here!

Thy gown should be snow-white silk,
And strings of orient pearls,
Like gossamers dipped in milk,
Should twine with thy raven curls!

Red rubies should deck thy hands,
And diamonds should be thy dower—
But Fairies have broke their wands,
And wishing has lost its power!

THE FAREWELL.

FOR A FRENCH AIR.

FARE thee well,
    Gabrielle!
Whilst I join France
With bright cuirass and lance,
    Trumpets swell,
    Gabrielle!
War-horses prance,
And cavaliers advance.

    In the night,
    Ere the fight,
    I'll think of thee!
    And in prayer,
    Lady fair,
    In thy prayer
    Think of me!

    Death may knell,
    Gabrielle!
When my plumes dance
By arquebus or lance,
    Then farewell,
    Gabrielle!
Take my last glance,
Fair maid of France.

ODE.

AUTUMN.

I.

I SAW old Autumn in the misty morn
Stand shadowless like Silence, listening
To silence, for no lonely bird would sing
Into his hollow ear from woods forlorn,
Nor lowly hedge nor solitary thorn ;
Shaking his languid locks all dewy bright
With tangled gossamer that fell by night,
    Pearling his coronet of golden corn.

II.

Where are the songs of Summer ?—With the sun,
Oping the dusky eyelids of the south,
Till shade and silence waken up as one,
And Morning sings with a warm odorous mouth.
Where are the merry birds ?—Away, away,
On panting wings through the inclement skies,
    Lest owls should prey
    Undazzled at noonday,
And tear with horny beak their lustrous eyes.

III.

Where are the blooms of Summer ?—In the west,
Blushing their last to the last sunny hours,
When the mild Eve by sudden Night is prest
Like tearful Proserpine, snatched from her flowers
    To a most gloomy breast.
Where is the pride of Summer,—the green prime,—
The many, many leaves all twinkling ?—Three
    On the mossed elm ; three on the naked lime
Trembling,—and one upon the old oak tree !
    Where is the Dryads' immortality ?
Gone into mournful cypress and dark yew,
Or wearing the long gloomy Winter through
    In the smooth holly's green eternity.

IV.

The squirrel gloats on his accomplished hoard,
The ants have brimmed their garners with ripe grain,
    And honey bees have stored
The sweets of Summer in their luscious cells;
The swallows all have winged across the main;
But here the Autumn melancholy dwells,
And sighs her tearful spells,
Amongst the sunless shadows of the plain.
      Alone, alone,
        Upon a mossy stone,
She sits and reckons up the dead and gone
With the last leaves for a love-rosary,
Whilst all the withered world looks drearily,
Like a dim picture of the drownèd past
In the hushed mind's mysterious far away,
Doubtful what ghostly thing will steal the last
Into that distance, grey upon the grey.

V.

O go and sit with her, and be o'ershaded
Under the languid downfall of her hair:
She wears a coronal of flowers faded
Upon her forehead, and a face of care;
There is enough of withered everywhere
To make her bower,—and enough of gloom;
There is enough of sadness to invite,
If only for the rose that died,—whose doom
Is Beauty's,—she that with the living bloom
Of conscious cheeks most beautifies the light;
There is enough of sorrowing, and quite
Enough of bitter fruits the earth doth bear,—
Enough of chilly droppings for her bowl;
Enough of fear and shadowy despair,
To frame her cloudy prison for the soul!

———◆———

BALLAD.

SPRING it is cheery,
Winter is dreary,
Green leaves hang, but the brown must fly;

When he's forsaken,
Withered and shaken
What can an old man do but die?

Love will not clip him,
Maids will not lip him,
Maud and Marian pass him by;
Youth it is sunny,
Age has no honey,—
What can an old man do but die?

June it was jolly,
O for its folly!
A dancing leg and a laughing eye;
Youth may be silly,
Wisdom is chilly,—
What can an old man do but die?

Friends, they are scanty,
Beggars are plenty,
If he has followers, I know why;
Gold's in his clutches,
(Buying him crutches!)—
What can an old man do but die?

———◆———

HYMN TO THE SUN.

GIVER of glowing light!
Though but a god of other days,
The kings and sages
Of wiser ages
Still live and gladden in thy genial rays!

King of the tuneful lyre,
Still poets' hymns to thee belong;
Though lips are cold
Whereon of old
Thy beams all turned to worshipping and song!

Lord of the dreadful bow,
None triumph now for Python's death :
    But thou dost save
    From hungry grave
The life that hangs upon a summer breath.

Father of rosy day,
No more thy clouds of incense rise ;
    But waking flowers
    At morning hours,
Give out their sweets to meet thee in the skies.

God of the Delphic fane,
No more thou listenest to hymns sublime ;
    But they will leave
    On winds at eve,
A solemn echo to the end of time.

TO A COLD BEAUTY.

I.

LADY, wouldst thou heiress be
    To Winter's cold and cruel part ?
When he sets the rivers free
    Thou dost still lock up thy heart ;
Thou that shouldst outlast the snow,
But in the whiteness of thy brow.

II.

Scorn and cold neglect are made
    For winter gloom and winter wind,
But thou wilt wrong the summer air,
    Breathing it to words unkind,—
Breath which only should belong
To love, to sunlight, and to song.

III.

When the little buds unclose,
　　Red, and white, and pied, and blue,
And that virgin flower, the rose,
　　Opes her heart to hold the dew,
Wilt thou lock thy bosom up
With no jewel in its cup?

IV.

Let not cold December sit
　　Thus in Love's peculiar throne ;
Brooklets are not prisoned now,
　　But crystal frosts are all agone,
And that which hangs upon the spray,
It is no snow, but flower of May !

AUTUMN.

I.

The Autumn skies are flushed with gold,
And fair and bright the rivers run ;
These are but streams of winter cold,
And painted mists that quench the sun.

II.

In secret boughs no sweet birds sing,
In secret boughs no bird can shroud ;
These are but leaves that take to wing,
And wintry winds that pipe so loud.

III.

'Tis not trees' shade, but cloudy glooms
That on the cheerless valleys fall,
The flowers are in their grassy tombs,
And tears of dew are on them all.

RUTH.

SHE stood breast high amid the corn,
Clasped by the golden light of morn,
Like the sweetheart of the sun,
Who many a glowing kiss had won.

On her cheek an autumn flush,
Deeply ripened;—such a blush
In the midst of brown was born,
Like red poppies grown with corn.

Round her eyes her tresses fell,
Which were blackest none could tell,
But long lashes veiled a light,
That had else been all too bright.

And her hat, with shady brim,
Made her tressy forehead dim;
Thus she stood amid the stooks,
Praising God with sweetest looks:

Sure, I said, heav'n did not mean,
Where I reap thou shouldst but glean,
Lay thy sheaf adown and come,
Share my harvest and my home.

THE SEA OF DEATH.

A FRAGMENT.

METHOUGHT I saw
Life swiftly treading over endless space:
And, at her foot-print, but a bygone pace,
The ocean-past, which, with increasing wave,
Swallowed her steps like a pursuing grave.

Sad were my thoughts that anchored silently
On the dead waters of that passionless sea,

Unstirred by any touch of living breath :
Silence hung over it, and drowsy Death,
Like a gorged sea-bird, slept with folded wings
On crowded carcases—sad passive things
That wore the thin grey surface, like a veil
Over the calmness of their features pale.

And there were spring-faced cherubs that did sleep
Like water-lilies on that motionless deep,
How beautiful ! with bright unruffled hair
On sleek unfretted brows, and eyes that were
Buried in marble tombs, a pale eclipse !
And smile-bedimpled cheeks, and pleasant lips,
Meekly apart, as if the soul intense
Spake out in dreams of its own innocence :
And so they lay in loveliness, and kept
The birth-night of their peace, that Life e'en wept
With very envy of their happy fronts ;
For there were neighbour brows scarred by the brunts
Of strife and sorrowing—where Care had set
His crooked autograph, and marred the jet
Of glossy locks, with hollow eyes forlorn,
And lips that curled in bitterness and scorn—
Wretched,—as they had breathed of this world's pain,
And so bequeathed it to the world again
Through the beholder's heart in heavy sighs.

So lay they garmented in torpid light,
Under the pall of a transparent night,
Like solemn apparitions lulled sublime
To everlasting rest,—and with them Time
Slept, as he sleeps upon the silent face
Of a dark dial in a sunless place.

————◆————

BALLAD.

She's up and gone, the graceless Girl !
    And robbed my failing years ;
My blood before was thin and cold
    But now 'tis turned to tears ;

My shadow falls upon my grave,
  So near the brink I stand,
She might have stayed a little yet,
  And led me by the hand !

Aye, call her on the barren moor,
  And call her on the hill,
'Tis nothing but the heron's cry,
  And plover's answer shrill ;
My child is flown on wilder wings,
  Than they have ever spread,
And I may even walk a waste
  That widened when she fled.

Full many a thankless child has been,
  But never one like mine ;
Her meat was served on plates of gold,
  Her drink was rosy wine,
But now she'll share the robin's food,
  And sup the common rill,
Before her feet will turn again
  To meet her father's will !

I REMEMBER, I REMEMBER.

I.

I REMEMBER, I remember,
The house where I was born,
The little window where the sun
Came peeping in at morn ;
He never came a wink too soon,
Nor brought too long a day,
But now I often wish the night
Had borne my breath away !

II.

I remember, I remember,
The roses, red and white,
The vi'lets, and the lily-cups,
Those flowers made of light !

The lilacs where the robin built,
And where my brother set
The laburnum on his birthday,—
The tree is living yet !

III.

I remember, I remember,
Where I was used to swing,
And thought the air must rush as fresh
To swallows on the wing ;
My spirit flew in feathers then,
That is so heavy now,
And summer pools could hardly cool
The fever on my brow !

IV.

I remember, I remember,
The fir trees dark and high ;
I used to think their slender tops
Were close against the sky :
It was a childish ignorance,
But now 'tis little joy
To know I'm farther off from heav'n
Than when I was a boy.

BALLAD.

Sigh on, sad heart, for Love's eclipse,
And Beauty's fairest queen,
Tho' 'tis not for my peasant lips
To soil her name between :
A king might lay his sceptre down,
But I am poor and nought,
The brow should wear a golden crown
That wears her in its thought.

The diamonds glancing in her hair,
Whose sudden beams surprise,
Might bid such humble hopes beware
The glancing of her eyes ;

Yet looking once, I looked too long,
    And if my love is sin,
Death follows on the heels of wrong,
    And kills the crime within.

Her dress seemed wove of lily leaves,
    It was so pure and fine,
O lofty wears, and lowly weaves,
    But hodden grey is mine ;
And homely hose must step apart,
    Where gartered princes stand,
But may he wear my love at heart
    That wins her lily hand !

Alas ! there's far from russet frieze
    To silks and satin gowns,
But I doubt if God made like degrees,
    In courtly hearts and clowns'.
My father wronged a maiden's mirth,
    And brought her cheeks to blame,
And all that's lordly of my birth,
    Is my reproach and shame !

'Tis vain to weep,—'tis vain to sigh,
    'Tis vain this idle speech,
For where her happy pearls do lie,
    My tears may never reach ;
Yet when I'm gone, e'en lofty pride
    May say of what has been,
His love was nobly born and died,
    Tho' all the rest was mean !

My speech is rude,—but speech is weak
    Such love as mine to tell,
Yet had I words, I dare not speak,
    So, lady, fare thee well ;
I will not wish thy better state
    Was one of low degree,
But I must weep that partial fate
    Made such a churl of me.

THE WATER LADY.

ALAS, the moon should ever beam
To show what man should never see !
I saw a maiden on a stream,
And fair was she !

I stayed awhile, to see her throw
Her tresses back, that all beset
The fair horizon of her brow
With clouds of jet.

I stayed a little while to view
Her cheek, that wore in place of red
The bloom of water, tender blue,
Daintily spread.

I stayed to watch, a little space,
Her parted lips if she would sing ;
The waters closed above her face
With many a ring.

And still I stayed a little more,
Alas ! she never comes again ;
I throw my flowers from the shore,
And watch in vain.

I know my life will fade away,
I know that I must vainly pine,
For I am made of mortal clay,
But she's divine !

THE EXILE.

THE swallow with summer
    Will wing o'er the seas,
The wind that I sigh to
    Will visit thy trees,

The ship that it hastens
    Thy ports will contain,
But me—I must never
    See England again !

There's many that weep there,
    But one weeps alone,
For the tears that are falling
    So far from her own ;
So far from thy own, love,
    We know not our pain ;
If death is between us,
    Or only the main.

When the white cloud reclines
    On the verge of the sea,
I fancy the white cliffs,
    And dream upon thee ;
But the cloud spreads its wings
    To the blue heav'n and flies,
We never shall meet, love,
    Except in the skies !

TO AN ABSENTEE.

O'ER hill and dale, and distant sea,
Through all the miles that stretch between,
My thought must fly to rest on thee,
And would though worlds should intervene.

Nay, thou art now so dear, methinks
The farther we are forced apart,
Affection's firm elastic links
But bind the closer round the heart.

For now we sever each from each,
I learn what I have lost in thee ;
Alas ! that nothing less could teach,
How great indeed my love should be !

Farewell! I did not know thy worth,
But thou art gone, and now 'tis prized ;
So angels walked unknown on earth,
But when they flew were recognised !

———◆———

SONG.

I.

THE stars are with the voyager
    Wherever he may sail ;
The moon is constant to her time ;
    The sun will never fail ;
But follow, follow round the world,
    The green earth and the sea ;
So love is with the lover's heart,
    Wherever he may be.

II.

Wherever he may be, the stars
    Must daily lose their light ;
The moon will veil her in the shade ;
    The sun will set at night.
The sun may set, but constant love
    Will shine when he's away ;
So that dull night is never night,
    And day is brighter day.

———◆———

ODE TO THE MOON.

I.

MOTHER of light ! how fairly dost thou go
Over those hoary crests, divinely led !
Art thou that huntress of the silver bow
Fabled of old ? Or rather dost thou tread
Those cloudy summits thence to gaze below,
Like the wild Chamois from her Alpine snow,

Where hunter never climbed,—secure from dread?
How many antique fancies have I read
Of that mild presence! and how many wrought!
      Wondrous and bright,
      Upon the silver light,
Chasing fair figures with the artist, Thought!

II.

What art thou like? Sometimes I see thee ride
A far-bound galley on its perilous way,
Whilst breezy waves toss up their silvery spray;
      Sometimes behold thee glide,
Clustered by all thy family of stars,
Like a lone widow, through the welkin wide,
Whose pallid cheek the midnight sorrow mars;
Sometimes I watch thee on from steep to steep,
Timidly lighted by thy vestal torch,
Till in some Latmian cave I see thee creep,
To catch the young Endymion asleep,—
Leaving thy splendour at the jagged porch!

III.

Oh, thou art beautiful, howe'er it be!
Huntress, or Dian, or whatever named;
And he, the veriest Pagan, that first framed
A silver idol, and ne'er worshipped thee!
It is too late, or thou shouldst have my knee;
Too late now for the old Ephesian vows,
And not divine the crescent on thy brows!
Yet, call thee nothing but the mere mild Moon,
      Behind those chestnut boughs,
Casting their dappled shadows at my feet;
I will be grateful for that simple boon,
In many a thoughtful verse and anthem sweet,
And bless thy dainty face whene'er we meet.

IV.

In nights far gone,—ay, far away and dead,—
Before Care-fretted with a lidless eye,—
I was thy wooer on my little bed,
Letting the early hours of rest go by,

To see thee flood the heaven with milky light,
And feed thy snow-white swans, before I slept;
For thou wert then purveyor of my dreams,—
Thou wert the fairies' armourer, that kept
Their burnished helms, and crowns, and corslets bright,
        Their spears, and glittering mails;
And ever thou didst spill in winding streams
        Sparkles and midnight gleams,
For fishes to new gloss their argent scales!

v.

Why sighs?—why creeping tears?—why claspèd hands?
Is it to count the boy's expended dower?
That fairies since have broke their gifted wands?
That young Delight, like any o'erblown flower,
Gave, one by one, its sweet leaves to the ground?
Why then, fair Moon, for all thou mark'st no hour,
Thou art a sadder dial to old Time
        Than ever I have found
On sunny garden-plot, or mossgrown tower,
Mottoed with stern and melancholy rhyme.

vi.

Why should I grieve for this?—O I must yearn,
Whilst Time, conspirator with Memory,
Keeps his cold ashes in an ancient urn,
Richly embossed with childhood's revelry,
With leaves and clustered fruits, and flowers eterne,—
(Eternal to the world, though not to me,)
Aye, there will those brave sports and blossoms be,
The deathless wreath, and undecayed festoon,
        When I am hearsed within,—
Less than the pallid primrose to the Moon,
That now she watches through a vapour thin.

vii.

So let it be:—Before I lived to sigh,
Thou wert in Avon, and a thousand rills,
Beautiful Orb! and so, whene'er I lie
Trodden, thou wilt be gazing from thy hills.
Blest be thy loving light, where'er it spills,

And blessed thy fair face, O Mother mild!
Still shine, the soul of rivers as they run,
Still lend thy lonely lamp to lovers fond,
And blend their plighted shadows into one:
Still smile at even on the bedded child,
And close his eyelids with thy silver wand!

TO ———.

WELCOME, dear Heart, and a most kind good-morrow;
The day is gloomy, but our looks shall shine:
Flow'rs I have none to give thee, but I borrow
Their sweetness in a verse to speak for thine.

Here are red roses, gathered at thy cheeks,—
The white were all too happy to look white:
For love the rose, for faith the lily speaks;
It withers in false hands, but here 'tis bright!

Dost love sweet Hyacinth? Its scented leaf
Curls manifold,—all love's delights blow double:
'Tis said this flow'ret is inscribed with grief,—
But let that hint of a forgotten trouble.

I plucked the Primrose at night's dewy noon;
Like Hope, it showed its blossoms in the night;
'Twas, like Endymion, watching for the Moon!
And here are Sunflowers, amorous of light!

These golden Buttercups are April's seal,—
The Daisy stars her constellations be:
These grew so lowly, I was forced to kneel,
Therefore I pluck no Daisies but for thee!

Here's Daisies for the morn, Primrose for gloom,
Pansies and Roses for the noontide hours:
A wight once made a dial of their bloom,—
So may thy life be measured out by flow'rs!

19

THE FORSAKEN.

THE dead are in their silent graves,
And the dew is cold above,
And the living weep and sigh,
Over dust that once was love.

Once I only wept the dead,
But now the living cause my pain :
How couldst thou steal me from my tears,
To leave me to my tears again ?

My Mother rests beneath the sod,—
Her rest is calm and very deep ;
I wished that she could see our loves,—
But now I gladden in her sleep.

Last night unbound my raven locks,
The morning saw them turned to grey,
Once they were black and well-beloved,
But thou art changed,—and so are they !

The useless lock I gave thee once,
To gaze upon and think of me,
Was ta'en with smiles,—but this was torn
In sorrow that I send to thee !

AUTUMN.

THE Autumn is old,
The sere leaves are flying ;
He hath gathered up gold,
And now he is dying ;
Old age, begin sighing !

The vintage is ripe,
The harvest is heaping ;
But some that have sowed
Have no riches for reaping ;
Poor wretch, fall a-weeping !

The year's in the wane,
There is nothing adorning,
The night has no eve,
And the day has no morning;
Cold winter gives warning.

The rivers run chill,
The red sun is sinking,
And I am grown old,
And life is fast shrinking;
Here's enow for sad thinking!

ODE TO MELANCHOLY.

COME, let us set our careful breasts,
Like Philomel, against the thorn,
To aggravate the inward grief,
That makes her accents so forlorn;
The world has many cruel points,
Whereby our bosoms have been torn,
And there are dainty themes of grief,
In sadness to outlast the morn,—
True honour's dearth, affection's death,
Neglectful pride, and cankering scorn,
With all the piteous tales that tears
Have watered since the world was born.

The world!—it is a wilderness
Where tears are hung on every tree;
For thus my gloomy phantasy
Makes all things weep with me!
Come let us sit and watch the sky,
And fancy clouds where no clouds be;
Grief is enough to blot the eye,
And make heav'n black with misery.
Why should birds sing such merry notes,
Unless they were more blest than we?
No sorrow ever chokes their throats,
Except sweet nightingale; for she

Was born to pain our hearts the more
With her sad melody.
Why shines the sun, except that he
Makes gloomy nooks for Grief to hide,
And pensive shades for Melancholy,
When all the earth is bright beside?
Let clay wear smiles, and green grass wave,
Mirth shall not win us back again,
Whilst man is made of his own grave,
And fairest clouds but gilded rain!

I saw my mother in her shroud,
Her cheek was cold and very pale;
And ever since I've looked on all
As creatures doomed to fail!
Why do buds ope, except to die?
Ay, let us watch the roses wither,
And think of our loves' cheeks;
And oh, how quickly time doth fly
To bring death's winter hither!
Minutes, hours, days, and weeks,
Months, years, and ages shrink to nought;
An age past is but a thought!

Ay, let us think of Him awhile,
That, with a coffin for a boat,
Rows daily o'er the Stygian moat,
And for our table choose a tomb:
There's dark enough in any skull
To charge with black a raven plume;
And for the saddest funeral thoughts
A winding sheet hath ample room,
Where Death, with his keen-pointed style,
Hath writ the common doom.
How wide the yew tree spreads its gloom,
And o'er the dead lets fall its dew,
As if in tears it wept for them,
The many human families
That sleep around its stem!

How cold the dead have made these stones,
With natural drops kept ever wet!

Lo! here the best, the worst, the world
Doth now remember or forget,
Are in one common ruin hurled,
And love and hate are calmly met;
The loveliest eyes that ever shone,
The fairest hands, and locks of jet.
Is't not enough to vex our souls,
And fill our eyes, that we have set
Our love upon a rose's leaf,
Our hearts upon a violet?
Blue eyes, red cheeks, are frailer yet;
And, sometimes, at their swift decay
Beforehand we must fret:
The roses bud and bloom again;
But love may haunt the grave of love,
And watch the mould in vain.

O clasp me, sweet, whilst thou art mine,
And do not take my tears amiss;
For tears must flow to wash away
A thought that shows so stern as this:
Forgive, if somewhile I forget,
In woe to come, the present bliss.
As frighted Proserpine let fall
Her flowers at the sight of Dis,
Ev'n so the dark and bright will kiss.
The sunniest things throw sternest shade,
And there is even a happiness
That makes the heart afraid!

Now let us with a spell invoke
The full-orbed moon to grieve our eyes;
Not bright, not bright, but, with a cloud
Lapped all about her, let her rise
All pale and dim, as if from rest
The ghost of the late buried sun
Had crept into the skies.
The Moon! she is the source of sighs,
The very face to make us sad;
If but to think in other times
The same calm quiet look she had,

As if the world held nothing base,
Of vile and mean, of fierce and bad ;
The same fair light that shown in streams,
The fairy lamp that charmed the lad ;
For so it is, with spent delights
She taunts men's brains and makes them mad.

All things are touched with Melancholy,
Born of the secret soul's mistrust,
To feel her fair ethereal wings
Weighed down with vile degraded dust ;
Even the bright extremes of joy
Bring on conclusions of disgust,
Like the sweet blossoms of the May,
Whose fragrance ends in must.
O give her, then, her tribute just,
Her sighs and tears, and musings holy !
There is no music in the life
That sounds with idiot laughter solely ;
There's not a string attuned to mirth,
But has its chord in Melancholy.

THE DREAM OF EUGENE ARAM.

'Twas in the prime of summer time,
    An evening calm and cool,
And four-and-twenty happy boys
    Came bounding out of school :
There were some that ran and some that leapt,
    Like troutlets in a pool.

Away they sped with gamesome minds,
    And souls untouched by sin ;
To a level mead they came, and there
    They drave the wickets in :
Pleasantly shown the setting sun
    Over the town of Lynn.

Like sportive deer they coursed about,
    And shouted as they ran,—

Turning to mirth all things of earth,
    As only boyhood can ;
But the Usher sat remote from all,
    A melancholy man !

His hat was off, his vest apart,
    To catch heaven's blessèd breeze ;
For a burning thought was in his brow,
    And his bosom ill at ease :
So he leaned his head on his hands, and read
    The book upon his knees !

Leaf after leaf he turned it o'er,
    Nor ever glanced aside,
For the peace of his soul he read that book
    In the golden eventide :
Much study had made him very lean,
    And pale, and leaden-eyed.

At last he shut the pond'rous tome,
    With a fast and fervent grasp
He strained the dusky covers close,
    And fixed the brazen hasp :
" Oh, God ! could I so close my mind,
    And clasp it with a clasp !"

Then leaping on his feet upright,
    Some moody turns he took,—
Now up the mead, then down the mead,
    And past a shady nook,—
And lo ! he saw a little boy
    That pored upon a book.

" My gentle lad, what is't you read—
    Romance or fairy fable ?
Or is it some historic page,
    Of kings and crowns unstable ?"
The young boy gave an upward glance,—
    " It is ' The Death of Abel.' "

The Usher took six hasty strides,
    As smit with sudden pain,—

Six hasty strides beyond the place,
    Then slowly back again;
And down he sat beside the lad,
    And talked with him of Cain;

And, long since then, of bloody men,
    Whose deeds tradition saves;
Of lonely folk cut off unseen,
    And hid in sudden graves;
Of horrid stabs, in groves forlorn,
    And murders done in caves;

And how the sprites of injured men
    Shriek upward from the sod,—
Ay, how the ghostly hand will point
    To show the burial clod:
And unknown facts of guilty acts
    Are seen in dreams from God!

He told how murderers walk the earth
    Beneath the curse of Cain,—
With crimson clouds before their eyes,
    And flames about their brain:
For blood has left upon their souls
    Its everlasting stain!

"And well," quoth he, "I know for truth,
    Their pangs must be extreme,—
Woe, woe, unutterable woe,—
    Who spill life's sacred stream!
For why? Methought, last night, I wrought
    A murder, in a dream!

"One that had never done me wrong—
    A feeble man and old;
I led him to a lonely field,
    The moon shown clear and cold:
Now here, said I, this man shall die,
    And I will have his gold!

"Two sudden blows with a ragged stick,
    And one with a heavy stone,

One hurried gash with a hasty knife,—
 And then the deed was done:
There was nothing lying at my foot
 But lifeless flesh and bone!

" Nothing but lifeless flesh and bone,
 That could not do me ill;
And yet I feared him all the more,
 For lying there so still:
There was a manhood in his look,
 That murder could not kill!

" And lo! the universal air
 Seemed lit with ghastly flame;
Ten thousand thousand dreadful eyes
 Were looking down in blame:
I took the dead man by his hand,
 And called upon his name!

" Oh God! it made me quake to see
 Such sense within the slain!
But when I touched the lifeless clay,
 The blood gushed out amain!
For every clot, a burning spot
 Was scorching in my brain!

" My head was like an ardent coal,
 My heart as solid ice;
My wretched, wretched soul, I knew,
 Was at the Devil's price:
A dozen times I groaned; the dead
 Had never groaned but twice!

" And now, from forth the frowning sky,
 From the Heaven's topmost height,
I heard a voice—the awful voice
 Of the blood-avenging sprite—
' Thou guilty man! take up thy dead
 And hide it from my sight!'

" I took the dreary body up,
 And cast it in a stream,—

A sluggish water, black as ink,
    The depth was so extreme :
My gentle Boy, remember this
    Is nothing but a dream !

"Down went the corse with a hollow plunge,
    And vanished in the pool ;
Anon I cleansed my bloody hands,
    And washed my forehead cool,
And sat among the urchins young,
    That evening in the school.

"Oh, Heaven ! to think of their white souls,
    And mine so black and grim !
I could not share in childish prayer,
    Nor join in Evening Hymn :
Like a Devil of the Pit I seemed,
    'Mid holy Cherubim !

"And peace went with them, one and all,
    And each calm pillow spread ;
But Guilt was my grim Chamberlain
    That lighted me to bed ;
And drew my midnight curtains round,
    With fingers bloody red !

"All night I lay in agony,
    In anguish dark and deep,
My fevered eyes I dared not close,
    But stared aghast at Sleep :
For Sin had rendered unto her
    The keys of Hell to keep !

"All night I lay in agony,
    From weary chime to chime,
With one besetting horrid hint,
    That racked me all the time ;
A mighty yearning, like the first
    Fierce impulse unto crime !

"One stern tyrannic thought, that made
    All other thoughts its slave ;

Stronger and stronger every pulse
    Did that temptation crave,—
Still urging me to go and see
    The Dead Man in his grave!

" Heavily I rose up, as soon
    As light was in the sky,
And sought the black accursèd pool
    With a wild misgiving eye;
And I saw the Dead in the river bed,
    For the faithless stream was dry.

" Merrily rose the lark, and shook
    The dewdrop from its wing;
But I never marked its morning flight,
    I never heard it sing:
For I was stooping once again
    Under the horrid thing.

"With breathless speed, like a soul in chase,
    I took him up and ran;
There was no time to dig a grave
    Before the day began:
In a lonesome wood, with heaps of leaves,
    I hid the murdered man!

" And all that day I read in school,
    But my thought was otherwhere;
As soon as the midday task was done,
    In secret I was there:
And a mighty wind had swept the leaves,
    And still the corse was bare!

" Then down I cast me on my face,
    And first began to weep,
For I knew my secret then was one
    That earth refused to keep:
Or land or sea, though he should be
    Ten thousand fathoms deep.

" So wills the fierce avenging Sprite,
    Till blood for blood atones!

Ay, though he's buried in a cave,
    And trodden down with stones,
And years have rotted off his flesh,—
    The world shall see his bones!

"Oh God! that horrid, horrid dream
    Besets me now awake!
Again—again, with dizzy brain,
    The human life I take;
And my red right hand grows raging hot,
    Like Cranmer's at the stake.

"And still no peace for the restless clay,
    Will wave or mould allow;
The horrid thing pursues my soul,—
    It stands before me now!"
The fearful Boy looked up, and saw
    Huge drops upon his brow.

That very night, while gentle sleep
    The urchin eyelids kissed,
Two stern-faced men set out from Lynn,
    Through the cold and heavy mist;
And Eugene Aram walked between,
    With gyves upon his wrist.*

BALLAD.

It was not in the winter
    Our loving lot was cast!
It was the time of roses,
    We plucked them as we passed'

---

* Admiral Burney (brother of Madame d'Arblay) went to school at an establishment where the unhappy Eugene Aram was usher subsequent to his crime. The admiral stated that Eugene was generally liked by the boys, and that he used to discourse to them about murder, in somewhat the spirit which is attributed to him in this poem.—*Gem*, 1829.

That churlish season never frowned
   On early lovers yet !
Oh no—the world was newly crowned
   With flowers, when first we met.

'Twas twilight, and I bade you go,
   But still you held me fast ;
It was the time of roses,—
   We plucked them as we passed !

What else could peer my glowing cheek
   That tears began to stud ?
And when I asked the like of Love
   You snatched a damask bud,—

And oped it to the dainty core
   Still glowing to the last :
It was the time of roses,
   We plucked them as we passed !

SONNETS.

SONNET

ON MISTRESS NICELY, A PATTERN FOR HOUSEKEEPERS.

Written after seeing Mrs. Davenport in the character, at Covent Garden.

SHE was a woman peerless in her station,
  With household virtues wedded to her name ;
  Spotless in linen, grass-bleached in her fame,
And pure and clear-starched in her conversation ;
Thence in my Castle of Imagination
  She dwells for evermore, the dainty dame,
  To keep all airy draperies from shame,
And all dream furnitures in preservation :
  There walketh she with keys quite silver bright,
In perfect hose, and shoes of seemly black,
  Apron and stomacher of lily-white,
And decent order follows in her track :
  The burnished plate grows lustrous in her sight,
And polished floors and tables shine her back.

SONNET.

WRITTEN IN A VOLUME OF SHAKSPEARE.

How bravely Autumn paints upon the sky
The gorgeous fame of Summer which is fled !
Hues of all flowers that in their ashes lie,
Trophied in that fair light whereon they fed,
Tulip, and hyacinth, and sweet rose red,—
Like exhalations from the leafy mould,
Look here how honour glorifies the dead,

And warms their scutcheons with a glance of gold !
Such is the memory of poets old,
Who on Parnassus' hill have bloomed elate ;
Now they are laid under their marbles cold,
And turned to clay, whereof they were create :
But God Apollo hath them all enrolled,
And blazoned on the very clouds of fate !

———◆———

SONNET

TO FANCY.

MOST delicate Ariel ! submissive thing,
Won by the mind's high magic to its hest,—
Invisible embassy, or secret guest,—
Weighing the light air on a lighter wing
Whether into the midnight moon, to bring
Illuminate visions to the eye of rest,—
Or rich romances from the florid West,—
Or to the sea, for mystic whispering,—
Still by thy charmed allegiance to the will,
The fruitful wishes prosper in the brain,
As by the fingering of fairy skill,—
Moonlight, and waters, and soft music's strain,
Odours, and blooms, and *my* Miranda's smile,
Making this dull world an enchanted isle.

———◆———

SONNET

TO AN ENTHUSIAST.

YOUNG ardent soul, graced with fair Nature's truth,
Spring warmth of heart, and fervency of mind,
And still a large late love of all thy kind,
Spite of the world's cold practice and Time's tooth,—
For all these gifts, I know not, in fair sooth,
Whether to give thee joy, or bid thee blind
Thine eyes with tears,—that thou hast not resigned
The passionate fire and freshness of thy youth :

For as the current of thy life shall flow,
Gilded by shine of sun or shadow-stained,
Through flow'ry valley or unwholesome fen,
Thrice blessed in thy joy, or in thy woe
Thrice cursed of thy race,—thou art ordained
To share beyond the lot of common men.

SONNET.

It is not death, that sometimes in a sigh
This eloquent breath shall take its speechless flight;
That sometimes these bright stars, that now reply
In sunlight to the sun, shall set in night:
That this warm conscious flesh shall perish quite,
And all life's ruddy springs forget to flow;
That thoughts shall cease, and the immortal sprite
Be lapped in alien clay and laid below;
It is not death to know this,—but to know
That pious thoughts, which visit at new graves
In tender pilgrimage, will cease to go
So duly and so oft,—and when grass waves
Over the past-away, there may be then
No resurrection in the minds of men.

SONNET.

By ev'ry sweet tradition of true hearts,
Graven by Time, in love with his own lore;
By all old martyrdoms and antique smarts,
Wherein Love died to be alive the more;
Yea, by the sad impression on the shore,
Left by the drowned Leander, to endear
That coast for ever, where the billow's roar
Moaneth for pity in the Poet's ear;
By Hero's faith, and the foreboding tear
That quenched her brand's last twinkle in its fall;
By Sappho's leap, and the low rustling fear
That sighed around her flight; I swear by all,
The world shall find such pattern in my act,
As if Love's great examples still were lacked

SONNET

ON RECEIVING A GIFT.

LOOK how the golden ocean shines above
Its pebbly stones, and magnifies their girth;
So does the bright and blessed light of love
Its own things glorify, and raise their worth.
As weeds seem flowers beneath the flattering brine,
And stones like gems, and gems as gems indeed,
Even so our tokens shine; nay, they outshine
Pebbles and pearls, and gems and coral weed;
For where be ocean waves but half so clear,
So calmly constant, and so kindly warm,
As Love's most mild and glowing atmosphere,
That hath no dregs to be upturned by storm?
Thus, sweet, thy gracious gifts are gifts of price,
And more than gold to doting Avarice.

SONNET.

THE curse of Adam, the old curse of all,
Though I inherit in this feverish life
Of worldly toil, vain wishes, and hard strife,
And fruitless thought, in Care's eternal thrall,
Yet more sweet honey than of bitter gall
I taste, through thee, my Eva, my sweet wife.
Then what was Man's lost Paradise!—how rife
Of bliss, since love is with him in his fall!
Such as our own pure passion still might frame,
Of this fair earth, and its delightful bowers,
If no fell sorrow, like the serpent, came
To trail its venom o'er the sweetest flowers;
But oh! as many and such tears are ours,
As only should be shed for guilt and shame!

SONNET.

LOVE,   st lady, such as I would speak,
Lives not   hin the humour of the eye;
Not being   an outward phantasy,
That skims   surface of a tinted cheek,—
Else it would wane with beauty, and grow weak,
As if the rose made summer,—and so lie
Amongst the perishable things that die,
Unlike the love which I would give and seek :
Whose health is of no hue—to feel decay
With cheeks' decay, that have a rosy prime.
Love is its own great loveliness alway,
And takes new lustre from the touch of time;
Its bough owns no December and no May,
But bears its blossom into Winter's clime.

SONNET.

SILENCE.

THERE is a silence where hath been no sound,
  There is a silence where no sound may be,
   In the cold grave—under the deep, deep sea,
Or in wide desert where no life is found,
Which hath been mute, and still must sleep profound ;
  No voice is hushed—no life treads silently,
  But clouds and cloudy shadows wander free,
That never spoke, over the idle ground :
But in green ruins, in the desolate walls
  Of antique palaces, where Man hath been,
Though the dun fox, or wild hyena, calls,
  And owls, that flit continually between,
Shriek to the echo, and the low winds moan,
There the true Silence is, self-conscious and alone.

COMIC POEMS.

A RETROSPECTIVE REVIEW.

OH, when I was a tiny boy
My days and nights were full of joy,
   My mates were blithe and kind!
No wonder that I sometimes sigh,
And dash the teardrop from my eye,
   To cast a look behind!

A hoop was an eternal round
Of pleasure. In those days I found
   A top a joyous thing;
But now those past delights I drop,
My head, alas! is all my top,
   And careful thoughts the string!

My marbles—once my bag was stored,—
Now I must play with Elgin's lord,
   With Theseus for a taw!
My playful horse has slipt his string,
Forgotten all his capering,
   And harnessed to the law!

My kite—how fast and far it flew!
Whilst I, a sort of Franklin, drew
   My pleasure from the sky!
'Twas papered o'er with studious themes,
The tasks I wrote—my present dreams
   Will never soar so high!

My joys are wingless all and dead;
My dumps are made of more than lead;
   My flights soon find a fall;
My fears prevail, my fancies droop,
Joy never cometh with a hoop,
   And seldom with a call!

shelf;

fro;

turned

sk;

My authorship's an endless task,
 My head's ne'er out of school:
My heart is pained with scorn and slight,
I have too many foes to fight,
 And friends grown strangely cool!

The very chum that shared my cake
Holds out so cold a hand to shake,
 It makes me shrink and sigh:
On this I will not dwell and hang,
The changeling would not feel a pang
 Though these should meet his eye!

No skies so blue or so serene
As then;—no leaves look half so green
 As clothed the playground tree!
All things I loved are altered so,
Nor does it ease my heart to know
 That change resides in me!

Oh, for the garb that marked the boy,
The trousers made of corduroy,
 Well inked with black and red;
The crownless hat, ne'er deemed an ill—
It only let the sunshine still
 Repose upon my head!

Oh, for the riband round the neck!
The careless dog's-ears apt to deck
 My book and collar both!
How can this formal man be styled
Merely an Alexandrine child,
 A boy of larger growth?

Oh, for that small, small beer anew !
And (heaven's own type) that mild sky-blue
   That washed my sweet meals down ;
The master even !—and that small Turk
That fagged me !—worse is now my work—
   A fag for all the town !

Oh, for the lessons learned by heart !
Ay, though the very birch's smart
   Should mark those hours again ;
I'd " kiss the rod," and be resigned
Beneath the stroke, and even find
   Some sugar in the cane !

The Arabian Nights rehearsed in bed
The Fairy Tales in school-time read,
   By stealth, 'twixt verb and noun !
The angel form that always walked
In all my dreams, and looked and talked
   Exactly like Miss Brown !

The *omne bene*—Christmas come !
The prize of merit, won for home—
   Merit had prizes then !
But now I write for days and days,
For fame—a deal of empty praise,
   Without the silver pen !

Then home, sweet home ! the crowded coach—
The joyous shout—the loud approach—
   The winding horns like rams' !
The meeting sweet that made me thrill,
The sweetmeats almost sweeter still,
   No " satis" to the "jams !"—

When that I was a tiny boy
My days and nights were full of joy,
   My mates were blithe and kind,—
No wonder that I sometimes sigh,
And dash the teardrop from my eye,
   To cast a look behind !

EPPING HUNT.

ADVERTISEMENT.

STRIDING in the Steps of Strutt—the historian of the old English Sports—the author of the following pages has endeavoured to record a yearly revel, already fast hastening to decay. The Easter Chase will soon be numbered with the pastimes of past times: its dogs will have had their day, and its Deer will be Fallow. A few more seasons, and this City Common Hunt will become uncommon.

In proof of this melancholy decadence, the ensuing epistle is inserted. It was penned by an underling at the Wells, a person more accustomed to riding than writing :—

"Sir,—About the Hunt. In anser to your Innqueries, their as been a great falling off laterally, so much so this year that there was nobody allmost. We did a mear nothing provisionally, hardly a Bottle extra, wich is a proof in Pint. In short our Hunt may be said to be in the last Stag of a decline.

"I am, Sir,
"With respects from your humble Servant,
"BARTHOLOMEW RUTT."

"On Monday they began to hunt."—*Chevy Chase.*

JOHN HUGGINS was as bold a man
　　As trade did ever know,
A warehouse good he had, that stood
　　Hard by the church of Bow.

There people bought Dutch cheeses round,
　　And single Glos'ter flat,—
And English butter in a lump,
　　And Irish—in a *pat.*

Six days a week beheld him stand,
　　His business next his heart,
At *counter* with his apron tied
　　About his *counter-part.*

The seventh in a sluice-house box,
   He took his pipe and pot;
On Sundays for *eel-piety*,
   A very noted spot.

Ah, blest if he had never gone
   Beyond its rural shed!
One Easter-tide, some evil guide
   Put Epping in his head!

Epping for butter justly famed,
   And pork in sausage popt;
Where winter time, or summer time,
   Pig's flesh is always *chopt*.

But famous more, as annals tell,
   Because of Easter Chase;
There ev'ry year, 'twixt dog and deer,
   There is a gallant race.

With Monday's sun John Huggins rose,
   And slapt his leather thigh,
And sang the burthen of the song,
   "This day a stag must die."

For all the livelong day before,
   And all the night in bed,
Like Beckford, he had nourished "Thoughts
   On Hunting" in his head.

Of horn and morn, and hark and bark,
   And echo's answering sounds,
All poets' wit hath every writ
   In *dog*-rel verse of *hounds*.

Alas! there was no warning voice
   To whisper in his ear,
Thou art a fool in leaving *Cheap*
   To go and hunt the *deer!*

No thought he had of twisted spine,
 Or broken arms or legs ;
Not *chicken-hearted* he, altho'
 'Twas whispered of his *eggs !*

Ride out he would, and hunt he would,
 Nor dreamt of ending ill ;
Mayhap with Dr. *Ridout's* fee,
 And Surgeon *Hunter's* bill.

So he drew on his Sunday boots,
 Of lustre superfine ;
The liquid black they wore that day,
 Was *Warren*-ted to shine.

His yellow buckskins fitted close,
 As once upon a stag ;
Thus well equipt he gaily skipt,
 At once, upon his nag.

But first to him that held the rein,
 A crown he nimbly flung ;
For holding of the horse ?—why, no—
 For holding of his tongue.

To say the horse was Huggins' own,
 Would only be a brag ;
His neighbour Fig and he went halves,
 Like Centaurs, in a nag.

And he that day had got the grey,
 Unknown to brother cit ;
The horse he knew would never tell,
 Altho' it was a *tit.*

A well-bred horse he was, I wis,
 As he began to show,
By quickly "rearing up within
 The way he ought to go."

But Huggins, like a wary man,
   Was ne'er from saddle cast ;
Resolved, by going very slow,
   On sitting very fast.

And so he jogged to Tot'n'am Cross
   An ancient town well known,
Where Edward wept for Eleanor
   In mortar and in stone.

A royal game of fox and goose,
   To play on such a loss ;
Wherever she set down her *orts,*
   Thereby he put a *cross.*

Now Huggins had a crony here,
   That lived beside the way ;
One that had promised sure to be
   His comrade for the day.

Whereas the man had changed his mind,
   Meanwhile upon the case !
And meaning not to hunt at all,
   Had gone to Enfield Chase.

For why, his spouse had made him vow
   To let a game alone,
Where folks that ride a bit of blood,
   May break a bit of bone.

" Now, be his wife a plague for life !
   A coward sure is he :"
Then Huggins turned his horse's head
   And crossed the bridge of Lea.

Thence slowly on thro' Laytonstone,
   Past many a Quaker's box,—
No friends to hunters after deer,
   Tho' followers of a *Fox.*

And many a score behind—before—
  The self-same route inclined,
And minded all to march one way,
  Made one great march of mind.

Gentle and simple, he and she,
  And swell, and blood, and prig;
And some had carts, and some a chaise,
  According to their gig.

Some long-eared jacks, some knacker's hacks,
  (However odd it sounds,)
Let out that day *to hunt*, instead
  Of going to the hounds !

And some had horses of their own,
  And some were forced to job it:
And some, while they inclined to *Hunt*,
  Betook themselves to *Cob-it.*

All sorts of vehicles and vans,
  Bad, middling, and the smart;
Here rolled along the gay barouche,
  And there a dirty cart !

And lo ! a cart that held a squad
  Of costermonger line ;
With one poor hack, like Pegasus,
  That slaved for all the Nine !

Yet marvel not at any load,
  That any horse might drag ;
When all, that morn, at once were drawn
  Together by a stag !

Now when they saw John Huggins go
  At such a sober pace ;
" Hallo !" cried they ; " come, trot away,
  You'll never see the chase !"

But John, as grave as any judge,
   Made answers quite as blunt ;
" It will be time enough to trot,
   When I begin to hunt !"

And so he paced to Woodford Wells,
   Where many a horseman met,
And letting go the *reins*, of course,
   Prepared for *heavy wet*.

And lo ! within the crowded door,
   Stood Rounding, jovial elf ;
Here shall the Muse frame no excuse,
   But frame the man himself.

A snow white head, a merry eye,
   A cheek of jolly blush ;
A claret tint laid on by health,
   With Master Reynard's brush ;

A hearty frame, a courteous bow,
   The prince he learned it from ;
His age about threescore and ten,
   And there you have Old Tom.

In merriest key I trow was he,
   So many guests to boast ;
So certain congregations meet,
   And elevate the host.

" Now welcome, lads," quoth he, " and prads,
   You're all in glorious luck :
Old Robin has a run to-day,
   A noted forest buck.

" Fair Mead's the place, where Bob and Tom,
   In red already ride ;
'Tis but a *step*, and on a horse
   You soon may go *a stride*."

So off they scampered, man and horse,
    As time and temper pressed—
But Huggins, hitching on a tree,
    Branched off from all the rest.

Howbeit he tumbled down in time
    To join with Tom and Bob,
All in Fair Mead, which held that day
    Its own fair meed of mob.

Idlers to wit—no Guardians some,
    Of Tattlers in a squeeze;
Ramblers, in heavy carts and vans,
    Spectators, up in trees.

Butchers on backs of butchers' hacks,
    That shambled to and fro!
Bakers intent upon a buck,
    Neglectful of the *dough!*

Change Alley Bears to speculate,
    As usual, for a fall;
And green and scarlet runners, such
    As never climbed a wall!

'Twas strange to think what difference
    A single creature made;
A single stag had caused a whole
    *Stag*nation in their trade.

Now Huggins from his saddle rose,
    And in the stirrups stood;
And lo! a little cart that came
    Hard by a little wood.

In shape like half a hearse,—tho' not
    For corpses in the least;
For this contained the *deer alive,*
    And not the *dear deceased!*

And now began a sudden stir,
    And then a sudden shout,
The prison-doors were opened wide,
    And Robin bounded out!

His antlered head shone blue and red,
    Bedecked with ribbons fine;
Like other bucks that come to 'list
    The hawbucks in the line.

One curious gaze of mild amaze,
    He turned and shortly took:
Then gently ran adown the mead,
    And bounded o'er the brook.

Now Huggins, standing far aloof,
    Had never seen the deer,
Till all at once he saw the beast
    Come charging in his rear.

Away he went, and many a score
    Of riders did the same,
On horse and ass—like high and low
    And Jack pursuing game!

Good Lord! to see the riders now,
    Thrown off with sudden whirl,
A score within the purling brook,
    Enjoyed their " early purl."

A score were sprawling on the grass,
    And beavers fell in showers;
There was another *Floorer* there,
    Beside the Queen of Flowers!

Some lost their stirrups, some their whips,
    Some had no caps to show;
But few, like Charles at Charing Cross,
    Rode on in *Statue* quo.

"O dear! O dear!" now might you hear,
  "I've surely broke a bone;"
"My head is sore,"—with many more
  Such speeches from the *thrown.*

Howbeit their wailings never moved
  The wide Satanic clan,
Who grinned, as once the Devil grinned,
  To see the fall of Man.

And hunters good, that understood,
  Their laughter knew no bounds,
To see the horses "throwing off,"
  So long before the hounds."

For deer must have due course of law,
  Like men the Courts among;
Before those Barristers the dogs
  Proceed to "giving tongue."

But now Old Robin's foes were set,
  That fatal taint to find,
That always is scent after him,
  Yet always left behind.

And here observe how dog and man
  A different temper shows,
What hound resents that he is sent
  To follow his own nose?

Towler and Jowler—howlers all,
  No single tongue was mute;
The stag had led a hart, and lo!
  The whole pack followed suit.

No spur he lacked, fear stuck a knife
  And fork in either haunch;
And every dog he knew had got
  An eye-tooth to his paunch!

Away, away ! he scudded like
    A ship before the gale ;
Now flew to " hills we know not of,"
    Now, nun-like, took the vale.

Another squadron charging now,
    Went off at furious pitch ;—
A perfect Tam o' Shanter mob,
    Without a single witch.

But who was he with flying skirts,
    A hunter did endorse,
And like a poet seemed to ride
    Upon a wingèd horse,—

A whipper in ? no whipper in :
    A huntsman ? no such soul :
A connoisseur, or amateur ?
    Why yes,—a Horse Patrol.

A member of police, for whom
    The county found a nag,
And, like Acteon in the tale,
    He found himself in stag !

Away they went then dog and deer,
    And hunters all away,—
The maddest horses never knew
    Mad staggers such as they !

Some gave a shout, some rolled about,
    And anticked as they rode,
And butchers whistled on their curs,
    And milkmen *tally-hoed !*

About two score there were, not more,
    That galloped in the race ;
The rest, alas ! lay on the grass,
    As once in Chevy Chase !

But even those that galloped on,
    Were fewer every minute,—
The field kept getting more select,
    Each thicket served to thin it.

For some pulled up, and left the hunt,
    Some fell in miry bogs,
And vainly rose and " ran a muck,"
    To overtake the dogs.

And some, in charging hurdle stakes,
    Were left bereft of sense,
What else could be premised of blades
    That never learned to fence?

But Rounding, Tom, and Bob, no gate,
    Nor hedge, nor ditch, could stay ;
O'er all they went, and did the work
    Of leap years in a day.

And by their side see Huggins ride,
    As fast as he could speed ;
For, like Mazeppa, he was quite
    At mercy of his steed.

No means he had, by timely check,
    The gallop to remit,
For firm and fast, between his teeth,
    The biter held the bit.

Trees raced along, all Essex fled
    Beneath him as he sate,—
He never saw a county go
    At such a county rate !

" Hold hard ! hold hard ! you'll lame the dogs :"
    Quoth Huggins, " So I do,—
I've got the saddle well in hand,
    And hold as hard as you !"

Good Lord! to see him ride along,
  And throw his arms about,
As if with stitches in the side,
  That he was drawing out!

And now he bounded up and down,
  Now like a jelly shook:
Till bumped and galled—yet not where **Gall**
  For bumps did ever look!

And rowing with his legs the while,
  As tars are apt to ride;
With every kick he gave a prick,
  Deep in the horse's side!

But soon the horse was well avenged,
  For cruel smart of spurs,
For, riding through a moor, he pitched
  His master in a furze!

Where sharper set than hunger is
  He squatted all forlorn;
And like a bird was singing out
  While sitting on a thorn!

Right glad was he, as well might be,
  Such cushion to resign:
" Possession is nine points," but his
  Seemed more than ninety-nine.

Yet worse than all the prickly points
  That entered in his skin,
His nag was running off the while
  The thorns were running in!

Now had a Papist seen his sport,
  Thus laid upon the shelf,
Altho' no horse he had to cross,
  He might have crossed himself.

Yet surely still the wind is ill
    That none can say is fair ;
A jolly wight there was, that rode
    Upon a sorry mare !

A sorry mare, that surely came
    Of pagan blood and bone ;
For down upon her knees she went,
    To many a stock and stone !

Now seeing Huggins' nag adrift,
    This farmer, shrewd and sage,
Resolved, by changing horses here,
    To hunt another stage !

Tho' felony, yet who would let
    Another's horse alone,
Whose neck is placed in jeopardy
    By riding on his own ?

And yet the conduct of the man
    Seemed honest-like and fair ;
For he seemed willing, horse and all,
    To go before the *mare !*

So up on Huggins' horse he got,
    And swiftly rode away,
While Huggins mounted on the mare
    Done brown upon a bay !

And off they set, in double chase,
    For such was fortune's whim,
The farmer rode to hunt the stag,
    And Huggins hunted him !

Alas ! with one that rode so well
    In vain it was to strive ;
A dab was he, as dabs should be—
    All leaping and alive !

And here of Nature's kindly care
  Behold a curious proof,
As nags are meant to leap, she puts
  A frog in every hoof!

Whereas the mare, altho' her share
  She had of hoof and frog,
On coming to a gate stopped short
  As stiff as any log;

Whilst Huggins in the stirrup stood
  With neck like neck of crane,
As sings the Scottish song—"to see
  The *gate* his *hart* had gane."

And lo! the dim and distant hunt
  Diminished in a trice:
The steeds, like Cinderella's team,
  Seemed dwindling into mice;

And, far remote, each scarlet coat
  Soon flitted like a spark,—
Tho' still the forest murmured back
  An echo of the bark!

But sad at soul John Huggins turned:
  No comfort could he find;
Whilst thus the " Hunting Chorus" sped,
  To stay five bars behind.

For tho' by dint of spur he got
  A leap in spite of fate—
Howbeit there was no toll at all,
  They could not clear the gate.

And, like Fitzjames, he cursed the hunt,
  And sorely cursed the day,
And mused a new Gray's elegy
  On his departed grey!

Now many a sign at Woodford town
   Its Inn-vitation tells :
But Huggins, full of ills, of course
   Betook him to the Wells,

Where Rounding tried to cheer him up
   With many a merry laugh :
But Huggins thought of neighbour Fig,
   And called for half-and-half.

Yet, spite of drink, he could not blink
   Remembrance of his loss ;
To drown a care like his, required
   Enough to drown a horse.

When thus forlorn, a merry horn
   Struck up without the door,—
The mounted mob were all returned ;
   The Epping Hunt was o'er !

And many a horse was taken out
   Of saddle, and of shaft ;
And men, by dint of drink, became
   The only " *beasts of draught.*"

For now begun a harder run
   On wine, and gin, and beer :
And overtaken men discussed
   The overtaken deer.

How far he ran, and eke how fast,
   And how at bay he stood,
Deerlike, resolved to sell his life
   As dearly as he could ;

And how the hunters stood aloof,
   Regardful of their lives,
And shunned a beast, whose very horns
   They knew could *handle* knives !

How Huggins stood when he was rubbed
    By help and ostler kind,
And when they cleaned the clay before,
    How worse " remained behind."

And one, how he had found a horse
    Adrift—a goodly grey !
And kindly rode the nag, for fear
    The nag should go astray.

Now Huggins, when he heard the tale,
    Jumped up with sudden glee ;
" A goodly grey ! why, then, I say
    That grey belongs to me !

" Let me endorse again my horse,
    Delivered safe and sound ;
And, gladly, I will give the man
    A bottle and a pound !"

The wine was drunk,—the money paid,
    Tho' not without remorse,
To pay another man so much,
    For riding on his horse ;

And let the chase again take place
    For many a long, long year—
John Huggins will not ride again
    To hunt the Epping Deer !

MORAL.

Thus pleasure oft eludes our grasp,
    Just when we think to grip her ;
And hunting after happiness,
    We only hunt a slipper.

ADVERTISEMENT TO THE SECOND EDITION OF EPPING HUNT.

The Publisher begs leave to say, that he has had the following letter from the Author of this little book :—

Dear Sir,—I am much gratified to learn from you, that the Epping Hunt has had *such a run*, that it is *quite exhausted*, and that you intend therefore to give the work what may be called "*second wind*," by a new impression.

I attended the last Anniversary of the Festival, and am concerned to say that the sport does not improve, but appears an ebbing as well as Epping custom. The run was miserable indeed ; but what was to be expected? The chase was a Doe, and, consequently, the Hunt set off with the *Hind* part before. It was, therefore, quite in character, for so many Nimrods to start, as they did, before the hounds, but which, as you know, is quite contrary to the *Lex Tallyho-nis*, or Laws of Hunting.

I dined with the Master of the Revel, who is as hale as ever, and promises to reside some time in the *Wells* ere he *kicks the bucket*. He is an honest, hearty, worthy man, and when he dies there will be "a cry of dogs" in his kennel.

I am, dear sir, yours, &c.

T. HOOD.

Winchmore Hill, June, 1830.

———◆———

NUMBER ONE.

VERSIFIED FROM THE PROSE OF A YOUNG LADY.

IT's very hard !—and so it is
To live in such a row,—
And witness this that every Miss
But me, has got a Beau.
For Love goes calling up and down,
But here he seems to shun ;
I am sure he has been asked enough
To call at Number One !

I'm sick of all the double knocks
That come to Number Four !
At Number Three, I often see
A lover at the door ;

And one in blue, at Number Two,
Calls daily like a dun,—
It's very hard they come so near
And not to Number One!

Miss Bell I hear has got a dear
Exactly to her mind,—
By sitting at the window pane
Without a bit of blind;
But I go in the balcony,
Which she has never done,
Yet arts that thrive at Number Five
Don't take at Number One!

'Tis hard with plenty in the street,
And plenty passing by,—
There's nice young men at Number Ten,
But only rather shy;
And Mrs. Smith across the way
Has got a grown-up son,
But la! he hardly seems to know
There is a Number One!

There's Mr. Wick at Number Nine,
But he's intent on pelf,
And though he's pious will not love
His neighbour as himself.
At Number Seven there was a sale—
The goods had quite a run!
And here I've got my single lot
On hand at Number One!

My mother often sits at work
And talks of props and stays,
And what a comfort I shall be
In her declining days:
The very maids about the house
Have set me down a nun,
The sweethearts all belong to them
That call at Number One.

Once only when the flue took fire,
One Friday afternoon,

Young Mr. Long came kindly in
And told me not to swoon :
Why can't he come again without
The Phœnix and the Sun !
We cannot always have a flue
On fire at Number One !

I am not old ! I am not plain !
Nor awkward in my gait—
I am not crooked like the bride
That went from Number Eight :
I'm sure white satin made her look
As brown as any bun—
But even beauty has no chance,
I think, at Number One !

At Number Six they say Miss Rose
Has slain a score of hearts,
And Cupid, for her sake, has been
Quite prodigal of darts.
The Imp they show with bended bow,
I wish he had a gun !
But if he had, he'd never deign
To shoot with Number One !

It's very hard and so it is
To live in such a row !
And here's a ballad singer come
To aggravate my woe :
O take away your foolish song,
And tones enough to stun—
There is " Nae luck about the house,"
I know, at Number One !

THOSE EVENING BELLS.

" I'D BE A PARODY."

THOSE Evening Bells, those Evening Bells,
How many a tale their music tells,

Of Yorkshire cakes and crumpets prime,
And letters only just in time!

The Muffin-boy has passed away,
The Postman gone—and I must pay,
For down below Deaf Mary dwells,
And does not hear those Evening Bells.

And so 'twill be when she is gone,
That tuneful peal will still ring on,
And other maids with timely yells
Forget to stay those Evening Bells.

THE DROWNING DUCKS.

AMONGST the sights that Mrs. Bond
    Enjoyed yet grieved at more than others,
Were little ducklings in a pond,
    Swimming about beside their mothers—
Small things like living water-lilies,
But yellow as the daffo-*dillies*.

"It's very hard," she used to moan,
    "That other people have their ducklings
To grace their waters—mine alone
    Have never any pretty chucklings."
For why!—each little yellow navy
Went down—all downy—to old Davy!

She had a lake—a pond I mean—
    Its wave was rather thick than pearly—
She had two ducks, their napes were green—
    She had a drake, his tail was curly,—
Yet spite of drake, and ducks, and pond,
No little ducks had Mrs. Bond!

The birds were both the best of mothers—
    The nests had eggs—the eggs had luck—
The infant D's came forth like others—
    But there, alas! the matter stuck!
They might as well have all died addle,
As die when they began to paddle!

For when, as native instinct taught her,
    The mother set her brood afloat,
They sank ere long right under water,
    Like any overloaded boat;
They were web-footed too to see,
As ducks and spiders ought to be!

No peccant humour in a gander
    Brought havoc on her little folks,—
No poaching cook—a frying pander
    To appetite,—destroyed their yolks,—
Beneath her very eyes, Od rot 'em!
They went, like plummets, to the bottom.

The thing was strange—a contradiction
    It seemed of nature and her works!
For little ducks, beyond conviction,
    Should float without the help of corks:
Great Johnson it bewildered him!
To hear of ducks that could not swim.

Poor Mrs. Bond! what could she do
    But change the breed—and she tried divers
Which dived as all seemed born to do;
    No little ones were e'er survivors—
Like those that copy gems, I'm thinking,
They all were given to die-sinking!

In vain their downy coats were shorn;
    They floundered still!—Batch after batch went!
The little fools seemed only born
    And hatched for nothing but a hatchment!
Whene'er they launched—O sight of wonder!
Like fires the water "got them under!"

No woman ever gave their lucks
    A better chance than Mrs. Bond did;
At last quite out of heart and ducks,
    She gave her pond up, and desponded;
For Death among the water-lilies,
Cried "*Duc* ad me" to all her dillies!

But though resolved to breed no more,
  She brooded often on this riddle—
Alas ! 'twas darker than before !
  At last about the summer's middle,
What Johnson, Mrs. Bond, or none did,
To clear the matter up the Sun did !

The thirsty Sirius, dog-like drank
  So deep, his furious tongue to cool,
The shallow waters sank and sank,
  And lo, from out the wasted pool,
Too hot to hold them any longer,
There crawled some eels as big as conger !

I wish all folks would look a bit,
  In such a case below the surface ;
But when the eels were caught and split
  By Mrs. Bond, just think of *her* face,
In each inside at once to spy
A duckling turned to giblet-pie !

The sight at once explained the case,
  Making the Dame look rather silly,
The tenants of that *Eely Place*
  Had found the way to *Pick a dilly*,
And so by under-water suction,
Had wrought the little ducks' abduction.

———◆———

A TRUE STORY.

WHOE'ER has seen upon the human face
The yellow jaundice and the jaundice black,
May form a notion of old Colonel Case
With nigger Pompey waiting at his back.

Case,—as the case is many time with folks
From hot Bengal, Calcutta, or Bombay,
Had tint his tint, as Scottish tongues would say,
And showed two cheeks as yellow as eggs' yolks.

Pompey, the chip of some old ebon block,
In hue was like his master's stiff cravat,
And might indeed have claimed akin to *that*,
Coming, as *he* did, of an old *black stock*.

Case wore the liver's livery that such
Must wear, their past excesses to denote,
Like Greenwich pensioners that take too much,
And then do penance in a yellow coat.
Pompey's, a deep and permanent jet dye,
A stain of nature's staining—one of those
We call *fast* colours—merely, I suppose,
Because such colours never *go* or *fly*.

Pray mark this difference of dark and sallow,
Pompey's black husk, and the old Colonel's yellow.

The Colonel, once a penniless beginner,
From a long Indian rubber rose a winner,
With plenty of pagodas in his pocket,
And homeward turning his Hibernian thought,
Deemed *Wicklow* was the very place that ought
To harbour one whose *wick* was in the socket.

Unhappily for Case's scheme of quiet,
Wicklow just then was in a pretty riot,
A fact recorded in each day's diurnals,
Things, Case was not accustomed to peruse,
          Careless of news ;
But Pompey always read those bloody journals,
Full of Killmany and of Killmore work,
The freaks of some O'Shaunessy's shillaly,
Or morning frays by some O'Brien Burke,
Or horrid nightly outrage by some Daly ;
How scums deserving of the Devil's ladle,
Would fall upon the harmless skull and knock it,
And if he found an infant in the cradle
Stern Rock would hardly hesitate to rock it ;
In fact, he read of burner and of killer,
And Irish ravages, day after day,
Till, haunting in his dreams, he used to say,
That " Pompey could not sleep on *Pompey's Pillar*."

Judge then the horror of the nigger's face
To find—with such impressions of that dire land—
That Case, his master,—was a packing case
      For Ireland !
He saw in fearful reveries arise,
Phantasmagorias of those dreadful men
Whose fame associate with Irish plots is,
Fitzgeralds—Tones—O'Connors—Hares—and then
" Those *Emmets*," not so " little in his eyes"
      As Doctor Watts's !
He felt himself piked, roasted,—carved and hacked,
His big black burly body seemed in fact
A pincushion for Terror's pins and needles,—
Oh, how he wished himself beneath the sun
Of Afric—or in far Barbadoes—one
Of Bishop Coleridge's new *black beadles.*

      Full of this fright,
With broken peace and broken English choking,
As black as any raven and as croaking,
Pompey rushed in upon his master's sight,
Plumped on his knees, and clasped his sable digits,
Thus stirring Curiosity's sharp fidgets—
" O Massa !—Massa !—Colonel ! – Massa Case,—
Not go to Ireland !—Ireland dam bad place ;
Dem take our bloods—dem Irish—every drop—
Oh why for Massa go so far a distance
To have him life ?"——Here Pompey made a stop,
Putting an awful period to existence.

" Not go to Ireland—not to Ireland, fellow,
And murdered—why should I be murdered, sirrah ?"
Cried Case, with anger's tinge upon his yellow,—
Pompey, for answer, pointing in a mirror
The Colonel's saffron, and his own japan,—
" Well, what has that to do—quick—speak outright, boy ?"
" O Massa"—(so the explanation ran)
" Massa be killed—'cause Massa *Orange Man*,
And Pompey killed—'cause Pompey not a *White Boy !*"

THE CARELESSE NURSE MAYD.

I SAWE a Mayd sitte on a Bank,
Beguiled by Wooer fayne and fond ;
And whiles His flatterynge Vowes She drank,
Her Nurselynge slipt within a Pond !

All Even Tide they Talkde and Kist,
For She was fayre and He was Kinde ;
The Sunne went down before She wist
Another Sonne had sett behinde !

With angrie Hands and frownynge Browe,
That deemd Her owne the Urchine's Sinne,
She pluckt Him out, but he was nowe
Past being Whipt for fallynge in.

She then beginnes to wayle the Ladde
With Shrikes that Echo answered round—
O ! foolishe Mayd to be soe sadde
The Momente that her Care was drownd !

ODE TO ST. SWITHIN.

" The rain it raineth every day."

THE dawn is overcast, the morning lowers,
On ev'ry window-frame hang beaded damps
Like rows of small illumination lamps
To celebrate the Jubilee of Showers !
A constant sprinkle patters from all leaves,
The very Dryads are not dry, but soppers,
   And from the Houses' eaves
   Tumble eaves-droppers.

The hundred clerks that live along the street,
Bondsmen to mercantile and city schemers,
With squashing, sloshing, and galloshing feet,
Go paddling. paddling, through the wet, like steamers,

Each hurrying to earn the daily stipend—
Umbrellas pass of every shade of green,
And now and then a crimson one is seen,
  Like an umbrella *ripened*.

    Over the way a waggon
Stands with six smoking horses, shrinking, blinking,
  While in the George and Dragon
The man is keeping himself dry—and drinking !
The butcher's boy skulks underneath his tray,
  Hats shine—shoes don't—and down droop collars,
And one blue Parasol cries all the way
  To school, in company with four small scholars !

Unhappy is the man to-day who rides,
Making his journey sloppier, not shorter ;
Ay, there they go, a dozen of outsides,
Performing on " a stage with real water !"
A dripping pauper crawls along the way,
  The only real willing out-of-doorer,
    And says, or seems to say,
" Well, I am poor enough—but here's a *pourer !*"

The scene in water colours thus I paint,
Is your own festival, you Sloppy Saint !
Mother of all the Family of Rainers !
    Saint of the Soakers !
    Making all people croakers,
Like frogs in swampy marshes, and complainers !
And why you mizzle forty days together,
Giving the earth your water-soup to sup,
I marvel—Why such wet, mysterious weather ?
    I wish you'd *clear it up !*

    Why cast such cruel dampers
On pretty Picnics, and against all wishes
Set the cold ducks a-swimming in the hampers,
And volunteer, unasked, to wash the dishes ?
Why drive the Nymphs from the selected spot,
  To cling like ladybirds around a tree—
    Why spoil a Gipsy party at their tea,
By throwing your cold water upon hot ?

Cannot a rural maiden, or a man,
Seek Hornsey Wood by invitation, sipping
   Their green with Pan,
But souse you come, and show their Pan all dripping !
Why upon snow-white tablecloths and sheets,
That do not wait, or want a second washing,
      Come squashing ?
Why task yourself to lay the dust in streets,
As if there were no water-cart contractors,
No potboys spilling beer, no shopboys ruddy
   Spooning out puddles muddy,
Milkmaids, and other slopping benefactors !

A Queen you are, raining in your own right,
Yet, oh ! how little flattered by report !
   Even by those that seek the Court,
Pelted with every term of spleen and spite.
Folks rail and swear at you in every place ;
They say you are a creature of no bowel ;
They say you're always washing Nature's face,
   And that you then supply her,
      With nothing drier,
Than some old wringing cloud by way of towel !
The whole town wants you ducked, just as you duck it,
They wish you on your own mud porridge suppered,
They hope that you may kick your own big bucket,
Or in your water-butt go souse ! heels up'ard !
They are, in short, so weary of your drizzle,
They'd spill the water in your veins to stop it—
Be warned !   You are too partial to a mizzle—
      Pray *drop it !*

———◆———

THE SCHOOLMASTER'S MOTTO.

"The Admiral compelled them all to strike."—*Life of Nelson*.

Hush ! silence in School—not a noise !
You shall soon see there's nothing to jeer at,
Master Marsh, most audacious of boys !
Come !—" Palmam qui meruit ferat !"

So this morn in the midst of the Psalm,
The Miss Siffkins's school you must leer at,
You're complained of—Sir ! hold out your palm—
There !—" Palmam qui meruit ferat !"

You wilful young rebel, and dunce !
This offence all your sins shall appear at,
You shall have a good caning at once—
There !—" Palmam qui meruit ferat !"

You are backward, you know, in each verb,
And your pronouns you are not more clear at,
But you're forward enough to disturb—
There !—" Palmam qui meruit ferat !"

You said Master Twig stole the plums,
When the orchard he never was near at,
I'll not punish wrong fingers or thumbs—
There !—" Palmam qui meruit ferat !"

You make Master Taylor your butt,
And this morning his face you threw beer at,
And you struck him— do *you* like a cut ?
There !—" Palmam qui meruit ferat !"

Little Biddle you likewise distress,
You are always his hair or his ear at—
He's my *Opt*, Sir, and you are my *Pess :*
There !—" Palmam qui meruit ferat !"

Then you had a pitched fight with young Rouse,
An offence I am always severe at !
You discredit to Cicero House !
There !—" Palmam qui meruit ferat !"

You have made too a plot in the night,
To run off from the school that you rear at !
Come, your other hand, now, Sir—the right,
There !—" Palmam qui meruit ferat !"

I'll teach you to draw, you young dog !
Such pictures as I'm looking here at !
" Old Mounseer making soup of a frog,"
There !—" Palmam qui meruit ferat !"

You have run up a bill at a shop,
    That in paying you'll be a whole year at—
You've but twopence a week, Sir, to stop!
    There!—" Palmam qui meruit ferat!"

Then at dinner you're quite cock-a-hoop,
    And the soup you are certain to sneer at—
I have sipped it—it's very good soup—
    There!—" Palmam qui meruit ferat!"

T'other day when I fell o'er the form,
    Was my tumble a thing, Sir, to cheer at?
Well for you that my temper's not warm—
    There!—" Palmam qui meruit ferat!"

Why, you rascal! you insolent brat!
    All my talking you don't shed a tear at,
There—take that, Sir! and that! that! and that!
    There!—" Palmam qui meruit ferat!"

THE SUPPER SUPERSTITION.

A PATHETIC BALLAD.

" Oh flesh, flesh, how art thou fishified!"—SHAKSPEARE.

I.

'TWAS twelve o'clock by Chelsea chimes,
    When all in hungry trim,
Good Mister Jupp sat down to sup
    With wife, and Kate, and Jim.

II.

Said he, " Upon this dainty cod
    How bravely I shall sup"—
When, whiter than the tablecloth,
    A GHOST came rising up!

III.

" O, father dear, O, mother dear,
    Dear Kate, and brother Jim—
You know when some one went to sea—
    Don't cry—but I am him!

IV.

" You hope some day with fond embrace
    To greet your absent Jack,
But oh, I am come here to say
    I'm never coming back !

V.

" From Alexandria we set sail,
    With corn, and oil, and figs,
But steering ' too much Sow,' we struck
    Upon the Sow and Pigs !

VI.

" The ship we pumped till we could see
    Old England from the tops ;
When down she went with all our hands,
    Right in the Channel's Chops.

VII.

" Just give a look in Norey's chart,
    The very place it tells ;
I think it says twelve fathom deep,
    Clay bottom, mixed with shells.

VIII.

" Well, there we are till ' hands aloft,'
    We have at last a call ;
The pug I had for brother Jim,
    Kate's parrot too, and all.

IX.

" But oh, my spirit cannot rest,
    In Davy Jones's sod,
Till I've appeared to you and said—
    Don't sup on that 'ere cod !

X.

" You live on land, and little think
    What passes in the sea ;
Last Sunday week, at 2 P.M.,
    That cod was picking me !

XI.

" Those oysters, too, that look so plump,
    And seem so nicely done,
They put my corpse in many shells,
    Instead of only one.

XII.

" Oh, do not eat those oysters then,
    And do not touch the shrimps ;
When I was in my briny grave,
    They sucked my blood like imps !

XIII.

" Don't eat what brutes would never eat,
    The brutes I used to pat,
They'll know the smell they used to smell,
    Just try the dog and cat !"

XIV.

The spirit fled—they wept his fate,
    And cried, Alack, alack !
At last up started brother Jim,
    " Let's try if Jack was Jack !"

XV.

They called the dog, they called the cat,
    And little kitten too,
And down they put the cod and sauce,
    To see what brutes would do.

XVI.

Old Tray licked all the oysters up,
    Puss never stood at crimps,
But munched the cod—and little kit
    Quite feasted on the shrimps !

XVII.

The thing was odd, and minus cod
    And sauce, they stood like posts ;
Oh, prudent folks, for fear of hoax,
    Put no belief in Ghosts !

A STORM AT HASTINGS,

AND THE LITTLE UNKNOWN.

'TWAS August—Hastings every day was filling—
Hastings, that " greenest spot on memory's waste !"
With crowds of idlers willing or unwilling
To be bedipped—be noticed—or be braced,
And all things rose a penny in a shilling.
Meanwhile, from window and from door, in haste
" Accommodation bills" kept coming down,
Gladding " the world of letters" in that town.

Each day poured in new coachfuls of new cits,
Flying from London smoke and dust annoying,
Unmarried Misses hoping to make hits,
And new-wed couples fresh from Tunbridge toying,
Lacemen and placemen, ministers and wits,
And Quakers of both sexes, much enjoying
A morning's reading by the ocean's rim,
That sect delighting in the sea's broad brim.

And lo ! amongst all these appeared a creature,
So small, he almost might a twin have been
With Miss Crachami—dwarfish quite in stature,
Yet well proportioned—neither fat nor lean,
His face of marvellously pleasant feature,
So short and sweet a man was never seen—
All thought him charming at the first beginning—
Alas, ere long they found him far too winning !

He seemed in love with chance—and chance repaid
His ardent passion with her fondest smile,
The sunshine of good luck, without a shade,
He staked and won—and won and staked—the bile
It stirred of many a man and many a maid,
To see at every venture how that vile
Small gambler snatched—and how he won them too—
A living Pam, omnipotent at loo !

Miss Wiggins set her heart upon a box,
'Twas handsome, rosewood, and inlaid with brass,

And dreamt three times she garnished it with stocks
Of needles, silks, and cottons—but, alas !
She lost it wide awake.　We thought Miss Cox
Was lucky—but she saw three caddies pass
To that small imp ;—no living luck could loo him !
Sir Stamford would have lost his Raffles to him !

And so he climbed—and rode—and won—and walked,
The wondrous topic of the curious swarm
That haunted the Parade.　Many were baulked
Of notoriety by that small form
Pacing it up and down : some even talked
Of ducking him—when lo ! a dismal storm
Stepped in—one Friday, at the close of day—
And every head was turned another way—

Watching the grander guest.　It seemed to rise
Bulky and slow upon the southern brink
Of the horizon—fanned by sultry sighs—
So black and threatening, I cannot think
Of any simile, except the skies
Miss Wiggins sometimes *shades* in Indian ink—
Miss-shapen blotches of such heavy vapour,
They seem a deal more solid than her paper.

As for the sea, it did not fret, and rave,
And tear its waves to tatters, and so dash on
The stony-hearted beach ;—some bards would have
It always rampant, in that idle fashion—
Whereas the waves rolled in, subdued and grave,
Like schoolboys, when the master's in a passion,
Who meekly settle in and take their places,
With a very quiet awe on all their faces.

Some love to draw the ocean with a head,
Like troubled table-beer—and make it bounce,
And froth, and roar, and fling—but this, I've said,
Surged in scarce rougher than a lady's flounce :
But then, a grander contrast thus it bred
With the wild welkin, seeming to pronounce
Something more awful in the serious ear,
As one would whisper that a lion's near—

Who just begins to roar : so the hoarse thunder
Growled long—but low—a prelude note of death,
As if the stifling clouds yet kept it under,
But still it muttered to the sea beneath
Such a continued peal, as made us wonder
It did not pause more oft to take its breath,
Whilst we were panting with the sultry weather,
And hardly cared to wed two words together,

But watched the surly advent of the storm,
Much as the brown-cheeked planters of Barbadoes
Must watch a rising of the Negro swarm :
Meantime it steered, like Odin's old Armadas,
Right on our coast ;—a dismal, coal-black form ;
Many proud gaits were quelled—and all bravadoes
Of folly ceased—and sundry idle jokers
Went home to cover up their tongs and pokers.

So fierce the lightning flashed.   In all their days
The oldest smugglers had not seen such flashing,
And they are used to many a pretty blaze,
To keep their Hollands from an awkward clashing
With hostile cutters in our creeks and bays :
And truly one could think without much lashing
The fancy, that those coasting clouds so awful
And black, were fraught with spirits as unlawful.

The gay Parade grew thin—all the fair crowd
Vanished—as if they knew their own attractions,—
For now the lightning through a near hand cloud
Began to make some very crooked fractions—
Only some few remained that were not cowed,
A few rough sailors, who had been in actions,
And sundry boatmen, that with quick yeo's,
Lest it should *blow*,—were pulling up the *Rose :*

(No flower, but a boat)—some more were hauling
The *Regent* by the head :—another crew
With that same cry peculiar to their *calling*—
Were heaving up the *Hope :*—and as they knew
The very gods themselves oft get a mauling
In their own realms, the seamen wisely drew

The *Neptune* rather higher on the beach,
That he might lie beyond his billows' reach.

And now the storm, with its despotic power,
Had all usurped the azure of the skies,
Making our daylight darker by an hour,
And some few drops—of an unusual size—
Few and distinct—scarce twenty to the shower,
Fell like huge teardrops from a giant's eyes—
But then this sprinkle thickened in a trice
And rained much *harder*—in good solid ice.

Oh! for a very storm of words to show
How this fierce crash of hail came rushing o'er us !
Handel would make the gusty organs blow
Grandly, and a rich storm in music score us :—
But ev'n his music seemed composed and low,
When we were *handled* by this Hailstone Chorus ;
Whilst thunder rumbled, with its awful sound,
And frozen comfits rolled along the ground—

As big as bullets :—Lord ! how they did batter
Our crazy tiles :—and now the lightning flashed
Alternate with the dark, until the latter
Was rarest of the two !—the gust too dashed
So terribly, I thought the hail must shatter
Some panes,—and so it did,—and first it smashed
The very square where I had chose my station
To watch the general illumination.

Another, and another, still came in,
And fell in jingling ruin at my feet,
Making transparent holes that let me win
Some samples of the storm :—Oh ! it was sweet
To think I had a shelter for my skin,
Culling them through these "loopholes of retreat"—
Which in a little we began to glaze—
Chiefly with a jacktowel and some baize !

By which, the cloud had passed o'erhead, but played
Its crooked fires in constant flashes still,
Just in our rear, as though it had arrayed
Its heavy batteries at Fairlight Mill,

So that it lit the town, and grandly made
The rugged features of the Castle Hill
Leap like a birth, from chaos into light,
And then relapse into the gloomy night—

As parcel of the cloud ;—the clouds themselves,
Like monstrous crags and summits everlasting,
Piled each on each in most gigantic shelves,
That Milton's devils were engaged in blasting.
We could e'en fancy Satan and his elves
Busy upon those crags, and ever casting
Huge fragments loose,—and that we *felt* the sound
They made in falling to the startled ground.

And so the tempest scowled away,—and soon
Timidly shining through its skirts of jet,
We saw the rim of the pacific moon,
Like a bright fish entangled in a net,
Flashing its silver sides,—how sweet a boon,
Seemed her sweet light, as though it would beget,
With that fair smile, a calm upon the seas—
Peace in the sky—and coolness in the breeze !

Meantime the hail had ceased :—and all the brood
Of glaziers stole abroad to count their gains ;
At every window there were maids who stood
Lamenting o'er the glass's small remains,—
Or with coarse linens made the fractions good,
Stanching the wind in all the wounded panes,—
Or, holding candles to the panes, in doubt :
The wind resolved—blowing the candles out.

No house was whole that had a southern front,—
No greenhouse but the same mishap befell ;
Bow-windows and *bell*-glasses bore the brunt,—
No sex in glass was spared !——For those who dwell
On each hill-side, you might have swum a punt
In any of their parlours ;—Mrs. Snell
Was slopped out of her seat,—and Mr. Hitchin
Had a *flower*-garden washed into a *Kitchen.*

But still the sea was mild, and quite disclaimed
The recent violence.—Each after each

A STORM AT HASTINGS.

The gentle waves a gentle murmur framed,
Tapping, like woodpeckers, the hollow beach.
Howbeit his *weather eye* the seaman aimed
Across the calm, and hinted by his speech
A gale next morning—and when morning broke,
There was a gale—" quite equal to bespoke."

Before high water—(it were better far
To christen it not *water* then but *waiter*,
For then the tide is *serving at the bar*)
Rose such a swell—I never saw one greater!
Black, jagged billows rearing up in war
Like ragged roaring bears against the baiter,
With lots of froth upon the shingle shed,
Like stout poured out with a fine *beachy head*.

No open boat was open to a fare,
Or launched that morn on seven-shilling trips;
No bathing woman waded—none would dare
A dipping in the wave—but waived their dips;
No seagull ventured on the stormy air,
And all the dreary coast was clear of ships;
For two *lea shores* upon the River Lea
Are not so perilous as one at sea.

Awe-struck we sat, and gazed upon the scene
Before us in such horrid hurly-burly,—
A boiling ocean of mixed black and green,
A sky of copper colour, grim and surly,—
When lo, in that vast hollow scooped between
Two rolling Alps of water,—white and curly!
We saw a pair of little arms a-skimming,
Much like a first or last attempt at swimming!

Sometimes a hand—sometimes a little shoe—
Sometimes a skirt—sometimes a hank of hair
Just like a dabbled seaweed rose to view,
Sometimes a knee, sometimes a back was bare—
At last a frightful summerset he threw
Right on the shingles. Anyone could swear
The lad was dead—without a chance of perjury,
And battered by the surge beyond all surgery!

However we snatched up the corse thus thrown,
Intending, Christian-like, to sod and turf it,
And after venting Pity's sigh and groan,
Then Curiosity began with *her* fit;
And lo ! the features of the Small Unknown !
'Twas he that of the surf had had this surfeit !
And in his fob, the cause of late monopolies,
We found a contract signed with Mephistopheles

A bond of blood, whereby the sinner gave
His forfeit soul to Satan in reversion,
Providing in this world he was to have
A lordship over luck, by whose exertion
He might control the course of cards and brave
All throws of dice,—but on a sea excursion
The juggling demon, in his usual vein,
Seized the last cast—and *Nicked* him in the *main !*

———◆———

LINES

TO A LADY ON HER DEPARTURE FOR INDIA.

Go where the waves run rather Holborn-hilly,
And tempests make a soda-water sea,
Almost as rough as our rough Piccadilly,
        And think of me !

Go where the mild Madeira ripens *her* juice,—
A wine more praised than it deserves to be !
Go pass the Cape, just capable of ver-juice,
        And think of me !

Go where the tiger in the darkness prowleth,
Making a midnight meal of he and she ;
Go where the lion in his hunger howleth,
        And think of me !

Go where the serpent dangerously coileth,
Or lies along at full length like a tree,
Go where the Suttee in her own soot broileth,
        And think of me !

Go where with human notes the parrot dealeth
In mono-*polly*-logue with tongue as free,
And like a woman, all she can revealeth,
    And think of me !

Go to the land of muslin and nankeening,
And parasols of straw where hats should be,
Go to the land of slaves and palankeening,
    And think of me !

Go to the land of jungles and of vast hills,
And tall bamboos—may none *bamboozle* thee !
Go gaze upon their elephants and castles,
    And think of me !

Go where a cook must always be a currier,
And parch the peppered palate like a pea,
Go where the fierce mosquito is a worrier,
    And think of me !

Go where the maiden on a marriage plan goes,
Consigned for wedlock to Calcutta's quay,
Where woman goes for mart, the same as mangoes,
    And think of me !

Go where the sun is very hot and fervent,
Go to the land of pagod and rupee,
Where every black will be your slave and servant,
    And think of me !

TO FANNY.

" Gay being, born to flutter !"—SALE's *Glee.*

Is this your faith, then, Fanny !
  What, to chat with every Dun !
I'm the one, then, but of many,
  Not of many, but the *One !*

Last night you smiled on all, ma'am,
  That appeared in scarlet dress ;
And your Regimental Ball, ma'am,
  Looked a little like a *Mess.*

I thought that of the Sogers
    (As the Scotch say) one might do,
And that I, slight Ensign Rogers,
    Was the chosen man and true.

But 'Sblood ! your eye was busy
    With that ragamuffin mob—
Colonel Buddell—Colonel Dizzy—
    And Lieutenant-Colonel Cobb.

General Joblin, General Jodkin,
    Colonels—Kelly, Felly, with
Majors—Sturgeon, Truffle, Bodkin,
    And the Quarter-master Smith.

Major Powderum—Major Dowdrum—
    Major Chowdrum—Major Bye—
Captain Tawney—Captain Fawney,
    Captain Any-one—but I !

Deuce take it ! when the regiment
    You so praised, I only thought
That you loved it in abridgment,
    But I now am better taught !

I went, as loving man goes,
    To admire thee in quadrilles ;
But Fan, you dance fandangoes
    With just any fop that wills !

I went with notes before us,
    On the lay of Love to touch ;
But with all the corps in chorus,
    Oh ! it is indeed too much !

You once—ere you contracted
    For the army—seemed my own ;
But now you laugh with all the staff,
    And I may sigh alone !

I know not how it chances,
    When my passion ever dares,
But the warmer my advances,
    Then the cooler are your airs.

I am, I don't conceal it,
 But I am a little hurt;
You're a Fan, and I must feel it,
 Fit for nothing but a *Flirt!*

I dreamt thy smiles of beauty
 On myself alone did fall;
But, alas! "Cosi Fan Tutti!"
 It is thus, Fan, thus with all!

You have taken quite a mob in
 Of new military flames;
They would make a fine Round Robin
 If I gave you all their names!

———◆———

THE ANGLER'S FAREWELL.

"Resigned, I kissed the rod."

WELL! I think it is time to put up!
For it does not accord with my notions,
 Wrist, elbow, and chine,
 Stiff from throwing the line,
To take nothing at last by my motions!

I ground-bait my way as I go,
And dip in at each watery dimple;
 But however I wish
 To inveigle the fish,
To my *gentle* they will not play *simple!*

Though my float goes so swimmingly on,
My bad luck never seems to diminish;
 It would seem that the Bream
 Must be scarce in the stream,
And the *Chub*, tho' it's chubby, be *thinnish!*

Not a Trout there can be in the place,
Not a Grayling or Rud worth the mention,
 And although at my hook
 With *attention* I look,
I can ne'er see my hook with *a Tench on!*

At a brandling once Gudgeon would gape,
But they seem upon different terms now;
   Have they taken advice
   Of the " *Council of Nice,*"
And rejected their " *Diet of Worms,*" now?

In vain my live minnow I spin,
Not a Pike seems to think it worth snatching;
   For the gut I have brought,
   I had better have bought
A good *rope* that was used to *Jack-ketching!*

Not a nibble has ruffled my cork,
It is vain in this river to search then;
   I may wait till it's night,
   Without any bite,
And at *roost-time* have never a *Perch* then!

No Roach can I meet with—no Bleak,
Save what in the air is so sharp now;
   Not a Dace have I got,
   And I fear it is not
" Carpe diem," a day for the Carp now!

Oh! there is not a one-pound prize
To be got in this fresh water-lottery!
   What then can I deem
   Of so fishless a stream
But that 'tis—like St. Mary's—*Ottery!*

For an Eel I have learned how to try,
By a method of Walton's own showing—
   But a fisherman feels
   Little prospect of Eels,
In a path that's devoted to towing!

I have tried all the water for miles,
Till I'm weary of dipping and casting,
   And hungry and faint—
   Let the Fancy just paint
What it is, *without Fish*, to be *Fasting!*

And the rain drizzles down very fast,
While my dinner-time sounds from a far bell—
   So, wet to the skin,
   I'll e'en back to my inn,
Where at least I am sure of a *Bar-bell!*

SEA SONG.

AFTER DIBDIN.

PURE water it plays a good part in
The swabbing the decks and all that—
And it finds its own level for sartin—
For it sartinly drinks very flat:
For my part a drop of the creatur
I never could think was a fault,
For if Tars should swig water by natur,
The sea would have never been salt!
Then off with it into a jorum,
And make it strong, sharpish, or sweet,
For if I've any sense of decorum,
It never was meant to be neat!

One day when I was but half sober—
Half measures I always disdain—
I walked into a shop that sold Soda,
And axed for some Water Champagne:
Well, the lubber he drew and he drew, boys,
Till I'd shipped my six bottles or more,
And blow off my last limb but it's true, boys,
Why, I warn't half so drunk as afore!
Then off with it into a jorum,
And make it strong, sharpish, or sweet,
For if I've any sense of decorum,
It never was meant to be neat.

THE KANGAROOS.

A FABLE.

A PAIR of married kangaroos
   (The case is oft a human one too)
Were greatly puzzled once to choose
   A trade to put their eldest son to :
A little brisk and busy chap,
   As all the little K's just then are—
About some two months off the lap,—
   They're not so long in arms as men are.

A twist in each parental muzzle
Betrayed the hardship of the puzzle—
   So much the flavour of life's cup
Is framed by early wrong or right,
And kangaroos we know are quite
   Dependent on their "rearing up."
The question, with its ins and outs,
Was intricate and full of doubts ;
   And yet they had no squeamish carings
For trades unfit or fit for gentry,
Such notion never had an entry,
   For they had no armorial bearings.
Howbeit they're not the last on earth
That might indulge in pride of birth ;
   Whoe'er has seen their infant young
Bob in and out their mother's pokes,
   Would own, with very ready tongue,
They are not born like common folks.
Well, thus the serious subject stood,
   It kept the old pair watchful nightly,
Debating for young hopeful's good,
That he might earn his livelihood,
   And go through life (like them) uprightly.
Arms would not do at all ; no, marry,
In that line all his race miscarry ;
   And agriculture was not proper,
Unless they meant the lad to tarry
   For ever as a mere clod-hopper.

23

He was not well cut out for preaching,
  At least in any striking style :
  And as for being mercantile—
He was not formed for over-reaching.

The law—while there still fate ill-starred him,
And plainly from the bar debarred him :
A doctor—who would ever fee him?
  In music he could scarce engage,
  And as for going on the stage,
In tragic socks I think I see him !

He would not make a rigging-mounter ;
  A haberdasher had some merit,
But there the counter still ran counter,
    For just suppose
    A lady chose
To ask him for a yard of ferret !

A gardener digging up his beds?
The puzzled parents shook their heads.

" A tailor would not do because—"
They paused and glanced upon his paws.
Some parish post,—though fate should place it
Before him, how could he embrace it?
In short, each anxious kangaroo
Discussed the matter through and through ;
By day they seemed to get no nearer,
    'Twas posing quite—
    And in the night
Of course they saw their way no clearer !
At last thus musing on their knees—
Or hinder elbows if you please—
It came—no thought was ever brighter !
In weighing every why and whether,
They jumped upon it both together—
" Let's make the imp a *shorthand writer !*"

MORAL.

I wish all human parents so
  Would argue what their sons are fit for ;
Some would-be critics that I know
  Would be in trades they have more wit for.

ODE

TO THE ADVOCATES FOR THE REMOVAL OF SMITHFIELD MARKET.

" Sweeping our flocks and herds."—*Douglas*.

O PHILANTHROPIC men !
For this address I need not make apology—
Who aim at clearing out the Smithfield pen,
And planting further off its vile Zoology—
 Permit me thus to tell,
 I like your efforts well,
For routing that great nest of Hornithology !

Be not dismayed, although repulsed at first,
And driven from their Horse, and Pig, and Lamparts,
Charge on !—you shall upon their hornworks burst,
And carry all their *Bull*-warks and their *Ram*-parts.

 Go on, ye wholesale drovers !
And drive away the Smithfield flocks and herds !
 As wild as Tartar-Curds,
That come so fat, and kicking, from their clovers ;
Off with them all !—those restive brutes, that vex
Our streets, and plunge, and lunge, and butt, and battle ;
 And save the female sex
From being cowed—like Iö—by the cattle !

 Fancy—when droves appear on
The hill of Holborn, roaring from its top,—
Your ladies—ready, as they own, to drop,
Taking themselves to Thomson's with a *Fear-on !*

 Or, in St. Martin's Lane,
Scared by a bullock, in a frisky vein,—
Fancy the terror of your timid daughters,
 While rushing souse
 Into a coffee-house,
 To find it—Slaughter's !

 Or fancy this :—
Walking along the street, some stranger miss,

Her head with no such thought of danger laden,
When suddenly 'tis " Aries Taurus Virgo !"
You don't know Latin, I translate it ergo,
Into your Areas a Bull throws the Maiden !

Think of some poor old crone
Treated, just like a penny, with a toss !
At that vile spot now grown
So generally known
For making a Cow Cross !

Nay, fancy your own selves far off from stall,
Or shed, or shop—and that an Ox infuriate
Just pins you to the wall,
Giving you a strong dose of *Oxy-Muriate !*

Methinks I hear the neighbours that live round
The Market-ground
Thus make appeal unto their civic fellows—
" 'Tis well for you that live apart—unable
To hear this brutal Babel,
But our *firesides* are troubled with their *bellows.*"

" Folks that too freely sup
Must e'en put up
With their own troubles if they can't digest ;
But we must needs regard
The case as hard
That *others'* victuals should disturb our rest,
That from our sleep *your* food should start and jump us !
We like, ourselves, a steak,
But, sirs, for pity's sake !
We don't want oxen at our doors to *rump-us !*

" If we *do* doze—it really is too bad !
We constantly are roared awake or rung,
Through bullocks mad
That run in all the ' Night Thoughts' of our Young !"

Such are the woes of sleepers—now let's take
The woes of those that wish to keep *a Wake !*

Oh, think! when Wombwell gives his annual feasts,
Think of these " Bulls of Basan," far from mild ones;
    Such fierce tame beasts,
That nobody much cares to see the Wild ones!
Think of the Show woman, " what shows a Dwarf,"
    Seeing a red Cow come
    To swallow her Tom Thumb,
And forced with broom of birch to keep her off!

Think, too, of Messrs. Richardson and Co.,
When looking at their public private boxes,
    To see in a back row
Three live sheeps' heads, a porker's and an Ox's!
Think of their Orchestra, when two horns come
Through, to accompany the double drum!
Or, in the midst of murder and remorses,
    Just when the Ghost is certain,
    A great rent in the curtain,
And enter two tall skeletons—of Horses!

Great Philanthropics! pray urge these topics
Upon the Solemn Council of the Nation,
Get a Bill soon, and give, some noon,
The Bulls, a Bull of Excommunication!
Let the old Fair have fair-play as its right,
    And to each show and sight
Ye shall be treated with a Free List latitude;
    To Richardson's Stage Dramas,
    Dio—and Cosmo—ramas,
    Giants and Indians wild,
    Dwarf, Sea Bear, and Fat Child,
And that most rare of Shows—a Show of Gratitude!

A GOOD DIRECTION.

A CERTAIN gentleman, whose yellow cheek
Proclaimed he had not been in living quite
    An Anchorite—
Indeed, he scarcely ever knew a well day;
At last, by friends' advice, was led to seek
A surgeon of great note—named Aberfeldie.

A very famous Author upon Diet,
Who, better starred than Alchemists of old,
By dint of turning mercury to gold,
Had settled at his country house in quiet.

Our Patient, after some impatient rambles
Thro' Enfield roads, and Enfield lanes of brambles,
At last, to make inquiry had the *nous*,—
      " Here, my good man,
      Just tell me if you can,
Pray which is Mr. Aberfeldie's house?"
The man thus stopped—perusing for awhile
The yellow visage of the man of bile,
At last made answer, with a broadish grin:
" Why, turn to right—and left—and right agin,
The road's direct—you cannot fail to go it."
" But stop—my worthy fellow!—one word more—
From other houses how am I to know it?"

" How!—why, you'll see *blue pillars* at the door!"

CONVEYANCING.

O, LONDON is the place for all,
    In love with loco-motion!
Still to and fro the people go
    Like billows of the ocean;
Machine or man, or caravan,
    Can all be had for paying,
When great estates, or heavy weights,
    Or bodies want conveying.

There's always hacks about in packs,
    Wherein you may be shaken,
And Jarvis is not always *drunk*,
    Tho' always *overtaken;*
In racing tricks he'll never mix,
    His nags are in their last days,
And *slow* to go, altho' they show
    As if they had their *fast days!*

Then if you like a single horse,
  This age is quite a *cab-age*,
A car not quite so small and light
  As those of our queen *Mab* age ;
The horses have been *broken well*,
  All danger is rescinded,
For some have *broken both their knees*,
  And some are *broken winded*.

If you've a friend at Chelsea end,
  The stages are worth knowing—
There is a sort, we call 'em short,
  Although the longest going—
For some will stop at Hatchett's shop,
  Till you grow faint and sicky,
Perched up behind, at last to find,
  Your dinner is all *dickey!*

Long stages run from every yard :
  But if you're wise and frugal,
You'll never go with any Guard
  That plays upon the bugle,
" Ye banks and braes," and other lays,
  And ditties everlasting,
Like miners going all your way,
  With *boring* and with *blasting.*

Instead of *journeys*, people now
  May go upon a *Gurney*,
With steam to do the horses' work,
  By *powers of attorney;*
Tho' with a load it may explode,
  And you may all be *un*-done !
And find you're going *up to heaven*,
  Instead of *up to London!*

To speak of every kind of coach,
  It is not my intention ;
But there is still one vehicle
  Deserves a little mention ;

The world a sage has called a stage,
　With all its living lumber,
And Malthus swears it always bears
　Above the proper number.

The law will transfer house or land
　For ever and a day hence,
For lighter things, watch, brooches, rings,
　You'll never want conveyance;
Ho! stop the thief! my handkerchief!
　It is no sight for laughter—
Away it goes, and leaves my nose
　To join in running after!

EPICUREAN REMINISCENCES OF A SENTIMENALIST.

"My *Tables! Meat* it is, *I set it* down!"—*Hamlet.*

I THINK it was Spring—but not certain I am—
　When my passion began first to work;
But I know we were certainly looking for lamb,
　And the season was over for pork.

'Twas at Christmas, I think, when I met with Miss Chase,
　Yes,—for Morris had asked me to dine,—
And I thought I had never beheld such a face,
　Or so noble a turkey and chine.

Placed close by her side, it made others quite wild,
　With sheer envy to witness my luck;
How she blushed as I gave her some turtle, and smiled
　As I afterwards offered some duck.

I looked and I languished, alas, to my cost,
　Through three courses of dishes and meats;
Getting deeper in love—but my heart was quite lost,
　When it came to the trifle and sweets!

With a rent-roll that told of my houses and land
　　To her parents I told my designs—
And then to herself I presented my hand,
　　With a very fine pottle of pines !

I asked her to have me for weal or for woe,
　　And she did not object in the least ;
I can't tell the date—but we married, I know,
　　Just in time to have game at the feast.

We went to ——, it certainly was the seaside ;
　　For the next, the most blessed of morns,
I remember how fondly I gazed at my bride,
　　Sitting down to a plateful of prawns.

O never may memory lose sight of that year,
　　But still hallow the time as it ought,
That season the " grass" was remarkably dear,
　　And the peas at a guinea a quart.

So happy, like hours, all our days seemed to haste,
　　A fond pair, such as poets have drawn,
So united in heart—so congenial in taste,
　　We were both of us partial to brawn !

A long life I looked for of bliss with my bride,
　　But then Death—I ne'er dreamt about that !
Oh there's nothing certain in life, as I cried,
　　When my turbot eloped with the cat !

My dearest took ill at the turn of the year,
　　But the cause no physician could nab ;
But something it seemed like consumption, I fear,
　　It was just after supping on crab.

In vain she was doctored, in vain she was dosed,
　　Still her strength and her appetite pined ;
She lost relish for what she had relished the most,
　　Even salmon she deeply declined.

For months still I lingered in hope and in doubt,
   While her form it grew wasted and thin ;
But the last dying spark of existence went out,
   As the oysters were just coming in !

She died, and she left me the saddest of men
   To indulge in a widower's moan,
Oh, I felt all the power of solitude then,
   As I ate my first natives alone !

But when I beheld Virtue's friends in their cloaks,
   And with sorrowful crape on their hats,
O my grief poured a flood ! and the out-of-door folks
   Were all crying—I think it was sprats !

I'M NOT A SINGLE MAN.

" Double, single, and the rub."—HOYLE.
" This, this is Solitude."—BYRON.

I.

WELL, I confess, I did not guess
   A simple marriage vow
Would make me find all women-kind
   Such unkind women now !
They need not, sure, as *distant* be
   As Java or Japan,—
Yet every Miss reminds me this—
   I'm not a single man !

II.

Once they made choice of my bass voice
   To share in each duet ;
So well I danced, I somehow chanced
   To stand in every set :
They now declare I cannot sing,
   And dance on Bruin's plan ;
Me draw !—me paint !—me any thing !—
   I'm not a single man !

III.

Once I was asked advice, and tasked
    What works to buy or not,
And "would I read that passage out
    I so admired in Scott?"
They then could bear to hear one read;
    But if I now began,
How they would snub, "My pretty page,"--
    I'm not a single man!

IV.

One used to stitch a collar then,
    Another hemmed a frill;
I had more purses netted then
    Than I could hope to fill.
I once could get a button on,
    But now I never can—
My buttons then were Bachelor's—
    I'm not a single man!

V.

Oh, how they hated politics
    Thrust on me by papa:
But now my chat—they all leave that
    To entertain mamma.
Mamma, who praises her own self,
    Instead of Jane or Ann,
And lays "her girls" upon the shelf—
    I'm not a single man!

VI.

Ah me, how strange it is the change,
    In parlour and in hall,
They treat me so, if I but go
    To make a morning call.
If they had hair in papers once,
    Bolt up the stairs they ran;
They now sit still in dishabille —
    I'm not a single man!

VII.

Miss Mary Bond was once so fond
　　Of Romans and of Greeks ;
She daily sought my cabinet
　　To study my antiques.
Well, now she doesn't care a dump
　　For ancient pot or pan,
Her taste at once is modernized—
　　I'm not a single man !

VIII.

My spouse is fond of homely life,
　　And all that sort of thing ;
I go to balls without my wife,
　　And never wear a ring :
And yet each Miss to whom I come,
　　As strange as Genghis Khan,
Knows by some sign, I can't divine—
　　I'm not a single man !

IX.

Go where I will, I but intrude,
　　I'm left in crowded rooms,
Like Zimmerman on Solitude,
　　Or Hervey at his Tombs.
From head to heel, they make me feel,
　　Of quite another clan ;
Compelled to own though left alone
　　I'm not a single man !

X.

Miss Towne the toast, though she can boast
　　A nose of Roman line,
Will turn up even that in scorn
　　At compliments of mine :
She should have seen that I have been
　　Her sex's partisan,
And really married all I could—
　　I'm not a single man !

XI.

'Tis hard to see how others fare,
  Whilst I rejected stand,—
Will no one take my arm because
  They cannot have my hand?
Miss Parry, that for some would go
  A trip to Hindostan,
With me don't care to mount a stair—
  I'm not a single man!

XII.

Some change, of course, should be in force,
  But, surely, not so much—
There may be hands I may not squeeze,
  But must I never touch?
Must I forbear to hand a chair
  And not pick up a fan?
But I have been myself picked up—
  I'm not a single man!

XIII.

Others may hint a lady's tint
  Is purest red and white—
May say her eyes are like the skies,
  So very blue and bright—
I must not say that she *has eyes*,
  Or if I so began,
I have my fears about my ears—
  I'm not a single man!

XIV.

I must confess I did not guess
  A simple marriage vow,
Would make me find all women-kind
  Such unkind women now;
I might be hashed to death, or smashed,
  By Mr. Pickford's van,
Without, I fear, a single tear—
  I'm not a single man!

THE BURNING OF THE LOVE-LETTER.

"Sometimes they were put to the proof, by what was called the Fiery
Ordeal."—*Hist. Eng.*

No morning ever seemed so long !
I tried to read with all my might !
In my left hand " My Landlord's Tales,"
And threepence ready in my right.

'Twas twelve at last—my heart beat high !
The Postman rattled at the door —
And just upon her road to church,
I dropt the " Bride of Lammermoor ! "

I seized the note—I flew upstairs—
Flung-to the door, and locked me in—
With panting haste I tore the seal—
And kissed the B in Benjamin !

'Twas full of love—to rhyme with dove—
And all that tender sort of thing—
Of sweet and meet—and heart and dart—
But not a word about a ring !

In doubt I cast it in the flame,
And stood to watch the latest spark—
And saw the love all end in smoke—
Without a Parson and a Clerk !

THE SUB-MARINE.

It was a brave and jolly wight,
    His cheek was baked and brown,
For he had been in many climes
    With captains of renown,
And fought with those who fought so well
    At Nile and Camperdown.

His coat it was a soldier coat,
    Of red with yellow faced,
But (merman-like) he looked marine
    All downward from the waist;
His trousers were so wide and blue,
    And quite in sailor taste!

He put the rummer to his lips,
    And drank a jolly draught;
He raised the rummer many times—
    And ever as he quaffed,
The more he drank, the more the Ship
    Seemed pitching fore and aft!

The Ship seemed pitching fore and aft,
    As in a heavy squall;
It gave a lurch and down he went,
    Head-foremost in his fall!
Three times he did not rise, alas!
    He never rose at all!

But down he went, right down at once,
    Like any stone he dived,
He could not see, or hear, or feel—
    Of senses all deprived!
At last he gave a look around
    To see where he arrived!

And all that he could see was green,
    Sea-green on every hand!
And then he tried to sound beneath,
    And all he felt was sand!
There he was fain to lie, for he
    Could neither sit nor stand!

And lo! above his head there bent
    A strange and staring lass!
One hand was in her yellow hair,
    The other held a glass;
A mermaid she must surely be
    If ever mermaid was!

Her fish-like mouth was open wide,
　　Her eyes were blue and pale,
Her dress was of the ocean green,
　　When ruffled by a gale;
Thought he " beneath that petticoat
　　She hides a salmon-tail !"

She looked as siren ought to look,
　　A sharp and bitter shrew,
To sing deceiving lullabies
　　For mariners to rue,—
But when he saw her lips apart,
　　It chilled him through and through !

With either hand he stopped his ears
　　Against her evil cry;
Alas, alas, for all his care,
　　His doom it seemed to die,
Her voice went ringing through his head,
　　It was so sharp and high !

He thrust his fingers further in
　　At each unwilling ear,
But still, in very spite of all,
　· The words were plain and clear;
" I can't stand here the whole day long,
　　To hold your glass of beer !"

With opened mouth and opened eyes,
　　Up rose the Sub-marine,
And gave a stare to find the sands
　　And deeps where he had been :
There was no siren with her glass !
　　No waters ocean-green !

The wet deception from his eyes
　　Kept fading more and more,
He only saw the barmaid stand
　　With pouting lip before—
The small green parlour of The Ship,
　　And little sanded floor !

PAIN IN A PLEASURE BOAT.

A SEA ECLOGUE.

"I apprehend you !"—*School of Reform.*

BOATMAN.

SHOVE off there !—ship the rudder, Bill—cast off ! she's under way !

MRS. F.

She's under what ?—I hope she's not ! good gracious, what a spray !

BOATMAN.

Run out the jib, and rig the boom ! keep clear of those two brigs !

MRS. F.

I hope they don't intend some joke by running of their rigs !

BOATMAN.

Bill, shift them bags of ballast aft—she's rather out of trim !

MRS. F.

Great bags of stones ! they're pretty things to help a boat to swim !

BOATMAN.

The wind is fresh—if she don't scud, it's not the breeze's fault !

MRS. F.

Wind fresh, indeed ! I never felt the air so full of salt !

BOATMAN.

That schooner, Bill, harn't left the roads, with oranges and nuts !

MRS. F.

If seas have roads, they're very rough—I never felt such ruts !

BOATMAN.

It's neap, ye see, she's heavy lade, and couldn't pass the bar.

MRS. F.

The bar ! what, roads with turnpikes too ? I wonder where they are !

24

BOATMAN.

Ho! Brig ahoy! hard up! hard up! that lubber cannot steer!

MRS. F.

Yes, yes—hard up upon a rock! I know some danger's near!
Lord, there's a wave! it's coming in! and roaring like a bull!

BOATMAN.

Nothing, Ma'am, but a little slop! go large, Bill! keep her full!

MRS. F.

What, keep her full! what daring work! when full, she must go
down!

BOATMAN.

Why, Bill, it lulls! ease off a bit—it's coming off the town!
Steady your helm! we'll clear the *Pint!* lay right for yonder pink!

MRS. F.

Be steady—well, I hope they can! but they've got a pint of drink!

BOATMAN.

Bill, give that sheet another haul—she'll fetch it up this reach.

MRS. F.

I'm getting rather pale, I know, and they see it by that speech!
I wonder what it is, now, but——I never felt so queer!

BOATMAN.

Bill, mind your luff—why, Bill, I say, she's yawing—keep her near!

MRS. F.

Keep near! we're going further off; the land's behind our backs.

BOATMAN.

Be easy, Ma'am, it's all correct, that's only 'cause we tacks;
We shall have to beat about a bit—Bill, keep her out to sea.

MRS. F.

Beat who about? keep who at sea?—how black they look at me!

BOATMAN.

It's veering round—I knew it would! off with her head! stand by!

Mrs. F.

Off with her head! who's? where? what with?—an axe I seem
to spy!

Boatman.

She can't keep her own, you see; we shall have to pull her in!

Mrs. F.

They'll drown me, and take all I have! my life's not worth a pin!

Boatman.

Look out you know, be ready, Bill—just when she takes the sand!

Mrs. F.

The sand—O Lord! to stop my mouth! how everything is planned!

Boatman.

The handspike, Bill—quick, bear a hand! now, Ma'am, just step
ashore!

Mrs. F.

What! ain't I going to be killed—and weltered in my gore?
Well, Heaven be praised! but I'll not go a sailing any more!

———◆———

LITERARY AND LITERAL.

The March of Mind upon its mighty stilts,
(A spirit by no means to fasten mocks on,)
In travelling through Berks, Beds, Notts, and Wilts,
    Hants—Bucks, Herts, Oxon,
Got up a thing our ancestors ne'er thought on,
A thing that, only in our proper youth,
We should have chuckled at—in sober truth,
A Conversazione at Hog's Norton!

A place whose native dialect, somehow,
Has always by an adage been affronted,
And that it is all *gutterals*, is now
      Taken for grunted.

Conceive the snoring of a greedy swine,
The slobbering of a hungry Ursine Sloth—
If you have ever heard such creature dine—
And—for Hog's Norton, make a mix of both!

O shades of Shakspeare! Chaucer! Spenser!
    Milton! Pope! Gray! Warton!
O Colman! Kenny! Planché! Poole! Peake!
    Pocock! Reynolds! Morton!
O Grey! Peel! Sadler! Wilberforce! Burdett!
    Hume! Wilmot Horton!
Think of your prose and verse, and worse—delivered in
    Hog's Norton!

The founder of Hog's Norton Athenæum
    Framed her society
    With some variety
From Mr. Roscoe's Liverpool museum;
Not a mere picnic, for the mind's repast,
But, tempting to the solid knife-and-forker,
It held its sessions in the house that last
    Had killed a porker.

It chanced one Friday,
One Farmer Grayley stuck a very big hog,
A perfect Gog or Magog of a pig-hog,
Which made of course a literary high day,——
Not that our Farmer was a man to go
With literary tastes—so far from suiting 'em,
When he heard mention of Professor *Crowe*,
Or Lalla-*Rookh*, he always was for shooting 'em!
In fact in letters he was quite a log,
    With him great Bacon
    Was literally taken,
And Hogg—the Poet—nothing but a Hog!
As to all others on the list of Fame,
Although they were discussed and mentioned daily,
He only recognised one classic name,
And thought that *she* had hung herself—*Miss Baillie!*

To balance this, our Farmer's only daughter
Had a great taste for the Castalian water—

A Wordsworth worshipper—a Southey wooer—
(Though men that deal in water-colour cakes
May disbelieve the fact—yet nothing's truer)
  She got the *bluer*
The more she dipped and dabbled in the *Lakes.*
The secret truth is, Hope, the old deceiver,
At future Authorship was apt to hint,
Producing what some call the *Type-us* Fever,
Which means a burning to be seen in print.

Of learning's laurels—Miss Joanna Baillie—
Of Mrs. Hemans—Mrs. Wilson—daily
Dreamt Anne Priscilla Isabella Grayley;
And Fancy hinting that she had the better
Of L. E. L. by one initial letter,
She thought the world would quite enraptured see

" Love Lays and Lyrics

BY

A. P. I. G."

Accordingly, with very great propriety,
She joined the H. N. B. and double S.,
That is—Hog's Norton Blue Stocking Society;
And saving when her Pa his pigs prohibited,
  Contributed
Her pork and poetry towards the mess,

This feast, we said, one Friday was the case,
When farmer Grayley—from Macbeth to quote—
Screwing his courage to the "sticking place,"
Stuck a large knife into a grunter's throat:—
A kind of murder that the law's rebuke
Seldom condemns by shake of its peruke,
Showing the little sympathy of *big-wigs*
  With *pig-wigs !*

The swine—poor wretch !—with nobody to speak for it,
And beg its life, resolved to have a squeak for it ;
So—like the fabled swan—died singing out,
And, thus, there issued from the farmer's yard
A note that notified without a card,
An invitation to the evening rout.

And when the time came duly,—" at the close of
The day," as Beattie has it, "when the ham—"
Bacon, and pork were ready to dispose of,
And pettitoes and chit'lings too, to cram,—
Walked in the H. N. B. and double S.'s
All in appropriate and swinish dresses,
For lo ! it is a fact, and not a joke,
Although the Muse might fairly jest upon it,
They came—each " Pig-faced Lady," in that bonnet
   We call *a poke.*

The Members all assembled thus, a rare woman
At pork and poetry was chosen *chairwoman ;*
In fact, the bluest of the Blues, Miss Ikey,
Whose whole pronunciation was so piggy,
She always named the authoress of " *Psyche,*"—
   As Mrs. *Tiggey !*
And now arose a question of some moment,—
What author for a lecture was the richer,
Bacon or Hogg ? there were no votes for Beaumont,
   But some for *Flitcher ;*
While others, with a more sagacious reasoning,
   Proposed another work,
   And thought their pork
Would prove more relishing from Thomson's Season-ing!

But, practised in Shaksperian readings daily,—
O ! Miss Macaulay ! Shakspeare at Hog's Norton !—
Miss Anne Priscilla Isabella Grayley
Selected *him* that evening to snort on.
In short, to make our story not a big tale,
   Just fancy her exerting
   Her talents, and converting
The Winter's Tale to something like a pig-tale !
   Her sister auditory,
All sitting round, with grave and learned faces,
   Were very plauditory,
Of course, and clapped her at the proper places ;
Till fanned at once by fortune and the Muse,
She thought herself the blessedest of Blues.
But Happiness, alas ! has blights of ill,
And Pleasure's bubbles in the air explode ;—
There is no travelling through life but still

The ship will meet with breakers on the road !
      With that peculiar voice
Heard only from Hog's Norton throats and noses,
Miss G., with Perdita, was making choice
Of buds and blossoms for her summer posies,
When coming to that line, where Proserpine
Lets fall her flowers from the wain of Dis ;
      Imagine this—
Uprose on his hind legs old Farmer Grayley,
Grunting this question for the club's digestion,
" Do *Dis's Waggon* go from the Ould Bäaley ?"

ODE TO MADAME HENGLER,

FIREWORK-MAKER TO VAUXHALL.

OH, Mrs. Hengler !—Madame,—I beg pardon
Starry Enchantress of the Surrey Garden !
Accept an ode not meant as any scoff—
The Bard were bold indeed at thee to quiz,
Whose squibs are far more popular than his ;
Whose works are much more certain to go off.

Great is thy fame, but not a silent fame ;
With many a bang the public ear it courts ;
And yet thy arrogance we never blame,
But take thy merits from thy own reports.
Thou hast indeed the most indulgent backers,
We make no doubting, misbelieving comments,
Even in thy most bounceable of moments ;
But lend our ears implicit to thy crackers !—
Strange helps to thy applause too are not missing,
      Thy Rockets raise thee,
      And Serpents praise thee,
As none beside are ever praised—by hissing :

      Mistress of Hydropyrics,
Of glittering Pindarics, Sapphics, Lyrics,
Professor of a Fiery Necromancy,
Oddly thou charmest the politer sorts
      With midnight sports,
Partaking very much of *flash* and *fancy !*

What thoughts had shaken all
In olden time at thy nocturnal revels,
Each brimstone ball
They would have deemed an eyeball of the Devil's !
But now thy flaming Meteors cause no fright ;
A modern Hubert to the royal ear,
Might whisper without fear,
" My Lord, they say there were five moons to-night !"
Nor would it raise one superstitious notion
To hear the whole description fairly out :—
" One fixed—which t'other four whirled round about
With wondrous motion."

Such are the very sights
Thou workest, Queen of Fire, on earth and heaven,
Between the hours of midnight and eleven,
Turning our English to Arabian Nights,
With blazing mounts, and founts, and scorching dragons,
Blue stars and white,
And blood-red light,
And dazzling Wheels fit for Enchanters' waggons.
Thrice lucky woman ! doing things that be
With other folks past benefit of parson ;
For burning, no Burn's Justice falls on thee,
Altho' night after night the public see
Thy Vauxhall palaces all end in Arson !

Sure thou wast never born
Like old Sir Hugh, with water in thy head,
Nor lectured night and morn
Of sparks and flames to have an awful dread,
Allowed by a prophetic dam and sire
To play with fire.
O didst thou never, in those days gone by,
Go carrying about—no schoolboy prouder—
Instead of waxen doll a little Guy ;
Or in thy pretty pyrotechnic vein,
Up the parental pigtail lay a train,
To let off all his powder ?

Full of the wildfire of thy youth,
Didst never in plain truth,

Plant whizzing Flowers in thy mother's pots,
Turning the garden into powder plots?
  Or give the cook, to fright her,
Thy paper sausages well stuffed with nitre?
Nay, wert thou never guilty, now, of dropping
A lighted cracker by thy sister's Dear,
  So that she could not hear
  The question he was popping?

Go on, Madame!   Go on—be bright and busy
While hoaxed astronomers look up and stare
From tall observatories, dumb and dizzy,
To see a Squib in Cassiopeia's Chair!
A Serpent wriggling into Charles's Wain!
A Roman Candle lighting the Great Bear!
A Rocket tangled in Diana's train,
And Crackers stuck in Berenice's Hair!

There is a King of Fire—Thou shouldst be Queen!
Methinks a good connexion might come from it;
Couldst thou not make him, in the garden scene,
Set out per Rocket and return per Comet;
  Then give him a hot treat
Of Pyrotechnicals to sit and sup,
Lord! how the world would throng to see him eat,
He swallowing Fire, while thou dost throw it up!

One solitary night—true is the story,
Watching those forms that Fancy will create
Within the bright confusion of the grate,
I saw a dazzling countenance of glory!
  Oh Dei gratias!
  That fiery facias
'Twas thine, Enchantress of the Surrey Grove;
  And ever since that night,
  In dark and bright,
Thy face is *registered* within my *stove!*

Long may that starry brow enjoy its rays,
May no untimely *blow* its doom forestall;
But when old age prepares the friendly pall,
When the last spark of all thy sparks decays,
Then die lamented by good people all,
  Like Goldsmith's *Madam Blaize!*

A REPORT FROM BELOW.

"Blow high, blow low."—*Sea Song.*

As Mister B. and Mistress B.
One night were sitting down to tea,
With toast and muffins hot—
They heard a loud and sudden bounce,
That made the very china flounce;
They could not for a time pronounce
If they were safe or shot—
For Memory brought a deed to match
At Deptford done by night—
Before one eye appeared a Patch
In t'other eye a Blight!

To be belaboured out of life,
Without some small attempt at strife,
Our nature will not grovel;
One impulse moved both man and dame,
He seized the tongs—she did the same,
Leaving the ruffian, if he came,
The poker and the shovel.
Suppose the couple standing so,
When rushing footsteps from below
Made pulses fast and fervent,
And first burst in the frantic cat,
All steaming like a brewer's rat,
And then—as white as my cravat—
Poor Mary May, the servant!

Lord, how the couple's teeth did chatter,
Master and Mistress both flew at her,
"Speak! Fire? or Murder? What's the matter?"
Till Mary getting breath,
Upon her tale began to touch
With rapid tongue, full trotting, such
As if she thought she had too much
To tell before her death:—

"We was both, ma'am, in the wash-house, ma'am, a standing at
  our tubs,
And Mrs. Round was seconding what little things I rubs;

' Mary,' says she to me, ' I say'—and there she stops for coughin',
' That dratted copper flue has took to smokin' very often,
But please the pigs,'—for that's her way of swearing in a passion,
' I'll blow it up, and not be set a coughin' in this fashion !'
Well, down she takes my master's horn—I mean his horn for
    loading,
And empties every grain alive for to set the flue exploding.
' Lawk, Mrs. Round!' says I, and stares, 'that quantum is unproper,
I'm sartin sure it can't not take a pound to sky a copper ;
You'll powder both our heads off, so I tells you, with its puff,'
But she only dried her fingers, and she takes a pinch of snuff.
Well, when the pinch is over—' Teach your grandmother to suck
A powder-horn,' says she—' Well,' says I, ' I wish you luck.'
Them words sets up her back, so with her hands upon her hips,
' Come,' says she, quite in a huff, ' come, keep your tongue inside
    your lips ;
Afore ever you was born, I was well used to things like these ;
I shall put it in the grate, and let it turn up by degrees.'
So in it goes, and bounce—O Lord ! it gives us such a rattle,
I thought we both were canonized, like sogers in a battle !
Up goes the copper like a squib, and us on both our backs,
And bless the tubs, they bundled off, and split all into cracks.
Well, there I fainted dead away, and might have been cut shorter,
But Providence was kind, and brought me to with scalding water.
I first looks round for Mrs. Round, and sees her at a distance,
As stiff as starch, and looked as dead as any thing in existence ;
All scorched and grimed, and more than that, I sees the copper
    slap
Right on her head, for all the world like a percussion copper cap.
Well, I crooks her little fingers, and crumps them well up to-
    gether,
As humanity pints out, and burnt her nostrums with a feather :
But for all as I can do, to restore her to her mortality,
She never gives a sign of a return to sensuality.
Thinks I, well there she lies, as dead as my own late departed
    mother,
Well, she'll wash no more in this world, whatever she does in
    t'other.
So I gives myself to scramble up the linens for a minute,
Lawk, sich a shirt ! thinks I, it's well my master wasn't in it ;
Oh ! I never, never, never, never, never, see a sight so shockin' ;
Here lays a leg, and there a leg—I mean, you know, a stocking—

Bodies all slit and torn to rags, and many a tattered skirt,
And arms burnt off, and sides and backs all scotched and black
    with dirt ;
But as nobody was in 'em—none but—nobody was hurt !
Well, there I am, a-scrambling up the things, all in a lump,
When, mercy on us ! such a groan as makes my heart to jump.
And there she is, a-lying with a crazy sort of eye,
A-staring at the wash-house roof, laid open to the sky ;
Then she beckons with a finger, and so down to her I reaches,
And puts my ear agin her mouth to hear her dying speeches,
For, poor soul ! she has a husband and young orphans, as I knew ;
Well, Ma'am, you wont believe it, but it's Gospel fact and true,
But these words is all she whispered—' Why, where *is* the powder
    blew ?' "

ODE TO M. BRUNEL.*

  " Well said, old mole ! canst work i' the earth so fast ? a worthy pioneer !"
                                    Hamlet.

WELL !—Monsieur Brunel,
  How prospers now thy mighty undertaking,
  To join by a hollow way the Bankside friends
  Of Rotherhithe and Wapping—
    Never be stopping,
  But poking, groping, in the dark keep making
  An archway, underneath the Dabs and Gudgeons,
  For Collier men and pitchy old Curmudgeons,
  To cross the water in inverse proportion,
  Walk under steamboats under the keel's ridge,
  To keep down all extortion,
  And without sculls to diddle London Bridge !
  In a fresh hunt, a new Great Bore to worry,
  Thou didst to earth thy human terriers follow,
  Hopeful at last from Middlesex to Surrey,
    To give us the " View Hollow."
  In short it was thy aim, right north and south,
  To put a pipe into old Thames's mouth ;
  Alas ! half-way thou hadst proceeded, when
  Old Thames, through roof, not water-proof,
  Came, like " a tide in the affairs of men ;"

---

* The architect of the Tunnel under the Thames.

And with a mighty stormy kind of roar,
    Reproachful of thy wrong,
    Burst out in that old song
Of Incledon's, beginning " Cease, rude Bore."
Sad is it, worthy of one's tears,
    Just when one seems the most successful,
To find one's self o'er head and ears
    In difficulties most distressful !
Other great speculations have been nursed,
    Till want of proceeds laid them on a shelf ;
But thy concern was at the worst,
    When it began to *liquidate* itself !
But now Dame Fortune has her false face hidden,
And languishes thy Tunnel—so to paint,
Under a slow incurable complaint,
        Bed-ridden !
Why, when thus Thames—bed-bothered—why repine !
Do try a spare bed at the Serpentine !
Yet let none think thee dazed, or crazed, or stupid ;
    And sunk beneath thy own and Thames's craft ;
Let them not style thee some Mechanic Cupid
    Pining and pouting o'er a broken shaft !
I'll tell thee with thy Tunnel what to do ;
Light up thy boxes, build a bin or two,
The wine does better than such water trades :
    Stick up a sign—the sign of the Bore's Head ;
    I've drawn it ready for thee in black lead,
And make thy cellar subterrane—Thy Shades !

ODE FOR ST. CECILIA'S EVE.

" Look out for squalls."— *The Pilot.*

O COME, dear Barney Isaacs, come,
Punch for one night can spare his drum
    As well as pipes of Pan !
Forget not, Popkins, your bassoon,
Nor, Mister Bray, your horn, as soon
    As you can leave the Van ;
    Blind Billy, bring your violin ;

Miss Crow, you're great in Cherry Ripe!
And Chub, your viol must drop in
Its bass to Soger Tommy's pipe.
　　　Ye butchers, bring your bones;
An organ would not be amiss
If grinding Jim has spouted his,
　　　Lend yours, good Mister Jones.
Do, hurdy-gurdy Jenny—do
Keep sober for an hour or two,
Music's charms to help to paint.
And, Sandy Gray, if you should not
Your bagpipes bring—O tuneful Scot!
　　　Conceive the feelings of the Saint!

Miss Strummel issues an invite,
For music, and turn-out to-night
In honour of Cecilia's session;
But ere you go, one moment stop,
And with all kindness let me drop
A hint to you, and your profession;
Imprimis then: Pray keep within
The bounds to which your skill was born;
　　　Let the one-handed let alone
　　　　　Trombone,
Don't—Rheumatiz! seize the violin,
Or Ashmy snatch the horn!

Don't ever to such rows give birth,
As if you had no end on earth,
Except to "wake the lyre;"
Don't "strike the harp," pray never do,
Till others long to strike it too,
Perpetual harping's apt to tire;
Oh I have heard such flat-and-sharpers,
　　　I've blest the head
　　　Of good King Ned,
For scragging all those old Welsh Harpers!

Pray, never, ere each tuneful doing,
Take a prodigious deal of wooing;
And then sit down to thrum the strain,
As if you'd never rise again—

The least Cecilia-like of things;
Remember that the Saint has wings.
I've known Miss Strummel pause an hour,
Ere she could " Pluck the Fairest Flower."
Yet without hesitation, she
Plunged next into the " Deep, Deep Sea."
When on the keys she *does* begin,
Such awful torments soon you share,
She really seems like Milton's "Sin,"
   Holding the keys of—you know where !

Never tweak people's ears so toughly,
That urchin-like they can't help saying—
" O dear ! O dear—you call this playing,
But oh, it's playing very roughly !"
Oft, in the ecstasy of pain,
I've cursed all instrumental workmen,
Wished Broadwood Thurtelled in a lane,
And Kirke White's fate to every Kirkman—
I really once delighted spied
" Clementi Collard in Cheapside."

Another word—don't be surprised,
Revered and ragged street musicians,
You have been only half-baptized,
And each name proper, or improper,
Is not the value of a copper,
Till it has had the due additions,
        Husky, Rusky,
        Ninny, Tinny,
        Hummel, Bummel,
        Bowsky, Wowsky,
All these are very good selectables ;
But none of your plain pudding-and-tames—
Folks that are called the hardest names
   Are music's most respectables.
      Ev'ry woman, ev'ry man,
      Look as foreign as you can,
      Don't cut your hair, or wash your skin,
      Make ugly faces and begin.

Each dingy Orpheus gravely hears.
And now to show they understand it !

Miss Crow her scrannel throttle clears,
And all the rest prepare to band it.
Each scraper right for concertante,
Rozins the hair of Rozinante :
Then all sound A, if they know which,
That they may join like birds in June ;
Jack Tar alone neglects to tune,
For he's all over concert-pitch.

A little prelude goes before,
Like a knock and ring at music's door,
Each instrument gives in its name ;
            Then sitting in
            They all begin
To play a musical round game.
Scrapenberg, as the eldest hand,
Leads a first fiddle to the band,
        A second follows suit ;
Anon the ace of horns comes plump
On the two fiddles with a trump,
            Puffindorf plays a flute.

This sort of musical revoke,
The grave bassoon begins to smoke
And in rather grumpy kind
Of tone begins to speak its mind ;
The double drum is next to mix,
Playing the Devil on Two Sticks—
            Clamour, clamour,
            Hammer, hammer,
While now and then a pipe is heard,
Insisting to put in a word,
    With all his shrilly best,
So to allow the little minion
Time to deliver his opinion,
        They take a few bars rest.

Well, little pipe begins—with sole
And small voice going thro' the *hole*,
            Beseeching,
            Preaching,
            Squealing,
            Appealing,

Now as high as he can go,
Now in language rather low,
And having done—begins once more,
Verbatim what he said before.
This twiddling, twaddling sets on fire,
All the old instrumental ire,
And fiddles for explosion ripe,
Put out the little squeaker's pipe;
This wakes bass viol—and viol for that,
Seizing on innocent little B flat,
Shakes it like terrier shaking a rat—
 They all seem miching malico!
To judge from a rumble unawares,
The drum has had a pitch downstairs:
   And the trumpet rash,
   By a violent crash,
Seems splitting somebody's calico!
The viol too groans in deep distress,
As if he suddenly grew sick;
And one rapid fiddle sets off express,—
    Hurrying,
    Scurrying,
    Spattering,
    Clattering,
To fetch him a Doctor of Music.
This tumult sets the Haut-boy crying,
Beyond the Piano's pacifying,
    The cymbal
    Gets nimble,
    Triangle
    Must wrangle,
The band is becoming most martial of bands,
   When just in the middle,
   A quakerly fiddle,
Proposes a general shaking of hands!
    Quaking,
    Shaking,
    Quivering,
    Shivering,
Long bow—short bow—each bow drawing:
Some like filing—some like sawing;

At last these agitations cease,
                And they all get
                The flageolet,
To breathe "a piping time of peace."

                Ah, too deceitful charm,
                Like lightning before death,
For Scrapenberg to rest his arm,
                And Puffindorf get breath!
Again without remorse or pity,
They play "The Storming of a City,"
Miss S. herself composed and planned it—
When lo! at this renewed attack,
Up jumps a little man in black,—
"The very Devil cannot stand it!"
                And with that,
                Snatching hat,
                (Not his own,)
                Off is flown,
                Thro' the door,
                In his black,
                To come back,
Never, never, never more!

O Music! praises thou hast had,
    From Dryden and from Pope,
For thy good notes, yet none I hope,
    But I, e'er praised the bad,
Yet are not saint and sinner even?
Miss Strummel on Cecilia's level?
One drew an angel down from heaven!
The other scared away the Devil!

A BLOW-UP.

"Here we go up, up, up."—*The Lay of the First Minstrel.*

NEAR Battle, Mr. Peter Baker
                Was Powder-maker,
Not Alderman Flower's flour,—the white that puffs
And primes and loads heads bald, or grey, or chowder,

Figgins and Higgins, Fippins, Filby, Crowder,—
Not vile apothecary's pounded stuffs,
But something blacker, bloodier, and louder,
   Gunpowder!

This stuff, as people know, is *semper*
Eadem ; very hasty in its temper—
Like Honour that resents the gentlest taps,
Mere semblances of blows, however slight ;
So powder fires, although you only p'rhaps
   Strike light.
To make it, therefore, is a ticklish business,
And sometimes gives both head and heart a dizziness;
For as all human flash and fancy minders,
Frequenting fights and Powder-works well know,
There seldom is a mill without a blow
Sometimes upon the grinders.
But then—the melancholy phrase to soften,
Mr. B.'s mill *transpired* so very often !
And advertised—than all Price Currents louder,
" Fragments look up—there is a rise in Powder,"
So frequently, it caused the neighbours' wonder,—
And certain people had the inhumanity
To lay it all to Mr. Baker's vanity,
That he might have to say—" That was my thunder !"
   One day—so goes the tale,
   Whether, with iron hoof,
   Not sparkle-proof,
Some ninny-hammer struck upon a nail,—
Whether some glowworm of the Guy Faux stamp,
Crept in the building, with Unsafety Lamp—
One day this mill that had by water ground,
Became a sort of windmill and blew round.
With bounce that went in sound as far as Dover, it
Sent half the workmen sprawling to the sky ;
Besides some visitors who gained thereby,
What they had asked—permission " to go over it !"
  Of course it was a very hard and high blow,
  And somewhat differed from what's called a fly-blow.
At Cowes' Regatta, as I once observed,
A pistol-shot made twenty vessels start ;
If such a sound could terrify oak's heart,

Think how this crash the human nerve unnerved.
In fact, it was a very awful thing,—
As people know that have been used to battle,
In springing either mine or mill, you spring
     A precious rattle !
The dunniest heard it—poor old Mr. F.
Doubted for once if he was ever deaf ;
Through Tunbridge town it caused most strange alarms,
    Mr. and Mrs. Fogg,
     Who lived like cat and dog,
Were shocked for once into each other's arms.
Miss M. the milliner—her fright so strong,
Made a great gobble-stitch six inches long ;
The veriest quakers quaked against their wish :
The " Best of Sons" was taken unawares,
And kicked the " Best of Parents" down the stairs :
The steadiest servant dropped the China dish ;
A thousand started, though there was but one
Fated to win, and that was Mister Dunn,
Who struck convulsively, and hooked a fish !

Miss Wiggins, with some grass upon her fork,
Tossed it just like a haymaker at work ;
Her sister not in any better case,
    For, taking wine,
     With nervous Mr. Pyne,
He jerked his glass of Sherry in her face.
    Poor Mistress Davy,
Bobbed off her bran-new turban in the gravy ;
While Mr. Davy at the lower end,
Preparing for a goose a carver's labour,
Darted his two-pronged weapon in his neighbour,
As if for once he meant to help a friend.

The nursemaid telling little " Jack-a-Norey,"
" Bo-peep," and " Blue-cap" at the house's top,
Screamed, and let Master Jeremiah drop
    From a fourth storey !
Nor yet did matters any better go
With cook and housemaid in the realms below ;
As for the laundress, timid Martha Gunning,

Expressing faintness and her fears by fits
And starts,—she came at last but to her wits,
By falling in the ale that John left running.
Grave Mr. Miles, the meekest of mankind,
Struck all at once, deaf, stupid, dumb, and blind,
Sat in his chaise some moments like a corse,
   Then coming to his mind,
   Was shocked to find,
Only a pair of shafts without a horse.
Out scrambled all the Misses from Miss Joy's !
From Prospect House, for urchins small and big,
   Hearing the awful noise,
   Out rushed a flood of boys,
Floating a man in black, without a wig ;
Some carried out one treasure, some another,—
 Some caught their tops and taws up in a hurry,
 Some saved Chambaud, some rescued Lindley Murray,
But little Tiddy carried his big brother !
   Sick of such terrors,
The Tunbridge folks resolved that truth should dwell
No longer secret in a Tunbridge Well,
But to warn Baker of his dangerous errors ;
Accordingly, to bring the point to pass,
They called a meeting of the broken glass,
The shattered chimney-pots, and scattered tiles,
   The damage of each part,
 And packed it in a cart,
Drawn by the horse that ran from Mr. Miles ;
While Dr. Babblethorpe, the worthy Rector,
And Mr. Gammage, cutler to George Rex,
And some few more, whose names would only vex,
Went as a deputation to the Ex-
Powder-proprietor and Mill-director.

Now Mr. Baker's dwelling-house had pleased
Along with mill-materials to roam,
And for a time the deputies were teased,
To find the noisy gentleman at home ;
At last they found him with undamaged skin,
Safe at the Tunbridge Arms—not out—but Inn.
The worthy Rector, with uncommon zeal,
Soon put his spoke in for the common weal—

A grave old gentlemanly kind of Urban,—
The piteous tale of Jeremiah moulded,
        And then unfolded,
By way of climax, Mrs. Davy's turban;
He told how auctioneering Mr. Pidding
    Knocked down a lot without a bidding,—
How Mr. Miles, in fright, had given his mare,
    The whip she wouldn't bear,
At Prospect House, how Dr. Oates, not Titus,
    Danced like Saint Vitus,—
And Mr. Beak, thro' Powder's misbehaving,
    Cut off his nose whilst shaving;
When suddenly, with words that seemed like swearing,
Beyond a Licenser's belief or bearing—
Broke in the stuttering, sputtering Mr. Gammage—
" Who is to pay us, sir"—he argued thus,
" For loss of cus-cus-cus-cus-cus-cus-cus—
Cus-custom, and the dam-dam-dam-dam-damage ?"

Now many a person had been fairly puzzled
By such assailants, and completely muzzled;
Baker, however, was not dashed with ease—
But proved he practised after their own system,
And with small ceremony soon dismissed 'em,
Putting these words into their ears like fleas :
" If I do have a blow, well, where's the oddity?
I merely do as other tradesmen do,
        You, sir,—and you—and you !
I'm only puffing off my own commodity !"

--------◆--------

SYMPTOMS OF OSSIFICATION.

" An indifference to tears, and blood, and human suffering, that could only belong to a *Boney-parte.*"—*Life of Napoleon.*

        TIME was, I always had a drop
        For any tale or sigh of sorrow;
        My handkerchief I used to sop
        Till often I was forced to borrow;

I don't know how it is, but now
My eyelids seldom want a drying;
The doctors, p'rhaps, could tell me how—
I fear my heart is ossifying!

O'er Goethe I used to weep,
With turnip cheeks and nose of scarlet,
When Werter put himself to sleep
With pistols kissed and cleaned by Charlotte;
Self-murder is an awful sin,
No joke there is in bullets flying,
But now at such a tale I grin—
I fear my heart is ossifying!

The Drama once could shake and thrill
My nerves, and set my tears a stealing,
The Siddons then could turn at will
Each plug upon the main of feeling;
At Belvidera now I smile,
And laugh while Mrs. Haller's crying;
'Tis odd, so great a change of style—
I fear my heart is ossifying!

That heart was such—some years ago,
To see a beggar quite would shock it,
And in his hat I used to throw
The quarter's savings of my pocket:
I never wish—as I did *then!*—
The means from my own purse supplying,
To turn them all to gentlemen:
I fear my heart is ossifying!

We've had some serious things of late,
Our sympathies to beg or borrow,
New melodrames, of tragic fate,
And acts, and songs, and tales of sorrow;
Miss Zouch's case, our eyes to melt,
And sundry actors sad good-bye-ing,
But Lord! so little have I felt,
I'm sure my heart is ossifying!

DOMESTIC ASIDES; OR, TRUTH IN PARENTHESES.

" I REALLY take it very kind,
This visit, Mrs. Skinner!
I have not seen you such an age—
(The wretch has come to dinner!)

" Your daughters, too, what loves of girls—
What heads for painters' easels!
Come here and kiss the infant, dears—
(And give it p'rhaps the measles!)

" Your charming boys I see are home
From Reverend Mr. Russell's;
'Twas very kind to bring them both—
(What boots for my new Brussels!)

" What! little Clara left at home?
Well now I call that shabby:
I should have loved to kiss her so—
(A flabby, dabby, babby!)

" And Mr. S., I hope he's well,
Ah! though he lives so handy,
He never now drops in to sup—
(The better for our brandy!)

" Come, take a seat—I long to hear
About Matilda's marriage;
You're come of course to spend the day!
(Thank Heaven, I hear the carriage!)

" What! must you go? next time I hope
You'll give me longer measure;
Nay—I shall see you down the stairs—
(With most uncommon pleasure!)

" Good-bye! good-bye! remember all,·
Next time you'll take your dinners!
(Now, David, mind I'm not at home
In future to the Skinners!")

FRENCH AND ENGLISH.

"Good heaven! Why, even the little children in France speak French!"
ADDISON.

I.

NEVER go to France
Unless you know the lingo,
If you do, like me,
You will repent by jingo.
Staring like a fool,
And silent as a mummy,
There I stood alone,
A nation with a dummy:

II.

Chaises stand for chairs,
They christen letters *Billies*,
They call their mothers *mares*,
And all their daughters *fillies;*
Strange it was to hear,
I'll tell you what's a good 'un,
They call their leather *queer*,
And half their shoes are wooden.

III.

Signs I had to make
For every little notion,
Limbs all going like
A telegraph in motion;
For wine I reeled about,
To show my meaning fully,
And made a pair of horns,
To ask for "beef and bully."

IV.

Moo! I cried for milk;
I got my sweet things snugger,
When I kissed Jeannette,
'Twas understood for sugar.

If I wanted bread,
My jaws I set a-going,
And asked for new-laid eggs
By clapping hands and crowing!

v.

If I wished a ride,
I'll tell you how I got it;
On my stick astride
I made believe to trot it;
Then their cash was strange,
It bored me every minute,
Now here's a *hog* to change,
How many *sows* are in it!

vi.

Never go to France,
Unless you know the lingo;
If you do, like me,
You will repent by jingo;
Staring like a fool,
And silent as a mummy,
There I stood alone,
A nation with a dummy!

————

THE DUEL.

A SERIOUS BALLAD.

"Like the two Kings of Brentford smelling at one nosegay."

In Brentford town, of old renown,
    There lived a Mister Bray,
Who fell in love with Lucy Bell,
    And so did Mr. Clay.

To see her ride from Hammersmith,
    By all it was allowed,
Such fair outsides are seldom seen,
    Such Angels on a Cloud.

Said Mr. Bray to Mr. Clay,
   You choose to rival me,
And court Miss Bell, but there your court
   No thoroughfare shall be.

Unless you now give up your suit,
   You may repent your love ;
I who have shot a pigeon match,
   Can shoot a turtle dove.

So pray before you woo her more,
   Consider what you do ;
If you pop aught to Lucy Bell—
   I'll pop it into you.

Said Mr. Clay to Mr. Bray,
   Your threats I quite explode ;
One who has been a volunteer
   Knows how to prime and load.

And so I say to you unless
   Your passion quiet keeps,
I who have shot and hit bulls' eyes,
   May chance to hit a sheep's.

Now gold is oft for silver changed,
   And that for copper red ;
But these two went away to give
   Each other change for lead.

But first they sought a friend apiece,
   This pleasant thought to give—
When they were dead, they thus should have
   Two seconds still to live.

To measure out the ground not long
   The seconds then forebore,
And having taken one rash step,
   They took a dozen more.

They next prepared each pistol-pan
   Against the deadly strife,
By putting in the prime of death
   Against the prime of life.

Now all was ready for the foes,
　But when they took their stands,
Fear made them tremble so they found
　They both were shaking hands.

Said Mr. C. to Mr. B.,
　Here one of us may fall,
And like St. Paul's Cathedral now,
　Be doomed to have a ball.

I do confess I did attach
　Misconduct to your name ;
If I withdraw the charge, will then
　Your ramrod do the same ?

Said Mr. B., I do agree—
　But think of Honour's Courts !
If we go off without a shot,
　There will be strange reports.

But look, the morning now is bright,
　Though cloudy it begun ;
Why can't we aim above, as if
　We had called out the sun ?

So up into the harmless air
　Their bullets they did send ;
And may all other duels have
　That upshot in the end !

TO A BAD RIDER.

I.

WHY, Mr. Rider, why
　Your nag so ill indorse, man ?
To make observers cry,
　You're mounted, but no horseman ?

II.

With elbows out so far,
 This thought you can't debar me—
Though no Dragoon—Hussar—
 You're surely of the army!

III.

I hope to turn M.P.,
 You have not any notion,
So awkward you would be
 At "seconding a motion!"

———◆———

MY SON AND HEIR.

I.

My mother bids me bind my heir,
But not the trade where I should bind;
To place a boy—the how and where—
It is the plague of parent-kind!

II.

She does not hint the slightest plan,
Nor what indentures to indorse;
Whether to bind him to a man,
Or, like Mazeppa, to a horse.

III.

What line to choose of likely rise,
To something in the stocks at last,—
"Fast bind, fast find," the proverb cries,
I find I cannot bind so fast!

IV.

A Statesman James can never be;
A Tailor?—there I only learn
His chief concern is cloth, and he
Is always cutting his concern.

V.

A Seedsman?—I'd not have him so ;
A Grocer's plum might disappoint ;
A Butcher?—no, not that—although
I hear " the times are out of joint !"

VI.

Too many of all trades there be,
Like Pedlars, each has such a pack ;
A merchant selling coals?—we see
The buyer send to cellar back.

VII.

A Hardware dealer?—that might please,
But if his trade's foundation leans
On spikes and nails, he wont have ease
When he retires upon his means.

VIII.

A Soldier?—there he has not nerves,
A Sailor seldom lays up pelf :
A Baker?—no, a baker serves,
His customer before himself.

IX.

Dresser of hair?—that's not the sort ;
A Joiner jars with his desire—
A Churchman?—James is very short,
And cannot to a church aspire.

X.

A Lawyer?—that's a hardish term !
A Publisher might give him ease,
If he could into Longman's firm,
Just plunge at once " in medias Rees."

XI.

A shop for pot, and pan, and cup,
Such brittle Stock I can't advise ;
A Builder running houses up,
Their gains are stories—maybe lies !

XII.

A Coppersmith I can't endure—
Nor petty Usher A, B, C-ing;
A Publican no father sure,
Would be the author of his being!

XIII.

A Paper-maker?—come he must
To rags before he sells a sheet;
A Miller?—all his toil is just
To make a meal he does not eat.

XIV.

A Currier?—that by favour goes—
A Chandler gives me great misgiving—
An Undertaker?—one of those
That do not hope to get their living!

XV.

Three Golden Balls?—I like them not;
An Auctioneer I never did—
The victim of a slavish lot,
Obliged to do as he is bid!

XVI.

A Broker watching fall and rise
Of stock?—I'd rather deal in stone:
A Printer?—there his toils comprise
Another's work beside his own.

XVII.

A Cooper?—neither I nor Jim
Have any taste or turn for that—
A Fish retailer?—but with him,
One part of trade is always flat.

XVIII.

A Painter?—long he would not live,
An Artist's a precarious craft—
In trade, Apothecaries give,
But very seldom take a draught.

XIX.

A Glazier ?—what if he should smash !
A Crispin he shall not be made—
A Grazier may be losing cash,
Although he drives " a roaring trade."

XX.

Well, something must be done ! to look
On all my little works around—
James is too big a boy, like book,
To leave upon the shelf unbound.

XXI.

But what to do ?—my temples ache
From evening's dew to morning's pearl,
What course to take my boy to make—
O could I make my boy—a girl !

———◆———

COCKLE v. CACKLE.

THOSE who much read advertisements and bills,
　　Must have seen puffs of Cockle's Pills,
　　　　Called Anti-bilious—
Which some Physicians sneer at, supercilious,
But which we are assured, if timely taken,
　　May save your liver and bacon ;
Whether or not they really give one ease,
　　I, who have never tried,
　　　　Will not decide ;
But no two things in union go like these—
Viz., Quacks and Pills—save Ducks and Peas.
Now Mrs. W. was getting sallow,
Her lilies not of the white kind, but yellow,
And friends portended was preparing for
　　A human Pâté Périgord ;
She was, indeed, so very far from well,
Her Son, in filial fear, procured a box
Of those said pellets to resist Bile's shocks—
And—tho' upon the ear it strangely knocks—
To save her by a Cockle from a shell !

But Mrs. W., just like Macbeth,
Who very vehemently bids us " throw
Bark to the Bow-wows," hated physic so,
It seemed to share " the bitterness of death :"
Rhubarb—Magnesia—Jalap, and the kind—
Senna—Steel—Assafœtida, and Squills—
Powder or Draught—but least her throat inclined
To give a course to Boluses or Pills ;
No—not to save her life in lung or lobe,
For all her lights' or all her liver's sake,
Would her convulsive thorax undertake,
Only one little uncelestial globe !

'Tis not to wonder at, in such a case,
If she put by the pill-box in a place
For linen rather than for drugs intended—
Yet for the credit of the pills let's say
    After they thus were stowed away,
    Some of the linen mended ;
But Mrs. W., by disease's dint,
Kept getting still more yellow in her tint,
When lo ! her second son, like elder brother,
Marking the hue on the parental gills,
Brought a new charge of Anti-turmeric Pills,
To bleach the jaundiced visage of his Mother—
Who took them—in her cupboard—like the other.

    " Deeper and deeper, still," of course,
    The fatal colour daily grew in force ;
Till daughter W., newly come from Rome,
Acting the self-same filial, pillial, part,
To cure Mamma, another dose brought home
Of Cockles ;—not the Cockles of her heart !
    These going where the others went before,
    Of course she had a very pretty store ;
And then—some hue of health her cheek adorning,
    The Medicine so good must be,
    They brought her dose on dose, which she
Gave to the upstairs cupboard, " night and morning."
Till wanting room at last, for other stocks,
Out of the window one fine day she pitched
The pillage of each box, and quite enriched
The feed of Mister Burrell's hens and cocks,—

A little Barber of a bygone day,
        Over the way,
Whose stock in trade, to keep the least of shops,
Was one great head of Kemble—that is, John,
Staring in plaster, with a *Brutus* on,
And twenty little Bantam fowls—with *crops*.

Little Dame W. thought when through the sash
        She gave the physic wings,
        To find the very things
So good for bile, so bad for chicken rash,
For thoughtless cock and unreflecting pullet!
But while they gathered up the nauseous nubbles,
Each pecked itself into a peck of troubles,
And brought the hand of Death upon its gullet.
They might as well have addled been, or ratted,
For long before the night—ah! woe betide
The Pills! each suicidal Bantam died
        Unfatted!

        Think of poor Burrell's shock,
Of Nature's debt to see his hens all payers,
And laid in death as Everlasting Layers
With Bantam's small ex-Emperor, the Cock,
In ruffled plumage and funereal hackle,
Giving, undone by Cockle, a last Cackle!
To see as stiff as stone his unlive stock,
It really was enough to move his block.

Down on the floor he dashed, with horror big,
Mr. Bell's third wife's mother's coachman's wig;
And with a tragic stare like his own Kemble,
Burst out with natural emphasis enough,
        And voice that grief made tremble,
Into that very speech of sad Macduff—
"What! all my pretty chickens and their dam,
        At one fell swoop!
        Just when I'd bought a coop
To see the poor lamented creatures cram!"

        After a little of this mood,
        And brooding over the departed brood,

With razor he began to ope each craw,
Already turning-black, as black as coals;
When lo! the undigested cause he saw—
    "Pisoned by goles!"

To Mrs. W.'s luck a contradiction,
Her window still stood open to conviction;
And by short course of circumstantial labour,
He fixed the guilt upon his adverse neighbour;
Lord! how he railed at her: declaring now,
He'd bring an action ere next Term of Hilary,
Then, in another moment, swore a vow,
He'd make her do pill-penance in the pillory!
She, meanwhile distant from the dimmest dream
Of combating with guilt, yard-arm or arm-yard,
Lapped in a paradise of tea and cream;
When up ran Betty with a dismal scream—
"Here's Mr. Burrell, ma'am, with all his farmyard!"
Straight in he came, unbowing and unbending,
    With all the warmth that iron and a barber
        Can harbour;
To dress the head and front of her offending,
The fuming phial of his wrath uncorking;
In short, he made her pay him altogether,
In hard cash, very *hard*, for every feather,
Charging, of course, each Bantam as a Dorking;
Nothing could move him, nothing make him supple,
So the sad dame unpocketing her loss,
Had nothing left but to sit hands across,
And see her poultry "going down ten couple."

Now birds by poison slain,
As venomed dart from Indian's hollow cane,
Are edible; and Mrs. W.'s thrift,—
    She had a thrifty vein,—
Destined one pair for supper to make shift,—
Supper as usual at the hour of ten:
But ten o'clock arrived and quickly passed,
Eleven—twelve—and one o'clock at last,
Without a sign of supper even then!
At length, the speed of cookery to quicken,
Betty was called, and with reluctant feet,

Came up at a white heat—
" Well, never I see chicken like them chicken !
My saucepans they have been a pretty while in 'em !
Enough to stew them, if it comes to that,
To flesh and bones, and perfect rags ; but drat
Those Anti-biling Pills ! there is no bile in 'em !"

ODE.

IMITATED FROM HORACE.

OH ! well may poets make a fuss
In summer time, and sigh *" O rus !"*
   Of London pleasures sick :
My heart is all at pant to rest
In greenwood shades,—my eyes detest
   This endless meal of brick !

What joy have I in June's return ?
My feet are parched—my eyeballs burn,
   I scent no flowery gust ;
But faint the flagging zephyr springs,
With dry Macadam on its wings,
   And turns me " dust to dust."

My sun his daily course renews,
Due east, but with no Eastern dews ;
   The path is dry and hot !
His setting shows more tamely still,
He sinks behind no purple hill,
   But down a chimney's pot !

Oh ! but to hear the milk-maid blithe,
Or early mower whet his scythe
   The dewy meads among !
My grass is of that sort—alas !
That makes no hay,—called sparrow-grass
   By folks of vulgar tongue !

Oh! but to smell the woodbine sweet!
I think of cowslip-cups—but meet
　　With very vile rebuffs!
For meadow buds, I get a whiff
Of Cheshire cheese,—or only sniff
　　The turtle made at Cuff's.

How tenderly Rousseau reviewed
His periwinkles!—mine are stewed!
　　My rose blooms on a gown!—
I hunt in vain for eglantine,
And find my blue-bell on the sign
　　That marks the Bell and Crown!

Where are ye, birds! that blithely wing
From tree to tree, and gaily sing
　　Or mourn in thickets deep?
My cuckoo has some ware to sell,
The watchman is my Philomel,
　　My blackbird is a sweep!

Where are ye, linnet! lark! and thrush!
That perch on leafy bough and bush,
　　And tune the various song?
Two hurdy-gurdists, and a poor
Street-Handel grinding at my door,
　　Are all my "tuneful throng."

Where are ye, early-purling streams,
Whose waves reflect the morning beams
　　And colours of the skies?
My rills are only puddle-drains
From shambles—or reflect the stains
　　Of calimanco-dyes.

Sweet are the little brooks that run
O'er pebbles glancing in the sun,
　　Singing in soothing tones:
Not thus the city streamlets flow;
They make no music as they go,
　　Tho' never "off the stones."

Where are ye, pastoral pretty sheep,
That wont to bleat, and frisk, and leap
   Beside your woolly dams?
Alas! instead of harmless crooks,
My Corydons use iron hooks,
   And skin—not shear—the lambs.

The pipe whereon, in olden day,
Th' Arcadian herdsman used to play
   Sweetly—here soundeth not;
But merely breathes unwelcome fumes,
Meanwhile the city boor consumes
   The rank weed—"piping hot."

All rural things are vilely mocked,
On every hand the sense is shocked
   With objects hard to bear:
Shades,—vernal shades!—where wine is sold!
And for a turfy bank, behold
   An Ingram's rustic chair!

Where are ye, London meads and bowers,
And gardens redolent of flowers
   Wherein the zephyr wons?
Alas! Moor Fields are fields no more!
See Hatton's Garden bricked all o'er;
   And that bare Wood—St. John's.

No pastoral scene procures me peace;
I hold no Leasowes in my lease,
   No cot set round with trees:
No sheep-white hill my dwelling flanks;
And omnium furnishes my banks
   With brokers—not with bees.

Oh! well may poets make a fuss
In summer time, and sigh "*O rus!*"
   Of city pleasures sick:
My heart is all at pant to rest
In greenwood shades—my eyes detest
   This endless meal of brick!

STANZAS TO TOM WOODGATE, OF HASTINGS.

I.

Tom !—are you still within this land
Of livers—still on Hastings' sand,
 Or roaming on the waves,—
Or has some billow o'er you rolled,
Jealous that earth should lap so bold
 A seaman in her graves ?

II.

On land the rush-light lives of men
Go out but slowly ; nine in ten,
 By tedious long decline,—
Not so the jolly sailor sinks,
Who founders in the wave, and drinks
 The apoplectic brine !

III.

Ay, while I write, mayhap your head
Is sleeping on an oyster-bed,—
 I hope 'tis far from truth !
With periwinkle eyes ;—your bone
Beset with mussels, not your own,
 And corals at your tooth !

IV.

Still does the " Chance " pursue the chance
The main affords—the " Aidant " dance
 In safety on the tide ?
Still flies that sign of my goodwill
A little *bunting* thing—but still
 To thee a flag of pride ?

V.

Does that hard, honest hand now clasp
The tiller in its careful grasp—

With every summer breeze
When ladies sail, in lady-fear—
Or, tug the oar, a gondolier
On smooth Macadam seas?

VI.

Or are you where the flounders keep,
Some dozen briny fathoms deep,
    Where sands and shells abound—
With some old Triton on your chest
And twelve grave mermen for a 'quest,
    To find that you are—drowned?

VII.

Swift is the wave, and apt to bring
A sudden doom—perchance I sing
    A mere funereal strain;
You have endured the utter strife—
And are—the same in death or life,
    A good man in the main!

VIII.

Oh, no—I hope the old brown eye
Still watches ebb and flood and sky;
    That still the old brown shoes
Are sucking brine up—pumps indeed!
Your tooth still full of ocean weed,
    Or Indian—which you choose.

IX.

I like you, Tom! and in these lays
Give honest worth its honest praise,
    No puff at honour's cost;
For though you met these words of mine,
All letter-learning was a line
    You, somehow, never crossed!

X.

Mayhap, we ne'er shall meet again,
Except on that Pacific main,
  Beyond this planet's brink ;
Yet as we erst have braved the weather,
Still we may float awhile together,
  As comrades on this ink !

XI.

Many a scudding gale we've had
Together, and, my gallant lad,
  Some perils we have passed ;
When huge and black the wave careered,
And oft the giant surge appeared
  The master of our mast :

XII.

'Twas thy example taught me how
To climb the billow's hoary brow,
  Or cleave the raging heap—
To bound along the ocean wild,
With danger only as a child
  The waters rocked to sleep.

XIII.

Oh, who can tell that brave delight,
To see the hissing wave in might,
  Come rampant like a snake !
To leap his horrid crest, and feast
One's eyes upon the briny beast,
  Left couchant in the wake !

XIV.

The simple shepherd's love is still
To bask upon a sunny hill,
  The herdsman roams the vale—
With both their fancies I agree ;
Be mine the swelling, scooping sea,
  That is both hill and dale !

XV.

I yearn for that brisk spray—I yearn
To feel the wave from stem to stern
    Uplift the plunging keel.
That merry step we used to dance,
On board the " Aidant" or the " Chance,"
    The ocean " toe and heel."

XVI.

I long to feel the steady gale,
That fills the broad distended sail—
    The seas on either hand !
My thought, like any hollow shell,
Keeps mocking at my ear the swell
    Of waves against the land.

XVII.

It is no fable—that old strain
Of sirens !—so the witching main
    Is singing—and I sigh !
My heart is all at once inclined
To seaward—and I seem to find
    The waters in my eye !

XVIII.

Methinks I see the shining beach ;
The merry waves, each after each,
    Rebounding o'er the flints ;
I spy the grim preventive spy !
The jolly boatmen standing nigh !
    The maids in morning chintz !

XIX.

And there they float—the sailing craft !
The sail is up—the wind abaft—
    The ballast trim and neat.
Alas ! 'tis all a dream—a lie !
A printer's imp is standing by,
    To haul my mizen sheet !

XX.

My tiller dwindles to a pen—
My craft is that of bookish men—
    My sale—let Longman tell !
Adieu the wave ! the wind ! the spray !
Men—maidens—chintzes—fade away !
    Tom Woodgate, fare thee well !

ON A PICTURE OF HERO AND LEANDER.

In the *Gem* for 1829. The subject is Leander just landing from the Hellespont ; Hero receiving him ; Cupid holding a torch above them ; and a girl
peeping at them from the top of the flight of steps.

WHY, Love, why
Such a water-rover ?
Would she love thee more
For coming half-seas over ?

Why, Lady, why
So in love with dipping ?
Must a lad of Greece
Come all over dripping ?

Why, Cupid, why
Make the passage brighter ?
Were not any boat
Better than a lighter ?

Why, Maiden, why
So intrusive standing ?
Must thou be on the stair,
When he is on the landing ?

SONNETS.

TO A DECAYED SEAMAN.

HAIL! seventy-four cut down! Hail, top and **lop**:
  Unless I'm much mistaken in my notion,
Thou wast a stirring tar, before that hop
  Became so fatal to thy locomotion;
Now, thrown on shore, like a mere weed of ocean,
  Thou readest still to men a lesson good,
To King and Country showing thy devotion,
  By kneeling thus upon a stump of wood!
Still is thy spirit strong as alcohol;
  Spite of that limb, begot of acorn-egg—
Methinks—thou Naval History in one vol.
  A virtue shines, e'en in that timber leg,
For unlike others that desert their Poll,
  Thou walkest ever with thy "Constant Peg!"

ON STEAM.

BY AN UNDER-OSTLER.

I WISH I livd a Thowsen year Ago
Wurking for Sober six and Seven milers
And dubble Stages runnen safe and slo
The Orsis cum in Them days to the Bilers
But Now by meens of Powers of Steem forces
A-turning Coches into Smoakey Kettls
The Bilers seam a Cumming to the Orses
And Helps and naggs Will sune be out of Vittels

Poor Bruits I wunder How we bee to Liv
When sutch a change of Orses is our Faits
No nothink need Be sifted in a Siv
May them Blowd ingins all Blow up their Grates
And Theaves of Oslers crib the Coles and Giv
Their blackgard Hannimuls a Feed of Slaits!

TO A SCOTCH GIRL, WASHING LINEN AFTER HER COUNTRY FASHION.

WELL done and wetly, thou Fair Maid of Perth:
    Thou mak'st a washing picture well deserving
    The pen and pencilling of Washington Irving:
Like dripping Naiad, pearly from her birth,
Dashing about the water of the Firth,
    To cleanse the calico of Mrs. Skirving,
    And never from thy dance of duty swerving
As there were nothing else than dirt on earth!
Yet what is thy reward? Nay, do not start!
    I do not mean to give thee a new damper,
But while thou fillest this industrious part
    Of washer, wearer, mangler, presser, stamper,
Deserving better character—thou art
    What Bodkin would but call—" a common tramper."

Allegory—A moral vehicle.—*Dictionary.*

I HAD a Gig-Horse, and I called him Pleasure,
    Because on Sundays, for a little jaunt,
He was so fast and showy, quite a treasure;
    Although he sometimes kicked and shied aslant.
I had a Chaise, and christened it Enjoyment,
    With yellow body, and the wheels of red,
Because 'twas only used for one employment,
    Namely, to go wherever Pleasure led.

I had a wife, her nickname was Delight :
  A son called Frolic, who was never still :
Alas ! how often dark succeeds to bright !
  Delight was thrown, and Frolic had a spill,
Enjoyment was upset and shattered quite,
  And Pleasure fell a splitter on *Paine's Hill !*

ADDITIONAL POEMS.

THE TWO SWANS.

A FAIRY TALE.

IMMORTAL Imogen, crowned queen above
The lilies of thy sex, vouchsafe to hear
A fairy dream in honour of true love—
True above ills, and frailty, and all fear—
Perchance a shadow of his own career
Whose youth was darkly prisoned and long twined
By serpent-sorrow, till white Love drew near,
And sweetly sang him free, and round his mind
A bright horizon threw, wherein no grief may wind.

I saw a tower builded on a lake,
Mocked by its inverse shadow, dark and deep—
That seemed a still intenser night to make,
Wherein the quiet waters sunk to sleep,—
And, whatsoe'er was prisoned in that keep,
A monstrous Snake was warden :—round and round
In sable ringlets I beheld him creep,
Blackest amid black shadows, to the ground,
Whilst his enormous head the topmost turret crowned :

From whence he shot fierce light against the stars,
Making the pale moon paler with affright ;
And with his ruby eye out-threatened Mars—
That blazed in the mid-heavens, hot and bright—
Nor slept, nor winked, but with a steadfast spite
Watched their wan looks and tremblings in the skies ;
And that he might not slumber in the night,
The curtain-lids were plucked from his large eyes,
So he might never drowse, but watch his secret prize.

Prince or princess in dismal durance pent,
Victims of old Enchantment's love or hate,
Their lives must all in painful sighs be spent,
Watching the lonely waters soon and late,
And clouds that pass and leave them to their fate,
Or company their grief with heavy tears :—
Meanwhile that Hope can spy no golden gate
For sweet escapement, but in darksome fears
They weep and pine away as if immortal years.

No gentle bird with gold upon its wing
Will perch upon the grate—the gentle bird
Is safe in leafy dell, and will not bring
Freedom's sweet keynote and commission-word
Learned of a fairy's lips, for pity stirred—
Lest while he trembling sings, untimely guest !
Watched by that cruel Snake and darkly heard,
He leave a widow on her lonely nest,
To press in silent grief the darlings of her breast.

No gallant knight, adventurous, in his bark,
Will seek the fruitful perils of the place,
To rouse with dipping oar the waters dark
That bear that serpent-image on their face.
And Love, brave Love ! though he attempt the base,
Nerved to his loyal death, he may not win
His captive lady from the strict embrace
Of that foul Serpent, clasping her within
His sable folds—like Eve enthralled by the old Sin.

But there is none—no knight in panoply,
Nor Love, entrenched in his strong steely coat :
No little speck—no sail—no helper nigh,
No sign—no whispering—no plash of boat :—
The distant shores show dimly and remote,
Made of a deeper mist,—serene and grey,—
And slow and mute the cloudy shadows float
Over the gloomy wave, and pass away,
Chased by the silver beams that on their marges play.

And bright and silvery the willows sleep
Over the shady verge—no mad winds tease
Their hoary heads ; but quietly they weep
Their sprinkling leaves—half fountains and half trees ;

There lilies be—and fairer than all these,
A solitary Swan her breast of snow
Launches against the wave that seems to freeze
Into a chaste reflection, still below,
Twin-shadow of herself wherever she may go.

And forth she paddles in the very noon
Of solemn midnight, like an elfin thing
Charmed into being by the argent moon—
Whose silver light for love of her fair wing
Goes with her in the shade, still worshipping
Her dainty plumage :—all around her grew
A radiant circlet, like a fairy ring ;
And all behind, a tiny little clue
Of light, to guide her back across the waters blue.

And sure she is no meaner than a fay
Redeemed from sleepy death, for beauty's sake,
By old ordainment :—silent as she lay,
Touched by a moonlight wand I saw her wake,
And cut her leafy slough, and so forsake
The verdant prison of her lily peers,
That slept amidst the stars upon the lake—
A breathing shape—restored to human fears,
And new-born love and grief—self-conscious of her tears.

And now she clasps her wings around her heart,
And near that lonely isle begins to glide,
Pale as her fears, and oft-times with a start
Turns her impatient head from side to side
In universal terrors—all too wide
To watch ; and often to that marble keep
Upturns her pearly eyes, as if she spied
Some foe, and crouches in the shadows steep
That in the gloomy wave go diving fathoms deep.

And well she may, to spy that fearful thing
All down the dusky walls in circlets wound ;
Alas ! for what rare prize, with many a ring
Girding the marble casket round and round ?
His folded tail, lost in the gloom profound,
Terribly darkeneth the rocky base ;
But on the top his monstrous head is crowned

27

With prickly spears, and on his doubtful face
Gleam his unwearied eyes, red watchers of the place.

Alas! of the hot fires that nightly fall,
No one will scorch him in those orbs of spite,
So he may never see beneath the wall
That timid little creature, all too bright,
That stretches her fair neck, slender and white,
Invoking the pale moon, and vainly tries
Her throbbing throat, as if to charm the night
With song—but, hush—it perishes in sighs,
And there will be no dirge sad-swelling, though she dies!

She droops—she sinks—she leans upon the lake,
Fainting again into a lifeless flower;
But soon the chilly springs anoint and wake
Her spirit from its death, and with new power
She sheds her stifled sorrows in a shower
Of tender song, timed to her falling tears—
That wins the shady summit of that tower,
And, trembling all the sweeter for its fears,
Fills with imploring moan that cruel monster's ears.

And lo! the scaly beast is all deprest,
Subdued like Argus by the might of sound—
What time Apollo his sweet lute addrest
To magic converse with the air, and bound
The many monster eyes, all slumber-drowned:—
So on the turret-top that watchful Snake
Pillows his giant head, and lists profound,
As if his wrathful spite would never wake,
Charmed into sudden sleep for Love and Beauty's sake!

His prickly crest lies prone upon his crown,
And thirsty lip from lip disparted flies,
To drink that dainty flood of music down—
His scaly throat is big with pent-up sighs—
And whilst his hollow ear entranced lies,
His looks for envy of the charmed sense
Are fain to listen, till his steadfast eyes,
Stung into pain by their own impotence,
Distil enormous tears into the lake immense.

Oh, tuneful Swan ! oh, melancholy bird !
Sweet was that midnight miracle of song,
Rich with ripe sorrow, needful of no word
To tell of pain, and love, and love's deep wrong—
Hinting a piteous tale—perchance how long
Thy unknown tears were mingled with the lake,
What time disguised thy leafy mates among—
And no eye knew what human love and ache
Dwelt in those dewy leaves, and heart so nigh to break.

Therefore no poet will ungently touch
The water-lily, on whose eyelids dew
Trembles like tears ; but ever hold it such
As human pain may wander through and through,
Turning the pale leaf paler in its hue—
Wherein life dwells, transfigured, not entombed,
By magic spells.   Alas ! who ever knew
Sorrow in all its shapes, leafy and plumed,
Or in gross husks of brutes eternally inhumed ?

And now the winged song has scaled the height
Of that dark dwelling, builded for despair,
And soon a little casement flashing bright
Widens self-opened into the cool air—
That music like a bird may enter there
And soothe the captive in his stony cage ;
For there is nought of grief, or painful care,
But plaintive song may happily engage
From sense of its own ill, and tenderly assuage.

And forth into the light, small and remote,
A creature, like the fair son of a king,
Draws to the lattice in his jewelled coat
Against the silver moonlight glistening,
And leans upon his white hand listening
To that sweet music that with tenderer tone
Salutes him, wondering what kindly thing
Is come to soothe him with so tuneful moan,
Singing beneath the walls as if for him alone !

And while he listens, the mysterious song,
Woven with timid particles of speech,
Twines into passionate words that grieve along
The melancholy notes, and softly teach

The secrets of true love,—that trembling reach
His earnest ear, and through the shadows dun
He missions like replies, and each to each
Their silver voices mingle into one,
Like blended streams that make one music as they run.

" Ah Love ! my hope is swooning in my heart."—
" Ay, sweet ! my cage is strong and hung full high."—
" Alas ! our lips are held so far apart,
Thy words come faint,—they have so far to fly !"—
" If I may only shun that serpent-eye !"—
" Ah me ! that serpent-eye doth never sleep."—
" Then nearer thee, Love's martyr, I will lie !"—
" Alas, alas ! that word has made me weep !
For pity's sake remain safe in thy marble keep !"

" My marble keep ! it is my marble tomb !"—
" Nay, sweet ! but thou hast there thy living breath."—
" Aye to expend in sighs for this hard doom."—
" But I will come to thee and sing beneath,
And nightly so beguile this serpent wreath."—
" Nay, I will find a path from these despairs."—
" Ah ! needs then thou must tread the back of death,
Making his stony ribs thy stony stairs ?—
Behold his ruby eye, how fearfully it glares !"

Full sudden at these words, the princely youth
Leaps on the scaly back that slumbers, still
Unconscious of his foot, yet not for ruth,
But numbed to dulness by the fairy skill
Of that sweet music (all more wild and shrill
For intense fear) that charmed him as he lay—
Meanwhile the lover nerves his desperate will,
Held some short throbs by natural dismay,
Then, down, down the serpent-track begins his darksome way

Now dimly seen—now toiling out of sight,
Eclipsed and covered by the envious wall ;
Now fair and spangled in the sudden light,
And clinging with wide arms for fear of fall :
Now dark and sheltered by a kindly pall
Of dusky shadow from his wakeful foe ;
Slowly he winds adown—dimly and small,

Watched by the gentle Swan that sings below,
Her hope increasing, still, the larger he doth grow.

But nine times nine the Serpent folds embrace
The marble walls about—which he must tread
Before his anxious foot may touch the base :
Long is the dreary path, and must be sped !
But Love, that holds the mastery of dread,
Braces his spirit, and with constant toil
He wins his way, and now, with arms outspread,
Impatient plunges from the last long coil :
So may all gentle Love ungentle Malice foil !

The song is hushed, the charm is all complete,
And two fair Swans are swimming on the lake :
But scarce their tender bills have time to meet,
When fiercely drops adown that cruel Snake—
His steely scales a fearful rustling make,
Like autumn leaves that tremble and foretell
The sable storm ;—the plumy lovers quake—
And feel the troubled waters pant and swell,
Heaved by the giant bulk of their pursuer fell.

His jaws, wide yawning like the gates of Death,
Hiss horrible pursuit—his red eyes glare
The waters into blood—his eager breath
Grows hot upon their plumes :—now, minstrel fair !
She drops her ring into the waves, and there
It widens all around, a fairy ring
Wrought of the silver light—the fearful pair
Swim in the very midst, and pant and cling
The closer for their fears, and tremble wing to wing.

Bending their course over the pale grey lake,
Against the pallid East, wherein light played
In tender flushes, still the baffled Snake
Circled them round continually, and bayed
Hoarsely and loud, forbidden to invade
The sanctuary ring : his sable mail
Rolled darkly through the flood, and writhed and made
A shining track over the waters pale,
Lashed into boiling foam by his enormous tail.

And so they sailed into the distance dim,
Into the very distance—small and white,
Like snowy blossoms of the spring that swim
Over the brooklets—followed by the spite
Of that huge Serpent, that with wild affright
Worried them on their course, and sore annoy,
Till on the grassy marge I saw them 'light,
And change, anon, a gentle girl and boy,
Locked in embrace of sweet unutterable joy!

Then came the Morn, and with her pearly showers
Wept on them, like a mother, in whose eyes
Tears are no grief; and from his rosy bowers
The Oriental sun began to rise,
Chasing the darksome shadows from the skies;
Wherewith that sable Serpent far away
Fled, like a part of night—delicious sighs
From waking blossoms purified the day,
And little birds were singing sweetly from each spray.

TO HOPE.

OH! take, young seraph, take thy harp,
    And play to me so cheerily;
For grief is dark, and care is sharp,
    And life wears on so wearily.
        Oh! take thy harp!
Oh! sing as thou wert wont to do,
    When, all youth's sunny season long,
    I sat and listened to thy song,
And yet 'twas ever, ever new,
With magic in its heaven-tuned string—
    The future bliss thy constant theme,
Oh! then each little woe took wing
    Away, like phantoms of a dream,
        As if each sound
        That fluttered round
    Had floated over Lethe's stream!

By all those bright and happy hours
We spent in life's sweet eastern bowers,

Where thou wouldst sit and smile, and show
Ere buds were come, where flowers would blow,
And oft anticipate the rise
Of life's warm sun that scaled the skies ;
By many a story of love and glory,
And friendships promised oft to me ;
By all the faith I lent to thee,—
Oh ! take, young seraph, take thy harp,
   And play to me so cheerily ;
For grief is dark, and care is sharp,
   And life wears on so wearily.
       Oh ! take thy harp !

Perchance the strings will sound less clear,
   That long have lain neglected by
In sorrow's misty atmosphere ;
It ne'er may speak as it hath spoken
   Such joyous notes so brisk and high ;
But are its golden chords all broken ?
Are there not some, though weak and low,
To play a lullaby to woe ?

But thou canst sing of love no more,
   For Celia showed that dream was vain ;
And many a fancied bliss is o'er,
   That comes not e'en in dreams again.
     Alas ! alas !
     How pleasures pass,
And leave thee now no subject, save
The peace and bliss beyond the grave !
Then be thy flight among the skies :
   Take, then, oh ! take the skylark's wing,
And leave dull earth, and heavenward rise
   O'er all its tearful clouds, and sing
      On skylark's wing !

Another life-spring there adorns
   Another youth, without the dread
Of cruel care, whose crown of thorns
   Is here for manhood's aching head.—
Oh ! there are realms of welcome day,
A world where tears are wiped away !

Then be thy flight among the skies :
　　Take, then, oh ! take the skylark's wing,
And leave dull earth, and heavenward rise
　　O'er all its tearful clouds, and sing
　　　　On skylark's wing !

TO CELIA.

OLD fictions say that Love hath eyes,
Yet sees, unhappy boy ! with none ;
Blind as the night ! but fiction lies,
For Love doth always see with one.

To one our graces all unveil,
To one our flaws are all exposed ;
But when with tenderness we hail,
He smiles and keeps the critic closed.

But when he's scorned, abused, estranged,
He opes the eye of evil ken,
And all his angel friends are changed
To demons—and are hated then !

Yet once it happed that, semi-blind,
He met thee on a summer day,
And took thee for his mother kind,
And frowned as he was pushed away.

But still he saw thee shine the same,
Though he had oped his evil eye,
And found that nothing but her shame
Was left to know his mother by !

And ever since that morning sun,
He thinks of thee, and blesses Fate
That he can look with both on one
Who hath no ugliness to hate.

ODE ON A DISTANT PROSPECT OF CLAPHAM ACADEMY.

AH me! those old familiar bounds!
That classic house, those classic grounds,
    My pensive thought recalls!
What tender urchins now confine,
What little captives now repine,
    Within yon irksome walls?

Ay, that's the very house!   I know
Its ugly windows, ten a-row!
    Its chimneys in the rear!
And there's the iron rod so high,
That drew the thunder from the sky,
    And turned our table-beer!

There I was birched! there I was bred!
There like a little Adam fed
    From Learning's woful tree!
The weary tasks I used to con!—
The hopeless leaves I wept upon!—
    Most fruitless leaves to me!—

The summoned class!—the awful bow!—
I wonder who is master now
    And wholesome anguish sheds!
How many ushers now employs,
How many maids to see the boys
    Have nothing in their heads!

And Mrs. S——?   Doth she abet
(Like Pallas in the parlour) yet
    Some favoured two or three,—
The little Crichtons of the hour,
Her muffin-medals that devour,
    And swill her prize—Bohea?

Ay, there's the playground! there's the lime,
Beneath whose shade in summer's prime

So wildly I have read !—
Who sits there *now*, and skims the cream
Of young Romance, and weaves a dream
    Of Love and Cottage-bread ?

Who struts the Randall of the walk ?
Who models tiny heads in chalk ?
    Who scoops the light canoe ?
What early genius buds apace ?
Where's Poynter ? Harris ? Bowers ? Chase ?
    Hal Baylis ? blithe Carew ?

Alack ! they're gone—a thousand ways !
And some are serving in " the Greys,"
    And some have perished young !—
Jack Harris weds his second wife ;
Hal Baylis drives the *wane* of life ;
    And Blithe Carew—is hung !

Grave Bowers teaches A B C
To savages at Owhyee ;
    Poor Chase is with the worms !—
All, all are gone—the olden breed !—
New crops of mushroom boys succeed,
    " And push us from our *forms !*"

Lo ! where they scramble forth, and shout,
And leap, and skip, and mob about,
    At play where we have played !
Some hop, some run (some fall), some twine
Their crony arms ; some in the shine,—
    And some are in the shade !

Lo ! there what mixed conditions run !
The orphan lad ; the widow's son ;
    And Fortune's favoured care—
The wealthy-born, for whom she hath
Mac-Adamized the future path—
    The Nabob's pampered heir !

Some brightly starred—some evil born,—
For honour some, and some for scorn,—

For fair or foul renown !
Good, bad, indifferent—none may lack !
Look, here's a White, and there's a Black !
   And there's a Creole brown !

Some laugh and sing, some mope and weep,
And wish *their* "frugal sires would keep
   Their only sons at home ;"—
Some tease the future tense, and plan
The full-grown doings of the man,
   And pant for years to come !—

A foolish wish ! There's one at hoop ;
And four at *fives !* and five who stoop
   The marble taw to speed !
And one that curvets in and out,
Reigning his fellow Cob about,—
   Would I were in his *steed !*

Yet he would gladly halt and drop
That boyish harness off, to swop
   With this world's heavy van
To toil, to tug. O little fool !
While thou canst be a horse at school,
   To wish to be a man !

Perchance thou deem'st it were a thing
To wear a crown,—to be a king !
   And sleep on regal down !
Alas ! thou know'st not kingly cares ;
Far happier is thy head that wears
   That hat without a crown !

And dost thou think that years acquire
New added joys ? Dost think thy sire
   More happy than his son ?
That manhood's mirth ?—Oh, go thy ways
To Drury Lane when —— *plays,*
   And see how *forced* our fun !

Thy taws are brave !—thy tops are rare !—
Our tops are spun with coils of care,

Our *dumps* are no delight !
The Elgin marbles are but tame,
And 'tis at best a sorry game
    To fly the Muse's kite :

Our hearts are dough, our heels are lead,
Our topmost joys fall dull and dead,
    Like balls with no rebound !
And often with a faded eye
We look behind, and send a sigh
    Towards that merry ground !

Then be contented.   Thou hast got
The most of heaven in thy young lot ;
    There's sky-blue in thy cup !
Thou'lt find thy Manhood all too fast—
Soon come, soon gone ! and Age at last
    A sorry *breaking-up !*

ADDRESS TO MR. CROSS, OF EXETER CHANGE,

ON THE DEATH OF THE ELEPHANT.

"'Tis *Greece*, but living *Greece* no more."—*Giaour.*

Oh, Mr. Cross !
Permit a sorry stranger to draw near,
            And shed a tear
(I've shed my shilling) for thy recent loss !
            I've been a visitor
Of old—a sort of a Buffon inquisitor
Of thy menagerie, and knew the beast
            That is deceased !
I was the Damon of the gentle giant,
            And oft have been,
            Like Mr. Kean,
Tenderly fondled by his trunk compliant.
Whenever I approached, the kindly brute
Flapped his prodigious ears, and bent his knees—
            It makes me freeze
To think of it !   No chums could better suit,
Exchanging grateful looks for grateful fruit,—

For so our former dearness was begun.—
I bribed him with an apple, and beguiled
The beast of his affection like a child ;
And well he loved me till his life was done
　　　　　(Except when he was wild).
It makes me blush for human friends—but none
I have so truly kept or cheaply won !

Here is his pen !
The casket—but the jewel is away !
The den is rifled of its denizen,—
　　　　　Ah, well-a-day !
This fresh free air breathes nothing of his grossness,
And sets me sighing even for its closeness.
　　　　　This light one-storey,
Where like a cloud I used to feast my eyes on
The grandeur of his Titan-like horizon,
Tells a dark tale of its departed glory ;—
The very beasts lament the change like me.
　　　　　The shaggy Bison
Leaneth his head dejected on his knee ;
The Hyæna's laugh is hushed ; the Monkey's pout ,
The Wild Cat frets in a complaining whine ;
The Panther paces restlessly about,
　　　　　To walk her sorrow out ;
The Lions in a deeper bass repine ;
The Kangaroo wrings its sorry short forepaws ;
　　　　　Shrieks come from the Macaws ;
The old bald Vulture shakes his naked head,
　　　　　And pineth for the dead ;
The Boa writhes into a double knot ;
　　　　　The Keeper groans
　　　　　Whilst sawing bones,
And looks askance at the deserted spot ;
Brutal and rational lament his loss,
The flower of thy beastly family !—
　　　　　Poor Mrs. Cross
Sheds frequent tears into her daily tea,
　　　　　And weakens her Bohea !
Oh, Mr. Cross, how little it gives birth
To grief when human greatness goes to earth ;

How few lament for Czars !—
But, oh, the universal heart o'erflowed
At his "high mass,"
Lighted by gas,
When, like Mark Antony, the keeper showed
The Elephantine scars !—
Reporters' eyes
Were of an egg-like size ;
Men that had never wept for murdered Marrs !
Hard-hearted editors, with iron faces
Their sluices all unclosed,—
And discomposed
Compositors went fretting to their cases !—
That grief has left its traces ;
The poor old Beef-eater has gone much greyer
With sheer regret ;
And the Gazette
Seems the least trouble of the beast's Purveyor !

And I too weep ! a dozen of great men
I could have spared without a single tear ;
But then
They are renewable from year to year !
Fresh Gents would rise though Gent resigned the pen
I should not wholly
Despair for six months of another C——,
Nor, though F—— lay on his small bier,
Be melancholy.
But when will such an elephant appear ?
Though Penley were destroyed at Drury Lane,
His like might come again ;
Fate might supply
A second Powell, if the first should die ;
Another Bennet, if the sire were snatched ;
Barnes—might be matched :
And Time fill up the gap
Were Parsloe laid upon the green earth's lap ;
Even Claremont might be equalled,—I could hope
(All human greatness is, alas, so puny !)
For other Egertons—another Pope,
But not another Chunee !

Well! he is dead!
And there's a gap in Nature of eleven
        feet high by seven—
Five living tons!—and I remain—nine stone
        Of skin and bone!
It is enough to make me shake my head
        And dream of the grave's brink—
        'Tis worse to think
How like the Beast's the sorry life *I've* led!-
        A sort of show
Of my poor public self and my sagacity,
        To profit the rapacity
Of certain folks in Paternoster Row,
A slavish toil to win an upper storey—
        And a hard glory
Of wooden beams about my weary brow!
        Oh, Mr. C.!
If ever you behold me twirl my pen
To earn a public supper, that is, eat
        In the bare street,—
Or turn about their literary den—
        Shoot *me!*

———◆———

ELEGY ON DAVID LAING, ESQ.

BLACKSMITH AND JOINER (WITHOUT LICENCE) AT GRETNA GREEN.

AH me! what causes such complaining breath,
    Such female moans, and flooding tears to flow?
It is to chide with stern, remorseless Death,
        For laying Laing low!
   From Prospect House there comes a sound of woe—
A shrill and persevering loud lament,
Echoed by Mrs. T.'s Establishment
        " For Six Young Ladies,
In a retired and healthy part of Kent."
   All weeping, Mr. L—— gone down to Hades!
Thoughtful of grates, and convents, and the veil!
        Surrey takes up the tale,

And all the nineteen scholars of Miss Jones,
With the two parlour-boarders and th' apprentice—
So universal this mis-timed event is—
   Are joining sobs and groans !
The shock confounds all hymeneal planners,
 And drives the sweetest from their sweet behaviours.
The girls at Manor House forget their manners,
 And utter sighs like paviours !
Down—down through Devon and the distant shires
 Travels the news of Death's remorseless crime ;
And in all hearts, at once, all hope expires
   Of *matches* against time !

   Along the northern route
The road is watered by postilions' eyes ;
 The topboot paces pensively about,
And yellow jackets are all stained with sighs.
There is a sound of grieving at the Ship,
And sorry hands are wringing at the Bell,
   In aid of David's knell.
The postboy's heart is cracking—not his whip—
 To gaze upon those useless empty collars
His wayworn horses seem so glad to slip—
 And think upon the dollars
That used to urge his gallop—quicker ! quicker !
   All hope is fled,
   For Laing is dead—
Vicar of Wakefield—Edward Gibbon's vicar !

   The barristers shed tears
Enough to feed a snipe (snipes live on suction)
   To think in after years
No suits will come of Gretna Green abduction,
   Nor knaves inveigle
Young heiresses in marriage scrapes or legal ;
   The dull reporters
Look truly sad and seriously solemn
   To lose the future column
On Hymen-Smithy and its fond resorters !
 But grave Miss Daulby and the teaching brood
Rejoice at quenching the clandestine flambeau—
 That never real beau of flesh and blood
Will henceforth lure young ladies from their *Chambaud.*

> Sleep—David Laing !—sleep
In peace, though angry governesses spurn thee !
O'er thy grave a thousand maidens weep,
> And honest postboys mourn thee !
Sleep, David !—safely and serenely sleep,
> Be-wept of many a learned legal eye !
To see the mould above thee in a heap
> Drowns many a lid that heretofore was dry !—
Especially of those that, plunging deep
> In love, would " ride and tie !"
Had I command thou should'st have gone thy ways
In chaise and pair—and lain in Père-la-Chaise !

A LAMENT FOR THE DECLINE OF CHIVALRY.

> WELL hast thou cried, departed Burke,
All chivalrous romantic work
> Is ended now and past !—
That iron age—which some have thought
Of metal rather over*wrought*
> Is now all over*cast*.

> Ay,—where are those heroic knights
Of old—those armadillo wights
> Who wore the plated vest,—
Great Charlemagne, and all his peers
Are cold—enjoying with their spears
> An everlasting rest !

> The bold King Arthur sleepeth sound,
So sleep his knights who gave that Round
> Old Table such éclat !
Oh Time has plucked that plumy brow !
And none engage *at turneys* now
> But those who go to law.

> Grim John o' Gaunt is quite gone by,
And Guy is nothing but a Guy,
> Orlando lies forlorn !—
Bold Sidney, and his kidney—nay,
Those " early Champions"—what are they
> But *Knights* without a morn !

28

No Percy branch now perseveres
Like those of old in breaking spears—
    The name is now a lie.
Surgeons, alone, by any chance,
Are all that ever couch a lance
    To couch a body's eye !

Alas for Lion-hearted Dick,
That cut the Moslem to the quick
    His weapon lies in piece,—
Oh, it would warm them in a trice,
If they could only have a spice
    Of his old mace in Greece !

The famed Rinaldo lies a-cold,
And Tancred too, and Godfrey bold,
    That scaled the holy wall !
No Saracen meets Paladin,
We hear of no great Saladin,
    But only grow the small.

Our Cressys too have dwindled since
To penny things—at our Black Prince
    Historic pens would scoff—
The only one we moderns had
Was nothing but a Sandwich lad,
    And measles took him off.

Where are those old and feudal clans,
Their pikes, and bills, and partizans,
    Their hauberks—jerkins—buffs ?
A battle was a battle then,
A breathing piece of work—but men
    Fight now with powder puffs !

The curtal-axe is out of date !
The good old cross-bow bends to Fate
    'Tis gone—the archer's craft !
No tough arm bends the springing yew,
And jolly draymen ride, in lieu
    Of Death, upon the shaft.

The spear—the gallant tilter's pride—
The rusty spear is laid aside,

Oh spits now domineer !
The coat of mail is left alone—
And where is all chain armour gone?
Go ask at Brighton Pier.

We fight in ropes and not in lists,
Bestowing hand-cuffs with our fists,
A low and vulgar art !
No mounted man is overthrown—
A tilt—it is a thing unknown,
Except upon a cart.

Methinks I see the bounding bard
Clad like his chief in steely garb
For warding steel's appliance !
Methinks I hear the trumpet stir,
'Tis but the guard to Exeter
That bugles the " Defiance."

In cavils when will cavaliers
Set ringing helmets by the ears,
And scatter plumes about?
Or blood—if they are in the vein—
That tap will never run again,
Alas the Casque is out.

No iron-crackling now is scored
By dint of battle-axe or sword
To find a vital place—
Though certain doctors still pretend
Awhile, before they kill a friend,
To labour through his case.

Farewell, then, ancient men of might—
Crusader, errant squire, and knight !
Our coats and customs soften.
To rise would only make ye weep—
Sleep on, in rusty iron sleep,
As in a safety coffin.

A PLAN FOR WRITING BLANK VERSE IN RHYME.

In a Letter to the Editor of the " Comic Annual" for 1832.

RESPECTED SIR,—In a morning paper justly celebrated for the acuteness of its reporters, and their almost prophetic insight into character and motives—the Rhodian length of their leaps towards results, and the magnitude of their inferences, beyond the drawing of Meux's dray-horses,—there appeared, a few days since, the following paragraph :—

" Mansion House. Yesterday, a tall, emaciated being, in a brown coat, indicating his age to be about forty-five, and the raggedness of which gave a great air of mental ingenuity and intelligence to his countenance, was introduced by the officers to the Lord Mayor. It was evident from his preliminary bow that he had made some discoveries in the art of poetry, which he wished to lay before his Lordship, but the Lord Mayor perceiving by his accent that he had already submitted his project to several of the leading Publishers, referred him back to the same jurisdiction, and the unfortunate Votary of the Muses withdrew, declaring by another bow, that he should offer his plan to the Editor of the 'Comic Annual.'"

The unfortunate above referred to, sir, is myself, and with regard to the Muses, indeed a votary, though not a 10*l.* one, if the qualification depends on my pocket—but for the idea of addressing myself to the Editor of the "Comic Annual," I am indebted solely to the assumption of the gentlemen of the Press. That I have made a discovery is true, in common with Hervey, and Herschel, and Galileo, and Roger Bacon,—or rather, I should say with Columbus—my invention concerning a whole hemisphere, as it were, in the world of poetry—in short, the whole continent of blank verse. To an immense number of readers this literary land has been hitherto a complete *terra incognita*, and from one sole reason,—the want of that harmony which makes the close of one line chime with the end of another. They have no relish for numbers that turn up blank, and wonder accordingly at the epithet of " Prize," prefixed to Poems of the kind which emanate in—I was going to say from—the University of Oxford. Thus many very worthy members of society are unable to appreciate the Paradise Lost, the Task, the Chase, or the

Seasons,—the Winter especially—without rhyme. Others, again, can read the Poems in question, but with a limited enjoyment; as certain persons can admire the architectural beauties of Salisbury steeple, but would like it better with a ring of bells. For either of these tastes my discovery will provide, without affronting the palate of any other; for although the lover of rhyme will find in it a prodigality hitherto unknown, the heroic character of blank verse will not suffer in the least, but each line will "do as it likes with its own," and sound as independently of the next as "milkmaid" and "water-carrier." I have the honour to subjoin a specimen—and if, through your publicity, Mr. Murray should be induced to make me an offer for an Edition of "Paradise Lost" on this principle, for the Family Library, it will be an eternal obligation on, Respected Sir, your most obliged, and humble servant,

* * *   * * *

A NOCTURNAL SKETCH.

EVEN is come ; and from the dark Park, hark,
The signal of the setting sun—one gun !
And six is sounding from the chime, prime time
To go and see the Drury-Lane Dane slain,—
Or hear Othello's jealous doubt spout out,—
Or Macbeth raving at that shade-made blade,
Denying to his frantic clutch much touch ;—
Or else to see Ducrow with wide stride ride
Four horses as no other man can span ;
Or in the small Olympic Pit, sit split
Laughing at Liston, while you quiz his phiz.
Anon Night comes, and with her wings brings things
Such as, with his poetic tongue, Young sung ;
The gas up-blazes with its bright white light,
And paralytic watchmen prowl, howl, growl,
About the streets and take up Pall-Mall Sal,
Who, hasting to her nightly jobs, robs fobs.

Now thieves to enter for your cash, smash, crash,
Past drowsy Charley, in a deep sleep, creep,
But frightened by Policeman B 3, flee,
And while they're going, whisper low, "No go !"

Now puss, while folks are in their beds, treads leads.
And sleepers waking, grumble—" Drat that cat !"
Who in the gutter caterwauls, squalls, mauls
Some feline foe, and screams in shrill ill-will.

Now Bulls of Bashan, of a prize size, rise
In childish dreams, and with a roar gore poor
Georgy, or Charley, or Billy, willy-nilly ;—
But Nursemaid, in a nightmare rest, chest-pressed,
Dreameth of one of her old flames, James Games,
And that she hears—what faith is man's !—Ann's banns
And his, from Reverend Mr. Rice, twice, thrice :
White ribbons flourish, and a stout shout out,
That upward goes, shows Rose knows those bows' woes !

JOHN DAY.

A PATHETIC BALLAD.

" A Day after the Fair."—Old Proverb.

JOHN DAY he was the biggest man
    Of all the coachman kind,
With back too broad to be conceived
    By any narrow mind.

The very horses knew his weight
    When he was in the rear,
And wished his box a Christmas-box
    To come but once a year.

Alas ! against the shafts of love
    What armour can avail ?
Soon Cupid sent an arrow through
    His scarlet coat of mail.

The barmaid of the Crown he loved,
    From whom he never ranged ;
For though he changed his horses there,
    His love he never changed.

He thought her fairest of all fares,
    So fondly love prefers ;
And often, among twelve outsides,
    Deemed no outside like hers.

One day as she was sitting down
    Beside the porter-pump,
He came, and knelt with all his fat,
    And made an offer plump.

Said she, " My taste will never learn
    To like so huge a man,
So I must beg you will come here
    As little as you can."

But still he stoutly urged his suit,
    With vows, and sighs, and tears,
    t could not pierce her heart, although
He drove the " Dart" for years.

In vain he wooed, in vain he sued ;
    The maid was cold and proud,
And sent him off to Coventry,
    While on his way to Stroud.

He fretted all the way to Stroud,
    And thence all back to town ;
The course of love was never smooth,
    So his went up and down.

At last her coldness made him pine
    To merely bones and skin,
But still he loved like one resolved
    To love through thick and thin.

" O Mary ! view my wasted back,
    And see my dwindled calf ;
Though I have never had a wife,
    I've lost my better half."

Alas ! in vain he still assailed,
    Her heart withstood the dint ;
Though he had carried sixteen stone,
    He could not move a flint.

Worn out, at last he made a vow
　　To break his being's link ;
For he was so reduced in size
　　At nothing he could shrink.

Now some will talk in water's praise,
　　And waste a deal of breath,
But John, though he drank nothing else,
　　He drank himself to death.

The cruel maid that caused his love
　　Found out the fatal close,
For looking in the butt, she saw
　　The butt-end of his woes.

Some say his spirit haunts the Crown,
　　But that is only talk—
For after riding all his life,
　　His ghost objects to walk.

THE FALL.

"Down, down, down, ten thousand fathoms deep."—*Count Fathom*

Who does not know that dreadful gulf, where Niagara falls,
Where eagle unto eagle screams, to vulture vulture calls ;
Where down beneath, Despair and Death in liquid darkness grope,
And upward, on the foam there shines a rainbow without Hope ;
While, hung with clouds of Fear and Doubt, the unreturning wave
Suddenly gives an awful plunge, like life into the grave ;
And many a hapless mortal there hath dived to bale or bliss ;
One—only one—hath ever lived to rise from that abyss !
O Heaven ! it turns me now to ice, with chill of fear extreme,
To think of my frail bark adrift on that tumultuous stream !
In vain with desperate sinews, strung by love of life and light,
I urged that coffin, my canoe, against the current's might :
On—on—still on—direct for doom, the river rushed in force,
And fearfully the stream of Time raced with it in its course.
My eyes I closed—I dared not look the way towards the goal ;
But still I viewed the horrid close, and dreamt it in my soul.
Plainly, as through transparent lids, I saw the fleeting shore,
And lofty trees, like winged things, flit by for evermore ;

Plainly— but with no prophet sense—I heard the sullen sound,
The torrent's voice—and felt the mist, like death-sweat gathering
   round.
O agony ! O life ! My home ! and those that made it sweet :
Ere I could pray, the torrent lay beneath my very feet.
With frightful whirl, more swift than thought, I passed the dizzy
   edge,
Bound after bound, with hideous bruise, I dashed from ledge to
   ledge,
From crag to crag,—in speechless pain,—from midnight deep to
   deep ;
I did not die,—but anguish stunned my senses into sleep.
How long entranced, or whither dived, no clue I have to find :
At last the gradual light of life came dawning o'er my mind ;
And through my brain there thrilled a cry,—a cry as shrill as birds'
Of vulture or of eagle kind,—but this was set to words :—
" It's Edgar Huntley in his cap and nightgown, I declares !
He's been a walking in his sleep, and pitched all down the stairs !"

A SINGULAR EXHIBITION AT SOMERSET HOUSE.

"Our Crummie is a dainty cow."—*Scotch Song.*

On that first Saturday in May,
   When Lords and Ladies, great and grand,
Repair to see what each R.A.
   Has done since last they sought the Strand,
In red, brown, yellow, green, or blue,
   In short, what's called the private view,—
Amongst the guests—the deuce knows how
   She got in there without a row—
There came a large and vulgar dame,
   With arms deep red, and face the same,
Showing in temper not a saint ;
   No one could guess for why she came,
   Unless perchance to " scour the paint."

From wall to wall she forced her way,
   Elbowed Lord Durham—poked Lord Grey—
Stamped Stafford's toes to make him move,
   And Devonshire's Duke received a shove ;

The great Lord Chancellor felt her nudge,
She made the Vice, his Honour, budge,
And gave a pinch to Park the Judge.
As for the ladies, in this stir,
The highest rank gave way to her.

From Number One and Number Two,
She searched the pictures through and through,
On benches stood to inspect the high ones,
And squatted down to scan the shy ones;
And as she went from part to part,
A deeper red each cheek became,
Her very eyes lit up in flame,
That made each looker-on exclaim,
" Really an ardent love of art !"
Alas ! amidst her inquisition,
Fate brought her to a sad condition;
She might have run against Lord Milton,
And still have stared at deeds in oil,
But ah ! her picture-joy to spoil,
She came full butt on Mr. Hilton.

The keeper, mute, with staring eyes,
Like a lay-figure for surprise,
At last thus stammered out, " How now !
Woman—where, woman, is your ticket,
That ought to let you through our wicket ?"
Says woman, " Where is David's Cow ?"
Said Mr. H., with expedition,
" There's no Cow in the Exhibition."
" No Cow !"—but here her tongue in verity
Set off with steam and rail celerity :—

" No Cow ! there an't no Cow ! then the more's the shame and pity,
Hang you and the R.A.'s, and all the Hanging Committee !
No Cow—but hold your tongue, for you needn't talk to me—
You can't talk up the Cow, you can't, to where it ought to be ;
I haven't seen a picture, high or low, or anyhow,
Or in any of the rooms, to be compared with David's Cow.
You may talk of your Landseers, and of your Coopers, and your
　　Wards,
Why, hanging is too good for them, and yet here they are on
　　cords !

They're only fit for window frames, and shutters, and street-
    doors—
David will paint 'em any day at Red Lions or Blue Boars ;
Why, Morland was a fool to him at a little pig or sow.
It's really hard it an't hung up —I could cry about the Cow !
But I know well what it is, and why—they're jealous of David's
    fame,
But to vent it on the Cow, poor thing, is a cruelty and a shame.
Do you think it might hang by-and-by, if you cannot hang it
    now ?
David has made a party up to come and see his Cow.
If it only hung three days a week, for an example to the learners,
Why can't it hang up, turn about, with that picture of Mr. Turner's?
Or do you think from Mr. Etty you need apprehend a row,
If now and then you cut him down to hang up David's Cow ?
I can't think where their tastes have been, to not have such a
    creature,
Although I say, that should not say, it was prettier than Nature ;
It must be hung—and shall be hung, for, Mr. H., I vow,
I daren't take home the catalogue, unless it's got the Cow !
As we only want it to be seen, I should not so much care,
If it was only round the stone man's neck, a-coming up the stair ;
Or down there in the marble room, where all the figures stand,
Where one of them Three Graces might just hold it in her hand ;
Or may be Bailey's Charity the favour would allow,
It would really be a charity to hang up David's Cow.
We haven't nowhere else to go if you don't hang it here,
The Water-Colour place allows no oilman to appear,
And the British Gallery sticks to Dutch, Teniers, and Gerard Douw,
And the Suffolk Gallery will not do—it's not a Suffolk Cow.
I wish you'd seen him painting her, he hardly took his meals
Till she was painted on the board correct from head to heels ;
His heart and soul was in his Cow, and almost made him shabby,
He hardly whipped the boys at all, or helped to nurse the babby.
And when he had her all complete and painted over red,
He got so grand, I really thought him going off his head,
Now hang it, Mr. Hilton, do just hang it anyhow :
Poor David, he will hang himself unless you hang his Cow ;
And if it's unconvenient, and drawn too big by half,
David shan't send next year except a very little calf."

I'M GOING TO BOMBAY.

"Nothing venture, nothing have."—*Old Proverb.*
"Every Indiaman has at least two mates." —*Falconer's Marine Guide.*

I.

My hair is brown, my eyes are blue,
And reckoned rather bright ;
I'm shapely, if they tell me true,
And just the proper height ;
My skin has been admired in verse,
And called as fair as day—
If I *am* fair, so much the worse,
I'm going to Bombay !

II.

At school I passed with some éclat ;
I learned my French in France ;
De Wint gave lessons how to draw,
And D'Egville how to dance :—
Crevelli taught me how to sing,
And Cramer how to play—
It really is the strangest thing—
I'm going to Bombay !

III.

I've been to Bath and Cheltenham Wells,
But not their springs to sip,—
To Ramsgate—not to pick up shells,—
To Brighton—not to dip.
I've toured the Lakes, and scoured the coast
From Scarboro' to Torquay—
But though of time I've made the most,
I'm going to Bombay !

IV.

By Pa and Ma I'm daily told
To marry now's my time,
For though I'm very far from old,
I'm rather in my prime.

They say while we have any sun
We ought to make our hay—
But India has so hot a one,
I'm going to Bombay!

V.

My cousin writes from Hyderapot
My only chance to snatch,
And says the climate is so hot,
It's sure to light a match.
She's married to a son of Mars,
With very handsome pay,
And swears I ought to thank my stars
I'm going to Bombay!

VI.

She says that I shall much delight
To taste their Indian treats;
But what she likes may turn me quite,
Their strange outlandish meats.
If I can eat rupees, who knows?
Or dine, the Indian way,
On doolies and on bungalows—
I'm going to Bombay!

VII.

She says that I shall much enjoy,—
I don't know what she means,—
To take the air and buy some toy,
In my own palankeens,—
I like to drive my pony chair,
Or ride our dapple grey—
But elephants are horses there—
I'm going to Bombay!

VIII.

Farewell, farewell, my parents dear!
My friends, farewell to them!
And oh, what costs a sadder tear,
Good-by, to Mr. M.!—

If I should find an Indian vault,
Or fall a tiger's prey,
Or steep in salt, it's all *his* fault
I'm going to Bombay!

IX.

That fine new teak-built ship, the Fox,
A 1—Commander Bird,
Now lying in the London Docks,
Will sail on May the third;
Apply for passage or for freight
To Nichol, Scott, & Gray—
Pa has applied and sealed my fate—
I'm going to Bombay!

X.

My heart is full—my trunks as well;
My mind and caps made up,
My corsets, shaped by Mrs. Bell,
Are promised ere I sup;
With boots and shoes, Rivarta's best
And dresses by Ducé,
And a special licence in my chest—
I'm going to Bombay!

THE GHOST.

A VERY SERIOUS BALLAD.

"I'll be your second."—LISTON.

IN Middle Row, some years ago,
  There lived one Mr. Brown;
And many folks considered him
  The stoutest man in town.

But Brown and stout will both wear out;
  One Friday he died hard,
And left a widowed wife to mourn,
  At twenty pence a yard.

Now Widow B. in two short months
    Thought mourning quite a tax,
And wished, like Mr. Wilberforce,
    To *manumit* her blacks.

With Mr. Street she soon was sweet;
    The thing thus came about:
She asked him in at home, and then
    At church he asked her out.

Assurance such as this the man
    In ashes could not stand;
So like a Phœnix he rose up
    Against the Hand in Hand.

One dreary night the angry sprite
    Appeared before her view;
It came a little after one,
    But she was after two!

"O Mrs. B.! O Mrs. B.!
    Are these your sorrow's deeds,
Already getting up a flame
    To burn your widow's weeds?

"It's not so long since I have left
    For aye the mortal scene;
My memory—like Rogers's,
    Should still be bound in green!

"Yet if my face you still retrace
    I almost have a doubt—
I'm like an old 'Forget-me-not,'
    With all the leaves torn out!

"To think that on that finger-joint
    Another pledge should cling;
O Bess! upon my very soul,
    It struck like 'Knock and Ring.'

"A ton of marble on my breast
    Can't hinder my return;
Your conduct, Ma'am, has set my blood
    A-boiling in my urn!

"Remember, oh ! remember, how
    The marriage rite did run,—
If ever we one flesh should be,
    'Tis now—when I have none !

"And you, sir—once a bosom friend—
    Of perjured faith convict,
As ghostly toe can give no blow,
    Consider you are kicked.

"A hollow voice is all I have,
    But this I tell you plain,
Marry come up !—you marry, Ma'am,
    And I'll come up again."

More he had said, but chanticleer
    The spritely shade did shock
With sudden crow, and off he went,
    Like fowling-piece at cock !

RHYME AND REASON.

To the Editor of the " Comic Annual."

Sir,—In one of your Annuals you have given insertion to " A Plan for Writing Blank Verse in Rhyme ;" but as I have seen no regular long poem constructed on its principles, I suppose the scheme did not take with the literary world. Under these circumstances I feel encouraged to bring forward a novelty of my own, and I can only regret that such poets as Chaucer and Cottle, Spenser and Hayley, Milton and Pratt, Pope and Pye, Byron and Batterbee, should have died before it was invented.

The great difficulty in verse is avowedly the Rhyme. Dean Swift says somewhere in his letters, " that a rhyme is as hard to find with him as a guinea,"—and we all know that guineas are proverbially scarce among poets. The merest versifier that ever attempted a Valentine must have met with this Orson, some untameable savage syllable that refused to chime in with society. For instance, what poetical Fox-hunter—a contributor to the Sporting Magazine—has not drawn all the covers of Beynard, Ceynard, Deynard, Feynard, Geynard, Heynard, Keynard, Leynard, Meynard, Neynard, Peynard, Queynard, to find a rhyme for

Reynard? The spirit of the times is decidedly against Tithe; and I know of no tithe more oppressive than that poetical one, in heroic measure, which requires that every tenth syllable shall pay a sound in kind. How often the Poet goes up a line, only to be stopped at the end by an impracticable rhyme, like a bull in a blind alley! I have an ingenious medical friend, who might have been an eminent poet by this time, but the first line he wrote ended in ipecacuanha, and with all his physical and mental power, he has never yet been able to find a rhyme for it.

The plan I propose aims to obviate this hardship. My system is, to take the bull by the horns; in short, to try at first what words will chime, before you go farther and fare worse. To say nothing of other advantages, it will at least have one good effect,— and that is, to correct the erroneous notion of the would-be poets and poetesses of the present day, that the great *end* of poetry is rhyme. I beg leave to present a specimen of verse, which proves quite the reverse, and am, Sir, Your most obedient servant,

JOHN DRYDEN GRUBB.

THE DOUBLE KNOCK.

RAT-TAT it went upon the lion's chin;
"That hat, I know it!" cried the joyful girl;
"Summer's it is, I know him by his knock;
Comers like him are welcome as the day!
Lizzy! go down and open the street-door;
Busy I am to any one but *him*.
Know him you must—he has been often here;
Show him upstairs, and tell him I'm alone."

Quickly the maid went tripping down the stair;
Thickly the heart of Rose Matilda beat;
"Sure he has brought me tickets for the play—
Drury—or Covent Garden—darling man!
Kemble will play—or Kean, who makes the soul
Tremble in Richard or the frienzied Moor—
Farren, the stay and prop of many a farce
Barren beside—or Liston, Laughter's Child—
Kelly the natural, to witness whom
Jelly is nothing to the public's jam—
Cooper, the sensible—and Walter Knowles
Super, in William Tell, now rightly told.

29

Better—perchance, from Andrews, brings a box,
Letter of boxes for the Italian stage—
Brocard! Donzelli! Taglioni! Paul!
No card,—thank Heaven—engages me to-night!
Feathers, of course—no turban, and no toque—
Weather's against it, but I'll go in curls.
Dearly I dote on white—my satin dress,
Merely one night—it wont be much the worse—
Cupid—the New Ballet I long to see—
Stupid! why don't she go and ope the door!"

Glistened her eye as the impatient girl
Listened, low bending o'er the topmost stair,
Vainly, alas! she listens and she bends,
Plainly she hears this question and reply:
"Axes your pardon, sir, but what d'ye want?"
"Taxes," says he, "and shall not call again!"

———————◆———————

BAILEY BALLADS.

To anticipate mistake, the above title refers not to Thomas Haynes
—or F. W. N.—or even to any publishers—but the original Old
Bailey. It belongs to a set of songs composed during the courtly
leisure of what is technically called a Juryman in Waiting—that is,
one of a *corps de réserve*, held in readiness to fill up the gaps which
extraordinary mental exertion—or sedentary habits—or starvation,
may make in the Council of Twelve. This wrong box it was once
my fortune to get into. On the 5th of November, at the 6th hour,
leaving my bed and the luxurious perusal of Taylor on Early Rising
—I walked from a yellow fog into a black one, in my unwilling way
to the New Court, which sweet herbs even could not sweeten, for
the sole purpose of making criminals uncomfortable. A neighbour,
a retired sea-captain with a wooden leg, now literally a jury-mast,
limped with me from Highbury Terrace on the same hanging
errand—a personified Halter. Our legal drill corporal was Serjeant
Arabin, and when our muster-roll without butter was over, before
breakfast, the uninitiated can form no idea of the ludicrousness of
the excuses of the would-be Nonjurors,—aggravated by the
solemnity of a previous oath, the delivery from a witness-box like
a pulpit, and the professional gravity of the Court. One weakly

old gentleman had been ordered by his physician to eat little, but often, and apprehended even fatal consequences from being locked up with an obstinate eleven; another conscientious demurrer desired time to make himself master of his duties, by consulting Jonathan Wild, Vidocq, Hardy Vaux, and Lazarillo de Tormes. But the number of deaf men who objected the hardness of their hearing criminal cases was beyond belief. The publishers of "Curtis on the Ear" and "Wright on the Ear"—(two popular surgical works, though rather suggestive of Pugilism)—ought to have stentorian agents in that Court. Defective on one side myself, I was literally ashamed to strike up singly in such a chorus of muffled double drums, and tacitly suffered my ears to be boxed with a common Jury. I heard, on the right hand, a Judge's charge—an arraignment and evidence to match, with great dexterity, but failing to catch the defence from the left hand, refused naturally to concur in any sinister verdict. The learned Serjeant, I presume, as I was only half deaf, only half discharged me,—committing me to the relay-box, as a Juror in Waiting,—and from which I was relieved only by his successor, Sir Thomas Denman, and to justify my dulness, I made even his stupendous voice to repeat my dismissal twice over!

It was during this compelled attendance that the project struck me of a Series of Lays of Larceny, combining Sin and Sentiment in the melodramatic mixture which is so congenial to the cholera-morbid sensibility of the present age and stage. The following are merely specimens, but a hint from the Powers that be,—in the Strand,—will promptly produce a handsome volume of the remainder, with a grateful Dedication to the learned Serjeant.

No. I.

LINES TO MARY.

(AT NO. 1 NEWGATE, FAVOURED BY MR. WONTNER.)

O Mary, I believed you true,
And I was blest in so believing;
But till this hour I never knew—
That you were taken up for thieving!

Oh! when I snatched a tender kiss,
Or some such trifle when I courted,
You said, indeed, that love was bliss,
But never owned you were transported!

But then, to gaze on that fair face,
It would have been an unfair feeling
To dream that you had pilfered lace—
And Flints had suffered from your stealing !

Or, when my suit I first preferred,
To bring your coldness to repentance,
Before I hammered out a word,
How could I dream you'd heard a sentence !

Or when, with all the warmth of youth,
I strove to prove my love no fiction,
How could I guess I urged a truth
On one already past conviction ?

How could I dream that ivory part,
Your hand—where I have looked and lingered,
Although it stole away my heart,
Had been held up as one light-fingered ?

In melting verse your charms I drew,
The charms in which my muse delighted—
Alas ! the lay, I thought was new,
Spoke only what had been *indicted !*

Oh ! when that form, a lovely one,
Hung on the neck its arms had flown to,
I little thought that you had run
A chance of hanging on your own too.

You said you picked me from the world—
My vanity it now must shock it—
And down at once my pride is hurled,—
You've picked me—and you've picked a pocket !

Oh ! when our love had got so far,
The banns were read by Dr. Daly,
Who asked if there was any *bar*—
Why did not some one shout, " Old Bailey ? "

But when you robed your flesh and bones
In that pure white that angel garb is,
Who could have thought you, Mary Jones
Among the Joans that link with *Darbies !*

And when the parson came to say
My goods were yours, if I had got any,
And you should honour and obey,
Who could have thought—" O Bay of Botany!"

But, oh! the worst of all your slips
I did not till this day discover—
That down in Deptford's prison-ships,
O Mary! you've a hulking lover!

No. II.

"Love, with a witness!"

HE has shaved off his whiskers and blackened his brows,
Wears a patch and a wig of false hair,—
But it's him—oh, it's him!—we exchanged lovers' vows
When I lived up in Cavendish Square.

He had beautiful eyes, and his lips were the same,
And his voice was as soft as a flute—
Like a Lord or a Marquis he looked, when he came
To make love in his master's best suit.

If I lived for a thousand long years from my birth,
I shall never forget what he told—
How he loved me beyond the rich women of earth,
With their jewels and silver and gold!

When he kissed me, and bade me adieu with a sigh,
By the light of the sweetest of moons;
Oh, how little I dreamt I was bidding good-by
To my Missis's teapot and spoons!

No. III.

" I'd be a parody."—BAILEY.

WE met—'twas in a mob—and I thought he had done me
I felt—I could not feel—for no watch was upon me;
He ran—the night was cold—and his pace was unaltered,
I too longed much to pelt—but my small-boned leg faltered.
I wore my brand-new boots—and unrivalled their brightness;
They fit me to a hair—how I hated their tightness!
I called, but no one came, and my stride had a tether—
Oh, *thou* hast been the cause of this anguish, my leather!

And once again we met—and an old pal was near him ;
He swore, a something low—but 'twas no use to fear him ;
I seized upon his arm—he was mine and mine only,
And stepped—as he deserved—to cells wretched and lonely :
And there he will be tried—but I shall ne'er receive her,
The watch that went too sure for an artful deceiver.
The world may think me gay,—heart and feet ache together—
Oh, *thou* hast been the cause of this anguish, my leather.

OUR VILLAGE.—BY A VILLAGER.

OUR village, that's to say, not Miss Mitford's village, but our
village of Bullock Smithy,
Is come into by an avenue of trees, three oak pollards, two elders,
and a withy ;
And in the middle there's a green of about not exceeding an acre
and a half ;
It's common to all, and fed off by nineteen cows, six ponies,
three horses, five asses, two foals, seven pigs, and a calf !
Besides a pond in the middle, as is held by a similar sort of
common-law lease,
And contains twenty ducks, six drakes, three ganders, two dead
dogs, four drowned kittens, and twelve geese.
Of course the green's cropt very close, and does famous for
bowling when the little village-boys play at cricket ;
Only some horse, or pig, or cow, or great jackass, is sure to come
and stand right before the wicket.
There's fifty-five private houses, let alone barns, and workshops,
and pigsties, and poultry huts, and such-like sheds ;
With plenty of public-houses—two Foxes, one Green Man, three
Bunch of Grapes, one Crown, and six King's Heads.
The Green Man is reckoned the best, as the only one that for
love or money can raise
A postilion, a blue-jacket, two deplorable lame white horses, and
a ramshackled "neat postchaise."
There's one parish church for all the people, whatsoever may be
their ranks in life or their degrees,
Except one very damp, small, dark, freezing-cold, little Methodist
Chapel of Ease ;

And close by the churchyard there's a stonemason's yard, that
    when the time is seasonable
Will furnish with afflictions sore and marble urns and cherubims
    very low and reasonable.
There's a cage, comfortable enough; I've been in it with Old Jack
    Jeffrey and Tom Pike;
For the Green Man next door will send you in ale, gin, or any-
    thing else you like.
I can't speak of the stocks, as nothing remains of them but the
    upright post;
But the pound is kept in repairs for the sake of Cob's horse, as is
    always there almost.
There's a smithy of course, where that queer sort of a chap in his
    way, Old Joe Bradley,
Perpetually hammers and stammers, for he stutters and shoes
    horses very badly.
There's a shop of all sorts, that sells everything, kept by the
    widow of Mr. Task;
But when you go there, it's ten to one she's out of everything you
    ask.
You'll know her house by the swarm of boys, like flies, about the
    old sugary cask:
There are six empty houses, and not so well papered inside as
    out,
For bill-stickers wont beware, but sticks notices of sales and
    election placards all about.
That's the Doctor's with a green door, where the garden pots in
    the windows are seen—
A weakly monthly rose that don't blow, and a dead geranium, and
    a tea-plant with five black leaves and one green.
As for hollyoaks at the cottage doors, and honeysuckles and
    jasmines, you may go and whistle;
But the tailor's front garden grows two cabbages, a dock, a
    ha'porth of pennyroyal, two dandelions, and a thistle.
There are three small orchards—Mr. Busby's the schoolmaster's
    is the chief—
With two pear-trees that don't bear; one plum and an apple, that
    every year is stripped by a thief.
There's another small day-school too, kept by the respectable
    Mrs. Gaby,
A select establishment, for six little boys and one big, and four
    little girls and a baby;

There's a rectory, with pointed gables and strange odd chimneys
  that never smokes,
For the rector don't live on his living like other Christian sort of
  folks ;
There's a barber's, once a week well filled with rough black-
  bearded, shock-headed churls,
And a window with two feminine men's heads, and two masculine
  ladies in false curls ;
There's a butcher's, and a carpenter's, and a plumber's, and a small
  greengrocer's, and a baker,
But he wont bake on a Sunday ; and there's a sexton that's a coal-
  merchant besides, and an undertaker ;
And a toyshop, but not a whole one, for a village can't compare
  with the London shops ;
One window sells drums, dolls, kites, carts, bats, Clout's balls, and
  the other sells malt and hops.
And Mrs. Brown, in domestic economy not to be a bit behind her
  betters,
Lets her house to a milliner, a watchmaker, a rat-catcher, a
  cobbler, lives in it herself, and it's the post-office for letters.
Now I've gone through all the village—ay, from end to end, save
  and except one more house,
But I haven't come to that—and I hope I never shall—and that's
  the Village Poorhouse !

ODE TO MR. MALTHUS.

My dear, do pull the bell,
  And pull it well,
And send those noisy children all upstairs,
  Now playing here like bears—
You George, and William, go into the grounds,
  Charles, James, and Bob are there,—and take your string,
  Drive horses, or fly kites, or anything,
You're quite enough to play at hare and hounds ;—
  You little May, and Caroline, and Poll,
    Take each your doll,
  And go, my dears, into the two-back pair,
    Your sister Margaret's there—
Harriet and Grace, thank God, are both at school,
  At far-off Ponty Pool—

I want to read, but really can't get on—
Let the four twins, Mark, Matthew, Luke, and John,
    Go—to their nursery—go—I never can
    Enjoy my Malthus among such a clan!

            Oh Mr Malthus, I agree
            In everything I read with thee!
            The world's too full, there is no doubt,
            And wants a deal of thinning out,—
            It's plain—as plain as Harrow's Steeple—
            And I agree with some thus far,
            Who say the King's too popular,
            That is,—he has too many people.
            There are too many of all trades,
                Too many bakers,
            Too many every-thing-makers,
            But not too many undertakers,—
                Too many boys,—
            Too many hobby-de-hoys,—
Too many girls, men, widows, wives, and maids,—
There is a dreadful surplus to demolish;
            And yet some Wrongheads,
            With thick not long heads,
            Poor metaphysicians!
            Sign petitions
Capital punishment to abolish;
And in the face of censuses such vast ones
            New hospitals contrive,
            For keeping life alive,
Laying first stones, the dolts! instead of last ones!—
Others, again, in the same contrariety,
Deem that of all Humane Society
            They really deserve thanks,
Because the two banks of the Serpentine
            By their design,
            Are Saving Banks.
    Oh! were it given but to me to weed
        The human breed,
And root out here and there some cumbering elf,
    I think I could go through it,
            And really do it
With profit to the world and to myself.—

For instance, the unkind among the Editors,
   My debtors, those I mean to say
   Who cannot or who will not pay,
      And all my creditors.
   These, for my own sake, I'd destroy;
   But for the world's, and every one's,
   I'd hoe up Mrs. G——'s two sons,
   And Mrs. B——'s big little boy,
   Called only by herself an " only joy."
   As Mr. Irving's chapel's not too full,
      Himself alone I'd pull—
But for the peace of years that have to run,
I'd make the Lord Mayor's a perpetual station,
   And put a period to rotation,
   By rooting up all Aldermen but one,—
These are but hints what good might thus be done !
   But ah ! I fear the public good
   Is little by the public understood,—
For instance—if with flint, and steel, and tinder,
Great Swing, for once a philanthropic man,
Proposed to throw a light upon thy plan,
No doubt some busy fool would hinder
His burning all the Foundling to a cinder.

Or, if the Lord Mayor, on an Easter Monday,
   That wine and bun-day,
Proposed to poison all the little Blue-coats,
Before they died by bit or sup,
Some meddling Marplot would blow up,
   Just at the moment critical,
   The economy political
Of saving their fresh yellow plush and new coats.

   Equally 'twould be undone,
   Suppose the Bishop of London,
      On that great day
      In June or May,
When all the large small family of charity,
   Brown, black, or carroty,
Walk in their dusty parish shoes,
In too, too many two-and-twos,

To sing together till they scare the walls
    Of old St. Paul's,
Sitting in red, grey, green, blue, drab, and white,
   Some say a gratifying sight.
     Tho' I think sad—but that's a schism—
     To witness so much pauperism—
Suppose, I say, the Bishop then, to make
In this poor crowded world more room,
    Proposed to shake
Down that immense extinguisher, the dome—
Some humane Martin in the charity *Gal*-way
    I fear would come and interfere,
    Save beadle, brat, and overseer,
    To walk back in their parish shoes,
    In too, too many two-and-twos,
Islington—Wapping—or Pall Mall way !

Thus, people hatched from goose's egg,
Foolishly think a pest, a plague,
And in its face their doors all shut,
On hinges oiled with cajeput—
Drugging themselves with drams well spiced and cloven,
    And turning pale as linen rags
    At hoisting up of yellow flags,
While you and I are crying " Orange Boven !"
Why should we let precautions so absorb us,
Or trouble shipping with a quarantine—
When if I understand the thing you mean,
We ought to *import* the Cholera Morbus !

THE COMPASS, WITH VARIATIONS.

" The Needles have sometimes been fatal to Mariners."
               Picture of Isle of Wight.

    ONE close of day—'twas in the Bay
    Of Naples—bay of glory !—
    While light was hanging crowns of gold
    On mountains high and hoary,
    A gallant bark got under weigh,
    And with her sails my story.

For Leghorn she was bound direct,
With wine and oil for cargo,
Her crew of men some nine or ten,
The captain's name Iago ;
A good and gallant bark she was,
La Donna (called) del Lago.

Bronzed mariners were hers to view,
With brown cheeks, clear or muddy,
Dark, shining eyes, and coal-black hair,
Meet heads for painter's study ;
But 'midst their tan there stood one man
Whose cheek was fair and ruddy ;

His brow was high, a loftier brow
Ne'er shone in song or sonnet,
His hair a little scant, and when
He doffed his cap or bonnet,
One saw that Grey had gone beyond
A premiership upon it !

His eye—a passenger was he,
The cabin he had hired it,—
His eye was grey, and when he looked
Around, the prospect fired it—
A fine poetic light, as if
The Appe-Nine inspired it.

His frame was stout—in height about
Six feet—well made and portly ;
Of dress and manner just to give
A sketch, but very shortly,
His order seemed a composite
Of rustic with the courtly.

He ate and quaffed, and joked and laughed,
And chatted with the seamen,
And often tasked their skill and asked,
" What weather is't to be, man ?"
No demonstration there appeared
That he was any demon.

No sort of sign there was that he
Could raise a stormy rumpus,
Like Prospero make breezes blow,
And rocks and billows thump us,—
But little we supposed what he
Could with the needle compass !

Soon came a storm—the sea at first
Seemed lying almost fallow—
When lo ! full crash, with billowy dash,
From clouds of black and yellow,
Came such a gale, as blows but once
A century, like the aloe !

Our stomachs we had just prepared
To vest a small amount in ;
When, gush ! a flood of brine came down
The skylight—quite a fountain,
And right on end the table reared,
Just like the Table Mountain.

Down rushed the soup, down gushed the wine,
Each roll its rôle repeating,
Rolled down—the round of beef declared
For parting—not for meating !
Off flew the fowls, and all the game
Was " too far gone for eating !"

Down knife and fork—down went the pork,
The lamb too broke its tether ;
Down mustard went—each condiment—
Salt—pepper—all together !
Down everything, like craft that seek
The Downs in stormy weather.

Down plunged the *Lady of the Lake*,
Her timbers seemed to sever ;
Down, down, a dreary derry down,
Such lurch she had gone never ;
She almost seemed about to take
A bed of down for ever !

Down dropped the captain's nether jaw,
Thus robbed of all its uses,
He thought he saw the Evil One
Beside Vesuvian sluices,
Playing at dice for soul and ship,
And throwing *Sink* and *Deuces.*

Down fell the steward on his face,
To all the Saints commending ;
And candles to the Virgin vowed,
As save-alls 'gainst his ending.
Down fell the mate, he thought his fate,
Check-mate, was close impending !

Down fell the cook—the cabin boy,
Their beads with fervour telling,
While alps of serge, with snowy verge,
Above the yards came yelling.
Down fell the crew, and on their knees
Shuddered at each white swelling !

Down sunk the sun of bloody hue,
His crimson light a cleaver
To each red rover of a wave :
To eye of fancy-weaver,
Neptune, the God, seemed tossing in
A raging scarlet fever !

Sore, sore afraid, each Papist prayed
To Saint and Virgin Mary ;
But one there was that stood composed
Amid the waves' vagary :
As staunch as rock, a true game cock
'Mid chicks of Mother Cary !

His ruddy cheek retained its streak,
No danger seemed to shrink him ;
His step still bold,—of mortal mould
The crew could hardly think him :
The Lady of the Lake, he seemed
To know, could never sink him.

Relaxed at last, the furious gale,
Quite out of breath with racing;
The boiling flood in milder mood,
With gentler billows chasing;
From stem to stern, with frequent turn,
The Stranger took to pacing.

And as he walked to self he talked,
Some ancient ditty thrumming,
In under tone, as not alone—
Now whistling, and now humming—
"You're welcome, Charlie," "Cowdenknowes,"
"Kenmure," or "Campbells' Coming."

Down went the wind, down went the wave,
Fear quitted the most finical;
The Saints, I wot, were soon forgot,
And Hope was at the pinnacle;
When rose on high, a frightful cry—
"The Devil's in the binnacle!"

"The Saints be near," the helmsman cried,
His voice with quite a falter—
"Steady's my helm, but every look
The needle seems to alter;
God only knows where China lies,
Jamaica, or Gibraltar!"

The captain stared aghast at mate,
The pilot at th' apprentice;
No fancy of the German Sea
Of Fiction the event is;
But when they at the compass looked,
It seemed non compass mentis.

Now north, now south, now east, now west,
The wavering point was shaken,
'Twas past the whole philosophy
Of Newton, or of Bacon;
Never by compass, till that hour,
Such latitudes were taken!

With fearful speech, each after each
Took turns in the inspection;
They found no gun—no iron—none
To vary its direction;
It seemed a new magnetic case
Of Poles in Insurrection!

Farewell to wives, farewell their lives,
And all their household riches;
Oh! while they thought of girl or boy,
And dear domestic niches,
All down the side which holds the heart,
That needle gave them stitches.

With deep amaze, the Stranger gazed
To see them so white-livered:
And walked abaft the binnacle,
To know at what they shivered:
But when he stood beside the card,
St. Josef! how it quivered!

No fancy-motion, brain
In eye of timid dreamer-
The nervous finger of a sot
Ne'er showed a plainer tremor;
To every brain it seemed too plain,
There stood th' Infernal Schemer!

Mixed brown and blue each visage grew,
Just like a pullet's gizzard;
Meanwhile the captain's wandering wit,
From tacking like an izzard,
Bore down in this plain course at last,
"It's Michael Scott—the Wizard!"

A smile passed o'er the ruddy face,
"To see the poles so falter
I'm puzzled, friends, as much as you,
For with no fiends I palter;
Michael I'm not—although a Scott—
My Christian name is Walter."

Like oil it fell, that name, a spell
On all the fearful faction ;
The captain's head (for he had read)
Confessed the Needle's action,
And bowed to HIM in whom the North
Has lodged its main attraction !

THERE'S NO ROMANCE IN THAT.

" So, while I fondly imagined we were deceiving my relations, and flattered myself that I should outwit and incense them all, behold, my hopes are to be crushed at once by my aunt's consent and approbation, and I am myself the only dupe. But here, sir—here is the picture !"—*Lydia Languish.*

O DAYS of old, O days of knights,
Of tourneys and of tilts,
When love was balked and valour stalked
On high heroic stilts—
Where are ye gone ?—adventures cease,
The world gets tame and flat,—
We've nothing now but New Police—
There's no Romance in that !

I wish I ne'er had learned to read,
Or Radcliffe how to write ;
That Scott had been a boor on Tweed,
And Lewis cloistered quite !
Would I had never drunk so deep
Of dear Miss Porter's vat ;
I only turn to life, and weep—
There's no Romance in that !

No bandits lurk—no turbaned Turk
To Tunis bears me off ;
I hear no noises in the night
Except my mother's cough ;
No Bleeding Spectre haunts the house ;
No shape, but owl or bat,
Come flitting after moth or mouse—
There's no Romance in that !

30

I have not any grief profound,
Or secrets to confess ;
My story would not fetch a pound
For A. K. Newman's press ;
Instead of looking thin and pale,
I'm growing red and fat,
As if I lived on beef and ale—
There's no Romance in that !

It's very hard, by land or sea
Some strange event I court,
But nothing ever comes to me
That's worth a pen's report :
It really made my temper chafe,
Each coast that I was at,
I vowed and railed, and came home safe—
There's no Romance in that !

The only time I had a chance,
At Brighton one fine day,
My chestnut mare began to prance,
Took fright, and ran away ;
Alas ! no Captain of the Tenth
To stop my steed came pat ;
A butcher caught the rein at length—
There's no Romance in that !

Love—even love—goes smoothly on
A railway sort of track—
No flinty sire, no jealous Don !
No hearts upon the rack ;
No Polydore, no Theodore—
His ugly name is Mat,
Plain Matthew Pratt, and nothing more—
There's no Romance in that !

He is not dark, he is not tall,
His forehead's rather low,
He is not pensive—not at all,
But smiles his teeth to show ;
He comes from Wales, and yet in size
Is really but a sprat,
With sandy hair and greyish eyes—
There's no Romance in that !

He wears no plumes or Spanish cloaks,
Or long sword hanging down ;
He dresses much like other folks,
And commonly in brown ;
His collar he will not discard,
Or give up his cravat
Lord Byron-like—he's not a bard—
There's no Romance in that !

He's rather bald, his sight is weak,
He's deaf in either drum ;
Without a lisp he cannot speak,
But then—he's worth a plum.
He talks of stocks and three per cents.
By way of private chat,
Of Spanish bonds, and shares, and rents—
There's no Romance in that !

I sing—no matter what I sing,
" Di Tanti," or " Crudel,"
"Tom Bowling," or " God save the King,"
" Di Piacer "—" All's well ;"
He knows no more about a voice
For singing than a gnat ;
And as to music " has no choice"—
There's no Romance in that !

Of light guitar I cannot boast,
He never serenades ;
He writes, and sends it by the post,
He doesn't bribe the maids :
No stealth, no hempen ladder—no !
He comes with loud rat-tat,
That startles half of Bedford Row—
There's no Romance in that !

He comes at nine in time to choose
His coffee—just two cups,
And talks with Pa about the news,
Repeats debates, and sups.
John helps him with his coat aright,
And Jenkins hands his hat ;
My lover bows, and says good-night—
There's no Romance in that !

I've long had Pa's and Ma's consent
My aunt she quite approves,
My brother wishes joy from Kent,
None try to thwart our loves ;
On Tuesday, Reverend Mr. Mace
Will make me Mrs. Pratt,
Of Number Twenty, Sussex Place—
There's no Romance in that.

SHOOTING PAINS.

"The charge is prepared."—*Macheath.*

IF I shoot any more I'll be shot,
For ill-luck seems determined to star me,
    I have marched the whole day
    With a gun,—for no pay—
Zounds, I'd better have been in the army !

What matters Sir Christopher's leave ;
To his manor I'm sorry I came yet !
    With confidence fraught,
    My two pointers I brought,
But we are not a point towards game yet !

And that gamekeeper too, with advice !
Of my course he has been a nice chalker,
    Not far, were his words,
    I could go without birds :
If my legs could cry out, they'd cry "Walker !"

Not Hawker could find out a flaw,—
My appointments are modern and Mantony,
    And I've brought my own man,
    To mark down all he can,
But I can't find a mark for my Antony !

The partridges,—where can they lie ?
I have promised a leash to Miss Jervas,
    As the least I could do ;
    But without even two
To brace me,—I'm getting quite nervous !

To the pheasants—how well they're preserved !
My sport's not a jot more beholden,
    As the birds are so shy,
    For my friends I must buy,
And so send " silver pheasants and golden."

I have tried every form for a hare,
Every patch, every furze that could shroud her,
    With toil unrelaxed,
    Till my patience is taxed,
But I cannot be taxed for hare-powder.

I've been roaming for hours in three flats
In the hope of a snipe for a snap at ;
    But still vainly I court
    The percussioning sport,
I find nothing for " setting my cap at !"

A woodcock,—this month is the time,—
Right and left I've made ready my lock for,
    With well-loaded double,
    But spite of my trouble,
Neither barrel can I find a cock for !

A rabbit I should not despise,
But they lurk in their burrows so lowly ;
    This day's the eleventh,
    It is not the seventh,
But they seem to be keeping it hole-y.

For a mallard I've waded the marsh,
And haunted each pool, and each lake—oh !
    Mine is not the luck,
    To obtain thee, O Duck,
Or to doom thee, O Drake, like a Draco !

For a field-fare I've fared far a-field,
Large or small I am never to sack bird,
    Not a thrush is so kind
    As to fly, and I find
I may whistle myself for a blackbird !

I am angry, I'm hungry, I'm dry,
Disappointed, and sullen, and goaded,
    And so weary an elf,
    I am sick of myself,
And with Number One seem o'erloaded.

As well one might beat round St. Paul's,
And look out for a cock or a hen there;
    I have searched round and round
    All the Baronet's ground,
But Sir Christopher hasn't a wren there!

Joyce may talk of his excellent caps,
But for nightcaps they set me desiring,
    And it's really too bad,
    Not a shot I have had
With Hall's Powder, renowned for " quick firing."

If this is what people call sport,
Oh ! of sporting I can't have a high sense,
    And there still remains one
    More mischance on my gun—
" Fined for shooting without any licence."

———◆———

THE BOY AT THE NORE.

" Alone I did it !—Boy !"—*Coriolanus.*

I say, little Boy at the Nore,
  Do you come from the small Isle of Man?
Why, your history a mystery must be,—
    Come tell us as much as you can,
        Little Boy at the Nore !

You live, it seems, wholly on water,
  Which your Gambier calls living in clover ;—
But how comes it, if that is the case,
    You're eternally half seas over,
        Little Boy at the Nore?

While you ride—while you dance—while you float—
  Never mind your imperfect orthography ;—
But give us as well as you can,
  Your watery auto-biography,
          Little Boy at the Nore !

LITTLE BOY AT THE NORE LOQUITUR.

I'm the tight little Boy at the Nore,
  In a sort of sea-negus I dwells,
Half and half 'twixt salt water and port ;
  I'm reckoned the first of the swells—
          I'm the Boy at the Nore !

I lives with my toes to the flounders,
  And watches through long days and nights ;
Yet, cruelly eager, men look—
  To catch the first glimpse of my lights—
          I'm the Boy at the Nore !

I never gets cold in the head,
  So my life on salt water is sweet ;
I think I owes much of my health
  To being well used to wet feet—
          As the Boy at the Nore !

There's one thing, I'm never in debt—
  Nay ! I liquidates more than I *oughter ;*
So the man to beat Cits as goes by,
  In keeping the head above water,
          Is the Boy at the Nore !

I've seen a good deal of distress,
  Lots of breakers in Ocean's *Gazette,*;
They should do as I do—rise o'er all,
  Ay, a good floating capital get,
          Like the Boy at the Nore !

---

* A word caught from some American trader in passing

I'm a'ter the sailor's own heart,
 And cheers him, in deep water rolling;
And the friend of all friends to Jack Junk,
 Ben Backstay, Tom Pipes, and Tom Bowling,
   Is the Boy at the Nore!

Could I e'er but grow up, I'd be off
 For a week to make love with my wheedles;
If the tight little Boy at the Nore
 Could but catch a nice girl at the Needles,
   We'd have *two* at the Nore.

They thinks little of sizes on water,
 On big waves the tiny one skulks—
While the river has men-of-war on it—
 Yes—the Thames is oppressed with great hulks,
   And the Boy's at the Nore!

But I've done—for the water is heaving
 Round my body as though it would sink it!
And I've been so long pitching and tossing,
 That sea-sick—you'd hardly now think it—
   Is the Boy at the Nore!

THE BROKEN DISH.

WHAT's life but full of care and doubt,
 With all its fine humanities;
With parasols we walk about,
 Long pigtails and such vanities.

We plant pomegranate trees and things,
 And go in gardens sporting,
With toys and fans of peacocks' wings
 To painted ladies courting.

We gather flowers of every hue,
 And fish in boats for fishes,
Build summer-houses painted blue,—
 But life's as frail as dishes.

Walking about their groves of trees,
　　Blue bridges and blue rivers,
How little thought them two Chinese
　　They'd both be smashed to shivers.

ODE TO PEACE.

WRITTEN ON THE NIGHT OF MY MISTRESS'S GRAND ROUT.

O PEACE! oh come with me and dwell—
　　But stop, for there's the bell.
O Peace! for thee I go and sit in churches,
　　On Wednesday, when there's very few
　　　In loft or pew—
Another ring, the tarts are come from Birch's.
O Peace! for thee I have avoided marriage—
　　Hush! there's a carriage.
O Peace! thou art the best of earthly goods—
　　The five Miss Woods.
O Peace! thou art the goddess I adore—
　　There come some more.
O Peace! thou child of solitude and quiet—
That's Lord Drum's footman, for he loves a riot.

　　　　O Peace!—
　　Knocks will not cease.
O Peace! thou wert for human comfort planned—
　　That's Weippert's band.
O Peace! how glad I welcome thy approaches—
　　I hear the sound of coaches.
O Peace! O Peace!—another carriage stops—
　　It's early for the Blenkinsops.

O Peace! with thee I love to wander,
But wait till I have showed up Lady Squander;
And now I've seen her up the stair,
O Peace!—but here comes Captain Hare.
O Peace! thou art the slumber of the mind,
Untroubled, calm and quiet, and unbroken—
If that is Alderman Guzzle from Portsoken,
Alderman Gobble wont be far behind.

O Peace ! serene in worldly shyness—
Make way there for his Serene Highness !

O Peace ! if you do not disdain
To dwell amongst the menial train,
I have a silent place, and lone,
That you and I may call our own,
Where tumult never makes an entry—
Susan, what business have you in my pantry ?

O Peace !—but there is Major Monk,
At variance with his wife.   O Peace !—
And that great German, Vander Trunk,
And that great talker, Miss Apreece.
O Peace ! so dear to poets' quills—
They're just beginning their quadrilles.
O Peace ! our greatest renovator—
I wonder where I put my waiter.
O Peace !—but here my ode I'll cease !
I have no peace to write of Peace.

HUGGINS AND DUGGINS.

A PASTORAL AFTER POPE.

Two swains or clowns—but call them swains—
While keeping flocks on Salisbury Plains—
For all that tend on sheep as drovers
Are turned to songsters or to lovers,—
Each of the lass he called his dear
Began to carol loud and clear.
First Huggins sang, and Duggins then,
In the way of ancient shepherd men ;
Who thus alternate hitched in song,
" All things by turns, and nothing long."

HUGGINS.

Of all the girls about our place,
There's one beats all in form and face ;
Search through all Great and Little Bumpstead
You'll only find one Peggy Plumstead.

DUGGINS.

To groves and streams I tell my flame,
I make the cliffs repeat her name :
When I'm inspired by gills and noggins,
The rocks re-echo Sally Hoggins !

HUGGINS.

When I am walking in the grove,
I think of Peggy as I rove :
I'd carve her name on every tree,
But I don't know my A, B, C.

DUGGINS.

Whether I walk in hill or valley,
I think of nothing else but Sally :
I'd sing her praise, but I can sing
No song, except " God save the King."

HUGGINS.

My Peggy does all nymphs excel,
And all confess she bears the bell ;
Where'er she goes swains flock together,
Like sheep that follow the bellwether.

DUGGINS.

Sally is tall and not too straight,—
Those very poplar shapes I hate ;
But something twisted like an S,—
A crook becomes a shepherdess.

HUGGINS.

When Peggy's dog her arms emprison,
I often wish my lot was hisn ;
How often I should stand and turn,
To get a pat from hands like hern.

DUGGINS.

I tell Sall's lambs how blest they be,
To stand about and stare at she ;
But when I look, she turns and shies,
And wont bear none but their sheep's-eyes !

HUGGINS.

Love goes with Peggy where she goes,—
Beneath her smile the garden grows,
Potatoes spring, and cabbage starts,
'Tatoes have eyes, and cabbage hearts!

DUGGINS.

Where Sally goes it's always Spring,
Her presence brightens everything;
The sun smiles bright, but where her grin is,
It makes brass farthings look like guineas.

HUGGINS.

For Peggy I can have no joy,
She's sometimes kind, and sometimes coy,
And keeps me, by her wayward tricks,
As comfortless as sheep with ticks.

DUGGINS.

Sally is ripe as June or May,
And yet as cold as Christmas Day;
For when she's asked to change her lot,
Lamb's wool,—but Sally, she wool not.

HUGGINS.

Only with Peggy and with health,
I'd never wish for state or wealth;
Talking of having health and more pence,
I'd drink her health if I had fourpence.

DUGGINS.

Oh, how that day would seem to shine,
If Sally's banns were read with mine;
She cries, when such a wish I carry,
" Marry come up !" but will not marry.

A FEW LINES ON COMPLETING FORTY-SEVEN.

WHEN I reflect, with serious sense,
   While years and years run on,
How soon I may be summoned hence—
   There's cook a-calling John.

Our lives are built so frail and poor,
   On sand, and not on rocks,
We're hourly standing at Death's door—
   There's some one double-knocks.

All human days have settled terms,
   Our fates we cannot force ;
This flesh of mine will feed the worms—
   They're come to lunch, of course.

And when my body's turned to clay,
   And dear friends hear my knell,
Oh, let them give a sigh and say—
   I hear the upstairs bell.

TO MARY HOUSEMAID,

ON VALENTINE'S DAY.

MARY, you know I've no love-nonsense,
   And, though I pen on such a day,
I don't mean flirting, on my conscience,
   Or writing in the courting way.

Though Beauty hasn't formed your feature,
   It saves you, p'rhaps, from being vain,
And many a poor unhappy creature
   May wish that she was half as plain.

Your virtues would not rise an inch,
   Although your shape was two foot taller,
And wisely you let others pinch
   Great waists and feet to make them smaller.

You never try to spare your hands
From getting red by household duty,
But, doing all that it commands,
Their coarseness is a moral beauty.

Let Susan flourish her fair arms,
And at your odd legs sneer and scoff;
But let her laugh, for you have charms
That nobody knows nothing of.

THE UNDYING ONE.

"He shall not die."—*Uncle Toby.*

I.

OF all the verses, grave or gay,
That ever whiled an hour,
I never knew a mingled lay,
At once so sweet and sour,
As that by Ladye Norton spun,
And christened "The Undying One."

II.

I'm very certain that she drew
A portrait when she penned
That picture of a perfect Jew,
Whose days will never end;
I'm sure it means my Uncle Lunn,
For he is an Undying One.

III.

These twenty years he's been the same,
And may be twenty more;
But Memory's pleasures only claim
His features for a score;
Yet in that time the change is none—
Th' image of th' Undying One!

IV.

They say our climate's damp and cold,
   And lungs are tender things ;
My uncle's much abroad and old,
   But when " King Cole" he sings,
A Stentor's voice, enough to stun,
Declares him an Undying One.

V.

Others have died from needle-pricks
   And very slender blows,
From accidental slips or kicks,
   Or bleedings at the nose ;
Or choked by grape-stone, or a bun—
But he is the Undying One !

VI.

A soldier once, he once endured
   A bullet in the breast—
It might have killed—but only cured
   An asthma in the chest ;
He was not to be slain with gun,
For he is the Undying One.

VII.

In water once too long he dived,
   And all supposed him beat,
He seemed so cold—but he revived
   To have another heat,
Just when we thought his race was run,
And came in fresh—th' Undying One !

VIII.

To look at Meux's once he went,
   And tumbled in the vat—
And greater Jobs their lives have spent
   In lesser boils than that :—
He left the beer quite underdone,
No bier to the Undying One !

IX.

He's been from strangulation black,
  From bile, of yellow hue,
Scarlet from fever's hot attack,
  From cholera-morbus blue ;
Yet with these dyes—to use a pun—
He still is the Undying One.

X.

He rolls in wealth, yet has no wife
  His Three per Cents. to share ;
He never married in his life,
  Or flirted with the fair ;
The sex he made a point to shun,
For beauty an Undying One.

XI.

To judge him by the present signs,
  The future by the past,
So quick he lives, so slow declines,
  The Last Man wont be last,
But buried underneath a ton
Of mould by the Undying One !

XII.

Next Friday week, his birthday boast,
  His ninetieth year he spends,
And I shall have his health to toast
  Amongst expectant friends,
And wish—it really sounds like fun—
Long life to the Undying One !

———◆———

ODE FOR THE NINTH OF NOVEMBER.

O Lud ! O Lud ! O Lud !
I mean, of course, that venerable town,
Mentioned in stories of renown,
  Built formerly of mud ;—

O Lud, I say, why didst thou e'er
    Invent the office of a mayor,
An office that no useful purpose crowns,
But to set aldermen against each other,
That should be brother unto brother,—
Sisters at least, by virtue of their gowns?

But still, if one must have a mayor
        To fill the civic chair,
        O Lud, I say,
    Was there no better day
To fix on than November Ninth so shivery,
And dull for showing off the Livery's livery?
           Dimming, alas!
           The Brazier's brass,
Soiling th' Embroiderers and all the Saddlers,
          Sopping the Furriers,
          Draggling the Curriers,
And making Merchant Tailors dirty paddlers;
Drenching the Skinners' Company to the skin,
    Making the crusty Vintner chiller,
    And turning the Distiller
To cold without instead of warm within;—
    Spoiling the brand-new beavers
    Of Wax-chandlers and Weavers,
      Plastering the Plasterers and spotting Mercers,
    Hearty November-cursers—
    And showing Cordwainers and dapper Drapers
Sadly in want of brushes and of scrapers;
Making the Grocer's Company not fit
    For company a bit;
Dyeing the Dyers with a dingy flood,
    Daubing incorporated Bakers,
    And leading the Patten-makers
Over their very pattens in the mud,-
      O Lud! O Lud! O Lud!

"This is a sorry sight,"
To quote Macbeth—but oh, it grieves me quite,
To see your wives and daughters in their plumes—
    White plumes not white—
    Sitting at open windows catching rheums,

Not "angels ever bright and fair,"
But angels ever brown and sallow,
With eyes—you cannot see above one pair,
　　　For city clouds of black and yellow---
And artificial flowers, rose, leaf, and bud,
　　　Such sable lilies
　　　And grim daffodillies,
Drooping, but not for drought—O Lud ! O Lud !

I may as well, while I'm inclined,
Just go through all the faults I find :—
　　　O Lud ! then, with a better air, say June,
　　　Could'st thou not find a better tune
　　　To sound with trumpets and with drums
　　　Than "See the Conquering Hero comes,"
　　　　When he who comes ne'er dealt in blood?
　　　Thy may'r is not a war-horse, Lud,
　　　That ever charged on Turk or Tartar,
　　　And yet upon a march you strike
　　　　That treats him like—
　　　　A little French if I may martyr—
Lewis Cart-horse or Henry Carter !

　　　　O Lud ! I say
　　　　Do change your day
To some time when your Show can really show ;
When silk can seem like silk, and gold can glow.
　　　Look at your Sweepers, how they shine in May !
　　　Have it when there's a sun to gild the coach,
　　　And sparkle in tiara—bracelet—brooch—
Diamond—or paste—of sister, mother, daughter ;
　　　When grandeur really may be grand—
　　　But if thy pageant's thus obscured by land—
O Lud ! it's ten times worse upon the water !
　　　Suppose, O Lud, to show its plan,
　　　I call, like Blue Beard's wife, to Sister Anne,
　　　Who's gone to Beaufort Wharf with niece and aunt
　　　To see what she can see—and what she can't ;
　　　Chewing a saffron bun by way of cud,
　　　To keep the fog out of a tender lung,
　　　While perched in a verandah nicely hung
　　　　Over a margin of thy own black mud,
　　　　　O Lud !

Now Sister Anne, I call to thee,
        Look out and see :
Of course about the bridge you view them rally
            And sally,
With many a wherry, sculler, punt, and cutter ;
The Fishmongers' grand boat, but not for butter,
        The Goldsmiths' glorious galley ;—
Of course you see the Lord Mayor's coach aquatic,
        With silken banners that the breezes fan,
            In gold all glowing,
            And men in scarlet rowing,
        Like Doge of Venice to the Adriatic ;
Of course you see all this, O Sister Anne ?

    " No, I see no such thing !
I only see the edge of Beaufort Wharf,
With two coal-lighters fastened to a ring ;
        And, dim as ghosts,
Two little boys are jumping over posts ;
        And something, farther off,
That's rather like the shadow of a dog,
        And all beyond is fog.
If there be anything so fine and bright,
To see it I must see by second sight.
Call this a Show ?   It is not worth a pin !
        I see no barges row,
        No banners blow ;
The Show is merely a gallanty-show,
Without a lamp or any candle in."

    But Sister Anne, my dear,
        Although you cannot see, you still may hear ?
Of course you hear, I'm very sure of that,
        The " Water Parted from the Sea," in C,
        Or " Where the Bee sucks," set in B ;
Or Huntsman's chorus from the Freischutz frightful,
Or Handel's Water Music in A flat.
Oh, music from the water comes delightful ;
        It sounds as nowhere else it can :
            You hear it first
            In some rich burst,

Then faintly sighing,
Tenderly dying,
Away upon the breezes, Sister Anne.

" There is no breeze to die on ;
And all their drums and trumpets, flutes and harps,
Could never cut their way with ev'n three sharps
Through such a fog as this, you may rely on.
I think, but am not sure, I hear a hum,
Like a very muffled double drum,
And then a something faintly shrill,
Like Bartlemy Fair's old buz at Pentonville.
And now and then I hear a pop,
As if from Pedley's soda-water shop.
I'm almost ill with the strong scent of mud,
And, not to mention sneezing,
My cough is more than usual teasing ;
I really fear that I have chilled my blood,
O Lud ! O Lud ! O Lud ! O Lud ! O Lud !"

LINES TO A FRIEND AT COBHAM.

'Tis pleasant, when we've absent friends,
Sometimes to hob and nob 'em
With memory's glass—at such a pass,
Remember me at Cobham !

Have pigs you will, and sometimes kill,
But if you sigh and sob 'em,
And cannot eat your home-grown meat,
Remember me at Cobham !

·Of hen and cock, you'll have a stock,
And death will oft unthrob 'em—
A country chick is good to pick—
Remember me at Cobham !

Some orchard trees of course you'll lease,
And boys will sometimes rob 'em,
A friend (you know) before a foe—
Remember me at Cobham !

You'll sometimes have wax-lighted rooms,
    And friends of course to mob 'em;
Should you be short of such a sort,
    Remember me at Cobham!

ODE TO PERCIVAL SPENCER, Esq., M.P.

    OH, Mr. Spencer!—
    I mean no offence, sir—
Retrencher of each trencher, man or woman's;
    Maker of days of ember,
    Eloquent member
Of the House of Com—— I mean to say *short* commons.
Thou, Long Tom Coffin, singing out, "Hold fast,"
        Avast!
    Oh! Mr. Percival, I'll bet a dollar a
    Great growth of cholera,
    And new deaths reckoned,
Will mark thy lenten twenty-first and -second.
The best of our physicians, when they con it,
    Depose the malady is in the air:
    Oh, Mr. Spencer!—if the ill is there,
Why should you bid the people live upon it?

Why should you make discourses against courses;
While Doctors, though they bid us rub and chafe,
    Declare, of all resources,
The man is safest who gets in the safe?
And yet you bid poor suicidal sinners
    Discard their dinners!
Thoughtless how Heaven above will look upon't,
For men to die so wantonly of want!

    By way of a variety,
    Think of the ineffectual piety
Of London's Bishop, at St. Faith's or Bride's,
Lecturing such chameleon insides,
    Only to find
    He's preaching to the wind.

Whatever others do, or don't,
I cannot—dare not, must not—fast, and wont,
Unless by night your day you let me keep,
    And fast asleep;
My constitution can't obey such censors:
    I must have meat
    Three times a day to eat,
    My health's of such a sort,
The *coats* of my stomach are not *Spencers*.

A HAPPY NEW YEAR.

" If th' affairs of this world did not make us so sad,
  'Twould be easy enough to be merry." - *Old Song.*

THERE'S nothing but plague in this house !
    There's the turbot is stole by the cat,
The Newfoundland has eat up the grouse,
    And the haunch has been gnawed by a rat !
It's the day of all days when I wished
    That our friends should enjoy our good cheer,
Mr. Wiggins—our dinner is dished,—
    But I wish you a Happy New Year !

Mr. Rudge has not called, but he will,
    For his rates, church, and highway, and poor ;
And the butcher has brought in his bill,
    Twice as much as the quarter before.
Little Charles is come home with the mumps,
    And Matilda with measles, I fear,
And I've taken two sovereigns like dumps—
    But I wish you a Happy New Year !

Your poor brother is in the *Gazette,*
    And your banker is off to New York ;
Mr. Bigsby has died in your debt,
    And the *Wiggins* has foundered near Cork.
Mr. Merrington's bill has come back,
    You are chosen to serve overseer,
The new wall is beginning to crack—
    But I wish you a Happy New Year !

The best dinner set's fall'n to the ground,
   The militia's called out, and you're drawn,
Not a piece of our plate can be found,
   But there's marks of men's feet on the lawn ;
Two anonymous letters have come
   That declare you shall die like a Weare,*
And it may—or may not—be a hum,—
   But I wish you a Happy New Year !

The old lawsuit with Levy is lost,
   You are fined for not cleansing the street,
And the water-pipe's burst with the frost,
   And the roof lets the rain in and sleet.
Your old tenant at Seventy-Four,
   Has gone off in the night with his gear,
And has taken the key of the door,—
   But I wish you a Happy New Year !

There's the Sun and the Phœnix to pay,
   For the chimney has blazed like Old Nick,
The new gig has been jammed by a dray,
   And the old horse has taken to kick ;
We have hardly a bushel of small,
   And now coal is extravagant dear,
Your great-coat is stole out of the hall,—
   But I wish you a Happy New Year !

The whole greenhouse is smashed by the hail,
   And the plants have all died in the night,
The magnolia's blown down by the gale,
   And the chimney looks far from upright ;
And the deuce take the man from the shop,
   That hung up the new glass chandelier,
It has come in the end to one drop,—
   But I wish you a Happy New Year !

There's misfortune wherever we dodge,
   It's the same in the country and town,
There's the porter has burned down his lodge,
   While he went off to smoke at the Crown ;

---

* Murdered by Thurtell.

The fat butler makes free with your wine,
 And the footman has drunk the small beer,
And the coachman can't walk in a line,—
 But I wish you a Happy New Year

I have doubts if your clerk is correct,
 There are hints of a mistress at Kew,
And some day he'll abscond, I expect.
 Mr. Brown has built out your back view ;
The new housemaid's the greatest of flirts,
 She has men in the house, that is clear,
And the laundress has pawned all your shirts,—
 But I wish you a Happy New Year !

Your "Account of a Visit to Rome,"
 Not a critic on earth seems to laud,
And old Huggins is lately come home,
 And will swear that your Claude isn't Claude ;
Your election is far from secure,
 Though it's likely to cost very dear,
You've come out in a caricature,—
 But I wish you a Happy New Year !

You've been christened an ass in the "Times,"
 And the "Chronicle" calls you a fool,
And that dealer in boys, Dr. Ghrimes,
 Has engaged the next house for a school ;
And the playground will run by the bow'r,
 That you took so much trouble to rear,
We shall never have one quiet hour,—
 But I wish you a Happy New Year !

Little John will not take to his book,
 He's come home black and blue from the cane ;
There's your uncle is courting his cook,
 And your mother has married again !
Jacob Jones will be tried with his wife,
 And against them you'll have to appear,
If they're hung you'll be wretched for life,—
 But I wish you a Happy New Year !

A CHARITY SERMON.

I'M an extremely charitable man—no collar and long hair, though
    a little carroty ;
Demure, half-inclined to the unknown tongues, but I never gained
    anything by Charity—
I got a little boy into the Foundling, but his unfortunate mother
    was traced and baited,
And the overseers found *her* out—and she found *me* out—and the
    child was affiliated.
        Oh, Charity will come home to roost,
        Like curses and chickens is Charity.

I once, near Whitehall's very old wall, when ballads danced over
    the whole of it,
Put a bad five-shilling piece into a beggar's hat, but the old hat
    had got a hole in it ;
And a little boy caught it in his little hat, and an officer's eye
    seemed to care for it,
As my bad crownpiece went through *his* bad crownpiece, and
    they took me to Queen's Square for it.
        Oh, Charity, &c.

I let my very old (condemned) old house to a man at a rent that
    was shockingly low,
So I found a roof for his ten motherless babes—all defunct and
    fatherless now ;
For the plaguey one-sided party-wall fell in, so did the roof, on son
    and daughter,
And twelve jurymen sat on eleven bodies, and brought in a very
    personal verdict of manslaughter.
        Oh, Charity, &c.

I picked up a young well-dressed gentleman, who had fallen in a
    fit in St. Martin's Court,
And charitably offered to see him home, for charity always seemed
    to be my forte,
And I've had presents for seeing fallen gentlemen home ; but this
    was an unlucky job,—
Do you know, he got my watch, my purse, and my handkerchief,
    for it was one of the swell mob.
        Oh, Charity, &c.

Being four miles from town, I stopped a horse that had run away
    with a man, when it seemed that they must be dashed to
    pieces,
Though several kind people were following him with all their
    might ; but such following a horse his speed increases.
I held the horse while he went to recruit his strength ; I meant to
    ride home, of course ;
But the crowd came up and took me up, for it turned out the man
    had run away with the horse.
        Oh, Charity, &c.

I watched last month all the drovers and drivers about the suburbs,
    for it's a positive fact,
That I think the utmost penalty ought always to be enforced against
    everybody under Mr. Martin's Act.
But I couldn't catch one hit over the horns, or over the shins, or
    on the ears, or over the head ;
And I caught a rheumatism from early wet hours, and got five
    weeks of ten swelled fingers in bed.
        Oh, Charity, &c.

Well, I've utterly done with Charity, though I used so to preach
    about its finest fount ;
Charity may do for some that are more lucky, but *I* can't turn it
    to any account.
It goes so the very reverse way—even if one chirrups it up with a
    dust of piety ;
That henceforth, let it be understood, I take my name entirely out
    of the list of the subscribers to the Humane Society.
        Oh, Charity, &c.

ODE TO ADMIRAL LORD GAMBIER, **G.C.B.**

"Well, if you reclaim such as Hood, your Society will deserve the thanks of the country."—*Temperance Society's Herald*, vol. i. No. I. p. 8.

> "My father, when last I from Guinea
>   Came home with abundance of wealth,
> Said, 'Jack, never be such a ninny
>   As to drink——' says I, 'Father, your health.'"
>
> Nothing like Grog.

I.

OH! Admiral Gam—— I dare not mention *bier*,
In such a temperate ear;
Oh! Admiral Gam—— an Admiral of the Blue,
Of course, to read the Navy List aright,
For, strictly shunning wine of either hue,
You can't be Admiral of the Red or White;
Oh, Admiral Gam! consider ere you call
On merry Englishmen to wash their throttles
With water only, and to break their bottles,
To stick, for fear of trespass, on the wall,
        Of Exeter Hall.

II.

Consider, I beseech, the contrariety
Of cutting off our brandy, gin, and rum
And then by tracts inviting us to come
And "mix" in your society!
In giving rules to dine, or sup, or lunch,
Consider Nature's ends before you league us
To strip the Isle of Rum of all its punch,
To dock the Isle of Mull of all its negus,
Or doom—to suit your milk-and-water view—
The Isle of Skye to nothing but sky-blue!

III.

Consider,—for appearance' sake, consider—
The sorry figure of a spirit-ridder,
Going on this crusade against the suttler,
A sort of Hudibras—without a Butler!

IV.

Consider,—ere you break the ardent spirits
Of father, mother, brother, sister, daughter;
What are your beverage's washy merits:
Gin may be low—but I have known low-water!

V.

Consider well before you thus deliver
With such authority your sloppy canon,
Should British tars taste nothing but the *river*,
Because the *Chesapeake* once fought the *Shannon*?

VI.

Consider too—before all Eau-de-vie,
Schiedam, or other drinkers you rebut,
To bite a bitten dog all curs agree;
But who would cut a man, because he's cut?

VII.

Consider—ere you bid the poor to fill
Their murmuring stomachs with the "murmuring rill,"
Consider that their streams are not like ours,
Reflecting heaven, margined by sweet flowers;
On their dark pools by day no sun reclines,
By night no Jupiter, no Venus shines;
Consider life's sour taste, that bids them mix
Rum with their Acheron, or gin with Styx:
If you must pour out water to the poor, oh!
        Let it be aqua d'oro!

VIII.

Consider,—ere as furious as a griffin,
Against a glass of grog you make such work,
A man may like a stiff 'un,
And yet not be a Burke.

IX.

Consider, too, before you bid all skinkers
Turn water-drinkers,
What sort of fluid fills their native rivers,
Their Mudiboos, and Niles, and Guadalquivers.

How should you like yourself, in glass or mug,
        The Bog—the Bug,
The Maine, the Weser, or that freezer Neva?
Nay, take the very rill of classic ground—
        Lord Byron found
Ev'n Castaly the better for Geneva.

x.

Consider—if to vote Reform's arrears,
His Majesty should please to make you peers,
Your titles would be very far from trumps
To figure in a book of blue and red :
    The Duke of Drawwell—what a name to dread !
Marquis of Mainpipe ; Earl of New River Head
And Temperance's chief, the Prince of Pumps.

A PUBLIC DINNER.

" ' Sit down and fall to,' said the Barmecide."—*Arabian Nights.*

At seven you nick it,
Give card—get wine ticket ;
Walk round through the Babel,
From table to table,
To find—a hard matter—
Your name in a platter.
Your wish was to sit by
Your friend, Mr. Whitby ;
But stewards' assistance
Has placed you at distance ;
And, thanks to arrangers,
You sit among strangers.
But too late for mending,
Twelve sticks come attending—
A stick of a chairman,
A little, dark, spare man,
With bald shining nob,
'Mid Committee swell mob,
In short, a short figure—
You thought the Duke bigger.

Then silence is wanted,
Non Nobis is chanted;
Then chairman reads letter,
The Duke's a regretter
A promise to break it,
But chair, he can't take it;
Is grieved to be from us,
But sends friend Sir Thomas,
And, what is far better,
A cheque in the letter;
Hear! hear! and a clatter,
And there ends the matter.
Now soups come and fish in,
And C—— brings a dish in.
Then rages the battle—
Knives clatter, forks rattle,
Steel forks with black handles
Under fifty wax-candles.
Your soup-plate is soon full,
You sip just a spoonful:
Mr. Roe will be grateful
To send him a plateful;
And then comes the waiter,
" Must trouble for 'tater;"
And then you drink wine off
With somebody—nine off—
Bucellas, made handy
With Cape and bad brandy,
Or East India sherry
That's very hot—very.
You help Mr. Myrtle,
Then find your mock turtle
Went off while you lingered
With waiter light-fingered.
To make up for gammon,
You order some salmon,
Which comes to your fauces
With boats without sauces.
You then make a cut on
Some lamb, big as mutton,
And ask for some grass too,
But that you must pass too—

It served the first twenty—
But toast there is plenty;
Then while lamb gets coldish,
A goose that is oldish—
At carving not clever—
You're begged to dissever;
And when thus you treat it,
Find no one will eat it.
So, hungry as glutton,
You turn to your mutton;
But—no sight for laughter—
The soup it's gone after.
Mr. Green then is very
Disposed to take sherry,
And next Mr. Nappy
Will feel very happy;
And then Mr. Conner
Requests the same honour;
Mr. Clarke, when at leisure,
Will really feel pleasure.
Then waiter leans over
To take off a cover
From fowls, which all beg of
A wing or a leg of;
And while they all peck bone,
You take to a neck bone.
But even your hunger
Declares for a younger;
A fresh plate you call for,
But vainly you bawl for;
Now taste disapproves it,
No waiter removes it.
Still hope, newly budding,
Relies on a pudding;
But critics each minute
Set fancy agin it—
" That's queer vermicelli;
" I say, Vizetelly,"
" There's glue in that jelly."
" Tarts bad altogether;"
" That crust's made of leather."
" Some custard, friend Vesey?"

" No—batter made easy."
" Some cheese, Mr. Foster ?"—
" Don't like single Gloucester."
Meanwhile, to top table,
Like fox in the fable,
You see silver dishes
With those little fishes
The whitebait delicious,
Borne past you officious ;
And near, rather plainish,
A sound that's champagnish ;
And glimpse certain bottles
Made long in the throttles,
And sniff—very pleasant—
Grouse, partridge, and pheasant,
And see mounds of ices,
For Patrons and Vices ;
Pine-apple, and bunches
Of grapes for sweet munches,
And fruits of all virtue
That really *desert* you ;
You've nuts, but not *crack* ones,
Half empty and black ones ;
With oranges sallow,
They can't be called yellow ;
Some pippins well wrinkled,
And plums almond sprinkled ;
Some rout cakes, and so on,
Then with business to go on.
Long speeches are stuttered,
And toasts are well buttered,
While dames in the gallery,
All dressed in fallallery,
Look on at the mummery,
And listen to flummery.
Hip, hip, and huzzaing,
And singing and saying
Glees, catches, orations,
And lists of donations.
Hush ! a song—Mr. Tinney—
" Mr. Benbow, one guinea,"
" Mr. Frederick Manual

One guinea, and annual ;"
Song—Jockey and Jenny—
" Mr. Markham, one guinea ;"
" Have you all filled your glasses ?
Here's a health to good lasses."
The subscription still skinny,
" Mr. Franklin, one guinea ;"
Franklin looks like a ninny.
" Mr. Boreham, one guinea ;
Mr. Blogg ; Mr. Finny ;
Mr. Tempest, one guinea ,"
Mr. Merrington, twenty,"
Rough music in plenty.
Away toddles Chairman,
The little dark spare man,
Not sorry at ending,
With white sticks attending
And some vain Tom Noldy
Votes in his own body
To fill the void seat up,
And get on his feet up.
To say, with voice squeaking,
" Unaccustomed to speaking"—
Which sends you off seeking
Your hat, number thirty.
No coach—very dirty,—
So hungry and fevered,
Wet footed, spoilt beavered,
Eyes aching in socket,
Ten pounds out of pocket,
To Brook Street the upper,
You haste home to supper.

THE CIGAR.

"Here comes Mr. Puff."—*The Critic.*

"I knew by the smoke that so gracefully curled."—MOORE.

SOME sigh for this and that,
    My wishes don't go far,
The world may wag at will,
    So I have my cigar.

Some fret themselves to death,
    With Whig and Tory jar;
I don't care which is in,
    So I have my cigar

Sir John requests my vote,
    And so does Mr. Marr;
I don't care how it goes,
    So I have my cigar.

Some want a German row,
    Some wish a Russian war,
I care not—I'm at peace—
    So I have my cigar

I never see the *Post*,
    I seldom read the *Star*,*
The *Globe* I scarcely heed,
    So I have my cigar.

They tell me that Bank Stock
    Is sunk much under par,
It's all the same to me,
    So I have my cigar.

Honours have come to men,
    My juniors at the Bar,
No matter—I can wait,
    So I have my cigar.

---

* The *Star* has set. The *Globe* still revolves on its axis.

Ambition frets me not ;
   A cab, or glory's car
Are just the same to me,
   So I have my cigar.

I worship no vain gods,
   But serve the household Lar ;
I'm sure to be at home,
   So I have my cigar.

I do not seek for fame :
   A General with a scar,
A Private let me be,
   So I have my cigar.

To have my choice among
   The toys of life's bazaar,
The deuce may take them all,
   So I have my cigar.

Some minds are often tost
   By tempests, like a tar ·
I always seem in port,
   So I have my cigar.

The ardent flame of love
   My bosom cannot char,
I smoke but do not burn,
   So I have my cigar.

They tell me Nancy Low
   Has married Mr. R——;
The jilt ! but I can live,
   So I have my cigar.

SONNET.

"Dornton & Co. may challenge the world, the house of Hope perhaps excepted."—*Road to Ruin.*

TIME was I sat upon a lofty stool,
At lofty desk, and with a clerkly pen,
Began each morning, at the stroke of ten,
To write in Bell & Co.'s commercial school;
In Warnford Court, a shady nook and cool,
The favourite retreat of merchant men;
Yet would my quill turn vagrant even then,
And take stray dips in the Castalian pool.
Now double entry—now a flowery trope,
Mingling poetic honey with trade wax.
Blogg Brothers—Milton—Grote & Prescott—Pope—
Bristles—and Hogg—Glyn, Mills, and Halifax—
Rogers—and Towgood—Hemp—the Bard of Hope—
Barilla—Byron—Tallow—Burns—and Flax!

SONNET.

TO LORD WHARNCLIFFE, ON HIS GAME BILL.

I'M fond of partridges, I'm fond of snipes,
I'm fond of blackcocks, for they're very good cocks—
I'm fond of wild ducks, and I'm fond of woodcocks,
And grouse, that set up such strange moorish pipes.
I'm fond of pheasants with their splendid stripes—
I'm fond of hares, whether from Whig or Tory—
I'm fond of capercailzies in their glory,—
Teal, widgeons, plovers, birds in all their types:
All these are in your care, law-giving Peer,
And when you next address your Lordly Babel,
Some clause put in your Bill, precise and clear,
With due and fit provision to enable
A man that holds all kinds of game so dear
To keep, like Crockford, a good Gaming Table.

RONDEAU.

[EXTRACTED FROM A WELL-KNOWN ANNUAL.]

O CURIOUS reader! didst thou ne'er
Behold a worshipful lord mayor
Seated in his great civic chair
    So dear?

Then cast thy longing eyes this way,
It is the ninth November day,
And in his new-born state survey
    One here!

To rise from little into great
Is pleasant; but to sink in state
From high to lowly is a fate
    Severe.

Too soon his shine is overcast,
Chilled by the next November blast;
His blushing honours only last
    One year!

He casts his fur and sheds his chains,
And moults till not a plume remains—
The next impending mayor distrains
    His gear.

He slips like water through a sieve—
Ah, could his little splendour live
Another twelvemonth—he would give
    One ear!

ON THE DEATH OF SIR WALTER SCOTT,

1833.

FAREWELL, Sir Walter Scott, secured
From Time—our greatest of Inditers!
No author's fame's so well *assured*
For all who wrote were *Underwriters*.

THE CHINA-MENDER.

GOOD morning, Mr. What-d'ye-call!   Well, here's another pretty
 job!
Lord help my Lady!—what a smash!—if you had only heard her
 sob!
It was all through Mr. Lambert: but for certain he was winy,
To think for to go to sit down on a table full of Chiny.
" Deuce take your stupid head!" says my Lady to his very face;
But politeness, you know, is nothing, when there's Chiny in the
 case:
And if ever a woman was fond of Chiny to a passion
It's my mistress, and all sorts of it, whether new or old fashion.
Her brother's a sea-captain, and brings her home ship-loads—
Such bonzes, and such dragons, and nasty, squatting things like
 toads;
And great nidnoddin mandarins, with palsies in the head:
I declare I've often dreamt of them, and had nightmares in my bed.
But the frightfuller they are—lawk! she loves them all the better:
She'd have Old Nick himself made of Chiny if they'd let her.
Lawk-a-mercy! break her Chiny, and it's breaking her very heart;
If I touch'd it, she would very soon say, " Mary, we must part."
To be sure she *is* unlucky: only Friday comes Master Randall,
And breaks a broken spout, and fresh chips a tea-cup handle:
He's a dear, sweet little child, but he will so finger and touch,
And that's why my Lady doesn't take to children much.
Well! there's stupid Mr. Lambert, with his two great coat flaps,
Must go and sit down on the Dresden shepherdess's laps,
As if there was no such things as rosewood chairs in the room;
I couldn't have made a greater sweep with the handle of the
 broom.
Mercy on us! how my mistress began to rave and tear!
Well! after all, there's nothing like good ironstone ware for wear.
If ever I marry, that's flat, I'm sure it wont be John Dockery,
I should be a wretched woman in a shop full of crockery.
I should never like to wipe it, though I love to be neat and tidy,
And afraid of mad bulls on market-days every Monday and Friday.
I'm very much mistook if Mr. Lambert's will be a catch;
The breaking the Chiny will be the breaking off of his own match.
Missis wouldn't have an angel, if he was careless about Chiny;
She never forgives a chip, if it's ever so small and tiny.

Lawk! I never saw a man in all my life in such a taking:
I could find in my heart to pity him for all his mischief-making.
To see him stand a-hammering and stammering, like a zany;
But what signifies apologies, if they wont mend old Chaney!
If he sent her up whole crates full, from Wedgwood's and Mr. Spode's,
He couldn't make amends for the cracked mandarins and smash'd toads.
Well! every one has their tastes, but, for my parts, my own self,
I'd rather have the figures on my poor dear grandmother's old shelf:
A nice pea-green poll-parrot, and two reapers with brown ears of corns,
And a shepherd with a crook after a lamb with two gilt horns,
And such a Jemmy Jessamy in top-boots and sky-blue vest,
And a frill and flowered waistcoat, with a fine bowpot at the breast.
God help her, poor old soul! I shall come into 'em at her death,
Though she's a hearty woman for her years, except her shortness of breath.
Well! you think the things will mend—if they wont, Lord mend us all!
My Lady will go in fits, and Mr. Lambert wont need to call:
I'll be bound in any money, if I had a guinea to give,
He wont sit down again on Chiny the longest day he has to live.
Poor soul! I only hope it wont forbid his banns of marriage,
Or he'd better have sat behind on the spikes of my Lady's carriage.
But you'll join 'em all of course, and stand poor Mr. Lambert's friend;
I'll look in twice a day, just to see, like, how they mend.
To be sure it is a sight that might draw tears from dogs and cats;
Here's this pretty little pagoda, now, has lost four of its cocked hats:
Be particular with the pagoda: and then here's this pretty bowl—
The Chinese Prince is making love to nothing because of this hole;
And here's another Chinese man, with a face just like a doll—
Do stick his pigtail on again, and just mend his parasol.
But I needn't tell you what to do; only do it out of hand,
And charge whatever you like to charge—my Lady wont make a stand.
Well! good morning, Mr. What-d'ye-call; for it's time our gossip ended:
And you know the proverb, the less as is said, the sooner the Chiny's mended.

A LAY OF REAL LIFE.

"Some are born with a wooden spoon in their mouths, and some witn a golden ladle."—GOLDSMITH.

"Some are born with tin rings in their noses, and some with silver ones."
SILVERSMITH.

WHO ruined me ere I was born,
Sold every acre, grass or corn,
And left the next heir all forlorn?
My Grandfather.

Who said my mother was no nurse,
And physicked me and made me worse,
Till infancy became a curse?
My Grandmother.

Who left me in my seventh year,
A comfort to my mother dear,
And Mr. Pope, the overseer?
My Father.

Who let me starve, to buy her gin,
Till all my bones came through my skin,
Then called me "ugly little sin?"
My Mother.

Who said my mother was a Turk,
And took me home—and made me work,
But managed half my meals to shirk?
My Aunt.

Who "of all earthly things" would boast,
"He hated others' brats the most,"
And therefore made me feel my post?
My Uncle.

Who got in scrapes, an endless score,
And always laid them at my door,
Till many a bitter bang I bore?
My Cousin.

Who took me home when mother died,
Again with father to reside,
Black shoes, clean knives, run far and wide?
My Stepmother.

Who marred my stealthy urchin joys,
And when I played cried " What a noise ."
Girls always hector over boys—
My Sister.

Who used to share in what was mine,
Or took it all, did he incline,
'Cause I was eight, and he was nine?
My Brother.

Who stroked my head, and said " Good lad,"
And gave me sixpence, " all he had ;"
But at the stall the coin was bad ?
My Godfather.

Who, gratis, shared my social glass,
But when misfortune came to pass,
Referr'd me to the pump?   Alas !
My Friend.

Through all this weary world, in brief,
Who ever sympathised with grief,
Or shared my joy—my sole relief?
Myself.

THE SWEEP'S COMPLAINT.

" I like to meet a sweep—such as come forth with the dawn, or somewhat
earlier, with their little professional notes, sounding like the *peep, peep,* of a
young sparrow."—*Essays of Elia.*

" A voice cried Sweep no more !
Macbeth hath murdered sweep."—SHAKSPEARE.

ONE morning, ere my usual time
I rose, about the seventh chime,
When little stunted boys that climb
    Still linger in the street ;
And as I walked, I saw indeed
A sample of the sooty breed,
Though he was rather run to seed,
    In height above five feet.

A mongrel tint he seemed to take,
Poetic simile to make,
DAY through his MARTIN 'gan to break,
   White overcoming jet.
From side to side he crossed oblique,
Like Frenchman who has friends to seek,
And yet no English word can speak,
   He walked upon the fret :
And while he sought the dingy job
His lab'ring breast appeared to throb,
And half a hiccup half a sob
   Betray'd internal woe.
To cry the cry he had by rote
He yearn'd, but law forbade the note,
Like Chanticleer with roupy throat,
   He gaped—but not a crow !
I watched him, and the glimpse I snatched
Disclosed his sorry eyelids patched
With red, as if the soot had catched
   That hung about the lid ;
And soon I saw the teardrop stray,
He did not care to brush away ;
Thought I, the cause he will betray—
   And thus at last he did.

Well, here's a pretty go ! here's a Gagging Act, if ever there was a
   gagging !
But I'm bound the members as silenced us, in doing it had
   plenty of magging.
They had better send us all off, they had, to the School for the
   Deaf and Dumb,
To unlarn us our mother tongues, and to make signs and be regu-
   larly mum.
But they can't undo natur—as sure as ever the morning begins to
   peep,
Directly I open my eyes, I can't help calling out Sweep
As natural as the sparrows among the chimbley-pots, that say Cheep !
For my own part I find my suppressed voice very uneasy,
And comparable to nothing but having your tissue stopt when
   you are sneezy.
Well, it's all up with us ! tho' I suppose we mustn't cry all up.
Here's a precious merry Christmas. I'm blest if I can earn either
   bit or sup !

If crying Sweep, of mornings, is going beyond quietness's border,
Them as pretends to be fond of silence oughtn't to cry hear, hear,
and order, order.
I wonder Mr. Sutton, as we've sut-on too, don't sympathise with us
As a Speaker what don't speak, and that's exactly our own cus.
God help us if we don't not cry, how are we to pursue our callings?
I'm sure we're not half so bad as other businesses with their bawlings.
For instance, the general postmen, that at six o'clock go about
ringing,
And wake up all the babbies that their mothers have just got to
sleep with singing.
Greens oughtn't to be cried no more than blacks—to do the
unpartial job,
If they bring in a Sooty Bill, they ought to have brought in a
Dusty Bob.
Is a dustman's voice more sweet than ourn, when he comes a
seeking arter the cinders,
Instead of a little boy, like a blackbird in spring, singing merrily
under your windows?
There's the omnibus cads as plies in Cheapside, and keeps calling
out Bank and City;
Let his worship, the Mayor, decide if our call of Sweep is not just
as pretty.
I can't see why the Jews should be let go about crying Old Close
thro' their hooky noses,
And Christian laws should be ten times more hard than the old
stone laws of Moses.
Why isn't the mouths of the muffin-men compell'd to be equally
shut?
Why, because Parliament members eat muffins, but they never
eat no sut.
Next year there wont be any May-day at all, we shan't have no
heart to dance,
And Jack in the Green will go in black like mourning for our
mischance,
If we live as long as May, that's to say, through the hard winter
and pinching weather,
For I don't see how we're to earn enough to keep body and soul
together.
I only wish Mr. Wilberforce, or some of them that pities the niggers,
Would take a peep down in our cellars, and look at our miserable
starving figures,

A-sitting idle on our empty sacks, and all ready to eat each
    other,
And a brood of little ones crying for bread to a heartbreaking
    Father and Mother.
They haven't a rag of clothes to mend, if their mothers had thread
    and needles,
But crawl naked about the cellars, poor things, like a swarm of
    common black beadles.
If they'd only inquired before passing the Act, and taken a few
    such peeps,
I don't think that any real gentleman would have set his face
    against sweeps.
Climbing's an ancient respectable art, and if History's of any
    vally,
Was recommended by Queen Elizabeth to the great Sir Walter
    Raleigh,
When he wrote on a pane of glass how I'd climb, if the way I only
    knew,
And she writ beneath, if your heart's afeard, don't venture up the
    flue.
As for me I was always loyal, and respected all powers that are
    higher,
But how can I now say God save the King, if I an't to be a Cryer?
There's London milk, that's one of the cries, even on Sunday the
    law allows,
But ought black sweeps, that are human beasts, to be worser off
    than black cows?
Do *we* go calling about, when it's church time, like the noisy
    Billingsgate vermin,
And disturb the parson with "All alive O!" in the middle of a
    funeral sermon?
But the fish wont keep, not the mackarel wont, is the cry of the
    Parliament elves,
Every thing, except the sweeps I think, is to be allowed to keep
    themselves!
Lord help us! what's to become of us if we mustn't cry no
    more?
We shan't do for black mutes to go a standing at a death's door.
And we shan't do to emigrate, no not even to the Hottentot
    nations,
For as time wears on, our black will wear off, and then think of
    our situations!

And we should not do, in lieu of black-a-moor footmen, to serve
    ladies of quality nimbly,
For when we were drest in our sky-blue and silver, and large
    frills, all clean and neat, and white silk stockings, if they
    pleased to desire us to sweep the hearth, we couldn't resist
    the chimbley.

I CANNOT BEAR A GUN.

" Timidity is generally reckoned an essential attribute of the fair sex, and
this absurd notion gives rise to more false starts, than . race for the Leger.
Hence screams at mice, fits at spiders, faces at toads, jumps at lizards, flights
from daddy longlegs, panics at wasps, *sauve qui peut* at sight of a gun. Surely,
when the military exercise is made a branch of education at so many ladies'
academies, the use of the musket would only be a judicious step further in the
march of mind. I should not despair, in a month's practice, of making the
most timid British female fond of small arms."—*Hints by a Corporal.*

IT can't be minced, I'm quite convinced,
    All girls are full of flam,
Their feelings fine and feminine
    Are nothing else but sham.
On all their tricks I need not fix,
    I'll only mention one,
How many a Miss will tell you this,
    " I cannot bear a gun !"

There's cousin Bell can't 'bide the smell
    Of powder—horrid stuff !
A single pop will make her drop,
    She shudders at a puff.
My Manton near, with aspen fear
    Will make her scream and run,
" It's always so, you brute, you know
    I cannot bear a gun !"

About my flask I must not ask,
    I must not wear a belt,
I must not take a punch to make
    My pellets, card or felt,
And if I just allude to dust,
    Or speak of Number one,
" I beg you'll not—don't talk of shot,
    I cannot bear a gun !"

Percussion cap I dare not snap,
  I may not mention Hall,
Or raise my voice for Mr. Joyce,
  His wadding to recall;
At Hawker's book I must not look,
  All shooting I must shun,
Or else—" It's hard, you've no regard,
  I cannot bear a gun !"

The very dress I wear no less
  Must suit her timid mind,
A blue or black must clothe my back,
  With swallow-tails behind,
By fustian, jean, or velveteen
  Her nerves are overdone,
" Oh do not, John, put gaiters on,
  I cannot bear a gun !"

Ev'n little James she snubs, and blames
  His Lilliputian train,
Two inches each from mouth to breech,
  And charged with half a grain—
His crackers stopped, his squibbing dropped,
  He has no fiery fun,
And all thro' her, " How dare you, Sir,
  I cannot bear a gun !"

Yet Major Flint,—the Devil's in't !
  May talk from morn to night,
Of springing mines, and twelves and nines
  And volleys left and right,
Of voltigeurs and tirailleurs,
  And bullets by the ton,
She never dies of fright, and cries
  " I cannot bear a gun !"

It stirs my bile to see her smile
  At all his bang and whiz,
But if I talk of morning walk,
  And shots as good as his,

I must not name the fallen game,
  As soon as I've begun,
She's in her pout, and crying out,
  " I cannot bear a gun !"

Yet underneath the rose her teeth
  Are false to match her tongue,
Grouse, partridge, hares, she never spares,
  Or pheasants, old or young—
On widgeon, teal, she makes a meal,
  And yet objects to none,
" What have I got, it's full of shot !
  I cannot bear a gun !"

At pigeon pie she is not shy,
  Her taste it never shocks,
Though they should be from Battersea,
  So famous for blue rocks ;
Yet when I bring the very thing
  My markmanship has won,
She cries, " Lock up that horrid cup,
  I cannot bear a gun !"

Like fool and dunce I got her once
  A box at Drury Lane,
And by her side I felt a pride
  I ne'er shall feel again :
To read the bill it made her ill,
  And this excuse she spun,
" Der Freyshütz, oh, seven shots, you know.
  I cannot bear a gun !"

Yet at a hint from Major Flint,
  Her very hands she rubs,
And quickly drest in all her best,
  Is off to Wormwood Scrubs.
The whole review she sits it through,
  With noise enough to stun,
And never winks, or even thinks,
  " I cannot bear a gun !"

She thus may blind the Major's mind
    In mock-heroic strife,
But let a bout at war break out,
    And where's the soldier's wife,
To take his kit and march a bit
    Beneath a broiling sun?
Or will she cry, " My dear, good-by,
    I cannot bear a gun!"

If thus she doats on army coats,
    And regimental cuffs,
The yeomanry might surely be
    Secure from her rebuffs;
But when I don my trappings on,
    To follow Captain Dunn,
My carbine's gleam provokes a scream,
    " I cannot bear a gun!"

It can't be minced, I'm quite convinced,
    All girls are full of flam,
Their feelings fine, and feminine,
    Are nothing else but sham;
On all their tricks I need not fix,
    I'll only mention one,
How many a Miss will tell you this,
    " I cannot bear a gun!"

TRIMMER'S EXERCISE,

FOR THE USE OF CHILDREN.

Here, come, Master Timothy Todd,
    Before we have done you'll look grimmer,
You've been spelling some time for the rod,
    And your jacket shall know I'm a Trimmer.

You don't know your A from your B,
    So backward you are in your Primer,
Don't kneel—you shall go on *my* knee.
    For I'll have you to know I'm a Trimmer.

This morning you hindered the cook,
    By melting your dumps in the skimmer,
Instead of attending your book,
    But I'll have you to know I'm a Trimmer.

To-day, too, you went to the pond,
    And bathed, though you are not a swimmer,
And with parents so doting and fond—
    But I'll have you to know I'm a Trimmer.

After dinner you went to the wine,
    And helped yourself—yes, to a brimmer;
You couldn't walk straight in a line,
    But I'll make you to know I'm a Trimmer.

You kick little Tomkins about,
    Because he is slighter and slimmer;
Are the weak to be thump'd by the stout?
    But I'll have you to know I'm a Trimmer.

Then you have a sly pilfering trick,
    Your school-fellows call you the nimmer,—
I will cut to the bone if you kick!
    For I'll have you to know I'm a Trimmer.

To-day you made game at my back,
    You think that my eyes are grown dimmer,
But I watched you, I've got a sly knack,
    And I'll have you to know I'm a Trimmer.

Don't think that my temper is hot,
    It's never beyond a slow simmer,
I'll teach you to call me Dame Trot,
    But I'll have you to know I'm a Trimmer.

Miss Edgeworth, or Mrs. Chapone,
    Might melt to behold your tears glimmer;
Mrs. Barbauld would let you alone,
    But I'll have you to know I'm a Trimmer.

ODE TO J. S. BUCKINGHAM, Esq., M.P.

ON THE REPORT OF THE COMMITTEE ON DRUNKENNESS.

"Steady, boys, steady."—*Sea Song*.

"*Then did they fall upon the chat of drinking;* and forthwith began Flaggons to go, Goblets to fly, great Bowls to ting, Glasses to ring, draw, reach, fill, mix, give it me without water ; so, my Friend, so ; whip me off this Glass neatly, bring me hither some Claret, a full weeping Glass till it run over !"

Rabelais.

"Now, seeing that every Vessel was empty, great and small, with not so much at the Bottom as would half befuddle or muddle even a Fly, such as are the Flies of Baieux, I say, seeing this lamentable sight, Gargantua leapt up on one of the Tables, and with tears in his Eyes as big as Cannon Bullets, did pathetically beseech Pantagruel, as well as he could for the Hiccups and the Drinking Cups, and all sorts of Cups, as he valued his precious Body and Soul, one or both, never to drink more than became a reasonable Man, and not a Hog and a Beast. And the Stint of a reasonably reasonable Man is thus much, to wit, seven Thousand three Hundred and fifty-three Hogsheads, twice as many Kilderkins, thrice as many little Kegs, and as many Flaggons, Bottles, and Tankards as you will, beside. A Christian ought not to drink more. As Gargantua said these Words his Voice grew thick, his Tongue being as it were too huge for his Mouth ; and on a sudden he turned dog-sick, and fell off the Table a prodigious Fall, whereby there was a horrible Earthquake, from Paris even unto Turkey in Asia, as is remembered unto this day."—*Rabelais*.

O, Mr. Buckingham, if I may take
The liberty with you and your Committee,
Some observations I intend to make,
I hope will prove both pertinent and pretty,
On Drunkenness you've held a special court,
But is consistency, I ask, your forte,
When after (I must say) much Temperance swaggering,
  You issue a Report,
  That's staggering !

Of course you laboured without drop or sup,
Yet certain parts of that Report to read,
  Some men might think indeed,
A corkscrew, not a pen, had drawn it up.

For instance, was it quite a sober plan
On such a theme as drunkenness to trouble
  A poor old man,
Who could not e'en see single, much less double ?

Blind some six years
As it appears,
He gives in evidence, and you receive it,
A flaming picture of a flaming palace
Where gin-admirers sipped the chalice
And then, (the banter is not bad,)
Thinks fit to add,
You really should have seen it to believe it.*

That *he* could see such sights I must deny,
Unless he borrowed Betty Martin's eye.
A man that is himself walks in a line,
One, not himself, goes serpentine,
And as he rambles
In crablike scrambles,
The while his body works in curves,
His intellect as surely swerves,
And some such argument as this he utters,
" While men get *cut* we must have cutters,
As long as Jack will have his rum,
We must have pink, corvette, and bomb,
Each sort of craft
Since Noah's old raft,
Frigate and brig,
Ships of all rig,
We must have fleets, because our sailors swig,
But only get our tars to broths and soups,
And see how slops will do away with sloops !

---

* What is your occupation ?—My occupation has been in the weaving line ; *but having the dropsy six years ago, I am deprived of my eyesight.*
2734. Did you not once *see* a gin-shop burnt down ?—*About nine months ago* there was the sign of the Adam and Eve at the corner of Church Street, at Bethnal Green, burnt down, and they had such a quantity of spirits in the house at the time that it was such a terrible fire, that they were obliged to throw everything into the middle of the road to keep it away from the liquor, and it was all in flames in the road ; and the gin-shop opposite was scorched and broke their windows ; and there was another gin-shop at the opposite corner ; at three corners there were gin-shops, and was, from the fire, just like a murdering concern, for you could not get round the corner at all, it was so thronged that *a man could not believe it unless he saw it.*

Turn flip to flummery, and grog to gravy,
And then what need has England of a navy?"*
Forgive my muse ; she is a saucy hussy,
But she declares such reasoning sounds muzzy,
And that, as sure as Dover stands at Dover,
The man who entertains so strange a notion
  Of governing the ocean,
Has been but half seas over.

Again : when sober people talk
On soberness, would not their words all walk
Straight to the point, instead of zigzag trials,
Of both sides of the way, till having crost
And crost, they find themselves completely lost
Like gentlemen,—rather cut—in Seven Dials?
Just like the sentence following in fact:
  " Every Act†
Of the Legislature," (so it *runs*) " should flow
Over the bed"——of what ?—begin your guesses.
  The Bed of Ware ?
  The State Bed of the May'r ?
One at the Hummums?   Of MacAdam's?   No
  A parsley bed ?
  Of cabbage, green or red ?
Of onions ? daffodils ? of watercresses ?
A spare-bed with a friend—one full of fleas ?
At Bedford, or Bedhampton ?—None of these.
The Thames bed?   The bed of the New River ?
A kennel? brick-kiln? or a stack of hay ?
  Of churchyard clay,
The bed that's made for ev'ry mortal liver ?
No—give it up,—all guessing I defy in it,
It is the bed of " Truth,"—" inspired" forsooth
As, if you gave your best best-bed to Truth,
  She'd *lie* in it!

---

 * 3893. *If temperance were universal, do you think we should need any line-of-battle ships ?*—It would be very unsafe for us to be without them.

 † 1686. Do you mean to infer from that, that the law in all its branches should be in accordance with the Divine command ?—I do ; every Act of the Legislature should flow over the bed of inspired truth, and receive the impregnation of its righteous and holy principles.

Come, Mr. Buckingham, be candid, come,
Didn't that metaphor want " seeing home?"

What man, who did not see far more than real,
  Drink's beau ideal,—
Could fancy the mechanic so well thrives,
  In these hard times,
  The source of half his crimes
Is going into gin-shops changing fives!*
Whate'er had washed such theoretic throats,
After a soundish sleep, till twelve next day,
And, perhaps, a gulp of soda—did not *they*
  All change their notes?

Suppose, mind, Mr. B., I say, suppose
You were the landlord of the Crown—the Rose—
The Cock and Bottle, or the Prince of Wales,
The Devil and the Bag of Nails,
  The Crown and Thistle,
  The Pig and Whistle,
Magpie and Stump—take which you like,
The question equally will strike;
Suppose your apron on—top-boots,—fur cap—
  Keeping an eye to bar and tap,
When in comes, muttering like mad,
The strangest customer you ever had!
Well, after rolling eyes and mouthing,
  And calling for a go of nothing,
He thus accosts you in a tone of malice:
" Here's pillars, curtains, gas, plate-glass—What not?
Zounds! Mr. Buckingham, the shop you've got
  Beats Buckingham Palace!
It's not to be allowed, Sir; I'm a Saint,
So I've brought a paint-brush, and a pot of paint,—
  You deal in Gin, Sir,
  Glasses of Sin, Sir;
No words—Gin wholesome?—You're a story-teller—

---

* **2512.** Are they in the habit of bringing £5 notes to get changed, as well
as sovereigns?—Very rarely; *I should think a £5 note is an article they
seldom put in their pockets.*

I don't mind Satan standing at your back,
The Spirit moveth me to go about,
And paint your premises inside and out,
          Black, Sir, coal black,
Coal black, Sir, from the garret to the cellar.
I'll teach you to sell gin—and, what is more,
To keep your wicked customers therefrom,
I'll paint a Great Death's Head upon your door—
Write underneath it, if you please—Old Tom !" *

Should such a case occur,
How would you act with the intruder, Sir ?
Surely, not cap in hand, you'd stand and bow,
But after hearing him proceed thus far,
(Mind—locking up the bar)
          You'd seek the first policeman near,
     " Here, take away this fellow, here,
The rascal is as drunk as David's Sow !"

If I may ask again—between
Ourselves and the General Post, I mean—
What was that gentleman's true situation
Who said—but could he really stand
To what he said ?—" In Scottish land
The cause of Drunkenness was education." †

Only, good Mr. Buckingham, conceive it !
In modern Athens, a fine classic roof,
Christened the *High* School—that is, *over proof !*
Conceive the sandy laddies ranged in classes,
With quaichs and bickers, drinking-horns and glasses,
Ready to take a lesson in Glenlivet !
Picture the little Campbells and M'Gregors,
Dancing half fou', by way of learning figures ;
And Murrays,—not as Lindley used to teach—
Attempting verbs when past their parts of speech—

---

* 3006. Do you think it would be of good effect, were the Legislature to
order that those houses should be painted all black, with a large death's head
and cross-bones over the door ?—I wish they would do even so much.

† 4502. What are the remote causes that have influenced the habit of
drinking spirits among all classes of the population ?—One of the causes of
drunkenness in Scotland is education.

Imagine Thompson, learning A B C,
　　By O D V.
Fancy a dunce that will not drink his wash,—
And Master Peter Alexander Weddel
　　Invested with a medal
For getting on so very far-in-tosh.
Fancy the Dominie—a drouthy body,
Giving a lecture upon making toddy,
Till having emptied every stoup and cup,
He cries, "Lads! go and play—the school is up!

To Scotland, Ireland is akin
In drinking, like as twin to twin,—
When other means are all adrift,
A liquor-shop is Pat's last shift,
Till reckoning Erin round from store to store,
　　There is one whisky shop in four.*
Then who, but with a fancy rather frisky,
And warm besides, and generous with whisky,
Not seeing most particularly clear,
Would recommend to make the drunkards thinner,
By shutting up the publican and sinner
With pensions each of fifty pounds a year?†
Ods! taps and topers! private stills and worms!
What doors you'd soon have open to your terms!

To men of common gumption,
　　How strange, besides, must seem
　　At this time any scheme
To put a check upon potheen's consumption,
When all are calling out for Irish Poor Laws!
Instead of framing *more* laws,

---

* 3804. Did you observe the drinking of spirits very general in Ireland?—
In Ireland, I think, upon a moderate calculation, one shop out of every four
is a whisky-shop, throughout the whole kingdom. Those who have been
unsuccessful in every other employment, and those who have no capital for
any employment, fly to the selling of whisky as the last shift.

† 773. Now, suppose we were to give £50 a-year to every spirit-seller in
Belfast, to pension them off, (and I am sure it would be much better for the
country that they should be paid for doing nothing than for doing mischief).

To pauperism if you'd give a pegger,
Don't check, but patronise their " Kill-the-Beggar !"*
If Pat is apt to go in *Irish linen,*
(Buttoning his coat, with nothing but his skin in)
Would any Christian man—that's quite himself,
His wits not floor'd, or laid upon the shelf—
While blaming Pat for raggedness, poor boy,
Would he deprive him of his " Corduroy !" †

Would any gentleman, unless inclining
To tipsy, take a board upon his shoulder,
Near Temple Bar, thus warning the beholder,

" BEWARE OF TWINING ?"

Are tea-dealers, indeed, so deep-designing,
As one of your select would set us thinking,
That to each tea-chest we should say Tu Doces,
    (Or doses,)
Thou tea-chest drinking ? ‡
    What would be said of *me*
Should I attempt to trace
The vice of drinking to the high in place,
    And say its *root* was on the *top o' the tree* ?§
But *I* am not pot-valiant, and I shun
To say how high potheen might have a *run*. ‖

---

* 794. We have in our neighbourhood a species of whisky of this kind called " Kill-the-Beggar."

† 795. Another description of what would be termed adulterated spirits, is by the vulgar termed " Corduroy."

‡ 798. It is quite common, in Dublin particularly, to have at one end of the counter a large pile of tea-chests for females to go behind, to be hid from sight : but the dangerous secrecy arises chiefly from the want of suspicion in persons going into grocers' shops.

788. It is a well-known fact, that mechanics' wives not unfrequently get potions of spirituous liquors at grocers' shops, and have them set down to their husbands' accounts as soap, sugar, tea, &c.

§ 816. Do you ascribe the great inclination for whisky at present existing among the lower classes, originally to the use of it by the higher classes as a favourite drink ?—I attribute a very large portion of the evil arising from the use of spirituous liquors to the sanction they have received from the higher classes ; the respectable in society I hold to be the chief patrons of drunkenness.

‖ 759. What do you mean by the phrase run ?—It means, according to a common saying, that *for one gallon made for the King, another is made for the Queen.*

What would *you* think if, talking about stingo,
I told you that a lady friend of mine,
    By only looking at her wine
Flushed in her face as red as a flamingo ?*
Would you not ask of me, like many more,—
" Pray, Sir, what had the lady had before ?"

    Suppose at sea, in Biscay's bay of bays,—·
    A rum cask bursting in a blaze,—
Should *I* be thought half tipsy or whole drunk,
If running all about the deck I roar'd
" I say is ever a Cork man aboard ?"
Answered by some Hibernian Jack Junk,
While hitching up his tarry trouser,—
How would it sound in sober ears, O how, Sir,
If I should bellow with redoubled noise,
" Then sit upon the bung-hole, broth of boys." †

When men—the fact's well known—reel to and fro,
A little what is called how-come-you-so,
They think themselves as steady as a steeple,
And lay their staggerings on other people—
    Taking that fact in pawn,
What proper inference would then be drawn
By e'er a dray-horse with a head to his tail,
    Should anybody cry,
    To some one going by,
    " O fie ! O fie ! O fie !
You're drunk—you've *nigh* had *half a pint of ale !*" ‡

---

* 4627. A lady informed me lately, that in dining out, although she should not taste a drop in the hob and nob at dinner, yet the lifting of the glass as frequently as etiquette requires, generally flushed her face a good deal before dinner was ended.

† 3901. Are you aware of the cause of the burning of the Kent East Indiaman in the Bay of Biscay ?—Holding a candle over the bung-hole of a cask of spirits, the snuff fell into the cask and set it on fire. They had not presence of mind to put in the bung, which would have put out the fire ; *and if a man had sat on the bung-hole it would not have burnt him*, and it would have put it out.

‡ 4282. Do many young men visit those houses ?—A very great many have done, more so than what visit the regular public-houses. I was in one of those places about twelve months ago, waiting for a coach, and there came into the beer-shop twenty-two boys, who called for half a gallon of ale, which they drank, and then they called for another.

One certain sign of fumes within the skull
They say is being rather slow and dull,
Oblivious quite of what we are about—
    No one can doubt
Some weighty queries rose, and yet you missed 'em
For instance, when a Doctor so bethumps
What he denominates the " forcing system,"
Nobody asks him about *forcing pumps !**
Oh say, with hand on heart,
    Suppose that I should start
      Some theory like this,
       " When Genesis
Was written,—before man became a glutton,
And in his appetites ran riot,
Content with simple vegetable diet,
Eating his turnips without leg of mutton,
His spinach without lamb—carrots sans beef,
     'Tis my belief
He was a polypus, and I'm convinced
Made other men when he was hashed or minced,"—
Did I in such a style as this proceed,
Would you not say I was *Farre gone*, indeed?†

Excuse me, if I doubt at each Assize
How sober it would look in public eyes,
For our King's Counsel and our learned Judges
When trying thefts, assaults, frauds, murders, arsons,
To preach from texts of temperance like parsons,
By way of giving tipplers gentle nudges.
Imagine my Lord Bayley, Parke, or Park,‡
Donning the fatal sable cap, and hark,

---

* 1211. The over-stimulation, which too frequently ends in the habit of drunkenness in Great Britain in every class, is the result of the British *forcing system* simply.

† 1282. Was not vegetable food prescribed in the first chapter of Genesis?— Vegetable food was appointed when the restorative power of man was complete. The restorative power in some of the lower animals is still complete. If a polypus be truncated or cut into several pieces, each part will become a perfect animal.—*Vide Evidence of Dr. Farre.*

‡ 975. What happy opportunities, for example, are offered to each Judge and King's Counsellor at every assize, to denounce all customary use of distilled spirit as the great excitement to crime. The proper improvement of such opportunities would do much for temperance.

"These sentences must pass, howe'er I'm panged,
You Brandy must return—and Rum the same—
To the Goose and Gridiron, whence you came—
Gin !—Reverend Mr. Cotton and Jack Ketch
   Your spirit jointly will despatch—
      Whisky be hanged !"

Suppose that some fine morning,
Mounted upon a pile of Dunlop cheeses,
I gave the following as public warning,
Would there not be sly winking, coughs and sneezes?
Or dismal hiss of universal scorn—
   "My brethren, don't be born,—
But if you're born, be well advised—
   Don't be baptized.
If both take place, still at the worst
   Do not be nursed,—
At every birth each gossip dawdle
   Expects her caudle,
At christenings, too, drink always hands about,
Nurses will have their porter or their stout,—
Don't wear clean linen, for it leads to sin,—
   All washerwomen make a stand for gin—
If you're a minister—to keep due stinting,
Never preach sermons that are worth the printing,*
Avoid a steamboat with a lady in her,†
And when you court, watch Miss well after dinner,‡
Never run bills, or if you do don't pay,§
And *give* your butter and your cheese away,‖

---

* 4642. When a clergyman gets a new manse he is fined in a bottle of wine ; when he has been newly married, this circumstance subjects him to the same amicable penalty ; the birth of a child also costs one bottle, and the publication of a sermon another.—*By J. Dunlop, Esq.*

† 4637. The absolute necessity of treating females in the same manner, in steamboat jaunts, is lamentable.

‡ 4637. Some youths have been known to defer their entrance into a temperate society till after their marriage, lest failure in the usual compliments should be misconstrued, and create a coldness with their future wives.

§ 1635. It (drinking) is employed in making bargains, at the payment of accounts.

‖ 4639. A landlady, in settling with a farmer for his butter and cheese, brings out the bottle and the glass with her own hands, and presses it on his acceptance. How can he refuse a lady soliciting him to do what he is, perhaps, unfortunately already more than half inclined to?

Build yachts and pleasure-boats, if you are rich,
But never have them launched, or payed with pitch,*
In fine, for Temperance if you stand high,
    " Don't die !" †
Did I preach thus, Sir, should I not appear
Just like the " parson much bemused with beer ?"

Thus far, O Mr. Buckingham, I've gathered,
But here, alas ! by space my pen is tethered,
And I can merely thank you all in short,
The witnesses that have been called in court,
And the Committee for their kind Report,
Whence I have picked and puzzled out this moral,
With which you must not quarrel,
'Tis based in charity—*That men are brothers,*
     And those who make a fuss,
     About their Temperance thus,
Are not so much more temperate than others.

——◆——

THE UNITED FAMILY.

    " We stick at nine."
       MRS. BATTLE.

    " Thrice to thine,
      And thrice to mine,
      And thrice again,
      To make up nine."
        The Weird Sisters in Macbeth.

How oft in families intrudes
The demon of domestic feuds,
One liking this, one hating that,
Each snapping each, like dog and cat,

---

* 4640. The launching bowl is a bonus of drink, varying from £2 to £10, according to the size of the ship, bestowed by the owners on the apprentices of a ship-building yard at the launch of a vessel. The graving bowl is given to the journeyman after a vessel is payed with tar.

† 4386. On the event of a decease, every one gets a glass who comes within the door until the funeral, and for six weeks after it.

With divers bents and tastes perverse,
One's bliss, in fact, another's curse
How seldom anything we see
Like our united family!

Miss Brown of chapels goes in search,
Her sister Susan likes the church;
One plays at cards, the other don't;
One will be gay, the other wont;
In pray'r and preaching one persists,
The other sneers at Methodists;
On Sundays ev'n they can't agree
Like our united family.

There's Mr. Bell, a Whig at heart,
His lady takes the Tories' part,
While William, junior, nothing loth,
Spouts Radical against them both.
One likes the News, one takes the Age,
Another buys the unstamp'd page;
They all say *I*, and never *we*,
Like our united family.

Not so with us;—with equal zeal
We all support Sir Robert Peel:
Of Wellington our mouths are full,
We dote on Sundays on John Bull,
With Pa and Ma on selfsame side,
Our house has never to divide—
No opposition members be
In our united family.

Miss Pope her "Light Guitar" enjoys,
Her father "cannot bear the noise,"
Her mother's charm'd with all her songs,
Her brother jangles with the tongs:
Thus discord out of music springs,
The most unnatural of things,
Unlike the genuine harmony
In our united family!

We *all* on vocal music dote,
To each belongs a tuneful throat,

And all prefer that Irish boon
Of melody—" The Young May Moon"—
By choice we all select the harp,
Nor is the voice of one too sharp,
Another flat—all in one key
Is our united family.

Miss Powell likes to draw and paint,
But then it would provoke a saint,
Her brother takes her sheep for pigs,
And says her trees are periwigs.
Pa' praises all, black, blue, or brown ;
And so does Ma'—but upside down !
They cannot with the same eyes see,
Like our united family.

Miss Patterson has been to France,
Her heart's delight is in a dance ;
The thing her brother cannot bear,
So she must practise with a chair.
Then at a waltz her mother winks ;
But Pa' says roundly what he thinks,
All dos-à-dos, not vis-à-vis,
Like our united family.

We none of us that whirling love,
Which both our parents disapprove,
A hornpipe we delight in more,
Or graceful Minuet de la Cour.
A special favourite with Mamma,
Who used to dance it with Papa,
In this we still keep step, you see,
In our united family.

Then books—to hear the Cobbs' debates !
One worships Scott—another hates,
Monk Lewis Ann fights stoutly for,
And Jane likes Bunyan's " Holy War."
The father on Macculloch pores,
The mother says *all* books are bores ;
But blue serene as heav'n are we,
In our united family.

We never wrangle to exalt
Scott, Banim, Bulwer, Hope, or Galt,
We care not whether Smith or Hook,
So that a novel be the book,
And in one point we all are fast,
Of novels we prefer the last,—
In that the very Heads agree
Of our united family!

To turn to graver matters still,
How much we see of sad self-will,
Miss Scrope, with brilliant views in life,
Would be a poor lieutenant's wife,
A lawyer has her pa's good word,
Her ma' has looked her out a Lord,
What would they not all give to be
Like our united family!

By one congenial taste allied,
Our dreams of bliss all coincide,
We're all for solitudes and cots,
And love, if we may choose our lots—
As partner in the rural plan
Each paints the same dear sort of man;
One heart alone there seems to be
In our united family.

One heart, one hope, one wish, one mind,—
One voice, one choice, all of a kind,—
And can there be a greater bliss—
A little heav'n on earth—than this?
The truth to whisper in your ear,
It must be told!—we are not near
The happiness that ought to be
In our united family!

Alas! 'tis our congenial taste
That lays our little pleasures waste—
We all delight, no doubt, to sing,
We all delight to touch the string,
But where's the harp that nine may touch?
And nine " May Moons" are eight too much—
Just fancy nine, all in one key,
Of our united family!

The play—O how we love a play !
But half the bliss is shorn away ;
On winter nights we venture nigh,
But think of houses in July !
Nine crowded in a private box,
Is apt to pick the stiffest locks—
Our curls would all fall out, though we
Are one united family.

In art the selfsame line we walk,
We all are fond of heads in chalk,
We one and all our talent strain
Adelphi prizes to obtain ;
Nine turban'd Turks are duly sent,
But can the Royal Duke present
Nine silver palettes—no, not he—
To our united family.

Our eating shows the very thing,
We all prefer the liver-wing,
Asparagus when scarce and thin,
And peas directly they come in,
The marrow-bone—if there be one,—
The ears of hare when crisply done,
The rabbit's brain—we all agree
In our united family.

In dress the same result is seen,
We all so dote on apple-green ;
But nine in green would seem a school
Of charity to quizzing fool—
We cannot all indulge our will
With " that sweet silk on Ludgate Hill,"
No *remnant* can sufficient be
For our united family.

In reading hard is still our fate,
One cannot read o'erlooked by eight,
And nine " Disowned"—nine " Pioneers,"
Nine " Chaperons," nine " Buccaneers,"
Nine " Maxwells," nine " Tremaines," and such,
Would dip into our means too much—
Three months are spent o'er volumes three,
In our united family.

Unhappy Muses ! if the Nine
Above in doom with us combine,—
In vain we breathe the tender flame,
Our sentiments are all the same,
And nine complaints address'd to Hope
Exceed the editorial scope,
One in, and eight *put out*, must be
Of our united family.

But this is nought—of deadlier kind,
A ninefold woe remains behind.
Oh why were we so art and part?
So like in taste, so one in heart?
Nine cottages may be to let,
But here's the thought to make us fret,
We cannot each add Frederick B.
To our united family.

THE COMET,

AN ASTRONOMICAL ANECDOTE.

" I cannot fill up a blank better than with a short history of this selfsame *Star*ling."—STERNE'S *Sentimental Journey.*

AMONGST professors of astronomy,
Adepts in the celestial economy,
    The name of H******l's* very often cited ;
And justly so, for he is hand and glove
With ev'ry bright intelligence above ;
Indeed, it was his custom so to stop,
Watching the stars upon the house's top,
    That once upon a time he got be-knighted.

In his observatory thus coquetting,
    With Venus— or with Juno gone astray,
All sublunary matters quite forgetting
In his flirtations with the winking stars,
Acting the spy—it might be upon Mars—
    A new André ;

---

* Herschel.

Or, like a Tom of Coventry, sly peeping
   At Dian sleeping ;
    Or ogling through his glass
    Some heavenly lass
  Tripping with pails along the Milky Way;
Or looking at that Wain of Charles the Martyr's :—
 Thus he was sitting, watchman of the sky,
When lo ! a something with a tail of flame
   Made him exclaim
  " *Mȳ* stars !"—he always puts that stress on *my*—
   " *My* stars and garters !"

  " A comet, sure as I'm alive !
A noble one as I should wish to view !
It can't be Halley's though, *that* is not due
   Till eighteen thirty-five.
Magnificent !—how fine his fiery trail !
Zounds ! 'tis a pity, though, he comes unsought—
Unasked—unreckoned,—in no human thought—
   He ought—he ought—he ought
   To have been caught
With scientific salt upon his tail !"
" I looked no more for it, I do declare,
  Than the Great Bear !
   As sure as Tycho Brahe is dead,
   It really entered in my head,
 No more than Berenice's Hair !"

Thus musing, Heaven's Grand Inquisitor
Sat gazing on the uninvited visitor
Till John, the serving-man, came to the upper
Regions, with " Please your Honour, come to supper."

" Supper ! good John, to-night I shall not sup
Except on that phenomenon—look up !"
" Not sup !" cried John, thinking with consternation
That supping on a *star* must be *star*vation,
   Or ev'n to batten
On Ignes Fatui would never fatten.
His visage seemed to say,—that very odd is,—
But still his master the same tune ran on,
" I can't come down,—go to the parlour, John,
And say I'm supping with the heavenly bodies."

"The heavenly bodies!" echoed John, "Ahem!"
His mind still full of famishing alarms,
"Zooks, if your Honour sups with *them*,
In helping, somebody must make long arms!"
He thought his master's stomach was in danger,
But still in the same tone replied the Knight,
        "Go down, John, go, I have no appetite,
Say I'm engaged with a celestial stranger."—
Quoth John, not much au fait in such affairs,
"Wouldn't the stranger take a bit downstairs?"

"No," said the master, smiling, and no wonder,
        At such a blunder,
"The stranger is not quite the thing you think,
He wants no meat or drink,
And one may doubt quite reasonably whether
        He has a mouth,
Seeing his head and tail are joined together,
Behold him,—there he is, John, in the South."

John, looking up with his portentous eyes,
Each rolling like a marble in its socket,
At last the fiery tad-pole spies,
And, full of Vauxhall reminiscence, cries,
        "A rare good rocket!"

"A what! A rocket, John! Far from it!
    What you behold, John, is a comet;
One of those most eccentric things
                That in all ages
                Have puzzled sages
                And frightened kings,
With fear of change, that flaming meteor, John,
Perplexes sovereigns, throughout its range"—
            "Do he?" cried John,
            "Well, let him flare on,
I haven't got no sovereigns to change!"

THE LAMENT OF TOBY,

THE LEARNED PIG.

"A little learning is a dangerous thing."—POPE.

O HEAVY day ! oh day of woe !
 To misery a poster,
Why was I ever farrowed—why
 Not spitted for a roaster ?

In this world, pigs, as well as men,
 Must dance to fortune's fiddlings,
But must I give the classics up,
 For barley-meal and middlings ?

Of what avail that I could spell
 And read, just like my betters,
If I must come to this at last,
 To litters, not to letters ?

O, why are pigs made scholars of ?
 It baffles my discerning,
What griskins, fry, and chitterlings
 Can have to do with learning.

Alas ! my learning once drew cash,
 But public fame's unstable,
So I must turn a pig again,
 And fatten for the table.

To leave my literary line
 My eyes get red and leaky ;
But Giblett doesn't want me *blue*,
 But red and white, and streaky.

Old Mullins used to cultivate
 My learning like a gard'ner ;
But Giblett only thinks of lard,
 And not of Doctor Lardner.

He does not care about my brain
   The value of two coppers,
All that he thinks about my head
   Is, how I'm off for choppers.

Of all my literary kin
   A farewell must be taken,
Good-bye to the poetic Hogg!
   The philosophic Bacon!

Day after day my lessons fade,
   My intellect gets muddy;
A trough I have, and not a desk,
   A stye—and not a study!

Another little month, and then
   My progress ends, like Bunyan's;
The seven sa:es that I loved
   Will be chopped up with onions!

Then over head and ears in brine
   They'll souse me, like a salmon,
My mathematics turned to brawn,
   My logic into gammon.

My Hebrew will all retrograde,
   Now I'm put up to fatten,
My Greek, it will all go to grease,
   The dogs will have my Latin!

Farewell to Oxford!—and to Bliss!
   To Milman, Crowe, and Glossop,—
I now must be content with chats,
   Instead of learned gossip!

Farewell to "Town!" farewell to "Gown!"
   I've quite outgrown the latter,—
Instead of Trencher-cap my head
   Will soon be in a platter!

O why did I at Brazen-Nose
   Rout up the roots of knowledge?
A butcher that can't read will kill
   A pig that's been to college!

For sorrow I could stick myself,
　　But conscience is a clasher;
A thing that would be rash in man
　　In me would be a rasher!

One thing I ask—when I am dead,
　　And past the Stygian ditches—
And that is, let my schoolmaster
　　Have one of my two flitches.

'Twas he who taught my letters so
　　I ne'er mistook or missed 'em,
Simply by *ringing* at the nose,
　　According to *Bell's* system.

———◆———

JOHN JONES.

A PATHETIC BALLAD.

"I saw the iron enter into his soul."—STERNE.

JOHN JONES he was a builder's clerk
　　On ninety pounds a year,
Before his head was engine-turned
　　To be an engineer.

For finding that the iron rods
　　Were quite the public tale,
Like Robin Redbreast, all his heart
　　Was set upon a rail.

But, oh! his schemes all ended ill,
　　As schemes must come to nought
With men who try to make short cuts
　　When cut with something short.

His altitudes he did not take
　　Like any other elf;
But first a spirit-level took
　　That levelled him himself.

Then getting up, from left to right
　　So many tacks he made,
The ground he meant to go upon
　　Got very well surveyed.

How crows may fly he did not care
　　A single fig to know—
He wished to make an iron road,
　　And not an iron crow :

So, going to the Rose and Crown
　　To cut his studies short,
The nearest way from *pint* to *pint*
　　He found was through a quart.

According to this rule, he planned
　　His railway o'er a cup ;
But when he came to lay it down,
　　No soul would take it up !

Alas ! not his the wily arts
　　Of men as shrewd as rats,
Who out of one sole *level* make
　　A precious lot of *flats !*

In vain from Z to crooked S
　　His devious line he showed ;
Directors even seemed to wish
　　For some directer road.

The writers of the public press
　　All sneered at his design ;
And penny-a-liners wouldn't give
　　A penny for his line !

Yet still he urged his darling scheme
　　In spite of all the fates;
Until at last his zigzag ways
　　Quite brought him into *straits.*

His money gone, of course he sank
　　In debt from day to day—
His way would not pay *him,* and so
　　He could not pay his way.

Said he, "All parties run me down,—
　　How bitter is my cup!
My landlord is the only man
　　That ever runs me up!

"And he begins to talk of scores,
　　And will not draw a cork."
And then he railed at Fortune, since
　　He could not rail at York!

The morrow in a fatal noose
　　They found him, hanging fast;
This sentence scribbled on the wall,
　　"I've got my line at last!"

Twelve men upon the body sate,
　　And thus on oath did say,
"We find he got his *gruel* 'cause
　　He couldn't have his *way!*"

THE END.

DALZIEL BROTHERS, CAMDEN PRESS, LONDON, N.W.